Financial Social Media

Ying Zhang

Financial Social Media

A Quantitative Approach to Measuring Investor Sentiment

Second Edition

palgrave
macmillan

Ying Zhang
Fairfield University
Fairfield, CT, USA

ISBN 978-3-032-09331-8 ISBN 978-3-032-09332-5 (eBook)
https://doi.org/10.1007/978-3-032-09332-5

This Palgrave Macmillan imprint is published by the registered company Springer Nature Switzerland AG
The registered company address is: Gewerbestrasse 11, 6330 Cham, Switzerland

To Biyun Huang, Aiwei (Ivy), Aike (Ike), and Ion Zhang.
To my parents, Shuwen Zhang and Shulian Deng.

Contents

1	**Why Pay Attention to Financial Social Media?**	1
	The Impact of the Internet	1
	The Impact of Social Media	3
	The Impact of Online Customer Reviews	4
	The Impact of the Internet and Financial Social Media on Financial Markets	7
	The Impact of Financial Social Media on Stock Trading	10
	Final Thoughts	12
2	**A Variety of Financial Social Media**	17
	Introduction	17
	Stock Chat Rooms	19
	Stock Trading Board	23
	Stock-Specific (Topic-Specific) Board	28
	Board of Boards	33
	Final Thoughts	35
3	**About Financial Social Media Posters**	37
	Introduction	37
	How to Learn a Poster's True Identity	38
	Who Posts Messages on Financial Social Media Platforms?	40
	Demographics of Posters	43

Measures and Determinants of Poster Credibility 46
Reputation Systems and Collaborative Filtering 47
Who Is Keener to Post What Messages? 48

4 Why Do People Post Messages on Financial Social Media Platforms? 51
Commonly Known Motivations 51
Motivations Pertinent to Financial Social Media Platforms 54
Final Thought 57

5 Modeling the Value of Financial Social Media Platforms 59
Introduction 59
Advantageous Selection 60
Adverse Selection 62
Theoretical Construct 63
Moral Hazard and its Implications 83
Herding Behavior 85
Final Thoughts 86

6 How to Measure Financial Social Media Activities? 89
Financial Social Media Data Structure 89
How a Text Classifier Works 92
Issues in Constructing the Training Dataset 95
A Variety of Text Classifiers 98
Class Assignment 109
Which Text Classifier is Most Suitable for Financial Social Media Data? 111
Financial Social Media Activity Measures 113

7 Patterns in Financial Social Media Posting Activities 119
Message-Related Patterns 119
Poster-Related Patterns 125
Stock-Related Patterns 135
Other Stock-Related Patterns 142

8 Online Talk: Does It Matter at All? 151
Introduction 151
Methodologies 152
Empirical Evidence 157

9 **Trading Strategies Based on Financial Social Media Information** 173
Introduction 173
Pump-and-Dump Strategy 174
Contrarian Trading Strategy 176
Long–Short Hedging Strategy 177
Event-Trading Strategy 178
Momentum or Trend-Trading Strategy 180
Continuous Trading Strategy Based on Financial Social Media Feeds 182
Volatility Play 183
Trading Strategies Based on Other Financial Social Media 185

10 **Legal Issues Associated with Financial Social Media Posting** 187
Introduction 187
Ten Famous Lawsuits Related to Financial Social Media Posting 188
Freedom of Speech, Securities Fraud, and Anonymity in Cyberspace 191
The Role of the SEC in Monitoring Online Securities Fraud 193
Use of Disclosure and/or Disclaimer 195
How to Spot Financial Social Media Manipulators 196
How to Avoid Financial Social Media Scams 197
How to Report Securities Fraud 200

11 **Whisperers Versus Analysts and Implications for Market Efficiency** 203
Market Efficiency 203
Stock Recommendations from Financial Analysts 206
Measure of Analyst Consensus, Security Recommendation Accuracy, and Earnings Forecast Accuracy 211
When Whisperers Talk, Who Listens? 214
Whisperers Versus Analysts: Whose Information Is more Accurate? 215
Trading Profits Based on Whisperer or Analyst Recommendations 217

12 **Alternative Information on the Internet** 221
Finding Free Information 221
Financial Social Media Platforms outside the United States 234
Platforms for a Variety of Financial Assets 236

13 **Implications of Financial Social Media** 241
Introduction 241
Implications for Individual Investors 241
Implications for Financial Institutions 243
Implications for Businesses 245
Implications for Regulators 247
Implications for Financial Markets 248
Implications for Researchers 250
Implications for Educators 253

14 **GameStop and Other Meme Stocks' Short Squeeze Frenzy** 257
Introduction 257
WallStreetBets: The Epicenter of the Meme Stock Frenzy 258
The Mechanics of Short Selling and Short Squeezes 259
Gamma Squeezes: The Role of Options Trading 260
The Fallout for Hedge Funds 261
The Broader Meme Stock Movement: AMC, Nokia, and beyond 262
The Robinhood Controversy: Market Manipulation or Risk Management? 263
The Long-Term Performance of Meme Stocks 264
Regulatory Responses: The Future of Retail Trading and Market Oversight 266
Final Thoughts: A Turning Point in Retail Trading 267
Academic Perspectives on the GameStop Short Squeeze 269

15 **How Metaverse Will Change Financial Social Media** 271
Introduction 271
Metaverse as a New Medium for Financial Social Interaction 272
Trading Simulations and Financial Education in Metaverse 277
Integration of Decentralized Finance (DeFi) and Digital Assets 281

Challenges and Risks in the Financial Metaverse 285
The Future of Financial Social Media in Metaverse 289
Final Thoughts 293

16 How Artificial Intelligence Will Affect Financial Social Media 295
Introduction 295
AI-Powered Chatbots: Revolutionizing User Engagement 296
The Dark Side of AI: Fake Content and Misinformation 299
Detecting and Mitigating AI-Generated Threats 302
Ethical Implications and Regulatory Challenges 305
Final Thoughts 309

17 How Financial Social Media Affects Corporate Value and Governance 313
Introduction 313
Impact on Corporate Image 314
The Role of Viral Content 315
Real-Time Crisis Management 317
Influence on Corporate Value 318
Transformation of Investor Relations 319
Challenges in Real-Time Communication 320
Managing Misinformation and Strategic Response in the Digital Era 321
Implications for Corporate Governance 322
Leveraging Sentiment Analysis 323
Financial Social Media and Initial Public Offerings (IPOs) 324

18 Financial Social Media Risk Management 327
Introduction 327
Understanding the Risks of Financial Social Media 328
Risk Management Strategies 331
Crisis Management in the age of Financial Social Media 333
Ethical Considerations and Regulatory Frameworks 336
International Approaches to Regulating Financial Social Media 337
Ethical Use of Algorithms in Financial Social Media 339

Challenges of Algorithmic Transparency 341
Establishing Ethical Guidelines for Financial Influencers 342
Collaborative Frameworks between Regulators and Platforms 344
Final Thoughts 346

19 The Future of Financial Social Media 349
Introduction 349
Trend 1: User-Rating System 350
Trend 2: Moderation Tools 350
Trend 3: Value-Added Services 351
Trend 4: Multimedia Sharing 353
Trend 5: Combination of Stock-Trading and Stock-Specific Boards 355
Trend 6: Multi-Assets Boards 356
Trend 7: Search Engine 357
Trend 8: Social Media Aggregation 357
Trend 9: Revenue-Generating Models 358
Trend 10: Mergers and Acquisitions 360
Trend 11: AI and the Future of Financial Social Media 361

20 Literature Review for Financial Social Media Studies 363
Future Research about FSM Platforms 389

Bibliography 393

About the Author

Ying Zhang Associate Professor of Finance, Department of Finance, Dolan School of Business, Fairfield University. Website: https://www.fairfield.edu/faculty-and-staff/profile/?username=yzhang1. Scholar link: http://scholar.google.com/citations?hl=en&user=bxZLJo8AAAAJ. Personal website: https://sites.google.com/view/ying-clement-zhang.

List of Figures

Fig. 2.1	Screen Capture of Post Message on Hotcopper	27
Fig. 2.2	Screen Capture of YingZhang's Member Profile on Hotcopper.com.au	29
Fig. 5.1	Linear Relationship between messages M and time t	67
Fig. 5.2	Linear relationship between probability of right messages Pr and rank r with a positive a	70
Fig. 5.3	Linear relationship between probability of right messages Pr and rank r with a negative a	71
Fig. 5.4	Linear relationship between rank r and time t	72
Fig. 5.5	Nonlinear relationship between value of an author v and time t with a positive a	74
Fig. 5.6	Nonlinear relationship between value of an author v and time t with a negative a	75
Fig. 5.7	Linear relationship between number of authors N and time t	78
Fig. 5.8	Nonlinear relationship between value of platform V and time t with a positive a	81
Fig. 5.9	Nonlinear relationship between value of platform V and time t with a negative a	82
Fig. 6.1	Screen capture of my Microsoft access database	90
Fig. 6.2	Screen capture of my text files folder	93
Fig. 6.3	Flowchart for using a text classifier	95
Fig. 7.1	Message length measured in number of characters	120
Fig. 7.2	Messages posted by hours (EST)	122
Fig. 7.3	Messages posted by day	123

Fig. 7.4	Messages posted by day within a month	124
Fig. 7.5	Messages posted by month	126
Fig. 7.6	Distribution of self-disclosed sentiment	127
Fig. 7.7	Number of messages posted by authors	128
Fig. 7.8	Authors' number of postings when starting a new message	129
Fig. 7.9	Authors' credit scores when leaving a message	131
Fig. 7.10	Number of watchers when authors leave messages	132
Fig. 7.11	Distribution of messages according to stock prices	134
Fig. 7.12	Stock's raw return mentioned in a message	136
Fig. 7.13	Number of outstanding shares	138
Fig. 7.14	Stock's market capitalization	140
Fig. 7.15	Daily trading volume when the stock was mentioned in a message	141
Fig. 7.16	Average numbers of messages and number of posters from t–5 to t+5	142
Fig. 7.17	Sentiment and disagreement indexes	145
Fig. 7.18	Event study on abnormal return from t–30 to t+30	146
Fig. 7.19	Event study on abnormal volume from t–30 to t+30	147
Fig. 7.20	Abnormal return from t–5 to t+5	148
Fig. 7.21	Abnormal volume from t–5 to t+5	148
Fig. 20.1	Number of papers per year	364

List of Tables

Table 2.1	An Example of Activetrader Chat Room	21
Table 2.2	User yingzhang's Profile on Activetrader	22
Table 2.3	An Example of the "Short Term Trading" Board on HotCopper	26
Table 2.4	Complete Content of Message Number 43464 on Hotcopper	28
Table 2.5	An Example of the AAPL Message Board on Siliconinvestor	31
Table 2.6	Message Number 168596 on the AAPL Message Board on Siliconinvestor	32
Table 2.7	User YingZhang's Profile on Siliconinvestor	33
Table 3.1	Demographics of Posters Based on Quantcast Analysis	45
Table 6.1	An example of confusion matrix	111

CHAPTER 1

Why Pay Attention to Financial Social Media?

The Impact of the Internet

Imagine life without the Internet. Initially, even its inventors could not have foreseen the profound impact it would have on our daily lives. Since its inception in the United States in 1983, the Internet has revolutionized not only social interactions but also economic activities. More than forty years later, its influence is so pervasive that it is almost impossible to envision a world without it. As a primary source of information and an efficient communication tool, the Internet has enhanced the convenience, vibrancy, and quality of life in ways previously unimaginable. In today's fast-paced knowledge economy, where the demand for instant information is paramount, the Internet is not just a tool but an essential part of everyday life.

In this connected world, web applications such as browsers, email, search engines, online gaming, online shopping, and online dating affect almost every aspect of daily life. We rely on the Internet for a multitude of tasks: from retrieving information to sharing opinions, from online shopping to stock trading, from e-commerce to e-banking, and from emailing to video conferencing. These activities can all be accomplished with just a click.

Informational websites can generally be categorized into three main types:

Y. Zhang, *Financial Social Media*,
https://doi.org/10.1007/978-3-032-09332-5_1

- Information-Service Sites: These websites serve as primary news portals, offering free information to users. Although they may be perceived as simple and low-tech, they attract a large audience. Compared to traditional media like newspapers and magazines, which are often criticized for outdated information, new media provide real-time updates at minimal cost.
- Function-Service Sites: Websites like ChatGPT, Google.com, MapQuest.com, and Zillow.com provide specific services, often free of charge. The rapid development of the Internet and technological advances have led to the emergence of these sites. They are typically high-tech, with a loyal user base, relying on their unique online functions and services. The success of function-service sites reflects the growing acceptance of the Internet and the recognition that information technology has indeed enhanced quality of life.
- Life-Service Sites: Platforms such as Facebook.com, X.com, Reddit.com, and TheLion.com allow users to not only consume content but also create it. These Web 2.0 sites have transformed the previously one-dimensional and unilateral online world into a dynamic and multilateral one. Unlike Web 1.0, where information flow was one-way and users were passive consumers, Web 2.0 connects vast audiences and empowers them to generate content.

As the Internet continues to evolve, these categories are becoming increasingly blurred due to the rise of multifunctional and multilateral services. For example, Yahoo.com is not merely an information-service site but a comprehensive platform that integrates all three service types—information, function, and life. This convergence is mutually beneficial: information-service sites seek the powerful capabilities of life-service platforms, while life-service platforms benefit from the large user base of information-service portals.

The rise of mega-sites like Yahoo.com and Google.com is also driven by the integration of advanced web applications designed to meet higher user expectations. In recent years, web functions have significantly improved, making the Internet more user-friendly and attractive. This positive feedback loop is not just a trend but an inevitable result of the Internet's ongoing development.

The Impact of Social Media

The rise of life-service sites and multifunctional mega-sites has significantly enriched and empowered the digital world. Unlike traditional Web 1.0 sites, Web 2.0 platforms allow users to interact and collaborate, creating user-generated content within virtual communities. Social media, often referred to as new media, encompasses a range of Internet-based applications built on Web 2.0 technologies, enabling people to create, share, and exchange information and ideas within these online communities.

In contrast, old media refers to traditional forms of communication that existed before the Internet, such as radio, television, and print publications like newspapers and magazines. With the vast number of social media users and the rapid speed of information dissemination, social media is now seen as a faster and more dynamic means of breaking news and analysis compared to traditional media. Additionally, with the widespread use of computers, tablets, and smartphones, users are continuously receiving, contributing, creating, and sharing information through social media, redefining the concept of media as a medium for information dissemination.

The rapid growth of the Internet and social media has fundamentally changed how we interact with the world, leaving a profound impact on society. Social media can be categorized into seven major forms: blogs/microblogs (e.g., X.com, formerly Twitter), wikis (e.g., Wikipedia), social networking sites (e.g., Facebook), bulletin board systems (e.g., TheLion.com), podcasts (e.g., Apple Podcasts), virtual game worlds (e.g., World of Warcraft), and content communities (e.g., Pinterest).

As a new type of online media, social media is characterized by five distinct features that set it apart from traditional websites:

- Participation: Social media platforms are open to everyone, encouraging users to actively engage, contribute, provide feedback, and share information online. Whether an individual, institution, association, or corporation, everyone can participate.
- Transparency and Openness: Social media promotes transparency, offering a wealth of services and content that are often free to users. Users are encouraged to participate, comment, respond, and share their opinions, with content easily shared through features like "share" or "like" buttons.

- Conversation: Unlike traditional media, where information flow was one-directional, social media facilitates bilateral communication, allowing for interaction and collaboration among users.
- Community Focus: Social media platforms make it easy for users to create groups, categorize communities and subcommunities, and connect with others who share similar interests. For example, stock traders might gather on financial social media (FSM, hereafter) or follow StockTwits, while golf enthusiasts can join Facebook's "The Golfing Society" group or follow "The Golf Digest" on X. This grouping enhances efficient communication.
- Universal Connectivity: Although no single social media platform meets all user needs, features such as mass texting, multimedia messages, and sharing functions enable connectivity across multiple platforms. For example, an individual's updates can be shared simultaneously on Facebook, X.com, TikTok, and LinkedIn. Clicking the "Like" button on a webpage can trigger a story in the user's Facebook news feed, linking back to the original webpage.

These five characteristics have led to the widespread acceptance and use of social media by the public. Its popularity continues to grow, becoming an integral part of daily life for many. The idea of life without social media now seems unimaginable.

As social media rapidly evolves globally, many corporations and organizations are adopting social business models. The use of social media platforms in advertising, recruitment, and customer service has seen significant growth in recent years, with an increasing number of companies being followed on platforms like X.com (formerly Twitter).

The Impact of Online Customer Reviews

Social media has become increasingly popular and has had a significant impact on the economy, particularly in areas such as commerce, marketing, and customer relations. Before making a purchase, whether online or offline, many consumers now expect to thoroughly understand product details and consider the opinions of other consumers. Today's purchase decisions have evolved from a simple, linear process into a complex, interconnected model, influenced heavily by peer recommendations.

Online customer reviews come in various forms. For example, Amazon.com allows customers to leave detailed feedback along with a rating from one to five stars and provides an average rating based on all reviews. On HealthGrades.com, patients can rate and comment on their doctors, with each doctor receiving an average rating. RateMyProfessors.com enables students to rate their professors and share reviews, while TripAdvisor.com facilitates the gathering of travel information, reviews, and opinions, hosting over 100 million reviews on hotels, restaurants, and other travel-related businesses.

Social media users can be classified into four levels of engagement, enthusiasm, and credibility:

- Inactive Users: Those who rarely visit social media sites.
- Fans: Individuals who frequently engage in online activities.
- Masters: Active participants who regularly share their opinions and engage in discussions.
- Gurus: Highly credible community members with many followers who provide insights and frequent reviews.

From the perspective of online activities, social media users can also be distinguished by their functional roles:

- Posters: Individuals who post messages, create blogs, upload files, and share content.
- Readers: Users who consume content such as blogs, discussions, videos, and reviews, but do not actively participate. In Internet culture, these users are often referred to as "lurkers."
- Responders: Those who respond to and comment on content posted by others.
- Researchers or analysts: Individuals who collect, aggregate, and analyze information from social media for personal or commercial purposes.

With the growth of network communication, word-of-mouth now spreads through various forms, with technology greatly enhancing its speed, reach, and impact. Opinion leaders in virtual communities play a crucial role in this social media landscape, sharing their shopping experiences, product reviews, and service ratings. Followers and newcomers who trust these reviews are often influenced in their purchase decisions.

While the views of opinion leaders carry significant weight, every consumer review matters. Websites typically display an average rating score based on all reviews, and these ratings are considered unbiased and more reliable than the information provided by manufacturers. Forums and other social media platforms significantly contribute to the dissemination of consumer reviews, which have a notable impact on sales. Companies are increasingly aware of this dynamic, with many actively monitoring online discussions to gauge customer sentiment.

Today, many companies are emphasizing the use of social media to build brand reputation and encourage information sharing. Social media has become an essential marketing channel, and businesses can no longer afford to ignore its influence. For instance, when promoting a new brand, it is common practice for companies to establish X.com, Instagram, and Facebook accounts, create brand forums, hire an Internet influencer for live-streaming product promotion, and engage with consumers as active participants in online communities.

Consumers are spending more time on social media than ever before. According to a 2025 Empathica survey of U.S. consumers, about 67% consult Facebook when making decisions about retail purchases or restaurants, and roughly 33% have tried new brands based on social media recommendations. The 2025 Accenture Interactive Survey found that over 60% of U.S. consumers follow at least one brand on social media, and 40% are more likely to buy from companies that utilize mobile applications. Additionally, more than 55% of U.S. consumers compare prices on their phones or tablets while in-store, and showrooming, which is inspecting a product in store but ultimately purchasing it online, has become a mainstream practice.

Online customer reviews and ratings have a profound influence on brand introduction, promotion, reputation, and sales. By collecting and analyzing these reviews, businesses can gain valuable insights into consumer needs and buying habits. This understanding helps companies generate more discussions around their products, attract more attention, engage opinion leaders in virtual communities, and reach more potential buyers. Ultimately, customer reviews play a critical role in how consumers discover, purchase, and promote brands and products.

The Impact of the Internet and Financial Social Media on Financial Markets

The Internet has been one of the most revolutionary technologies in history, profoundly impacting how we acquire information, communicate, and invest. It has been particularly transformative for individual investors. The widespread availability of information is perhaps the most significant benefit the Internet has brought to investing and trading. Before the Internet, individuals primarily relied on newspapers, magazines, financial literature, or direct contact with companies to access financial information and analyze securities.

With the advent of the Internet, investors can now easily access a publicly traded company's reports, such as Form 8-K and Form 10-Q, directly from the Securities and Exchange Commission (SEC) website immediately after they are released. Platforms like Yahoo! Finance provide daily press releases, analyst opinions, and estimates for free, along with financial statements from the past three years. For a fee, investors can purchase and download financial research reports on Yahoo! Finance, searchable by keywords, topics, and specific analyst recommendations. From a company's perspective, the Internet is a cost-effective way to maintain online investor relations and broadcast earnings conference calls.

Numerous financial websites, such as ValueLine.com, ValuEngine.com, Morningstar.com, and Bloomberg.com, compile financial information and offer stock recommendations. For example, Zhang et al. (2010) report that Value Line, an independent investment research firm, began announcing changes in its stock recommendations online on June 9, 2005. This accelerated online delivery system, as opposed to the traditional newspaper method, offers benefits such as quicker dissemination of information and more rapid incorporation of that information into stock prices, thus promoting overall market efficiency.

Today, many websites, such as Yahoo! Finance and CNNMoney, provide financial information for free, while others, like ValueLine.com and ValuEngine.com, charge nominal fees for specialized data. For instance, as of 2025, Value Line currently charges individual investors $598 per year for its standard Value Line Investment Survey (VLIS) service.

Another significant benefit the Internet has brought is the reduction in trading costs for most financial market participants. Over the years, there has been a dramatic decline in commission fees for trading securities. For example, as of 2025, Interactive Brokers "IBKR Lite" offers commission-free trading, while "IBKR Pro" provides tiered or fixed commission options. Options contracts are priced from \$0.15 to \$0.65 per contract, depending on volume. Before the rise of discount brokers, full-service brokers charged high commissions, sometimes reaching several hundred dollars per trade, which included advice on security selection and financial planning. However, while lower commission fees have made trading more accessible, they have also led to an increase in trading frequency, which can be detrimental to investor returns.

Research by Odean (1999) found that excessive trading by individual investors with discount brokerage accounts often reduces returns. Barber and Odean (2000) further concluded that active trading imposes a significant performance penalty on individual investors, highlighting that trading can be detrimental to wealth accumulation. In sum, the Internet's influence on financial markets is double-edged and continues to evolve.

Social media activity is also having a measurable impact on financial markets. This influence can be understood in at least three ways:

- Corporate Disclosures: Since April 2, 2013, the SEC has allowed public companies to use social media sites like X.com and Facebook to disclose corporate information in compliance with Regulation Fair Disclosure, if investors are informed where to find it. This means that instead of searching company websites for news, investors can now easily receive the latest corporate updates directly on their social media accounts.
- Investor Sentiment: Social media provides a platform for investors to share opinions about securities and markets. Sites like Yahoo! Finance, Raging Bull, Motley Fool, TheLion, Google Finance, X.com, and Facebook allow investors to express sentiment (e.g., buy, hold, sell) and comments. Social media has been shown to significantly influence stock prices. Bollen et al. (2011) demonstrated that the emotions expressed in online posts have a high correlation with near-term stock movements. They also found that X.com could predict swings in the Dow Jones Industrial Average (DJIA) with 87.6% accuracy. Additionally, popularity on social networks, measured by fan count, has been found to be a good predictor of stock prices, according to O'Connor (2013). Derwent Capital Markets even launched a hedge fund in 2012 that used signals derived from X.com to inform its trading strategy. The fund, which

operated for one month, reportedly returned 1.86%, outperforming the broader market and the average hedge fund. In May 2013, Paul Hawtin, the founder of Derwent Capital Markets, launched Cayman Atlantic, an investment management firm that uses real-time social media data to identify trading opportunities.

- High-Frequency Trading (HFT): Institutional investors, such as hedge funds, are increasingly using high-frequency trading (HFT) based on vast amounts of data from social media sites. Many HFT algorithms are programmed to trade based on aggregated and quantified news (e.g., good news = 1, neutral news = 0, bad news = −1) within milliseconds. Automated HFT now accounts for about half of daily stock market trading volume, and the use of social media information in trading is growing (Kirilenko et al. 2011). In 2012, Thomson Reuters MarketPsych Indices (TRMIs) began offering insights into the emotions and sentiments associated with specific countries, commodities, currencies, and economic sectors based on the analysis of news and social media.

In 2013, Bloomberg introduced a feature on its financial data terminals that streams relevant X.com messages to hedge funds, investment banks, and other investors. The financial industry continues to explore new ways to profit from the vast amount of information generated on social media platforms like message boards, chat rooms, Facebook, and Twitter. Park et al. (2013) reported that Seeking Alpha and other leading business magazines analyze and report on comments made on message boards or blogs. Similarly, several online services, such as PredictWallStreet.com, Marketwatch.com, SocialPicks.com, and Stockpkr.com, aggregate stock sentiments from these message boards and make the information available to online brokerages and other financial intermediaries.

However, it is undeniable that social media has also had some negative impacts on financial markets, including online securities fraud. For example, in September 2000, the SEC alleged that a 15-year-old used Internet FSM to manipulate stock prices in a classic "pump-and-dump" scheme. In 2007, during a lawsuit aimed at blocking Whole Foods' acquisition of Wild Oats Markets, the FTC alleged that John Mackey, the CEO of Whole Foods, anonymously attacked Wild Oats on Internet message boards to lower its price, making it easier for Whole Foods to acquire the company.

HFT has also been criticized for increasing market volatility and the probability of market crashes. Although it may seem unlikely that a single tweet could significantly impact a stock price, large-scale social media activity does appear to have this effect, particularly when linked to HFT. Bad news now spreads faster than ever, often magnified by investor reactions on social media. For example, on April 23, 2013, a fake report on X.com about a bomb at the White House caused a brief stock market panic, largely due to program trading. The Dow Jones Industrial Average (DJIA) dropped more than 143 points in two minutes but quickly recovered after the tweet was revealed to be false, and the Associated Press Twitter account was confirmed to have been hacked. The rapid plunge and rebound of the DJIA index displayed a V-shape within minutes.

This incident may signal an increasing reliance on social media platforms by traders. However, there is currently insufficient evidence to conclude that social media has a significant and sustained impact on financial markets and stock prices. What is clear is that automated trading exacerbates market fluctuations, particularly during market crashes. Computer programs now sift through millions of social media messages for early warnings about news that may move markets, and in some cases, these programs initiate trades automatically, without human involvement.

The Impact of Financial Social Media on Stock Trading

FSM refers to platforms where users discuss and share information related to financial markets, investments, and economic trends. It serves as a space for individuals to exchange ideas, seek advice, and stay updated on financial news. The social aspect allows for real-time discussions and diverse perspectives, contributing to a dynamic and interactive financial community.

With Web 2.0 technology, a specialized form of social media, FSM exert a significant influence on online trading. Their precursor, the stock chat room, whether private or public, facilitated synchronous web conferencing that allowed online investors to discuss topics such as stock holdings, personal opinions, trading strategies, and investment results, primarily through text. The term “online investors” refers to those who actively engage in online trading and frequently seek and share stock information via the Internet. In stock chat rooms, participants engage in real-time text-based discussions, interacting with other members via instant messaging, with the most recent messages visible to all participants.

FSM sites are more structured and offer a variety of value-added services compared to chat rooms. For instance, TheLion.com provides an all-in-one search service that allows users to view all messages related to a specific stock, enabling quick and efficient retrieval of historical posts—something not available in traditional chat rooms, where old messages are not archived. Additionally, TheLion.com allows users to add specific posters to a watchlist, highlighting their messages and sending instant email alerts whenever they post. This feature helps users closely monitor key contributors, particularly those with high credibility within the community. Yahoo! Finance, another prominent platform, allows users to rate messages with a thumbs-up or thumbs-down and displays the ratio of likes to dislikes, providing insight into both the popularity and perceived value of the message content.

Not all FSM sites are created equal; each has its unique structure and functions. FSM can be categorized in several ways:

- Membership Focus: Private boards, such as ValueForum.com, are typically invitation-based and may require membership fees, while public boards, like Raging Bull, are free to join.
- Structural Focus: Some platforms, like chat rooms, offer real-time discussions but do not archive past messages. Others, like TheLion.com, list messages in reverse chronological order with full retrievability. Stock-specific boards, such as those on Yahoo! Finance, provide separate pages for each stock and allow access to historical messages. Aggregators like BoardCentral.com compile real-time or historical streams from various message boards.
- Asset Type Focus: Boards may specialize in different asset types, such as stocks, stock warrants, options, bond funds, ETFs, retirement funds, currencies, commodities, or a mix of these.
- Liquidity Focus: Some boards concentrate on specific asset liquidity, focusing exclusively on common stocks (liquid), investment-grade bonds (liquid), or less liquid assets like penny stocks, cryptocurrencies, pink sheet stocks, and over-the-counter bulletin board stocks.
- Industry Focus: Certain boards are dedicated to specific sectors, such as biotech, real estate, or finance.

- Region and Language Focus: Boards may cater to different regions and languages, with platforms hosted in countries like the United States, United Kingdom, Japan, China, and Korea.

Public online FSM platforms, which have been around since the late 1990s, have grown exponentially in users and services. Information from these boards can alter investors' perceptions of a security or the broader market. Studies by Antweiler and Frank (2004), Sabherwal et al. (2011), and Zhang et al. (2012) have demonstrated that parameters such as the number of messages, posters, sentiment, and disagreement on FSM significantly influence trading decisions. These, in turn, impact stock prices, trading volumes, return volatility, and liquidity.

Institutional investors, such as hedge funds, also consider aggregate investor sentiment from FSM when making trading decisions. Given the interconnectedness of various message boards and social media channels, the aggregate sentiment reflects the overall mood of online investors at any given time, affecting event-driven trading strategies based on large volumes of posted messages.

The increasing popularity of FSM among online investors is clear. Platforms like TheLion.com have tracked over 100 million message postings from more than 25,000 message boards, attracting over 250 million page views and two million monthly visitors as of June 2007 (Sabherwal et al. 2011).

But why should we pay such close attention to FSM? For many investors, the primary goal is to achieve the highest return on their capital. Access to real-time and accurate information is crucial to this end. To gauge market consensus on a particular security, opinions from experienced investors and discussions among peers are invaluable. Often, the prevailing investor sentiment can be sensed from these boards.

While a single message might sometimes inform a trading decision, investors are advised to gather as much relevant information as possible before executing a trade. This is why institutional investors base their decisions on the aggregate sentiment from millions of online messages at a specific point in time.

Final Thoughts

There are also compelling reasons for practitioners, researchers, and policymakers to pay attention to FSM:

For Practitioners:

- Skill Enhancement: Participating in online discussions allows for feedback that can enhance trading skills. Contributing insights and offering comments can also help build reputation and credibility within the virtual financial community (Zhang 2009).
- Convenient Information Access: FSM provides a low-cost or even no cost way to search for real-time stock and market information. Participants often share and discuss breaking news and stock-related headlines. Value-added services, such as TheLion.com's all-in-one service, help gauge overall investor mood quickly (Depken and Zhang 2010).
- Impact on Stock Prices: Online discussions are not mere noise; they can influence stock prices. Antweiler and Frank (2004) found that online talk has a statistically significant, though economically small, impact on stock returns. Sabherwal et al. (2008) reported that the number of messages posted about a particular fringe stock on a given day is positively related to that stock's abnormal return and can predict the next day's return.
- Volume and Volatility Impacts: Extensive studies have shown that FSM activities, such as the number of messages, posters, message length, and overall sentiment, significantly impact trading volume, return volatility, and liquidity (Koski et al. 2004; Antweiler and Frank 2004; Sabherwal et al. 2011; Delort et al. 2011; Zhang et al. 2012).
- Trading Strategies: Given their impact on stock prices, volume, volatility, and liquidity, it is wise to incorporate trading strategies based on information from FSM. For instance, Gu, Konana et al. (2006) found that sentiments from investors who correctly predicted current stock movements are negatively associated with future movements, suggesting a strategy of buying stocks with low sentiment and selling those with high sentiment. Zhang et al. (2012) also observed a negative relationship between online sentiment and subsequent returns, offering potential opportunities for traders interested in short positions.

For Researchers:

Studying FSM activities helps determine whether posted messages contain valuable information or are merely noise. It also provides insights into why day traders might recommend certain stocks online. Although FSM research dates back to Wysocki's 1998 study, the field is still in its infancy. With advanced data analytics and AI tools, more research in this area is expected.

For Policymakers:

The impact of online message postings on stock trading is of particular interest to policymakers, such as the SEC and FTC. Monitoring FSM helps protect investors by identifying and mitigating securities fraud. Sabherwal et al. (2011) found that fringe stocks with no fundamental news, but high message activity often exhibit a pump-and-dump pattern, underscoring the potential for online manipulation. As a result, the SEC closely monitors FSM activities to safeguard market integrity.

While FSM offer many benefits, they also have drawbacks:

- Anonymity and Low-Quality Information: The anonymity of message authors often leads to low-quality information. Depken and Zhang (2010) argue that opinions on these boards are mostly unsolicited and anonymous, which can result in factually incorrect or misleading information intended to manipulate stock prices (Vilardo 2004).
- Duplicate Accounts: Posters can register multiple accounts under different screen names, making it difficult to track whether multiple identities belong to the same person. This practice can be used to amplify the influence of one's opinions, increasing the potential for securities fraud.
- Stock Price Manipulation: Low-priced stocks with thin floats and limited ownership are particularly vulnerable to manipulation through FSM. Studies by Wysocki (1998) and Aggarwal and Wu (2006) highlight this risk, and Sabherwal et al. (2011) confirm the existence of a pump-and-dump pattern in such stocks.
- Investor Herding: Herding behavior, characterized by unified sentiment among posters, is often observed on FSM. This can lead to increased volatility and risk, as investors overreact to the news,

causing stock prices to deviate substantially from their fundamental values.

Finally, smartphones have greatly expanded the reach and impact of FSM by making market information, sentiment updates, and peer discussions instantly accessible anytime and anywhere. With dedicated apps from platforms such as StockTwits, Seeking Alpha, and Reddit, investors can receive real-time alerts on breaking news, price movements, and trending discussions directly on their mobile devices. Push notifications enable users to act quickly on time-sensitive information, while integrated trading features in some apps allow them to execute trades without leaving the platform. The portability of smartphones also supports richer participation in financial communities through instant sharing of charts, videos, and commentary, enabling a continuous flow of crowd-sourced insights. As a result, mobile access has turned FSM from a desktop-based research tool into a dynamic, always-on ecosystem that actively shapes market sentiment and trading behavior.

In conclusion, FSM have a profound impact on stock trading and financial markets, offering more benefits than drawbacks. This chapter has explored the influence of the Internet, social media, and particularly FSM on financial markets. The next chapter will delve deeper into the structure, functions, and potential issues of various FSM.

CHAPTER 2

A Variety of Financial Social Media

Introduction

Today, a single message posted on the Internet can have a profound impact on financial markets. For example, as mentioned in Chapter 1, a false report of a bomb explosion on X.com (formerly Twitter) on April 23, 2013, caused the Dow Jones Industrial Average to drop by more than one percent, erasing $200 billion in market value in just two minutes.

Historically, financial social media (FSM, hereafter) platforms were not highly regarded by investment professionals and were often dismissed as sources of financial rumors. However, in the current financial landscape, fueled by automated trading and herding behaviors, it is not surprising that a single post on a FSM platform can significantly influence a company's share price, like the butterfly effect in chaos theory.

Today's investors have access to a vast array of digital resources and a large online financial community, which provide them with valuable tools for success in the financial market. FSM platforms allow investors to communicate and share information that may not be readily available elsewhere. The collective knowledge shared across these platforms can be extensive, enabling investors to identify which securities are worth paying attention to and to stay informed about market developments, sometimes even before major news outlets report them. While there is no guarantee of profit, these platforms keep investors alert to market conditions, improving their efficiency and profitability.

Y. Zhang, *Financial Social Media*,
https://doi.org/10.1007/978-3-032-09332-5_2

At its core, an FSM platform is an online bulletin board where users can read, analyze, reply to, and expect responses to their messages. Many websites, such as Yahoo.com and MarketWatch.com, host FSM platforms where users can exchange information and opinions. An FSM platform, specifically, serves as a specialized forum where users can share ideas, charts, strategies, and observations on an ongoing basis. These virtual meeting places have become essential tools for online investors to exchange financial information.

If you spend any time researching stock picks or trading tips online, you will undoubtedly come across some FSM platforms used by traders to share ideas. Not all FSM platforms are created equal. While most FSM platforms provide a useful way to exchange stock-related information, stock chat rooms are perhaps the most effective means of discussing trades in real time with other traders. Unlike other FSM platforms, stock chat rooms are designed exclusively for trading, with participants primarily focused on current market trends and stock movements.

In this chapter, I will introduce four major types of online FSM platforms, categorized by their structure and function: (1) stock chat rooms, (2) stock-trading boards, (3) stock-specific (topic-specific) boards, and (4) board of boards. Stock chat rooms, the predecessors of modern FSM platforms, emerged in the mid-1980s and became popular during the first wave of day trading in the late 1990s. However, due to drawbacks such as anonymity, lack of record retention, and disorganized message threads, chat rooms have declined in popularity, though they are still used by some day traders.

In the late 1990s and early 2000s, stock-trading boards emerged as a more efficient and powerful alternative to stock chat rooms. Despite their advantages, these boards still list messages in reverse chronological order, making it difficult to organize related messages. To address this issue, stock-specific (topic-specific) boards were developed. These boards allow investors to focus on one stock or topic at a time. However, stock-trading boards still have an edge over stock-specific boards because they allow users to discover hot stocks without prior knowledge, whereas stock-specific boards require users to already know the stock's ticker symbol.

When placing a trade order, knowing just the stock ticker symbol, number of shares, trade type, and order type is sufficient. Interestingly, many noise traders make trades with little knowledge of the company, relying only on its ticker symbol. For instance, Rashes (2001) found a significant correlation between the returns, volume, and volatility of stocks with similar ticker symbols, such as MCI and MCIC. Understanding investor sentiment and identifying hot stocks are crucial for swing and momentum traders who make speculative decisions based on market volatility. It is not difficult to observe a "clientele effect" between stock-trading boards and stock-specific boards. Mid- to long-term investors tend to prefer stock-specific boards, while day and short-term traders gravitate towards stock-trading boards. Both types of boards have coexisted and thrived due to the diverse needs of investors.

Later, the advent of powerful search engine technologies has given rise to a new type of FSM platform known as a "board of boards." These platforms aggregate real-time activity from various FSM platforms for a particular security, combining original content with messages sourced from other platforms such as FSM platforms, X.com, Facebook, and Google Plus. The board of boards also provides user-friendly tools, including search engines and sentiment indexes, to help investors access and analyze the vast amount of security-related information and investor sentiment available online.

Stock Chat Rooms

Stock chat rooms are virtual spaces within computer networks specifically designed for real-time conversations. These platforms allow participants to exchange messages instantly, making them a valuable tool for discussing stock-trading topics. A stock chat room functions much like an electronic bulletin board, where users can share investing tips, trading strategies, market insights, and commentaries related to the stock market.

While some stock chat rooms offer valuable insights on stock selection and trading strategies, others may be filled with noise and irrelevant chatter. The capacity of a stock chat room is generally determined by the moderators, who manage the flow of messages that appear simultaneously on all participants' screens as they are typed. Although the earliest stock chat rooms were text-based, many modern platforms now support both text and voice communication.

The primary purpose of a stock chat room is to facilitate the sharing of information related to stock trading, such as price forecasts, trading volume alerts, and news releases, among a group of online investors. These investors can be either registered acquaintances or complete strangers. For example, a penny stock chat room would typically focus solely on discussions related to penny stocks, while large-cap stock chat rooms would rarely entertain discussions about small-cap stocks, thanks to the vigilance of moderators who oversee the content in real time.

To maintain integrity, fairness, and safety, stock chat rooms usually enforce strict rules. Impersonation, racism, harassment, rudeness, and serious typographical errors are generally prohibited. Most chat rooms are well monitored to minimize the use of profanity and personal attacks. Additionally, advertising and flooding (repeatedly posting the same content) are typically banned. Multiple violations of these rules can result in the immediate and permanent suspension of a user account and a ban on the user's IP address.

In stock chat rooms, participants are usually anonymous, identified only by a screen name or alias of their choosing. However, these screen names are not unique and can be used by different individuals at different times, as name registration is often not required. This lack of consistent identity makes it challenging to distinguish between experienced and inexperienced investors.

Despite these challenges, stock chat rooms offer several advantages. They allow participants to pool their knowledge, making it easier to stay informed about current market conditions. The high level of interaction and collaboration is also a significant benefit, as questions posed in a chat room often receive answers within seconds, much faster than on other FSM platforms. In many ways, a stock chat room is like having a free trading customer service department at your fingertips.

One of the most well-known public stock chat rooms is Activetrader, which is the largest chat room managed through the Financialchat.com network. Unlike most FSM platforms, Activetrader does not require users to log in or register a unique screen name. Instead, users select a screen name each time they visit. Once inside, they see two separate screens: one displaying a list of text messages sorted chronologically, with the newest post first, and the other listing active participants. In Table 2.1, I demonstrate the kind of information captured with an example:

In Table 2.1, we can see that each text message is concise, informal, and presented in a dialogue-like format. Long messages in a chat room are not recommended, as few traders are willing to read lengthy posts. During trading hours, people are primarily focused on stock price movements, the trades they have made, and their target prices. It is only after trading hours that discussions may shift to topics less directly related to trading.

Table 2.1 An Example of Activetrader Chat Room

9:58	*LyndaR*	*spoos, uvxy both red?*	*Chatting*
9:58	ANEK2	immu6	ANEK2
9:59	Canuk	FSLR still nice	aNx
10:01		*** beausal Est parti (ping timeout)	BADDBILL
10:01	LyndaR	Bernanke speak today? Time?	Bizee
10:02	LyndaR	10:02ET U.S. BUSINESS INVENTORIES RISE 0.1% IN MAY [MW]	Blue
10:03	Remley	Wed.0.2 day testimony I think..Ben	Callsandputs
10:05		*** mikep a rejoint #ActiveTrader	Canuk
10:05	LyndaR	Inv expected 0.0%	Cwj
10:05	Gold‘	RVLT heads up	Deeps
22:05	Canuk	Need dx to lose this support	Delby
10:05		*** weregain Est parti (QUIT: User exited)	Gold‘
10:06	Canuk	FLSR on fire... Sweet move	Idlers
10:06		*** yoke101 a rejoint #ActiveTrader	Losap
10:07	LyndaR	BBL: u know the deal: (	LyndaR
10:08	LyndaR	Be back later; looks like a symbol stock, sorry	Metro
10:09	tool6	Oil slipping a bit	Mikep
10:09	tool6	i want 107$$$$	Remley
10:10		*** yeel a rejoint #ActiveTrader	Supreme15
10:11	Canuk	dx trying to lose it.. Cmon pop my euro to the moon please	tool6
10:12	Canuk	Ok. Ill take too the top of the hill. Forget the moon	Yingzhang

Since there are only 21 messages per screen, the influx of new messages quickly pushes older posts off the screen, making it difficult to keep up with the conversation. While users can scroll up to view previous posts, most do not, as outdated information holds little value for day traders. Additionally, once the chat window is closed, all chat records are lost and cannot be retrieved. The chat room is monitored by a team of moderators to ensure compliance with its rules.

Users can view the background of other participants by clicking on their screen names and selecting the “Whois” option. Additional features include “PM” (private messaging) for direct communication and “Ignore” to hide a user’s messages from your screen. For instance, Table 2.2 shows my account details:

The effectiveness of stock chat rooms varies, with some providing valuable information and others serving as little more than noise. This

Table 2.2 User yingzhang's Profile on Activetrader

Who is yingzhang?	
Nickname:	*yingzhang*
Username:	ae8bd1aa
Hostname:	109.169.29.gs91=
Real name:	174.139.209.170
Server:	ny.ny.us.financialchat.com
Server info:	Financial chat: NY, NY server
Idle time:	3 minutes
Channels:	#ActiveTrader

inconsistency has led practitioners, researchers, and policymakers to question the true impact of discussions in stock chat rooms. Academic research has provided some insights. Mizrach and Weerts (2009) conducted the first empirical study on the Activetrader chat room and found that more than half of the traders in the room made profits after accounting for transaction costs, with a statistically significant abnormal return of 0.17 percent per day, equivalent to 53.4 percent annually, after controlling for conventional risk factors. This result is surprising given that other studies, such as Barber and Odean (2000), report that average retail traders underperform the market by 1.5 percent annually, with the most active traders experiencing even worse returns. Lu and Mizrach (2011) further demonstrated that less skilled traders in the chat room benefited from following the strategies of more experienced traders. This evidence suggests that stock chat rooms can be valuable tools for improving trading skills and achieving higher-than-average returns.

However, stock chat rooms are not without risks. As with any online platform, there are individuals who attempt to manipulate stock prices for personal gain. These bad actors may spread false or misleading information to influence others' trading decisions. A notable example is the 2008 pump-and-dump scheme involving Rudy Nutrition (RUNU) stock, where Stephen DeCesare and his partners used chat rooms to artificially inflate the stock's price and volume before selling their shares at a profit. The SEC eventually charged those involved, but similar cases have occurred throughout the history of online trading.[1] The phrase "garbage in, garbage out" is particularly relevant in the context of stock chat rooms. Most chat rooms are free, and the information shared within them is often speculative. While subscription-based chat rooms are generally considered to be of higher quality, users should still approach the advice they receive with caution. Public access chat rooms differ from fee-based chat rooms, where traders pay for tips from expert traders or analysts. These fee-based chat rooms often come with memberships that provide exclusive benefits and support.

It is important to remember that you are not limited to a single chat room, whether public or private. You can register with as many as you wish and stick with those that provide the best information and trading advice. However, even in fee-based chat rooms, there have been cases of stock price manipulation. A well-known example is Yun Soo Oh Park, also known as "Tokyo Joe," who ran a stock-tipping website and private chat room. The SEC fined him in 2001 for front-running the picks he made in his chat room, highlighting the importance of doing your homework before acting on any advice.[2] There are numerous cases of securities fraud related to stock chat rooms, underscoring the need for vigilance. Richard H. Walker, former SEC director of enforcement, advised investors to protect themselves against Internet fraud, including pump-and-dump schemes, by conducting thorough research and being skeptical of information received from strangers online. Ultimately, the best protection is to be well-informed and cautious, regardless of the source of your trading advice.

Stock Trading Board

The second type of FSM platform is the stock-trading board, which has evolved from the stock chat room. Stock chat rooms, while useful, have several limitations, including poster anonymity, irretrievable past messages, unorganized message threads, implicit sentiment, and lack of poster credibility. Modern stock-trading boards, however, have addressed all these issues effectively.

Firstly, stock-trading boards, as more advanced web-based systems, require users to register with a unique screen name. Registered users, referred to as members, can then submit and send electronic messages. While this does not eliminate anonymity, it ensures that no one else can register the same screen name, allowing a user to build a recognizable reputation within the community as long as the account remains secure.

Account registration significantly enhances the overall information quality on stock-trading boards. For instance, research by Depken and Zhang (2009) found that registration reduces the likelihood of users manipulating stock prices through multiple usernames, as maintaining multiple accounts diminishes the reputation of any single account. Additionally, with their registered accounts, users are incentivized to post quality messages to build their reputation within the community.

A key distinction between stock chat rooms and trading boards is the ability to access past messages on trading boards at any time. This feature is invaluable for long-term investors and automated trading, as historical messages can provide useful insights. Gu, Konana, Liu, Rajagopalan, and Ghosh (2006) argue that some posters on FSM platforms possess information not fully reflected in stock prices, making a trading strategy based on these posters' past sentiments potentially profitable. Furthermore, the ability to retrieve past messages does not disadvantage day traders, who can still monitor the latest posts on the main page, similar to a stock chat room.

Another advantage of trading boards is the organized structure of messages. Unlike stock chat rooms, where messages are sorted chronologically and not grouped by relevance, trading boards link messages according to their relevance and topics. Each message is clearly identified as either a reply or an original post, making it easier to search for and find information.

In terms of sentiment disclosure, stock-trading boards offer a significant improvement over chat rooms. In chat rooms, users must interpret the mood of the poster by reading the message content without any explicit sentiment indicators, which can lead to subjective and inconsistent interpretations. To reduce this bias, stock-trading boards began introducing sentiment functions in the early 2000s, allowing posters to explicitly label their opinions. For example, TheLion.com allows users to select sentiments such as Strong Buy, Buy, Hold, Scalp, Sell, Strong Sell, Short, or to leave it undisclosed by default. This feature supports the construction of an aggregate sentiment index, as demonstrated by Zhang, Swanson, and Prombutr (2012).

Modern FSM platforms also attach a rating score or rank (scaled from low to high) next to a screen name, helping users gauge the quality of information provided by a poster. Many stock-trading boards have adopted similar reputation systems that rank posters based on their portfolio performance and forecast accuracy. According to Gregg and Scott (2006) and Depken and Zhang (2009), posters accumulate reputation credit for posting quality messages, which reduces the incentive to create and use multiple accounts, a problem identified by Vilardo (2004). This credit score system helps to reduce stock manipulation and increases the incentives for providing accurate information. Researchers studying investor behavior on FSM platforms often rely on credibility-weighted measures of investor sentiment, which are considered more reliable than traditional equally weighted sentiment indices, see Zhang et al. (2022).

Stock-trading boards also commonly feature "watch" and "ignore" functions. The "watch list" allows users to highlight all messages from a particular author, making it easier to track their contributions. The more followers a user has, the larger the impact their opinions may have on stock prices. Depken and Zhang (2010) interpret this as a non-monetary reputation measure, serving as a surrogate for popularity within the community. Conversely, the "ignore list" allows users to hide messages from specific authors, helping them manage and filter out disruptive, advertising, or spam messages. These user-friendly functions empower forum participants to tailor the information they receive according to their preferences.

There are several notable stock-trading boards, such as TheLion, HotCopper, Trade2Win, and StockReads. To illustrate the differences between a stock-trading board and a stock chat room, consider the "Short Term Trading" board on HotCopper.com.au, the largest stock market forum in the Southern Hemisphere. The "Short Term Trading" board is dedicated to discussions on short-term trading, particularly on the Australian Securities Exchange (ASX).

As shown in Table 2.3, all messages on the "Short Term Trading" board are listed in reverse chronological order based on their posting date and time, displayed in the "Date" column. The most recent message appears at the top of the screen, and each message is assigned a unique number in the "Msg. #" column.

If a message references a stock, the ticker symbol entered by the author is displayed in the "Sym." column. Some messages may not reference any stock, leaving the "Symbol" column empty (e.g., see Msg. #43377).

The first few words of each message are shown as a hyperlink in the "Subject" column, giving readers a quick glimpse of the content. By clicking the hyperlink, users can view the complete message. However, most authors aim to be concise, so the entire message often fits within the subject line. The "Posted by" column shows the author ID of each message, while the "Views" column indicates how many times the message has been read. HotCopper also allows peer reviewing through the "Rating" column, which displays how many users recommend a post.

Table 2.3 An Example of the "Short Term Trading" Board on HotCopper

Msg. #	*Sym.*	*Subject*	*View As*	*Posted by*	*Views*	*Rating*	*Date*
43,465	AAC	Aac good earnings this week.	Thread	YingZhang	7		27/04/14 04:20
43,464	GAM	Gam looks bullish	Thread	YingZhang	10		27/04/14 04:11
43,377		Re: Easter lounge short term trading 19th- 21 apr	Thread	MithridatesVI	352		20/04/14 15:37
43,376		Re: Easter lounge short term trading 19th- 21 apr	Thread	3500	451	+4	19/04/14 17:57
43,375	BNE	Re: Entry for stt list; bne	Thread	J8	178		19/04/14 15:47
43,374	BNE	Re: Entry for stt list; bne	Thread	J8	164		19/04/14 15:44
43,373	BNE	Entry for stt list; bne	Thread	Deltatrader	177		19/04/14 11:00
43,372		Re: Easter lounge short term trading 19th- 21 apr	Thread	3500	482	+1	18/04/14 21:27

For instance, a "+4" rating for message #43376 means four other readers gave it a "Thumbs Up." Messages without endorsements do not display a rating number.

As depicted in Fig. 2.1, when posting a new message, users must disclose whether they hold a position in the stock they are discussing. This disclosure is crucial as it reveals any potential conflicts of interest. It's common sense that a poster's sentiment may be biased if they have a vested interest in the stock. Users can also select one of eight sentiments: None, Buy, ST Buy, LT Buy, Hold, Sell, ST Sell, and LT Sell, where ST stands for short-term and LT for long-term.

Let us focus on Msg. #43464, posted by the author. Below is a detailed printout of its content:

In Table 2.4, Msg. #43464 on the "Forum: Short Term Trading" board starts a new thread. The title of the message is "gam looks bullish (YingZhang)," indicating it was posted by the author YingZhang. The

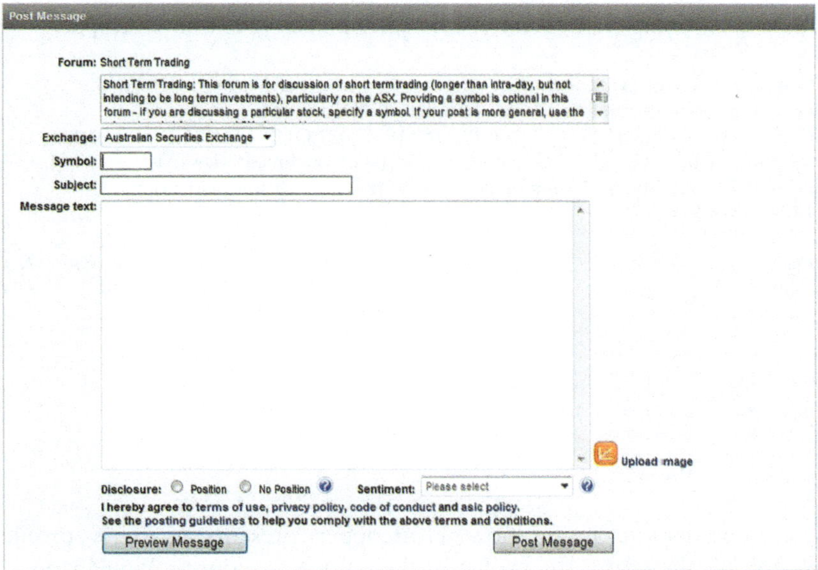

Fig. 2.1 Screen Capture of Post Message on Hotcopper

stock symbol "GAM" refers to the company "GAMING & ENTERTAINMENT GROUP LIMITED," listed on the Australian Securities Exchange (ASX). Users can click on "Price Chart" to view the price chart of GAM or "Announcements" to see market news about the company. The sentiment for this post is "LT Buy," signaling a long-term bullish outlook. The "Disclosure: Stock Held" note indicates that the poster "YingZhang" held a position in the stock at the time of posting. Notably, the first five digits (142.54) of the poster's IP address are visible, helping readers identify the poster and reduce account abuse. The complete content of Msg. #43464 is displayed in the center of the table, allowing readers to review the original message. By clicking "Post Reply," users can respond to this message in a new "Post Reply Message" window, as shown in Fig. 2.1. The "Thread View" option displays the original message and all subsequent replies on one page, arranged in reverse chronological order. Each post also includes a "Report Post" link, enabling readers to report inappropriate content to forum moderators.

Table 2.4 Complete Content of Message Number 43464 on Hotcopper

Gam looks bullish (YingZhang)
Forum: Short term trading (Back | return to CFDs forum)
Code: GAM - GAMING & ENTERTAINMENT GROUP LIMITED (Price chart | announcements | Google GAM) post: 43464 (start of thread) views: 10
Posted: 27/04/14 04:11 sentiment: LT buy disclosure: Stock held from: 142.54.Xxx.Xxx

Post Reply	*Thread View*	*Back*	*(0)*	*Thumbs Up / Thumbs Down*	*Report Post*	*Previous Post*	*Next Post*

GAM looks bullish. Test message.

Add user to Favorites	Add stock to Favorites	Email to Friend	Ignore Member	Ignore Stock

Finally, let's examine how HotCopper presents a user's profile. Figure 2.2 showcases the profile of the author's account—YingZhang.

The profile information is comprehensive. We learn that "YingZhang" joined the HotCopper community on April 18, 2014, and has posted two messages. By default, HotCopper displays the last 10 posts by each user, along with the corresponding forum, stock symbol, subject, number of views, and posting date. The author's first message was posted on April 27, 2014, at 04:11, and the second one was posted on April 27, 2014, at 04:20.

Stock-Specific (Topic-Specific) Board

In contrast to the stock chat room, the stock-trading board has been significantly enhanced in almost every aspect. However, due to its nature as a trading board, messages are typically listed according to the time of posting, as it is crucial for active short-term traders to know which stocks are currently "hot" and worthy of attention. A traditional trading board does not aggregate messages related to a particular stock on a separate page.

As a competitor, another type of FSM platform, the stock-specific board, was developed and has gained popularity among longer-term investors who typically focus on one stock at a time. Although stock-specific boards have a different structure for presenting messages, they are

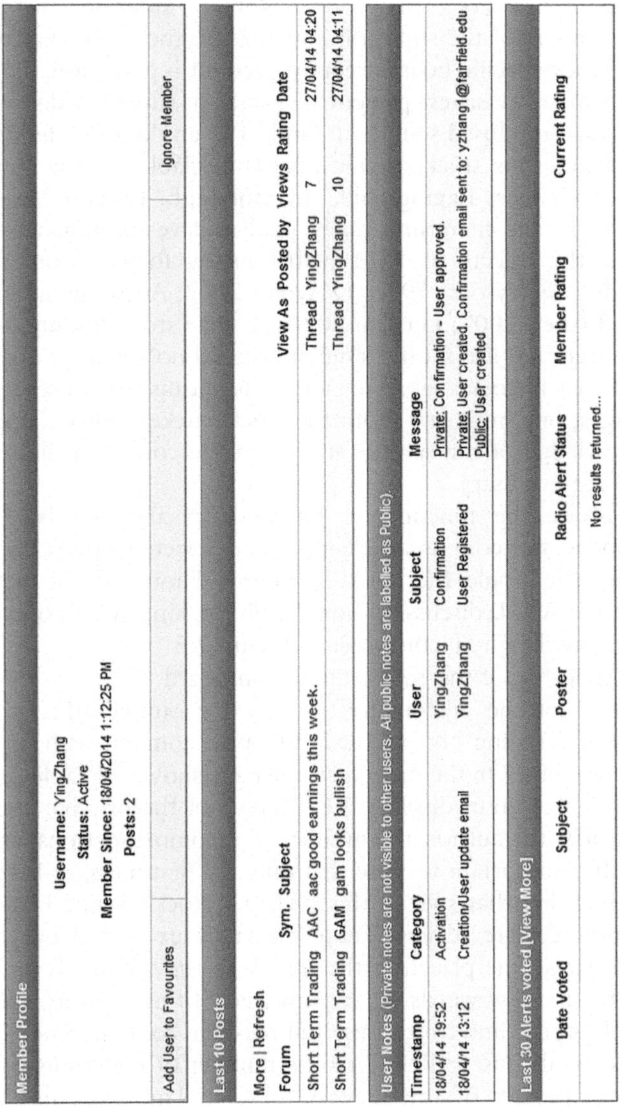

Fig. 2.2 Screen Capture of YingZhang's Member Profile on Hotcopper.com.au

equipped with similar functions to those found on stock-trading boards. For this reason, a stock-specific board is also considered a more advanced FSM platform than a stock chat room. Notably, stock-specific boards have addressed many of the shortcomings that plague stock chat rooms. For instance, stock-specific boards require account registration, allow for the retrieval of past messages, present messages in threaded discussions, enable explicit self-disclosed sentiment, and offer an "ignore" function.

There are numerous stock-specific boards available on the Internet, such as Yahoo! Finance, Raging Bull, InvestorsHub, InvestorLinks, and SiliconInvestor. In the literature, many studies have examined investor behaviors and the effects of FSM platforms by focusing on Yahoo! Finance boards (see Wysocki 1998; D'Avolio 2002; Antweiler and Frank 2004; Das and Chen 2007; Lerman 2020). Unlike stock-trading boards, where all messages are listed on a single page, Yahoo! Finance organizes messages under each stock's separate page. This means that to read stock-related messages, one must first input the stock's ticker symbol, implying that prior knowledge of the specific stock and the correct spelling of its ticker symbol are necessary.

To demonstrate the functionality of stock-specific boards, I have chosen SiliconInvestor.com as an example and selected one of its most visited boards—the Apple Inc. (AAPL) board. Thousands of messages are posted on the AAPL discussion board daily, making AAPL one of the most discussed stocks on SiliconInvestor. Figure 2.5

provides a snapshot of the AAPL discussion board.

The structure of the SiliconInvestor board is simpler than that of the "Short Term Trading" board on HotCopper.com.au, with only five columns in the layout. On the main message page shown in Table 2.5, the first row from left to right displays the "Reply" of the original message, a message preview, the author, the number of recommendations, and the posting date. It is important to note that only the first message is considered the original one that started this "AAPL" stock-specific board. All subsequent messages are replies. These messages are sorted by posting time, with the latest one placed at the top. Like the "Short Term Trading" board, the first few words are hyperlinked in this column, allowing readers to click on the link to read the full message content. The SiliconInvestor platform also uses "Recs," or the number of recommendations, to indicate the popularity of a message. A "-" symbol indicates the absence of any endorsements.

Table 2.5 An Example of the AAPL Message Board on Siliconinvestor

Reply	*Message Preview*	*From*	*Recs*	*Date*
168,596	I am so bullish about apple company. I give a strong buy sentiment.	YingZhang	–	4/20/2014 15:22
168,595	Got it, thanks! A very happy Easter to you too!	J.F. Sebastian	–	4/20/2014 14:07
168,594	Cleaning out a drawer... found an old iTunes gift card that an American friend aw	Yofal	–	4/20/2014 14:05
168,593	Meanwhile, handset shipments in China totaled over 100 million units in the fir	Pyslent	–	4/20/2014 12:58
168,592	I think the biggest error they made in their recent upgrades was hiding by defa	J.F. Sebastian	–	4/20/2014 11:38
168,591	Some things are nice, but I really miss things like cover flow and the ease of n	Yofal	1	4/20/2014 11:09
168,590	Which is one of the big reasons I don't upgrade iTunes. Why should I? All	Doren	1	4/19/2014 21:14
168,589	I completely agree with your assessment about the bloated nature of iTunes. The	J.F. Sebastian	1	4/19/2014 16:57
168,588	iTunes does a good job of managing media files, but I can't say it does an e	HerbVic	1	4/19/2014 15:30
168,587	Now this is a much better number from China Mobile. digitimes.com China	slacker711	1	4/19/2014 13:21
168,586	Exactly. End user sell-through is always a better metric of end user demand than	MGV	–	4/19/2014 12:58
168,585	Right! So why would Nike keep the software team on board, when they fired most o	Stock puppy	4	4/19/2014 12:02

Table 2.6 Message Number 168596 on the AAPL Message Board on Silicon-investor

Technology Stocks: Apple Inc. AAPL 524.94 0.0% Apr 17 8:10 PM EDT News
Public reply | Prvt reply | mark as last read | file |keep | previous 10 |previous |next From: YingZhang 4/20/2014 15:22 168,596 of 168,596 I am so bullish about apple company. I give a strong buy sentiment. Report TOU violation Public reply | Prvt reply | mark as last read | file |keep | previous 10 |previous |next

Next, let's click on the hyperlink of message #168596, titled "I am so bullish about Apple company. I give a Strong Buy sentiment," to review its detailed content. Table 2.6 shows the complete content of the message.

This message was written by me, under the username "YingZhang," on April 20, 2014, at 15:22. The content of the message is the same as the preview because it is only 67 characters long. Other users can reply to me via "Public Reply" or "Prvt Reply." Additionally, any user can report a message by clicking the "Report TOU Violation" button, where TOU stands for "Terms of Use."

Unlike TheLion.com, SiliconInvestor presents a more concise author profile. As shown in Table 2.7, SiliconInvestor provides only basic details such as the author's name, total posts, last activity time, and the date they joined. In this case, the "Date Joined" (a proxy for membership duration) might be loosely used as a measure of the poster's credibility—the longer the membership duration, the higher the credibility. SiliconInvestor displays all messages written by the poster in reverse chronological order, from the most recent to the oldest.

Stock-specific and stock-trading boards share several common features:

- Each message is accompanied by a detailed posting date and time.
- The corresponding stock ticker symbol is displayed (if applicable).
- Past information is stored and can be retrieved at any time in the future.
- Data is structured in an organized manner.
- Reply and non-reply messages are distinctly differentiated.

Table 2.7 User YingZhang's Profile on Siliconinvestor

Site Participation			
Date Joined	*Apr 20 2014*	*User Level*	*1*
Posts	5	Boards moderated	0
PeopleMarks	0	Bans issued	0
Ignored by	0	Bans received	0
Personal information			
25 Most recent subjects	Last post	Posts	
Google	4/20/2014 16:23	1	
2014 biotech charity contest	4/20/2014 16:00	1	
Weibo	4/20/2014 15:57	1	
Apple Inc.	4/20/2014 15:22	1	
Posts by YingZhang			
Message	Subject	Recs	Posted
GOOG and GOOGL are both bullish in the short and long run.	Google	–	4/20/2014 16:23
Bio tech sector will go up from here after the selloff last month.	2014 biotech charity contest	–	4/20/2014 16:00
Weibo is similar to twitter which is a popular social media site in China.	Weibo	–	4/20/2014 15:57
I am so bullish about apple company. I give a strong buy sentiment.	Apple Inc.	–	4/20/2014 15:22

- Self-disclosed sentiments are displayed, providing a method to quantify text messages.

Board of Boards

FSM platforms offer investors a platform to communicate and exchange valuable information. However, with the vast number of posts across various platforms, searching for and reading messages about just one stock, let alone multiple stocks, can be an overwhelming task. For an astute trader, manually processing a large volume of posts while making trades is simply impractical.

To address this challenge, search engines within "Board of Boards" systems efficiently gather data from popular FSM platforms, chat rooms, financial blogs, Facebook pages, and X.com accounts. This information is then organized and categorized by stock, topic, popularity, or other relevant criteria, significantly reducing the time needed to gauge investor sentiment on a specific stock or the market. With quick access to comprehensive data, an increasing number of investors are turning to "Board of Boards" platforms to identify potential winning stocks. This innovative application represents a significant advancement over traditional FSM platforms.

Due to the complexities involved in developing sophisticated search engine technologies, there are fewer aggregator boards compared to other types of FSM platforms. Among these, BoardCentral.com is the most visited and serves as an excellent example of the structure and functions of a "Board of Boards."

BoardCentral.com was designed to provide investors with comprehensive access to FSM platforms and X.com content. Its unique and effective search engine aggregates and presents this information to users at no cost, simplifying the process of finding relevant data and saving valuable time. Users can tailor their searches by specifying individual sites, the number of messages per page, and the timeframe for search queries. In addition to aggregating data from external sources, BoardCentral.com also allows its users to contribute content. Consequently, the platform tracks the most popular ticker symbols across its own site and affiliated sources, offering a wide range of financial data and tools for the online financial community.

BoardCentral.com provides real-time streams of feeds, FSM activities, and market news related to over-the-counter (OTC) stocks, NASDAQ, and NYSE-listed stocks, ETFs, and Forex securities. For instance, users can search for messages related to AAPL across 13 different source boards, including Yahoo! Finance, Google, Market Rap, Motley Fool, TheLion.com, ItsAllBull, FreeRealTime, ADVFN InvestorsHub, Stockhouse, The Stock Roach, Investor Village, Raging Bull, and Silicon Investor. Users can select one or a combination of these sources for their searches.

Beyond FSM platforms and X.com, BoardCentral.com enables users to search for stock information from social profiles. The platform categorizes news into two groups: news from the web and news from the company. The first group aggregates stock-related news from various web sources such as TheStreet.com, Seeking Alpha, and MarketWatch.com. The second group collects company news from major portals like NASDAQ.com and Reuters.com. This news is provided in real time, with clickable titles that redirect users to the original articles on their respective websites. Given these features, investors seeking in-depth research, supported by detailed resources from the two largest online financial communities, frequently turn to BoardCentral.com.

Finally, BoardCentral.com offers real-time and historical buzz indexes that highlight the most researched and discussed stocks within the FSM sphere. By monitoring these indexes, investors can identify stocks that warrant attention, often before news is publicly released.

Final Thoughts

FSM platforms have developed from small online rumor forums into influential channels that can move markets within minutes. They provide real-time communication, explicit sentiment sharing, and access to the collective knowledge of investors, often delivering market-relevant information before traditional news outlets. This chapter introduces four main types of FSM platforms: stock chat rooms, stock-trading boards, stock-specific boards, and the aggregator board of boards. Stock chat rooms offer immediate interaction and quick responses but lack message archives, consistent identity verification, and content organization, which can lead to misinformation and manipulation. Stock-trading boards improve on these weaknesses by requiring account registration, storing past messages, organizing discussions by topic, and including sentiment indicators and reputation systems that enhance information quality. Stock-specific boards focus on a single security and are favored by long-term investors who want in-depth discussion, although they require prior knowledge of the ticker symbol. Aggregator boards, such as BoardCentral.com, compile content from multiple FSM sources, using advanced search and sentiment tools to help investors track market buzz and identify opportunities quickly. While these platforms can improve market awareness, trading skills, and decision-making, they also carry risks including bias, low-quality information, and deliberate market manipulation, making cautious and informed participation essential.

Notes

1. SEC's official press release, titled *SEC Charges Daniel "Rudy" Ruettiger and 12 Others in Scheme to Pump Stock in Sports Drink Company*, provides a comprehensive overview. This Litigation Release (No. 22198, dated December 16, 2011) explains how DeCesare and others used Internet chat rooms, promotional mailers, SEC filings, and press releases to manipulate RUNU's price and volume while selling unregistered shares, resulting in over $11 million in illicit profits. It also details the engagement of chat rooms in disseminating misleading information to investors.
2. Litigation Release No. 16399 (January 5, 2000)-SEC vs. Yun Soo Oh Park a/k/a Tokyo Joe and Tokyo Joe's Societe Anonyme Corp. This official SEC complaint details how Park ran a stock-tipping website and private chat room while trading ahead of his recommendations (i.e., front-running), posting misleading performance results, and failing to disclose conflicts of interest.

CHAPTER 3

About Financial Social Media Posters

Introduction

Web operators, including major companies like Google and Yahoo, along with Internet service providers (ISPs) such as America Online (AOL) and Comcast, routinely track Internet users' IP addresses. In many cases, they may also collect personal information like email addresses, dates of birth, and home addresses during the registration process. These operators typically disclose that they may share personal information to law enforcement agencies or other relevant parties if they suspect any form of misconduct, including securities fraud.

For instance, if you attempt to post on a Yahoo! Finance discussion board, Yahoo expects compliance with its Terms of Service (TOS). You will likely encounter a notice indicating that, although your IP address is not visible in your post, Yahoo does record your Yahoo! ID and IP address to combat abuse. This information may be disclosed to law enforcement or other entities if necessary. Similar terms of service are standard across nearly all financial social media (FSM, hereafter) platforms.

While defamatory and libelous postings are prohibited, web operators are not necessarily required to reveal the identity of anonymous posters. Even in cases where they do, operators must balance various considerations, including free speech, public safety, and the need to foster an online community. Nevertheless, there have been lawsuits against posters for

Y. Zhang, *Financial Social Media*,
https://doi.org/10.1007/978-3-032-09332-5_3

defamatory and libelous content. These lawsuits have generally favored the defendants, largely due to their anonymity status (see Lidsky, 2009).

However, the scenario changes in cases of securities fraud. Courts can compel web operators to disclose the identities of anonymous posters through legal orders. It is well known that FSM platforms are under scrutiny by market regulators and law enforcement agencies, including the Securities and Exchange Commission (SEC), Federal Trade Commission (FTC), and Federal Bureau of Investigation (FBI). These entities monitor both public and private FSM platforms regularly and maintain extensive records of chat logs.

How to Learn a Poster's True Identity

Let us begin with an example: online securities fraud. As previously discussed, stock manipulators often create websites to disseminate inaccurate or misleading information about companies, intending to manipulate stock prices. To reach a broader audience, they may use email (often spam) to spread fraudulent information, post false press releases on FSM platforms, and use online auction sites to market fraudulent or unregistered securities to unsuspecting investors.

One common tactic used by stock manipulators is the "pump-and-dump" scheme. In this scheme, they purchase shares of a stock at a low price, hype it on FSM platforms with false and misleading information, and encourage honest investors to buy the stock, inflating its price. The manipulators then sell their shares at the peak, causing the stock price to plummet. Using data from TheLion.com platform, Saberwal, Sarkar, and Zhang (2011) documented a two-day pump followed by a two-day dump manipulation pattern by online traders. They found that small, thinly traded stocks with weak financials and low institutional holdings are more susceptible to manipulation, even in the absence of market news about these companies.

Once stock manipulation is under investigation, the SEC may file a lawsuit against the poster(s), alleging securities fraud. In such cases, courts can compel web operators and ISPs to disclose the identity of anonymous posters. Most web operators or ISPs are willing to provide a poster's IP address, which can usually be traced back to the poster's ISP account information. Once the poster(s) are identified, the SEC may examine their trading records alongside chat logs. If sufficient evidence is found, the SEC will charge the poster(s) with fraud for manipulating stocks. Violators of securities laws often face imprisonment.

This example underscores the lack of "absolute privacy" on the Internet. Users should not assume anonymity when posting online, as it is technologically simple to trace the source of messages and identify posters. Here's how it works: All communications between computers via the Internet involve IP addresses, which may be static or dynamic. Static IP addresses are permanent. An IP address is a numeric address consisting of four sets of numbers separated by periods, such as 123.123.123.123, and it can typically be traced back to the ISP. The ISP holds the poster's personal information, including their email account, home address, and telephone number. When a computer user posts a message online, the data transmission includes the computer's IP address, which is recorded by the website operator. Even when using a public computer, the poster's identity can be traced through their login credentials and the recorded time of use.

Defamatory or libelous postings present a different challenge. While the right to speak anonymously is recognized, it is not absolute. Posters cannot use anonymity as a shield against liability for defamation. However, defamation cases are often difficult to pursue because defamatory statements on FSM platforms can be framed as opinions, which are protected by the First Amendment. Moreover, a law requiring anonymous posters to voluntarily reveal their identities would likely be unconstitutional, as the U.S. Supreme Court has ruled against such requirements. This is why web operators that allow users to post anonymously do not have to disclose the identities of posters in defamation cases.

Additionally, FSM platforms' hosts are not held liable for false or defamatory statements made by others. Under Section 230(c) (1) of the Communications Decency Act (CDA Sec. 230), "No provider or user of an interactive computer service shall be treated as the publisher or speaker of any information provided by another information content provider." For example, in the case of Green v. AOL, John Green alleged that AOL failed to adequately monitor its services, allowing third parties to defame him and cause intentional emotional distress. However, the court upheld immunity for AOL against negligence claims.

Section 230 of the Communications Decency Act of 1996 thus grants most FSM platforms' hosts the discretion to manage postings in response to claims of defamation or misleading content Most hosts include terms of service that grant them the right to delete or retain messages at their discretion, and these terms have generally been upheld as enforceable under the law. TheLion.com's "User Agreement & Disclaimer" is a prime example.

Who Posts Messages on Financial Social Media Platforms?

There is no absolute privacy on the Internet. While law enforcement entities can compel web operators to reveal a poster's identity through legal channels, it remains nearly impossible for an ordinary individual, including researchers, to obtain this information. As we study the behavior of posters on FSM platforms, our understanding of their backgrounds is limited. However, before performing quantitative analyses and building econometric models to study posting activities, it is crucial to categorize different types of posters. We also need to consider their motivations, habits, preferences, and posting patterns. Based on my years of observation, documentation, and research, I have identified eight categories of posters, each characterized by distinct backgrounds, behaviors, and typical contributions to FSM platforms.

A. Sincere Online Investors: These make up the majority of posters, and their primary purpose is to share information and express opinions. Each poster registers with a unique alias, posts messages, and responds to others. Consistent with prior classifications of social media users, sincere online investors can be subdivided into four categories based on their level of engagement, enthusiasm, and credibility:

- Infrequent posters: Occasionally visit and post messages.
- Frequent posters: Regularly participate in discussions and contribute a significant number of messages.
- Masters: Highly active participants who frequently share opinions about financial securities and markets.
- Gurus: Respected masters with high credibility within the community, possessing many followers. They frequently post messages, answer questions, provide comments, and share their sentiments.

Das, Martinez-Jerez, and Tufano (2005) noted that there are relatively few frequent posters, while occasional posters are far more numerous. Some posters may register multiple screen names. However, as discussed in Chapter 2, many stock-trading boards implement reputation systems to reduce the incentive to use multiple accounts, thereby mitigating stock manipulation and encouraging the dissemination of accurate information.

B. Platform Hosts: It is understandable that FSM platform administrators, creators, and hosts also post messages. There are several reasons for this:

- System broadcasting: For example, moderators in the Activetrader chat room, whose screen names often have an "@" prefix, frequently post system-broadcast messages starting with "***." Similarly, on TheLion.com's WallStreetPit forum, announcements by hosts are usually tagged at the bottom of each page, often emphasizing rules and terms of service.
- Answering questions: It is common for users to leave questions for administrators. Platform administrators generally prefer responding directly on the platform rather than through private emails.
- Generating posting activity: The primary role of FSM platform hosts is to maintain engagement with regular updates. High traffic and valuable posts are essential for a forum's success, so frequent and quality communications are necessary. Consequently, it is not surprising to see stock-related messages posted by platform hosts to share opinions and information.
- Stock manipulation: Though uncommon, some hosts engage in pump-and-dump schemes on their forums. A notable example is the previously mentioned "Tokyo Joe." As always, verify everything you read online and beware of misleading content.

C. Regulators: It may come as a surprise, but market regulators also post messages on FSM platforms. The SEC, for example, has used the Internet to alert investors about potential problems with specific securities. In November 1996, the SEC posted information about the suspension of OmniGene Diagnostics, Inc. (stock symbol as "OMGD") in a chat room that discussed the stock, marking the first instance of such action.

D. Past and Present Employees: Employees, especially those working for publicly traded companies, often monitor FSM platforms to see what others are saying about their employer, whether it's truth or rumor.

Disgruntled investors and unhappy employees frequently use FSM platforms to vent, share opinions, reveal confidential insider information, and sometimes spread rumors or fake news. For example, in April 1999, an employee of PairGain Technologies Inc. posted a fake news report on the Yahoo! Finance discussion board, falsely claiming that the company was going to be acquired by an Israeli firm. The stock gained 31% within hours (see Kimmel, 2004). Felton and Kim (2002) also studied the Yahoo! Finance discussion board for Enron and found that it was full of messages from Enron employees, who warned of the company's impending collapse.

E. Company Representatives: Many companies are concerned about online postings and take active measures to address questions raised in those postings. Public relations and legal teams closely monitor FSM platforms and participate in online discussions to "set the record straight" and manage damage control (see Wysocki, 1999). Wysocki also suggested that message-posting activity is linked to a company's information environment; a sudden surge in postings may indicate investor discontent and signal the need to address an information gap.

F. Company Executives: You may recall the 2007 lawsuit aimed at blocking Whole Foods Market from acquiring Wild Oats Markets. The FTC alleged that John Mackey, the CEO of Whole Foods Market, anonymously attacked Wild Oats Markets on FSM platforms with an intention to push down its stock price, enabling Whole Foods Market to acquire it at a lower price. Following this scandal, Whole Foods Market amended its code of business conduct, prohibiting senior executives and directors from posting messages about the company, its competitors, and vendors on unsponsored Internet forums.

G. Paid Posters: Paid forum posters are often employed to generate traffic and activity on a forum, which is crucial to its success. On FSM platforms, however, some posters are paid to manipulate certain stocks. These individuals may use multiple aliases, posting and answering their own questions under different names to influence users' investment decisions and trading activities. Since they are viewed as deceptive, paid posters are careful not to reveal their status. Notable cases include SEC v. Jason A. Greg ("Greig"), SEC v. Eugene B. Martineau, and SEC v. David A. Wood, Jr.

H. Professionals and Institutions: It is often assumed that only retail investors post messages on FSM platforms, but there is evidence that market makers, securities brokers, and other financial institutions have also engaged in stock manipulation on these platforms. For example, the SEC brought action against Comparator Systems Corp. and three of its officers and directors, alleging that they sold tens of millions of shares of the company's stock while falsely claiming ownership of certain fingerprint technology. Touting on FSM platforms and television caused the stock price to rise from $0.06 to $1.88 in just three days. The SEC halted trading, and investors lost millions.

Another notable case involves Amir "Anthony" Elgindy, a broker who used public FSM platforms and an extortion scheme to manipulate stocks. The SEC charged him with stock manipulation. Numerous cases involve brokers or dealers using FSM platforms to influence stock prices (see Bagnoli, Beneish, and Watts, 1999; Bettman, Hallett, and Sault, 2011).

One more important issue is worth mentioning: it is not unusual to find the same or similar messages, even with identical titles, on multiple platforms, sometimes under different aliases. "Cross-posting" is quite common in online financial communities, though it is generally unwelcome to most users. Some posters work together to spread spam, using software to automatically post identical content across multiple platforms, or manually copying messages from one platform to another. Identifying the source of such activity is challenging because, alongside retail investors, FSM platforms also attract participation from market regulators, company representatives, corporate executives, brokers, and dealers.

Demographics of Posters

To analyze the demographics of FSM platforms' posters, I utilized data from Quantcast.com, a leading digital audience measurement company. Quantcast specializes in providing in-depth insights into the demographics of users on public websites. Given the vast number of popular FSM platforms available online, it is impractical and unnecessary to analyze them all. Instead, I selected five frequently visited FSM platforms to offer a representative view of poster demographics.

Quantcast evaluates digital audience demographics across six dimensions: gender, age, presence of children in the household, household income, education level, and ethnicity. As expected, and as shown in Table 3.1, the descriptive statistics across the five selected platforms are consistent, indicating that online posters share several common characteristics.

- Gender: Men account for 74% of posters on FSM platforms. Given that men generate only 49% of overall Internet activity, it is evident that FSM platform participation is predominantly male-driven.
- Age: Fifty-four percent of posters on FSM platforms are middle-aged adults, ranging from 34 to 54 years old. This stands in contrast to the relatively even age distribution among general Internet users.
- Children in Household: Sixty-four percent of FSM platforms' posters have no children, compared to 51% of all Internet users.
- Household Income: More than half of the posters on FSM platforms are affluent, with 31% reporting annual household incomes exceeding $150,000.
- Education Level: Nearly half of the posters on FSM platforms hold a college degree, which aligns with the average Internet user. Additionally, 21% of posters have postgraduate education, a figure twice as high as the general Internet population.
- Ethnicity: Approximately 80% of posters are Caucasian, a reflection of the fact that the selected FSM platforms are primarily used in and popular within the United States and the United Kingdom.

Further insights into FSM platforms' posters can be found in existing literature. Tancer (2007) reports that most FSM platforms' users are male (77%), over 55 years old (35.8%), and belong to the most affluent segments of suburban society. According to data from Hitwise and Claritas, which segments the U.S. population by consumer behavior, the typical FSM poster resides in a large home, wears expensive clothing, drives a luxury vehicle, travels internationally, and is considered wealthy.

Das, Martinez-Jerez, and Tufano (2005) interviewed Glenn R., the most prolific poster on the Amazon (AMZN) subforum on SiliconInvestor. In 1999, Glenn was in his late forties, held an undergraduate degree, owned a small chain of jewelry stores, including an online store, was self-employed, and spent approximately 30 hours a week, primarily at night and on weekends, engaging with the platforms. These details align closely with the demographic data presented in Table 3.1.

Researchers have also identified several patterns in the behavior of FSM platforms' posters. For instance, Wysocki (1999) found that while most messages are posted during regular stock exchange trading hours, active posters tend to post late at night, after trading has ended. Antweiler and Frank (2004) observed that posters' self-reported sentiments often

Table 3.1 Demographics of Posters Based on Quantcast Analysis

	TheLion (%)	*Raging Bull (%)*	*SiliconInvestor (%)*	*InvestorsHub (%)*	*Stockhouse (%)*	*Board Average (%)*	*Internet Average (%)*
Gender							
Male	80	66	70	68	87	74	49
Female	20	34	30	32	13	26	51
Age							
<18	9	5	4	6	9	7	18
18–24	4	4	3	2	8	4	12
25–34	22	13	8	12	16	14	17
35–44	19	44	30	32	21	29	19
45–54	21	19	33	27	23	25	17
55–64	15	11	14	15	15	14	10
64+	10	4	7	6	8	7	6
Children							
No Kids	74	72	64	53	58	64	51
Has Kids	26	28	36	47	42	36	49
Income							
$0-50 K	21	17	9	15	29	18	18
$50-100 K	15	28	17	23	36	24	27
$100-150 K	39	29	22	27	19	27	28
$150 K+	26	26	52	35	16	31	28
Education							
No College	32	38	20	23	34	29	45
College	56	45	54	56	36	49	41
Grad School	11	17	26	22	30	21	11
Ethnicity							
Caucasian	65	82	81	83	85	79	75
African American	6	5	9	13	4	7	9
Asian	8	5	7	1	5	5	4
Hispanic	20	5	2	1	5	7	9
Other	1	2	1	1	1	1	1

align with their actual trading positions, with predominant buy-side sentiments indicating that most online investors adopt a buy-and-hold trading strategy. These researchers also noted that small traders find it easier to maintain long positions than short ones, leading to a predominance of bullish discussions.

Furthermore, Zhang and Swanson (2010) reported that "Strong Buy" and "Buy" sentiments dominate other sentiment types, suggesting that FSM platforms' posters tend to be optimistic. Sabherwal, Sarkar, and Zhang (2008) found that posters often focus on thinly traded microcap stocks, while Zhang (2009) concluded that online posters generally promote risky, weakly fundamental, and overvalued stocks.

Measures and Determinants of Poster Credibility

Liu, Gu, Konana, and Ghosh (2006) argued that casual users often struggle to distinguish between online posters and evaluate their comments. As discussed in Chapter 2, FSM platforms' posters vary significantly in their backgrounds, experience, intentions, and knowledge. Thus, a standardized method to assess the quality of their commentary would be valuable.

Academic Approaches to Measuring Poster Credibility

Early studies on FSM platforms, such as those by Wysocki (1998), Tumarkin and Whitelaw (2001), and Antweiler and Frank (2004), assumed that all posters had equal credibility. However, this approach is problematic because not all posters possess the same level of insight and experience. For example, consider two posters who simultaneously express a "Strong Buy" sentiment for the same stock. If one poster is highly knowledgeable and the other is not, treating both sentiments equally and assigning them the same weight is inadequate. Intuitively, assigning greater weight to the more knowledgeable poster would more accurately reflect investor consensus.

Recognizing the limitations of equal weighting, Antweiler and Frank (2004) proposed two alternative weighting schemes. The first method suggests that longer messages might convey more information and thus should be given more weight. The second method aims to control for spam by weighting each message inversely to the total number of messages posted by the poster. Despite these refinements, Antweiler and Frank (2004) found that these alternative weighting schemes yielded results similar to the equal-weighting approach.

Later, Gu, Konana, Liu, Rajagopalan, and Ghosh (2006) introduced a more sophisticated approach by weighting average sentiment based on the message poster's reputation. A poster's reputation is calculated according to their past cumulative predictive accuracy, with greater weight given to messages from posters with higher predictive accuracy.

Later, Sabherwal, Sarkar, and Zhang (2011) developed a credit-weighted measure of investor sentiment based on a rewards system from TheLion.com. This system allows posters to earn reputation credits from other users by sharing high-quality information. A higher credit score reflects greater reputation within the financial community, enabling users to distinguish between experienced experts and newcomers; see Zhang et al. (2022).

Reputation Systems and Collaborative Filtering

There are various ways to determine a poster's reputation, ranging from imprecise to more accurate and efficient methods. A typical reputation system is often coupled with an incentive system designed to reward good stock recommendations and penalize poor recommendations or mere chatter. As discussed in Chapter 2, stock-trading boards frequently adopt reputation systems that rank posters based on factors such as information timing, content relevance, performance records, and forecast accuracy.

A typical reputation system is a type of collaborative filtering algorithm, and different algorithms can be employed to design such systems. These might include feedback systems, fixed formulas based on posting statistics, credit scores assigned by forum administrators, or user-reward systems. Zhang (2009) found that a poster's sentiment, popularity within the community, information quality (rather than quantity), and the follow-up opinions on the stock within the next 24 hours all positively affect a poster's reputation. Zhang (2009) also examined whether a poster's reputation is influenced by the characteristics of the stock being discussed, concluding that recommending stocks with a high price-to-earnings (P/E) ratio and a large percentage of institutional ownership reduces the likelihood of earning reputation credits, while promoting highly liquid stocks increases the likelihood of gaining reputation.

Understanding the determinants of poster reputation allows researchers to construct more efficient credit-weighted sentiment indices. By weighting each poster's sentiment contribution based on their reputation and analyzing interactions within a financial community, researchers can gain deeper insights. Sabherwal, Sarkar, and Zhang (2011) applied Zhang's (2009) research and weighting scheme to create and test an online trader's credit-weighted sentiment index. Their findings suggest that online trader sentiment, rather than the volume of postings, is positively associated with contemporaneous returns but negatively predicts returns over the following two trading days.

Who Is Keener to Post What Messages?

Posters exhibit different habits and preferences, reflecting their individual characteristics. For instance, some posters prefer lengthy messages, while others opt for shorter ones. Some consistently disclose their sentiments, while others rarely do. Additionally, sentiment expression varies—some prefer strong tones like "Strong Buy" or "Strong Sell," while others favor more moderate sentiments such as "Buy" and "Sell."

In this section, I explore who is more inclined to post what specific types of messages. The most effective way to address this question is by summarizing empirical findings from other scholars. First, Odean (1999) reported that 99 percent of small investors hold long positions and do not engage in short selling due to high costs, short-sell restrictions, and the inherent risks of shorting. Many online investors are day traders, momentum traders, swing traders, or short-term traders, typically small individual investors. Antweiler and Frank (2004) documented that current institutions (e.g., brokerage firms) make it significantly easier for small traders to hold long positions than short ones.

DeMarzo, Vayanos, and Zwiebel (2003) supported the idea that traders post on FSM platforms when they already hold positions in particular stocks. Since "posters put their money where their mouth is," many researchers believe that posters tend to disclose bullish sentiments. For example, Zhang and Swanson (2010) suggested that most posters on FSM platforms tend to express bullish sentiments, and the "Hold" sentiment they offer is often biased toward optimism. Other studies have also found that online posters generally display a bullish bias (see Tumarkin and Whitelaw 2001; Tumarkin 2002; Sabherwal, Sarkar, and Zhang 2011; and Zhang, Swanson, and Prombutr 2012).

Additionally, posters tend to avoid lengthy messages online due to time and space constraints. Admati and Pfleiderer (2001) initially suggested that forum messages posted by individual investors are typically style-free, short, elliptical, and formatted like a dialogue. In a sample of bulletin board messages analyzed by Antweiler and Frank (2004), it is evident that posters usually leave only one or two short sentences, rarely employing lengthy paragraphs. This is logical, as traders are unlikely to read lengthy messages filled with excessive information while trading. Sabherwal, Sarkar, and Zhang (2008) empirically demonstrated that the average message length is significantly negatively correlated with investor attention, further suggesting that online investors focus more on shorter, more concise messages.

Furthermore, TheLion.com has a reputation system that allows readers to reward posters with credits. Depken and Zhang (2010) proposed using a poster's average credit score per message (total credit score divided by the number of messages) as a measure of reputation and tested whether reputation influences the frequency and accuracy of voluntarily offered sentiments, such as "Buy," "Hold," and "Sell." They reached three key conclusions: First, posters with high reputations are less likely to offer sentiments randomly. In other words, posters with no established reputation (newbies) tend to offer more sentiments than those with established reputations. Newbies are generally less cautious because they have no credit to lose. Second, posters with no reputation at stake tend to be more bearish ("Sell," "Strong Sell," or "Short") in their sentiments, while those with better reputations lean toward bullish sentiments. Third, high-reputation posters tend to offer more accurate sentiments only on the day their message is posted, suggesting that their messages have limited predictive power for subsequent days.

Lastly, Wysocki (1999) made four important observations about individuals who post messages on Yahoo! Finance boards. First, the variation in posting volume across companies is related to the companies' fundamental characteristics; companies with a large investor base or an uncertain information environment tend to attract more messages. Second, the majority of messages are posted by a small number of individuals. For nearly all stock-specific discussion boards on Yahoo! Finance, fewer than 5 percent of posters contribute most messages. Third, frequent posters tend to post in tandem and enthusiastically respond to the messages of other frequent posters, suggesting possible collusion among active posters or posting under multiple aliases. Fourth, frequent posters are likely to be short sellers or "bashers" who collaborate to spread negative information about a company, as there is increased tandem posting during high short-sale months.

Finally, many participants are simply readers or browsers, known in Internet jargon as "lurkers." Lurkers typically observe but do not actively participate or contribute to the creation and measurement of investor sentiment. Since registration is generally not required to read messages, lurkers remain unobserved.

CHAPTER 4

Why Do People Post Messages on Financial Social Media Platforms?

Commonly Known Motivations

Many people have experience posting online through non-financial social media platforms such as blogs, forums, discussion groups, email lists, or other forms of mass communication. When leaving messages online, most of us give little thought to why we do it. Often, the reason is so straightforward that we do not even pause to consider it. For example, we might post to answer a question, share something we have seen or heard, forward timely news, or express our frustrations. It is not surprising that a single message can sometimes serve multiple purposes.

Do we really need a reason to post? Can we say anything we like online? Is it even worthwhile to discuss the motivations behind online posting? For many, understanding these motivations may not seem important, especially in a typical online forum. However, the combination of an online forum and security trading creates a unique environment, financial social media (FSM, hereafter) platforms, where financial considerations come into play. This makes FSM platforms inherently more complex than regular non-financial ones.

Before posters actively participate in online forums, there must be some motivation that drives them. Many economists believe such motivation can be used to interpret and predict human behavior. Spend enough time on FSM platforms, and you'll notice that most active posters hold positions in the stocks they recommend. DeMarzo, Vayanos, and Zwiebel

Y. Zhang, *Financial Social Media*,
https://doi.org/10.1007/978-3-032-09332-5_4

(2003), as well as Antweiler and Frank (2004), suggest that posters are unlikely to engage in online discussions about a particular stock unless they have a vested interest in it. Research also shows that these posters often put their money where their mouth is, as seen in studies by Depken and Zhang (2010), among others.

Since maximizing trading profits is typically the primary incentive for trading a stock (Lakonishok and Smidt, 1986), it's understandable that most FSM postings are aimed at maximizing the poster's trading profits. Unlike most non-financial online forums, FSM postings are not just a simple process of information sharing and exchange; they can also involve malicious collaboration and intentional stock manipulation. Understanding the motivations behind FSM posting is valuable for several reasons: it helps researchers better comprehend the psychology and behavior of online traders when they recommend stocks, aids investors in avoiding common trading mistakes, assists forum administrators in managing online postings, and helping regulators identify online securities fraud.

Understanding the motivations behind FSM postings is crucial, yet research in this area is lacking. This chapter aims to address that gap by discussing the motivations specific to these platforms. To fully grasp the motivations for FSM postings, it's helpful to first examine the motivations for message posting on non-financial online forums. These motivations can be categorized into five common types:

- Being Part of a Community:

  One of the most prevalent motivations for online message posting is the desire to be part of a community. This includes seeking help, providing feedback, participating in discussions, sharing information and experiences, obtaining opinions, making friends, and seeking validation from others. This motivation is prevalent across most online platforms, regardless of their structure. In fact, many platforms were originally created to cultivate a sense of community.

  Several studies have examined what drives people to participate in online communities, with a focus on community engagement as a primary motivation. Kollock (1999) suggests that individuals are motivated to contribute valuable information to a community with the expectation of receiving help and information in return (anticipated reciprocity). He also identifies two other major reasons: the desire for recognition (increased recognition) and the sense of efficacy, where individuals feel their contributions have an impact on the community. Butler (2001) and Bagozzi and Dholakia (2002) further suggest that both social and economic benefits—such as reciprocity, reputation, self-efficacy, and the enjoyment of helping others—play a key role in motivating participation.

- Trolling:

  Although forums are generally designed for discussions among like-minded individuals, some posters, known as trolls, deliberately disrupt the conversation. Trolls repeatedly breach the netiquette of an established online community by posting inflammatory, extraneous, or off-topic messages with the intent of provoking emotional responses or disrupting normal discussions.

  The prevalence of trolls can be attributed to various factors, including feelings of depression, attention-seeking, anger, jealousy, or narcissism. As mentioned in Chapter 3, most posters are anonymous, which allows trolls to hide behind their aliases and continue their behavior without facing real-world consequences. This anonymity makes trolling easy, as anyone can do it without fear of repercussions. Responding to trolls is often referred to as "feeding the troll" and is generally discouraged, as it can encourage further disruptive behavior. Instead, it's best to ignore trolls. In forums with administrators, you can gather evidence, report the troll, and request that they be banned.

- Sockpuppetry:

  A sockpuppet is an online identity used for deception or self-promotion. It refers to multiple aliases used by the same person on a particular FSM platform. The term "sockpuppet" comes from the image of a puppeteer manipulating both puppets simultaneously. A typical sockpuppet account might agree with or debate another sockpuppet account controlled by the same person, reinforcing the puppeteer's position in an argument. Another common use is to praise another sockpuppet account, boosting its popularity or credibility in the community.

  The key difference between using an alias and creating a sockpuppet account is that the sockpuppet poses as an independent third party, unaffiliated with the puppeteer. Sockpuppets are usually detected through IP address checks on forum accounts. However, as discussed in previous chapters, it can be challenging to identify sockpuppets since their IP addresses often remain undisclosed by ISPs. If IP addresses were publicly available, sockpuppets would likely disappear. Many online communities have policies against sockpuppetry, and users can report suspected sockpuppets to the webmaster.

- Spamming:

  Forum spamming involves repeatedly posting the same message within a short period. Like email spamming, forum spamming is a breach of netiquette and can be highly irritating to other users. Spamming is often a deliberate act, sometimes with malicious intent, and is also a common trolling technique. Certain spammers even use software to automate their spam posts. Common examples of forum spam include advertisements, solicitations, sales pitches, and recommendations.

  Flaming, a special case of forum spamming, occurs when a discussion becomes heated, and participants focus on personal attacks rather than engaging in constructive debate. Although flame wars are less common on FSM platforms, they can still occur. However, most online traders are too focused on maximizing their trading profits to engage in flaming. Nonetheless, it's important to recognize that any form of spamming is frowned upon by the community and is usually prohibited in online forums. To reduce spamming, for instance, TheLion.com limits users to no more than five messages per hour, while SiliconInvestor.com has a stricter rule of no more than five messages per day for non-advanced users.
- Compulsory Posting:

  Compulsory posting typically occurs in the form of replies. For example, you may encounter a post that only shows partial content, requiring you to reply before you can view the entire message. This tactic is used to increase forum membership and artificially boost engagement, as it forces users to reply to access the full content. However, this "trick" is often seen as irritating and is generally discouraged.

  Due to its unpopularity, compulsory posting has not been widely adopted. To the best of my knowledge, no FSM platform currently forces users to reply to read the content of a message.

Motivations Pertinent to Financial Social Media Platforms

In addition to the five motivations common to all online forums, this chapter discusses eight specific motivations that are particularly relevant to FSM platforms. These platforms are not just venues for sharing and exchanging stock-related information but can also be platforms for stock recommendations, manipulations, and even illegal stock sales. For most posters, after all, the primary motivation for posting is to maximize trading profits.

Below are eight special motivations for posting messages on FSM platforms:

- Earn a Reputation

  Reputation is highly valued in online financial communities. Respected posters, often referred to as "gurus" (as discussed in Chapter 1), typically attract more readers and followers, and their opinions can significantly influence stock trading. Studies by Cook and Lu (2009) and Depken and Zhang (2010) suggest that posters with a high reputation can impact stock prices more than those with lower reputations. Building a reputation is often part of a long-term strategy to attract followers, who can then amplify the impact of a poster's stock recommendations. Generally, building a good reputation requires active participation in discussions and frequent contributions of opinions and reviews. However, some individuals resort to using sockpuppet accounts, hiring agents, or even utilizing bots to artificially inflate their reputations in a short period. Although this behavior is also common in non-financial platforms, it's important to recognize that earning reputation is a primary motivation on FSM platforms.
- Pump

  A "pump" occurs when an individual promotes a security they already own to drive up its price, allowing them to sell it later at a higher price for a profit. This strategy involves expressing positive opinions about the stock in hopes of influencing other readers to buy. The success of this tactic often depends on the reputation of the pumper; those with larger followings are more likely to succeed. Pumpers typically target thinly traded penny stocks with low institutional holdings, minimal analyst coverage, and weak fundamentals, as these stocks are more susceptible to price manipulation. Blue-chip stocks, on the other hand, are less likely to be targeted because their prices are less influenced by online hype due to their solid fundamentals and institutional ownership. Common tactics used by pumpers include reposting old positive news without the original release date, spreading baseless rumors, and fabricating false news.

- Dump
  The counterpart to the pump, a "dump," involves spreading negative information about a stock to drive down its price, enabling the seller to buy shares at a lower price and profit when the price rebounds. In another scenario, a short seller can profit directly from the price decline caused by dumping. Dumpers may engage in a variety of activities to achieve their goal, such as sending baseless allegations to regulatory agencies, contacting the company's suppliers and customers with negative information, or posting negative messages on FSM platforms. Dumping is generally easier to accomplish than pumping because it is easier to scare investors into selling than to convince them to buy. Like pumpers, dumpers tend to target companies with weak fundamentals. Tactics used to dump stocks are like those used in pumping, including reposting old negative news, spreading false rumors, and making baseless allegations.
- Manipulate
  Manipulation combines the tactics of both pumping and dumping to maximize profits from both upward and downward price movements. In a typical pump-and-dump scheme, fraudsters first promote a stock they own to drive up the price, sell at the peak, then short the stock and begin spreading negative information to drive the price back down. The reverse process, dump-and-pump, involves driving the price down first and then buying shares at a low price before pumping the stock to sell at a higher price for a profit. Manipulation is easier to execute with low-priced, small-cap stocks that are more susceptible to price swings due to their weak fundamentals. Studies, such as those by Sabherwal, Sarkar, and Zhang (2011), have shown that FSM platforms can be used to manipulate stock prices and trading volumes temporarily.
- Spread Rumor
  The Internet is a fertile ground for the spread of rumors, which can have significant impacts on financial markets. Rumors can be fact-based or entirely fabricated, but they are often posted without confirmation. Financial communities are particularly concerned about rumors because they can cause substantial damage. Rumormongers may include stock manipulators, illegal securities sellers, company competitors, and even terrorists. Research by Clarkson, Joyce, and Tutticci (2006) and Bettman, Hallett, and Sault (2011) has shown that market reactions to rumors, such as takeover speculation, can result in abnormal returns and increased trading volumes.

Spreading rumors is often intertwined with other motivations, such as pumping or dumping stocks.

- Tell a Truth

  Not all posters on FSM platforms have malicious intentions. Some are well-meaning individuals who want to share quality information. For example, current or former employees may disclose insider information, as was the case with Enron in 2001 when anonymous posts on Yahoo! Finance warned the public of the company's impending collapse. Other posters might be sincere investors who have conducted thorough analyses and wish to share their findings. Replies to posts are generally more likely to be genuine, as they are often responses to questions or agreements/disagreements with previous posts.
- Gossip

  Some posters use FSM platforms to discuss non-financial topics like politics, sports, or movies. Certain forums even have designated spaces for such discussions. Additionally, some posters are paid to create meaningless content in order to increase forum activity, as higher activity levels can make a forum appear more successful. These posters, who often contribute little value, may be classified as honest since their information is genuine, but they typically do not aim to build a reputation or make trading profits.
- Cybersmear

  Cybersmearing involves spreading false or misleading information about a company to drive down its stock price. This tactic is like dumping but differs in that cybersmearers may not have any financial stake in the company. Instead, they may be disgruntled former employees, competitors, or individuals with other motivations. Cybersmearing can be challenging to prosecute because the false statements made can sometimes be framed as opinions protected by the First Amendment.

Final Thought

Finally, I argue that individuals with profit-related motivations for posting on FSM platforms typically already have, or are about to acquire, a trading position in the stock. They aim to influence trading-related metrics such as return, volume, volatility, and liquidity. The motivations previously discussed can be categorized into two main groups:

- Profit-Related Motivations

  These activities include pumping, dumping, manipulation, genuine contribution, and rumor spreading. It is important to note that stock manipulation through FSM platforms is not limited to the United States. Such practices are also common among publicly traded companies in China, Singapore, Vietnam, and Korea, where their impact can be even more severe than in the United States, in part due to lower market efficiency.
- Non-profit Motivations

  Posts not primarily driven by profit often involve trolling, sockpuppetry, spamming, compulsory posting, reputation-seeking, genuine contributions, gossip, cybersmearing, and those seeking community engagement. It is essential to recognize that these categories are not mutually exclusive. For instance, sockpuppeteers or spammers might also have stakes in the stock and seek to influence trading. In conclusion, you should never base your investment decisions solely on information posted on public FSM platforms. Instead, conduct your own research based on credible sources and insights before making investment decisions.

While online discussions can offer valuable information, it is crucial to exercise due diligence before trading securities, even when the information comes from financial professionals. Sometimes, even reputable sources make mistakes. A notable example occurred in March 2025, when Reuters reported that Google was expanding a data partnership with Reddit. The story was based on outdated information from a blog post that was nearly a year old. Once the mistake was recognized, Reuters issued a retraction, but not before Reddit's stock price surged and then sharply reversed. This case illustrates how even reputable news organizations like Reuters can inadvertently spread misinformation and how quickly such errors can influence markets. In summary, diverse motivations ranging from profit seeking to community engagement create a volatile information environment. As the Reuters and Reddit case demonstrates, a poster's incentive is the ultimate filter for credibility. While these platforms provide valuable real time data, investors must treat every post as an unverified data point requiring independent confirmation against fundamental research.

CHAPTER 5

Modeling the Value of Financial Social Media Platforms

Introduction

In the academic literature, there are theoretical models that explore how posters interact with one another, how they process and exchange information, and how they make trading decisions based on financial social media (FSM, hereafter) content (see Lu 2009; Lu and Mizrach 2011). Recently, a comprehensive theoretical model that captures the overall value of an FSM platform was developed by Zhang (2025).

Why is it important to construct such a model? Being able to quantify the value of an FSM platform as a whole would enable us to evaluate its popularity among users, its broader societal impact, potential longevity, and market value in the context of mergers and acquisitions. It would also allow for meaningful comparisons among different FSM platforms based on their estimated values.

In this chapter, I first explain the concepts of advantageous and adverse selection in intuitive terms. I then present a theoretical framework for evaluating the value of an individual message, a poster, and an entire platform. Finally, drawing on this model, I discuss potential moral hazard issues within FSM platforms and outline possible directions for their future development.

Y. Zhang, *Financial Social Media*,
https://doi.org/10.1007/978-3-032-09332-5_5

Advantageous Selection

Let us first assume there are two types of FSM posters: Superior Authors (SAs, hereafter) and Inferior Authors (IAs, hereafter). We also assume that both SAs and IAs put their money where their mouth is, meaning they trade based on their own recommendations.

In an advantageous selection scenario, each author's quality, competency, or credibility—measured by their rank—is made public to all platform users. The information about each poster's rank is symmetrically available to everyone on the FSM platform. With an effective and reliable user-rating system in place, a higher rank is associated with greater stock return forecast accuracy. This leads to an advantageous selection dynamic.

Even in cases where FSM platforms lack a formal reputation-recognition system, users can still indirectly assess a poster's credibility using other indicators—such as past recommendations and trading records, virtual portfolio returns, number of followers, thumbs-up/thumbs-down ratios, and the number of replies received.

I propose that, under an advantageous selection scenario, the long-term evolution of an FSM platform progresses through the following five stages:

- Initial Contributions and Credibility Building

  SAs recommend stocks with clear sentiments based on their research and insights. Their motivation is twofold: to build reputation within the community and to benefit from potentially higher short-term trading gains, triggered by other users acting on their sentiments. The resulting increase in trading liquidity and narrowing of bid-ask spreads, which imply lower transaction costs, are additional benefits of follower-driven herding behavior. Conversely, IAs, having low credibility scores, fail to attract significant interest. As a result, few readers act on their recommendations.
- Increasing Participation and Reputation Accumulation

  The combination of larger trading gains, higher liquidity, and lower transaction costs attracts more posters to share their insights. While SAs continue to benefit from their established reputation and influence, IAs are motivated to improve and keep up. To transition into SAs, IAs must go through a time-consuming process of building credibility by consistently contributing high-quality and valuable posts. Over time, as IAs produce more accurate and useful information, they gain recognition and eventually become SAs. Gradually, the platform becomes dominated by SAs.

- Competitive Contribution and Quality Enhancement

  SAs continue contributing to the platform, driven by the incentive of greater trading gains. IAs, too, remain active, disclosing their sentiments through legitimate accounts. In this competitive environment, IAs are motivated to conduct deeper research and more rigorous analysis to improve their forecast accuracy and gain credibility. As their reputation scores rise, they attract more followers. This long-term learning process fosters quality improvement and encourages all posters to contribute more frequently, share more insights, and strive for accuracy. Eventually, high-quality messages dominate the platform.

- Message Quality and Community Growth

  As the platform matures, the information posted becomes increasingly valuable and reliable. The user base expands, and members are more willing to participate and share insights. With an efficient rating system, high-ranking authors are associated with higher-quality content and greater forecast accuracy. Since rankings are publicly visible, information asymmetry is reduced. Messages from high-ranking authors receive more attention, and herding behavior among traders becomes more pronounced. This creates a virtuous cycle in which the volume and quality of high-value content increase, further promoting advantageous selection.

- Long-Term Value Creation

  In the long run, the value of the FSM platform grows significantly. Under an advantageous selection scenario, a rich pool of high-quality messages and an expanding member base emerge. SAs dominate the discussions, while IAs follow a constructive and motivating path to improvement. Followers benefit from trading on SAs' recommendations, and SAs, in turn, benefit from the higher trading liquidity and lower transaction costs driven by their followers. This results in a mutually beneficial environment. As more users achieve meaningful trading gains, participation increases, leading to a vibrant and flourishing FSM platform. Consequently, the long-term value of the platform becomes positive.

Adverse Selection

In this scenario, we assume that each author's quality, competency, or credibility cannot be identified due to the absence of an effective reputation-recognition system. As a result, general platform users are unable to distinguish experienced SAs from inexperienced IAs. At best, long-time users may be able to make informed judgments about who might be an SA, but more often than not, there is no reliable method to determine a poster's credibility.

Information about each author's ranking or credibility is either invisible to others, inaccurately reflected by the user-rating system, or misinterpreted by the community. Under such an inefficient and unreliable system, a higher rank may incorrectly signal lower forecast accuracy, thereby creating an adverse selection environment.

I propose that the long-term evolution of an FSM platform under an adverse selection scenario unfolds in the following five stages:

- Undistinguished Contributions

  SAs contribute stock recommendations based on research and thoughtful analysis. IAs, on the other hand, issue recommendations without any real basis or insight. Both groups aim to build reputations and benefit from trading gains driven by followers. However, in an adverse selection environment, general users are unable to distinguish between SAs and IAs, so the value of the recommendations becomes unclear. This undermines the incentives for quality contributions.
- Absence of a Reputation System and Account Manipulation

  Without an effective reputation-recognition system, IAs, who invest little or no effort in research, continue to post sentiments in the hope that others will follow them blindly. It becomes common for IAs to register multiple fake accounts to artificially boost their perceived credibility and manipulate sentiment, especially in thinly traded or vulnerable stocks.
- Capital Misallocation and Decline of SAs

  Since follower investors cannot distinguish SAs from IAs, their limited investment capital is partially diverted to poor-quality stock recommendations. As a result, SAs receive less attention, fewer followers, and diminished gains, both reputational and financial, compared to what they would receive in an advantageous selection scenario. Moreover, due to limited following, the liquidity of stocks recommended by SAs does not improve, and trading costs remain high. Over time, SAs become disillusioned and begin to exit the platform. IAs, who incur little cost and face little accountability, gradually take over the platform.

- Dominance of Low-Quality Content

  With fewer SAs contributing, the quality of posts declines sharply. IAs, lacking research ability and insight, flood the platform with low value or misleading content. Users who follow IA recommendations experience trading losses. As high-quality messages dwindle and low-quality messages dominate, the platform becomes increasingly noisy and unreliable. This mirrors the classic “lemon market” problem (Akerlof, 1970), where bad actors drive out the good.

- Erosion of Trust and Collapse of the Community

  As followers incur repeated losses from following poor advice, trust in the FSM platform erodes. User engagement drops, and more investors abandon the platform. This leads to a lose-lose situation: SAs have already exited, and IAs lose influence as their audience disappears. With little participation and no credible content, the platform becomes inactive and eventually fades away. In the end, the platform’s value approaches zero or even turns negative, considering the cumulative losses incurred by its users.

Theoretical Construct

To model the value of an FSM platform, we must first consider the value of an author (poster), as a discussion platform is fundamentally composed of user-generated messages or posts. Therefore, the overall value of an FSM platform can be understood as the sum of the values of its individual contributors. Furthermore, in order to assess the value of an author, we must first define the value of a message, since an author’s contribution is inherently reflected in the messages they produce. Accordingly, I define, in a logical sequence, the value of a message, the value of an author, and finally the value of the platform as a whole. In addition to modeling the platform’s static state at a given time t, I also examine its long-term evolution and value over time to provide a more comprehensive view of its development.

The Value of a Message M

I first assume that each message includes a stock symbol (e.g., IBM or WMT) and an explicit sentiment (e.g., Buy, Hold, or Sell), either self-disclosed by the poster or assigned by a third-party text classifier.[1] If an author shares a forecast on the overall stock market rather than on an individual stock, I assume the author is recommending a tradable market index fund with a specific ticker symbol, such as SPY or DIA.[2]

A sentiment forecasts the direction of a subsequent stock price movement or expected stock return. For simplicity, the sentiment is classified as one of the following: Optimistic (Buy), Neutral (Hold), or Pessimistic (Sell).[3] I define the value of a message as +1 (or positive one) if its sentiment correctly predicts the subsequent one-term stock return after the message is posted, and −1 (or negative one) otherwise.[4] The term "subsequent one term" is relative and can refer to any time interval, such as one minute, one hour, one day, one month, or even one year, after the sentiment is expressed. Its definition depends on how the forum developer configures it, how the researcher defines it, or how it is perceived by other online investors.

For example, if the sentiment expressed in a message is optimistic and the stock price subsequently rises over the defined one-term period, the message is considered to have positive value. This implies that an investor who follows the sentiment and purchases the stock after reading the message would profit. Conversely, if the sentiment is pessimistic and the stock price subsequently declines, the message is likewise considered to have positive value, as an investor who follows the sentiment and shorts or sells the stock would also gain or at least avoid a loss. In both cases, alignment between sentiment and subsequent stock movement indicates a valuable message.[5] Similarly, in a rare case, if a neutral sentiment is expressed and the subsequent stock price remains unchanged, the sentiment is considered accurate, and the message is also assigned a positive value.

In sum, the value of a message can be defined as either +1 (correct) or −1 (incorrect). It is important to note that a message that is noisy or irrelevant to a particular stock or the broader market is considered to have no impact and therefore no value. For example, an FSM platform cluttered with off-topic posts unrelated to financial matters would clearly undermine the platform's overall usefulness. As a result, such irrelevant messages are typically discouraged and may even be removed by forum administrators.

In practice, the value of a message can be quantified using a more granular scale. For instance, a message might be assigned a value of +10 if a bullish sentiment is matched by a subsequent 10% increase in stock price, based on a scale where each 1% return corresponds to one incremental unit of value. However, for simplicity, this model uses a binary scale: +1 for correct messages and −1 for incorrect ones.

The Value of an Author A

An author *A*'s current value at time *t* is determined by the total value of all the messages he or she has posted in FSM platform *F* since his or her first registration. Say he or she has posted *m* number of messages among which *r* messages were right (+1) and *w* messages were wrong (−1). We have:

$$m_t^A = r_t^A + w_t^A \tag{5.1}$$

For instance, if *A* has posted 100 messages among which 60 were right and 40 were wrong or irrelevant, *A*'s cumulative net contribution to the FSM platform is 60*(+1) + 40*(−1) = 20. In other words, his or her sentiment forecast accuracy is 60/100 = 0.6 or 60 percent. The general formula to measure author *A*'s forecast accuracy, $\Pr_{Right}^{A,t}$ at time *t* is as follows:

$$\Pr_{Right}^{A,t} = \frac{r_t^A}{r_t^A + w_t^A} = \frac{r_t^A}{m_t^A} \tag{5.2}$$

As we know, a purely random process would yield an accuracy of 50 percent, assuming there are only two possible outcomes: correct or incorrect. If a superior author (SA) has a forecast accuracy greater than 0.5, they are considered to make a positive contribution to the platform. Conversely, any poster whose forecast accuracy is equal to or less than 0.5 is classified as an inferior author (IA). An IA is assumed to make little or no contribution, or even a negative contribution, to the community.

I therefore propose a formula to measure the overall value (net contribution) of an author A at time t as follows:

$$v_t^A = r_t^A - w_t^A = \Pr_{Right}^{A,t} \cdot m_t^A - \left(1 - \Pr_{Right}^{A,t}\right) m_t^A = \left(2\Pr_{Right}^{A,t} - 1\right) m_t^A \tag{5.3}$$

I first assume there is no cost in posting messages and recommending stocks. In reality, however, an author would encounter various costs, such as research expenses, personal time, a membership fee, an information-acquiring fee, and an opportunity cost. Thus, an author's value could be extended to $v_t^A = r_t^A - w_t^A - k_t^A$, where k_t^A is the total cost that author A has undertaken at time t. I will discuss the value with costs at the end of this chapter. From Eq. 5.3, it is clear that SA would have a positive value if $\Pr_{Right}^{A,t} > 0.5$ while IA would have a non-positive value if $\Pr_{Right}^{A,t} > 0.5$.

Next, I will need to further discuss m_t^A and $\Pr_{Right}^{A,t}$ in Eq. 5.3. m_t^A is the cumulative number of messages posted by author A. It is obvious that m_t^A is a function of time t and m_t^A must be a non-negative integer {0, 1, 2, 3 …}. I first consider a simple linear relationship between m_t^A and time t, which can be written as

$$m_t^A = m_t^A = b_A t \tag{5.4}$$

where m_i^A is for author A at his or her initial registration time and $m_i^A = 0$. Over time, an author gradually posts more and more messages and b_A measures his or her willingness to post messages on the FSM platform.

Although different authors have different posting rates, b_A is set to be a positive number because m generally grows over time.[6] A graphical demonstration of Eq. 5.5 is presented in Fig. 5.1 where time is arbitrary set from 0 to 100 and b_A is set as 0.1, which is also an arbitrary positive number.

In Eq. 5.4, taking the first derivative with respect to time t, we have $b_A = \frac{dm_t^A}{dt}$, which measures the author A's marginal posting rate. Again, this marginal posting rate is dependent upon the author's posting habit or preference, thus it is assumed to be constant to a particular poster. Plugging Eq. 5.4 into 5.3, we have

$$v_t^A = \left(2\Pr_{Right}^{A,t} - 1\right) b_A t \tag{5.5}$$

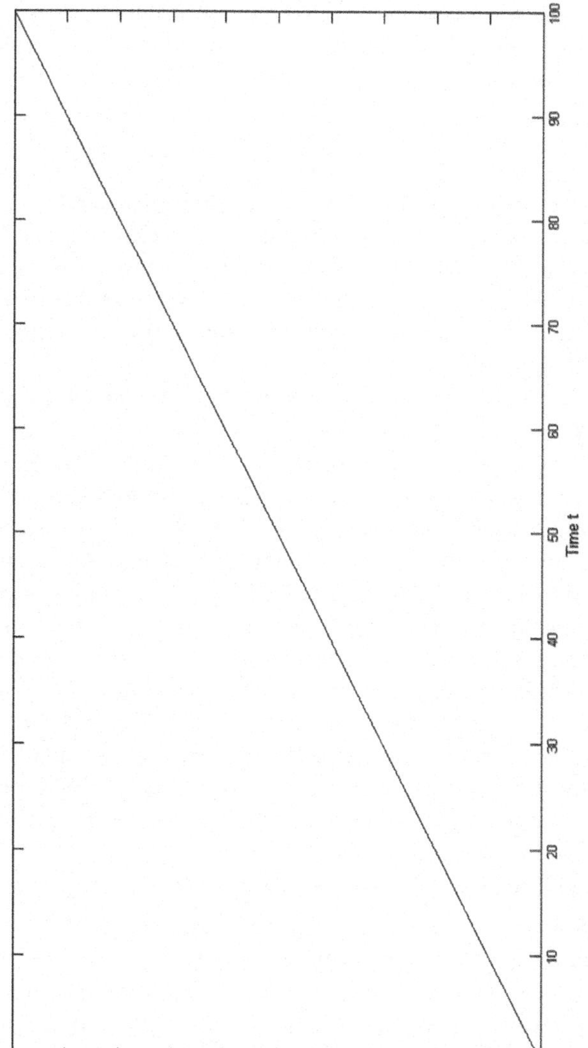

Fig. 5.1 Linear Relationship between messages M and time t

Next, I introduce an important concept, rank r, which is an author's reputation, credibility, or competency measure in a platform. Since we know that a random process would produce an accuracy of 50 percent (or 0.5) given two possible outcomes, I propose $\Pr_{Right}^{A,t}$ is a function of r and can be written as follows:

$$\Pr_{Right}^{A,t} = 0.5 + a_F r_t^A \tag{5.6}$$

where Eq. 5.6 can be interpreted as $\Pr_{Right}^{A,t}$ = random accuracy + forecast ability by author A at time t. Note that 0.5 is the critical value because any probability larger than 0.5 implies a positive value in Eq. 5.5, and vice versa. The coefficient, a_F, is the reputation-recognition mechanism by forum F. Note that a_F plays a crucial role in the derivation of the value of an FSM platform.

Let us take the first derivative with respect to rank r in the Eq. 5.6. We have $a_F = \frac{dPr_{Right}}{dr}$ and this is the marginal forecast accuracy per unit of increased rank in platform F. I propose if $a_F > 0$, this platform is effective. Positive a_F means a higher rank, recognized by the forum associates with the author's higher forecast accuracy.[7] With an effective reputation-recognition system, information asymmetry and adverse selection would be minimized (Depken and Zhang 2010). If $a \leq 0$, this platform would be ineffective. Negative a means a higher rank recognized by the FSM platform and implies lower forecast accuracy.

In the next section, I will demonstrate how the sign of a_F will lead to different selection scenarios. Similar to b_A in Eq. 5.4, a_F is also assumed to be a constant, which is determined by the platform F's reputation-recognition mechanism. Practically, different FSM platforms have different reputation-recognition mechanisms. Some have positive a_F while others have negative ones.

Since a probability must fall between 0 and 1, we have $0 \leq \Pr_{Right}^{A,t} \leq 1$. Based on Eq. 5.6, we can derive the following inequality: $-0.5 \leq a_F r_t^A \leq 0.5$, where rank r_t^A is non-negative integer {0, 1, 2, 3, …} and we must have $0 \leq r_t^A \leq \frac{0.5}{|a_F|}$.[8] Since an author's rank, r_t^A, could be a large number, $|a_F|$ is supposed to be small; that is, the marginal forecast accuracy per unit of increased rank should be small. A new registered member is given the lowest rank $r = 0$. Negative rank is not considered or eventually disappears because any poster who has a negative rank attracts no follower and therefore would reregister a new account and start it over again, assuming there is no cost to register. Figure 5.2 plots a linear relationship between probability $\Pr_{Right}^{A,t}$ and rank r_t^A setting $a_F = 0.001$ as an arbitrary positive number and rank r ranges from 0 to 100 (maximum value is $\frac{0.5}{|0.001|} = 500$).

Figure 5.3 plots a linear relationship between probability $\Pr_{Right}^{A,t}$ and rank r_t^A setting $a_F = -0.001$ as an arbitrary positive number and rank r ranges from 0 to 100 (maximum value is also $\frac{0.5}{|-0.001|} = 500$).

Plugging Eq. 5.6 into 5.5, we have

$$v_t^A = \left[2\left(0.5 + a_F r_t^A\right) - 1\right] b_A t = 2a_F r_t^A b_A t \tag{5.7}$$

where it is obvious that $a_F > 0 \Rightarrow v_t^A \geq 0$ given r_t^A is a non-negative term, b_A is set to be a positive number and time $t \in [0, +\infty)$, and vice versa. Thus, $a_F > 0$ implies an advantageous selection scenario for the platform when time goes by. Conversely, $a_F \leq 0$ gives rise to an adverse selection scenario for the platform in the long run.

I further propose that rank r_A itself is also a function of time t. Although coefficient a_F and b_A are both assumed to be constant in Eq. 5.7, r_t^A is a variable. It is reasonable to assume that an author's rank, based on his or her forecast accuracy, increases over time, assuming the author learns from other experienced posters and the platform's reputation-recognition mechanism is effective (see Lu and Mizrach [2011]). I propose a simple, linear relationship between r_t^A and time t as follows:

$$r_t^A = r_i^A + c_A t \tag{5.8}$$

where $r_i^A = 0$ because a user is initially given a rank 0 when he or she first registers. And we know that r_i^A is a non-negative integer as discussed above. c_A is author A's learning curve, which is determined by the individual's learning ability. I contend that c_A is a constant and positive term because it is unlikely for a normal person to become more skillful but meanwhile have his or her accuracy decrease over time. Here, b_A and c_A are assumed to be uncorrelated because b_A is based on the poster's posting habit, while c_A is based on the poster's forecasting ability. Figure 5.4 plots the linear relationship between rank r_t^A and time t, sets the $c_A = 0.5$ as an arbitrary positive number and t is from 0 to 100.

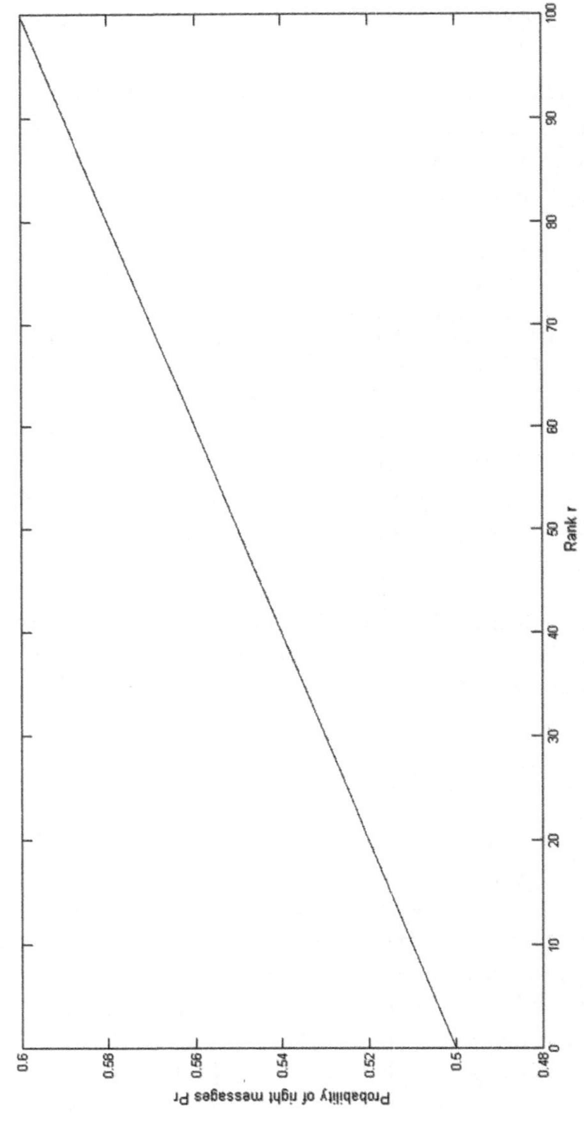

Fig. 5.2 Linear relationship between probability of right messages Pr and rank *r* with a positive *a*

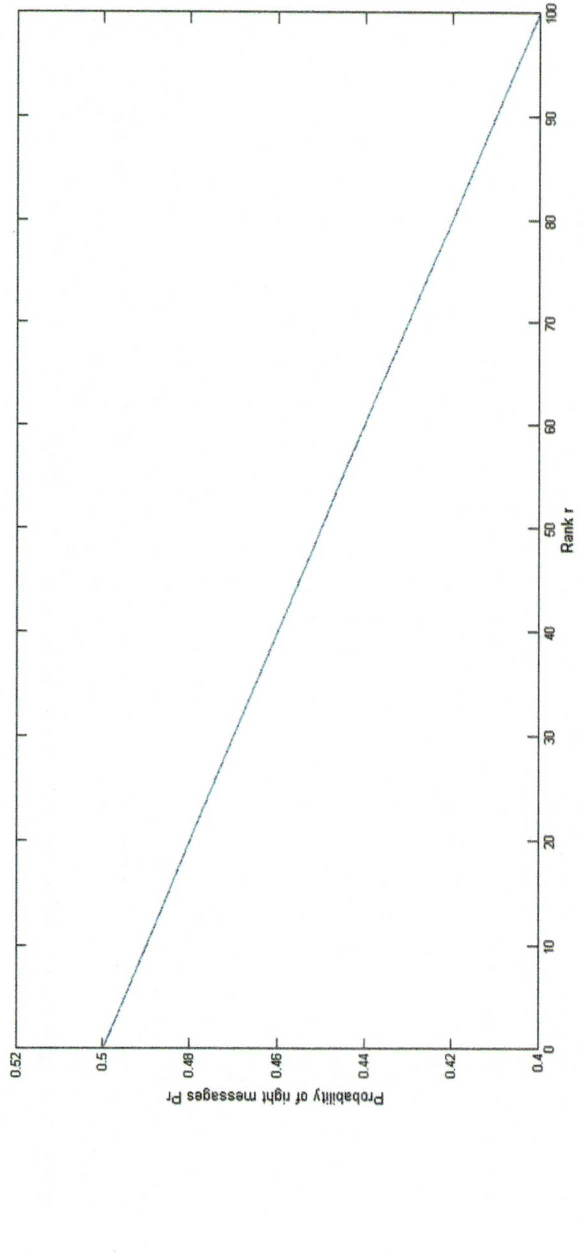

Fig. 5.3 Linear relationship between probability of right messages Pr and rank r with a negative a

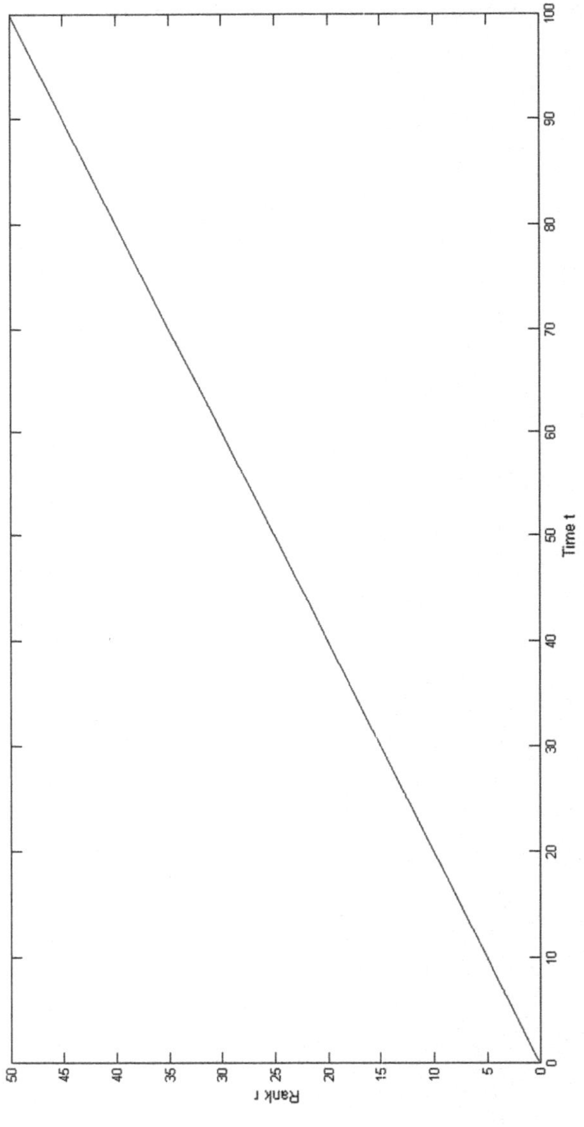

Fig. 5.4 Linear relationship between rank *r* and time *t*

Taking the first derivative with respect to time t, we have $c_A = \frac{dr_t^A}{dt}$, which is author A's marginal learning curve. Plugging Eq. 5.8 into 5.7 yields the value of author A:

$$v_t^A = 2a_F b_A c_A t^2 \tag{5.9}$$

where a_F is the reputation-recognition mechanism determined by platform F, b_A is the marginal posting rate determined by author A, and c_A is the marginal learning rate also determined by author A. a_F, b_A, and c_A are all constant in Eq. 5.9, which shows that the value of author A, v_t^A, is so far a quadratic function of time t. Because b_A and c_A are both non-negative terms, the sign of v_t^A is solely determined by the sign of a_F, that is a positive a_F determines a positive value of author A at time t, and vice versa. Figure 5.5 plots the value of author A from time 0 to 100 under an effective platform with $a_F = 0.001$, $b_A = 0.1$, and $c_A = 0.5$ set as arbitrary numbers.

By contrast, Fig. 5.6 plots the value of author A from time 0 to 100 under an ineffective platform with $a_F = -0.001$, $b_A = 0.1$, and $c_A = 0.5$ as arbitrary numbers.

The Value of a Financial Social Media Platform F

Equation 5.9 formulates the value generated by a single poster at time t. We further assume there are N_t posters at time t, and if all posters have the same activity history as the platform F (assuming all posters registered at the beginning of the platform when $t = 0$, and no new posters have been added since). Because a platform consists of N_t number of posters or authors at time t and the value of an FSM platform is the sum of N_t authors' total values $\sum_{A=1}^{N_t} v_t^A$, thus the value V_t^F at time t can be written as

$$V_t^F = \sum_{A=1}^{N_t} v_t^A = \sum_{A=1}^{N_t} 2a_F b_A c_A t^2 = 2a_F t^2 \left(\sum_{A=1}^{N_t} b_A c_A \right) \tag{5.10}$$

where a_F is a constant term in Eq. 5.10 because a_F is the programmed platform reputation-recognition system. We will later relax the assumption of equal activity history for all posters. Let us consider the value V_t^F generated by platform F when $a_F > 0$. In the scenario where $a_F > 0$, indicating an effective platform that accurately rewards posters' forecast accuracy, we assume that all posters will eventually converge to the platform-level

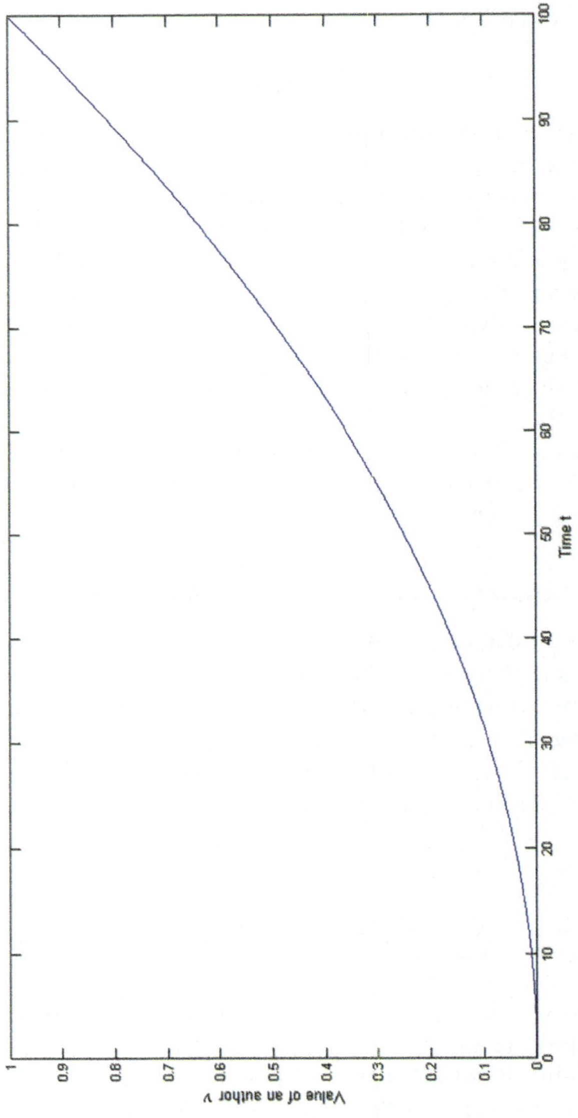

Fig. 5.5 Nonlinear relationship between value of an author v and time t with a positive a

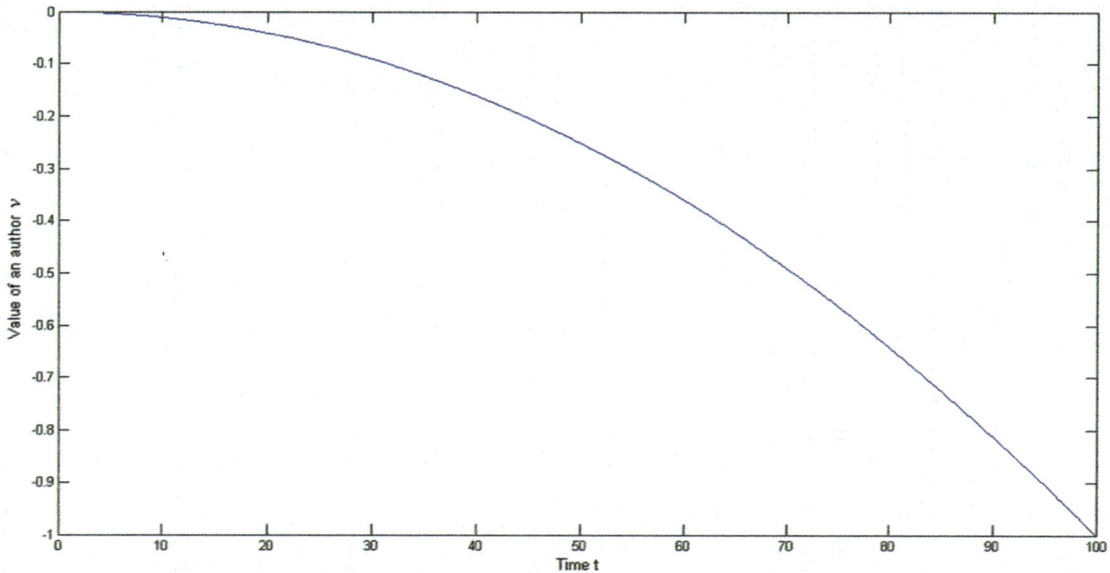

Fig. 5.6 Nonlinear relationship between value of an author v and time t with a negative a

posting rate, b_F, and to the platform-level learning ability, c_F, under a virtuous cycle or an advantageous selection scenario. The value V_t^F generated by platform F when $a_F \leq 0$ is not of interest, as it reflects an ineffective platform that inaccurately rewards posters' forecasting ability. This ultimately leads to a vicious cycle or an adverse selection scenario, as previously discussed. I acknowledge the limitation of assuming a uniform posting rate and learning ability across all users on the platform. This assumption implies that, in an idealized scenario, all posters would eventually converge to a similar level of engagement and knowledge acquisition. In a more realistic setting, however, the posting rate may represent an average across all users, and learning ability may similarly reflect the average level within the poster community. Thus, considering N_t as the total number of posters on platform F at time t, we therefore have:

$$b_1 = b_2 = \ldots = b_N = b_F, and\ c_1 = c_2 = \cdots = c_N = c_F, \tag{5.11}$$

and

$$b_1 c_1 = b_2 c_2 = \cdots = b_N c_N = b_F c_F \tag{5.12}$$

thus, we also have $b_F = \frac{\sum_{A=1}^{N} b_A}{N}$ and $c_F = \frac{\sum_{A=1}^{N} c_A}{N}$. Therefore, we have the following expression:

$$b_F \cdot c_F = \frac{\sum_{A=1}^{N} b_A}{N} \cdot \frac{\sum_{A=1}^{N} c_A}{N} = \frac{N b_F}{N} \cdot \frac{N c_F}{N} \tag{5.13}$$

thus, the total value the platform F can generate is rewritten as:

$$V_t^F = \sum_{A=1}^{N_t} v_t^A = 2a_F t^2 (b_1 c_1 + b_2 c_2 + \ldots b_N c_N) = 2a_F t^2 N_t b_F c_F \tag{5.14}$$

Next, assuming N_t represents the total number of authors in the platform F at time t and is also a function of time t, we have the following relationship:

$$N_t = N_0 + d_F t \tag{5.15}$$

N_t is assumed to increase over time given $N_0 = 0$. Note that a member who leaves the platform would make his or her account dormant, but would not reduce the total number of accounts. Taking the first derivative with respect to time t in Eq. 5.15, we have $d_F = \frac{dN_t}{dt}$, which is the average membership growth rate in platform F over time. Because the number of registered authors in a platform can only go up through time, d_F is set to be a positive term.

Figure 5.7 plots the linear relationship between the number of authors N_t and time t, setting $d_F = 2$ as an arbitrary positive number, which means two more new members at an incremental time.

Let us plus Eq. 5.15 into 5.14. Thus, at time t, under an unrealistic scenario, if all posters registered at the debut of platform F and no new poster added thereafter, the total value generated by platform F at time t would be:

$$V_t^F = 2a_F b_F c_F t^2 \cdot d_F t = 2a_F b_F c_F d_F t^3 \tag{5.16}$$

in which we can see that at the very beginning of the platform, when $t = 0$, there were no members, so the initial value was zero. Based on Eq. 5.16, the total value generated by platform F is a cubic function of time and increases as t gets larger.

However, not all posters have the same activity history. Since they join the discussion platform F at different times, each poster has a different time variable. Some posters have shorter activity history or registered later, while others have longer history due to earlier registration. According to Eq. 5.15, there are d_F additional posters at each incremental time interval. Meanwhile, the longer the activity history, the higher the poster's contribution or value v_t^A, as presented in Eq. 5.9. Thus, the total value platform F can generate at a specific time t is as follows, see Zhang (2025) for details of the derivation:

$$V_t^F = 2a_F b_F c_F d_F (\mathrm{t} \cdot (\mathrm{t} + 1) \cdot (2\mathrm{t} + 1)) \div 6 \tag{5.17}$$

where t is known and can be measured, it represents the history from the beginning of platform F to current. Thus, we can predict the expected total value platform F will generate at any future time t+n (n represents the number of periods after current t) as:

$$V_{t+n}^F = \frac{a_F b_F c_F d_F}{3} \cdot (t+n) \cdot \left[\left(t+n\right)+1\right] \cdot [2(t+n)+1] \tag{5.18}$$

Thus, the present value of V_{t+n}^F is calculated as $\frac{V_{t+n}^F}{(1+k)^n}$. Therefore, the sum of all future values that platform F will generate, discounted to the

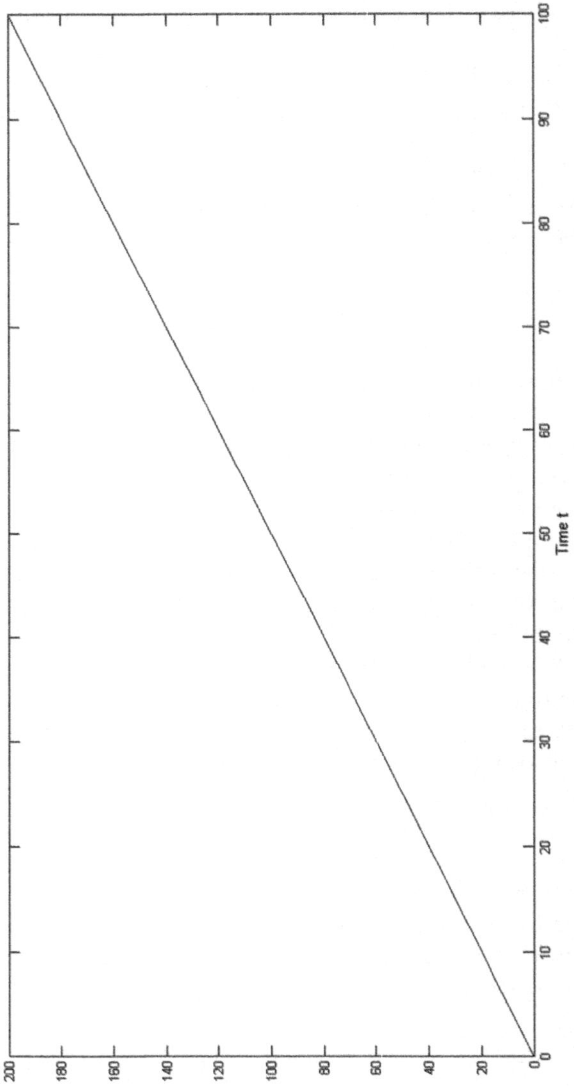

Fig. 5.7 Linear relationship between number of authors N and time t

present time t using a discount rate k, would be (excluding current value V_t^F):

$$PV_t^F = \sum_{n=1}^{+\infty} \frac{a_F b_F c_F d_F}{3} \cdot (t+n)(t+n+1)(2t+2n+1) \cdot \frac{1}{(1+k)^n} \tag{5.19}$$

where PV_t^F is the present value at time t based on all discounted future values that platform F will generate. Again, time t is known in the equation representing the history the platform from its debut to current, n ranges from 1 to infinity to represent future period (if n = 0, $PV_t^F = V_t^F$), k is the discount rate, representing the short-term traders' required rate of return. Firstly, we can prove that this series converges as n approaches infinity, see Zhang (2025) for the proof. Secondly, the closed-form solution for Eq. 5.19 is as follows (see Zhang (2025) for the proof):

$$PV_t^F = \frac{a_F b_F c_F d_F}{3} \cdot \left(\frac{2t^3 + 9t^2 + 13t + 6}{k} + \frac{6t^2 + 24t + 24}{k^2} + \frac{12t + 30}{k^3} + \frac{12}{k^4} \right) \tag{5.20}$$

where a_F, b_F, c_F, and d_F all are constant values that can be estimated through empirical analysis using statistical methods.

Continuous compounding represents the ultimate mathematical boundary for compound interest, achieved if it were calculated and reinvested into an investor's account balance over an infinite number of periods. Although this is infeasible in real-world scenarios, the idea of continuously compounded interest is crucial as it provides the lowest present value that platform F would generate at the current time based on all discounted future values. Therefore, the equation below offers a method to gauge the minimum theoretical present value, assuming it continuously generates value for its short-term investors and e is the Euler's number ≈ 2.718 (see Zhang (2025) for derivation):

$$\min\left(PV_t^F\right) = \frac{a_F b_F c_F d_F}{3} \cdot \left[\frac{2e^{3k} + 8e^{2k} + 2e^k}{\left(e^k - 1\right)^4} + \frac{(6t+3) \cdot \left(e^{2k} + e^k\right)}{\left(e^k - 1\right)^3} + \frac{\left(6t^2 + 6t + 1\right) \cdot e^k}{\left(e^k - 1\right)^2} + \frac{2t^3 + 3t^2 + t}{e^k - 1} \right] \tag{5.21}$$

Figure 5.8 plots the value of an effective platform F from time 0 to 100, setting $a_F = 0.001$, $b_F = 0.1$, $c_A = 0.5$, and $d_F = 2$ as arbitrary numbers.

By contrast, Fig. 5.9 plots the value of an ineffective platform F from time 0 to 100, setting $a_F = -0.001$, $b_F = 0.1$, $c_A = 0.5$, and $d_F = 2$ as arbitrary numbers.

In sum, the value of an FSM platform F, V_t^F shown in Eq. 5.17, is determined by four factors other than time t:

- a_F, which is platform F's reputation-recognition mechanism
- b_F, non-negative number, which is the platform F' average posting willingness
- c_F, non-negative number, which is the platform F' average marginal learning curve
- d_F, non-negative number, which is the membership growth rate on platform F.

It is not hard to see that a_F determines the sign of the value (direction of development) while a_F, b_F, c_F, d_F jointly affect the magnitude of the value. It is reasonable to assume that none of these four determinants are correlated, or are a function of each other. For instance, b_F is the average posting willingness while c_F is the average learning curve, so they are assumed to be uncorrelated with each other.

In an actual platform F, these four factors are empirically measurable. First a_F can be estimated by using a cross-sectional regression model between forecast accuracy and ranks among all authors at any static moment t. a_F is expected to be stable over time because it is the reputation-recognition mechanism implemented by the platform or accepted by all participants so that $a_{F,\, t} = a_{F,\, t+1}$. Second, b_F can be measured by a panel regression model given the number of messages posted by all authors over time. Third, a similar structured panel regression model can be conducted to estimate c_F for all posters over time. Finally, d_F can be calculated based on a time-series analysis, given the available number of users over time.

In addition, when considering a continuous regime, FSM activity can be modeled as growing exponentially, reflecting the exponential growth of both Internet usage and Internet-based stock trading (Loh and Ong, 1998; Teich, Wallenius, and Wallenius, 1999; Hong, 2000). As a result,

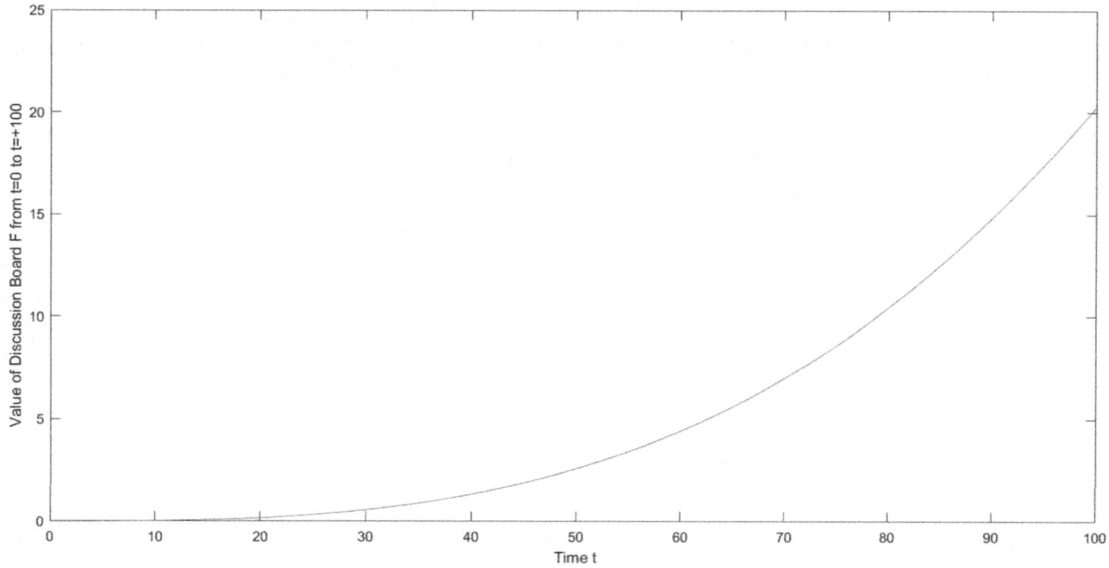

Fig. 5.8 Nonlinear relationship between value of platform V and time t with a positive a

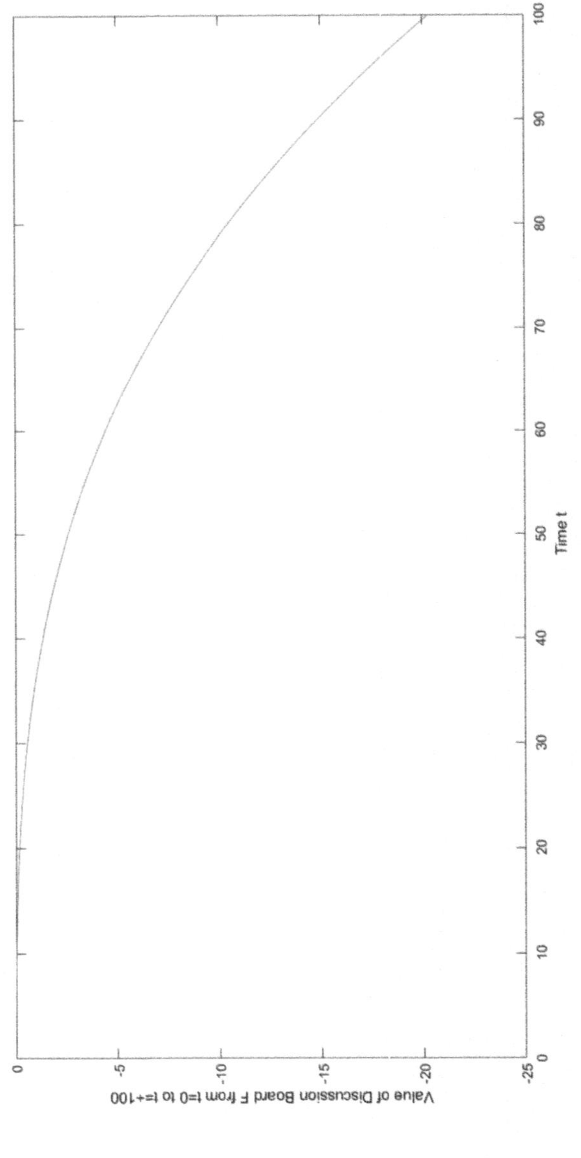

Fig. 5.9 Nonlinear relationship between value of platform *V* and time *t* with a negative *a*

the linear functions presented in the previous equations may be replaced with nonlinear functions without altering the underlying conclusions, even though the specific equations may differ. For nonlinear formulations, see Zhang (2025).

The derivation of the FSM platform valuation model has several practical implications. It demonstrates that an effective reputation-recognition mechanism can reduce information asymmetry among users and help prevent the adverse selection dynamics discussed earlier. The model offers guidance on how to design and maintain an effective platform. Furthermore, it suggests that reputation-recognition mechanisms need not rely solely on user ratings, as seen in systems like TheLion.com, eBay.com, and Amazon.com, but can also be implemented algorithmically by forum developers.

Therefore, it is both feasible and advisable to incorporate an algorithmic system that objectively ranks authors based on their sentiment forecasts and the subsequent performance of the relevant stocks. Such a system would be more reliable than traditional user-generated rating systems, which are vulnerable to manipulation, for example, through multiple account registrations used to inflate a primary account's credibility. When this occurs, an author's rating becomes unreliable, ultimately diminishing the value of the platform.

A more robust approach would involve displaying two distinct scores for each user: one reflecting peer-assigned credibility (for example: a score of 80), and the other reflecting the objectively calculated sentiment-performance accuracy (for example: a score of 95). This dual-score system can offer a more transparent and trustworthy reputation framework for FSM platforms.

Moral Hazard and its Implications

A problem of moral hazard may arise if the FSM platform lacks adequate oversight from its administrators and/or market regulators. Moral hazard can occur under both previously discussed scenarios, although it is more likely to emerge under an advantageous selection scenario. By reintroducing posting costs into Eq. 5.3, we have:

$$v_t^A = \left(2\Pr_{Right}^{A,t} - 1\right) m_t^A - cost_t^A \tag{5.22}$$

where $cost_t^A \geq 0$ represents the total costs that poster A has incurred at time t. To maximize v_t^A, A would minimize $cost_t^A$ regardless of the sign and magnitude of $\left(2\Pr_{Right}^{A,t} - 1\right)m_t^A$. In other words, any author would want to minimize cost in order to maximize his or her value v_t^A.

Any IA can easily and irresponsibly recommend stocks at no cost. However, this behavior does not contribute to building the IA's reputation. Even if an IA attempts to do so, the lack of followers means moral hazard is unlikely to occur. SAs, on the other hand, typically refrain from manipulating stocks due to their assumed ethical standards and the value they place on their reputations. Nevertheless, we cannot entirely rule out the possibility of moral hazard—particularly when one or more SAs become extremely powerful and influential within the community.

In practice, when a highly ranked poster becomes especially influential, any stock recommendation made by that poster is likely to attract a substantial number of followers who act on that sentiment. Over time, such a poster may realize that by selecting an easily manipulated target, they can trigger follower activity, enabling them to generate quick and substantial trading profits with minimal effort or risk—often without conducting any meaningful research or incurring any cost.

As a result, some influential posters may begin to abuse their power, leveraging their community influence to manipulate stocks for personal gain (Aggarwal and Wu, 2006). Moral hazard arises in these situations, where influential posters exploit their power to manipulate vulnerable stocks, maximizing their profits at little cost while exposing their followers to potential losses. A situation in which the influential SA spends no time or money on research or information gathering before issuing a stock recommendation represents a moral hazard scenario.

Moral hazard introduces market inefficiencies, exacerbates information asymmetries, and ultimately harms the interests of other investors. To maximize their returns with minimal investment, influential posters may target stocks with weak fundamentals and poor technical indicators (Sabherwal, Sarkar, and Zhang, 2012). Low-priced stocks are particularly susceptible to such manipulation, as they often lack broad ownership and have limited floating shares, making price movements easier to influence (Wysocki, 1998).

When moral hazard becomes widespread, regulatory intervention may be necessary. Policymakers such as the Securities and Exchange Commission (SEC) and the Federal Trade Commission (FTC) are expected to step in to protect market integrity. In extreme cases, if stock manipulation becomes rampant and unmanageable, the platform itself may face legal action, potentially leading to its shutdown. Legal proceedings against stock manipulators have already been documented in such contexts.[9]

Herding Behavior

There was a time when online FSM platforms were dismissed as little more than rumor mills. Today, they can move markets in minutes. A single post from a well-known figure, such as a tweet by Tesla's CEO Elon Musk, can send a stock price soaring or tumbling. The effect is even stronger when the poster has a large and loyal following. In 2021, for example, "Roaring Kitty" shared bullish views on GameStop (GME) in the WallStreetBets forum on Reddit, helping to spark a dramatic short squeeze that cost some hedge funds billions. Even without one central influencer, a steady stream of similar opinions from many posters can create the sense that the sentiment reflects the majority view, as seen with meme stocks like AMC Entertainment Holdings, Inc. (AMC). In such moments, many traders fall in line with the crowd.

Herding happens when investors base their decisions on what others are doing instead of their own analysis. It can be fueled by the lightning fast spread of news and rumors online, often leading to overreactions, price swings, and volatility. Although herding can briefly boost liquidity and narrow bid-ask spreads, these benefits are usually short lived. Over time, it can distort prices, create inefficiencies, and increase risk.

Studies have shown that online platforms can trigger herd like behavior, often leading to temporary price jumps followed by sharp reversals. Yet these platforms also provide a wealth of timely information, connecting investors to market developments that may not appear in traditional news for hours or even days. When participants are informed, herding is not necessarily harmful and can even be profitable.

In practice, the most pronounced herding occurs when trusted, highly ranked posters share their views, drawing in large numbers of followers. By contrast, posts from less credible voices tend to generate little reaction, making widespread herding far less likely.

Final Thoughts

In the future, as with many other industries, the FSM landscape is likely to consolidate, with a few dominant firms emerging through mergers and acquisitions. Currently, platforms such as Facebook, X.com (formerly Twitter), Google, LinkedIn, Reddit, and Yahoo rank among the most widely used social media sites across all age groups in the United States. Many of these tech giants host their own FSM platform, including Yahoo! Finance, Reddit, and Google Finance.

In addition to these structured platforms, stock-related discussions also occur within more informal communities, such as Facebook trading groups (Karabulut 2013; Simon and Heimer 2012) and Twitter-based investor circles (Bollen, Mao, and Zeng 2011; Thelwall, Buckley, and Paltoglou 2011). While there are still several popular stand-alone stock-trading boards, such as TheLion and Raging Bull, these platforms or their parent companies are typically not publicly traded and generally lack the financial strength of the major publicly listed social media giants.

It is therefore likely that we will witness mergers among these independent FSM platforms or acquisitions by larger social media firms. A relevant example is Google's acquisition of YouTube on October 9, 2006. Prior to the acquisition, YouTube operated as a successful stand-alone video-sharing website. Similar consolidation has already begun in the financial social media space. For instance, in September 2006, ADVFN.com, a UK-based financial market website, acquired InvestorsHub.com, a prominent online investment community serving the North American market. To help estimate the value of an FSM platform in the mergers and acquisitions process, the formula covered in this chapter would be very useful.

Notes

1. A text classifier uses its algorithm to assign a sentiment score to a non-self-disclosed message. Details of text classifiers will be discussed in the next chapter.
2. SPY is SPDR S&P 500 Exchanged Traded Fund while DIA is SPDR Dow Jones Industrial Average Exchanged Traded Fund.
3. Many FSM platforms provide a sentiment indicator for posters to explicitly disclose their sentiment on a voluntary basis. For instance,

Yahoo! Finance allows a poster to choose one of the following sentiments: Strong Buy, Buy, Hold, Sell, Strong Sell, or not disclose (by default). TheLion.com offers two more sentiments: Short and Scalp. The Short sentiment suggests short selling while the Scalp sentiment implies buying and selling quickly with the intent of a day-trade profit but without any specific sentiment. Raging Bull also requires the author to specify his or her short-term and long-term sentiments (Tumarkin and Whitelaw 2001).

4. To be more realistic, the value of a message could also depend on the author's reputation or credibility. Logically, a high-ranked author's message should contribute a higher value than that of a low-ranked author's, ceteris paribus. For example, when two social media accounts give out the same information and same recommendation, a higher value should be given to an Associated Press account than an unknown individual's account. Another example is, one author's credit score is 100 and the other author has just 1 credit score. If both of them are correct, we can define the value of a message's value to be $100(+1) = +100$ for the former author and $1(+1) = +1$ for the latter one. But to keep my derivation simple, I define the value is $+1$ unit if the message's sentiment is right and -1(stet) unit otherwise.
5. Shorting is the practice of selling securities or other financial instruments that are not currently owned, with the intention of subsequently repurchasing them ("Buy to cover") at a lower price.
6. In reality, it is possible for an author to have one or more messages deleted by the administrator. However, it is unlikely for one author's messages to be consistently deleted over a considerable amount of time by the administrator because this type of author would be blocked by the FSM platform. Thus, we do not consider a case with a negative b_A in the model.
7. A reputation-recognition mechanism could be implemented either mandatorily by the forum design or voluntarily by all participants in the FSM platform. An effective voluntary reputation-recognition mechanism would occur when an author makes a correct forecast and other participants grant him or her positive credit, and vice versa.
8. Rank's upper limit $1/|2a_F|$can be set by the platform developer. Each author's rank needs to be updated in real time based on his/her cumulative forecast accuracy.

9. http://www.sec.gov/news/headlines/intmm.htm and http://www.sec.gov/news/headlines/tokyojoe2.htm

CHAPTER 6

How to Measure Financial Social Media Activities?

Financial Social Media Data Structure

Researchers employ various web-crawling tools to extract financial social media (FSM hereafter) data and store it in different types of database systems. In my case, I developed custom software using Visual Basic to collect data from the WallStreetPit trading board hosted on TheLion.com. I also designed a Microsoft Access database to store the extracted text data.

There are several reasons for this design choice. First, my Visual Basic program automatically filters out any disclaimers or signature lines appended to messages, as well as any unrecognized or meaningless symbols. The database captures essential metadata for each post, including the message ID, posting date and time, author's name, credit score, and membership history, stock symbol and stock price (if disclosed), and the self-reported sentiment when available.

The textual content of each message is stored separately in a machine-readable text file, named according to its message ID. This design is intentional: the separate files serve as the foundation for building a training dataset, which is later used to construct and evaluate a text classifier. We will discuss that process in a later section.

Figure 6.1 shows a screenshot of the Microsoft Access database interface.

Y. Zhang, *Financial Social Media*,
https://doi.org/10.1007/978-3-032-09332-5_6

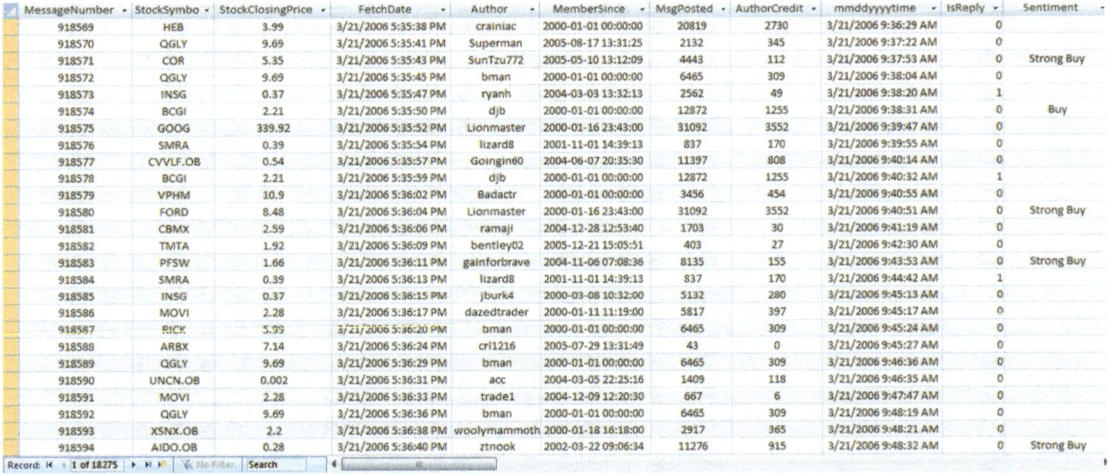

MessageNumber	StockSymbo	StockClosingPrice	FetchDate	Author	MemberSince	MsgPosted	AuthorCredit	mmddyyyytime	IsReply	Sentiment
918569	HEB	3.99	3/21/2006 5:35:38 PM	crainiac	2000-01-01 00:00:00	20819	2730	3/21/2006 9:36:29 AM	0	
918570	QGLY	9.69	3/21/2006 5:35:41 PM	Superman	2005-08-17 13:31:25	2132	345	3/21/2006 9:37:22 AM	0	
918571	COR	5.35	3/21/2006 5:35:43 PM	SunTzu772	2005-05-10 13:12:09	4443	112	3/21/2006 9:37:53 AM	0	Strong Buy
918572	QGLY	9.69	3/21/2006 5:35:45 PM	bman	2000-01-01 00:00:00	6465	309	3/21/2006 9:38:04 AM	0	
918573	INSG	0.37	3/21/2006 5:35:47 PM	ryanh	2004-03-03 13:32:13	2562	49	3/21/2006 9:38:20 AM	1	
918574	BCGI	2.21	3/21/2006 5:35:50 PM	djb	2000-01-01 00:00:00	12872	1255	3/21/2006 9:38:31 AM	0	Buy
918575	GOOG	339.92	3/21/2006 5:35:52 PM	Lionmaster	2000-01-16 23:43:00	31092	3552	3/21/2006 9:39:47 AM	0	
918576	SMRA	0.39	3/21/2006 5:35:54 PM	lizard8	2001-11-01 14:39:13	837	170	3/21/2006 9:39:55 AM	0	
918577	CVVLF.OB	0.54	3/21/2006 5:35:57 PM	Goingin60	2004-06-07 20:35:30	11397	808	3/21/2006 9:40:14 AM	0	
918578	BCGI	2.21	3/21/2006 5:35:59 PM	djb	2000-01-01 00:00:00	12872	1255	3/21/2006 9:40:32 AM	1	
918579	VPHM	10.9	3/21/2006 5:36:02 PM	Badactr	2000-01-01 00:00:00	3456	454	3/21/2006 9:40:55 AM	0	
918580	FORD	8.48	3/21/2006 5:36:04 PM	Lionmaster	2000-01-16 23:43:00	31092	3552	3/21/2006 9:40:51 AM	0	Strong Buy
918581	CBMX	2.59	3/21/2006 5:36:06 PM	ramaji	2004-12-28 12:53:40	1703	30	3/21/2006 9:41:19 AM	0	
918582	TMTA	1.92	3/21/2006 5:36:09 PM	bentley02	2005-12-21 15:05:51	403	27	3/21/2006 9:42:30 AM	0	
918583	PFSW	1.66	3/21/2006 5:36:11 PM	gainforbrave	2004-11-06 07:08:36	8135	155	3/21/2006 9:43:53 AM	0	Strong Buy
918584	SMRA	0.39	3/21/2006 5:36:13 PM	lizard8	2001-11-01 14:39:13	837	170	3/21/2006 9:44:42 AM	1	
918585	INSG	0.37	3/21/2006 5:36:15 PM	jburk4	2000-03-08 10:32:00	5132	280	3/21/2006 9:45:13 AM	0	
918586	MOVI	2.28	3/21/2006 5:36:17 PM	dazedtrader	2000-01-11 11:19:00	5817	397	3/21/2006 9:45:17 AM	0	
918587	RICK	5.99	3/21/2006 5:36:20 PM	bman	2000-01-01 00:00:00	6465	309	3/21/2006 9:45:24 AM	0	
918588	ARBX	7.14	3/21/2006 5:36:24 PM	crl1216	2005-07-29 13:31:49	43	0	3/21/2006 9:45:27 AM	0	
918589	QGLY	9.69	3/21/2006 5:36:29 PM	bman	2000-01-01 00:00:00	6465	309	3/21/2006 9:46:36 AM	0	
918590	UNCN.OB	0.002	3/21/2006 5:36:31 PM	acc	2004-03-05 22:25:16	1409	118	3/21/2006 9:46:35 AM	0	
918591	MOVI	2.28	3/21/2006 5:36:33 PM	trade1	2004-12-09 12:20:30	667	6	3/21/2006 9:47:47 AM	0	
918592	QGLY	9.69	3/21/2006 5:36:36 PM	bman	2000-01-01 00:00:00	6465	309	3/21/2006 9:48:19 AM	0	
918593	XSNX.OB	2.2	3/21/2006 5:36:38 PM	woolymammoth	2000-01-18 16:18:00	2917	365	3/21/2006 9:48:21 AM	0	
918594	AIDO.OB	0.28	3/21/2006 5:36:40 PM	ztnook	2002-03-22 09:06:34	11276	915	3/21/2006 9:48:32 AM	0	Strong Buy

Fig. 6.1 Screen capture of my Microsoft access database

As shown in Fig. 6.1, the database contains 18,275 records, each representing a unique message post. Below is a summary of the key columns visible in the figure:

- Message Number—This is the unique identification number assigned to each message. The messages are sorted in ascending order, from the top (e.g., Message Number 918,569) to the bottom (e.g., 918,594).
- Stock Symbol—The ticker symbol associated with the stock discussed in the message. (Note: Not all messages include a stock symbol.)
- Stock Price—The stock price at the time the message was posted.
- Download Time—The exact time the message was downloaded by my software.
- Author—The screen name of the author.
- Registration Time—The date and time the author first registered. This information is used to calculate the author's membership history measured in days.
- Message Count—The total number of messages posted by the author prior to the current message.
- Credit Score—The cumulative score received by the author, based on ratings from other users.
- Post Time—The actual timestamp of when the message was posted.
- Reply Status—Indicates whether the message is a reply or an original post. (This distinction is important. As noted by Zhang et al. [2012], replies may carry different informational value compared to original messages and should be treated differently when constructing sentiment indices.)
- Self-Disclosed Sentiment—The sentiment explicitly disclosed by the author in the message.

Due to space limitations, Fig. 6.1 displays only a subset of the full database, which actually includes 83 columns encompassing a wide range of posting-related, message-related, stock-related, and author-related variables. Still, even this abbreviated view highlights useful insights. For example, Columns 7 and 8 provide useful metrics for evaluating an author's popularity within the FSM platform.

It's important to note that not all messages contain explicit sentiment tags. For messages without self-disclosed sentiments, I employ a text classifier to infer and assign sentiment. These sentiments are then quantified based on a widely accepted coding standard. Following the methodology proposed by Tumarkin and Whitelaw (2001), Tumarkin (2002), and Zhang and Swanson (2009), the sentiment values are coded as follows: –3 = Short Sell; –2 = Strong Sell; –1 = Sell; 0 = Hold or Scalp; + 1 = Buy; + 2 = Strong Buy.

As previously mentioned, the content of each message is saved in a separate text file, named according to the Message Number (from the first column of the database). Figure 6.2 shows a screenshot of the folder containing all 18,275 text files, each corresponding directly to a record in the Microsoft Access database. These files are essential for the next step: building the training dataset used in text classification.

At this point, we have established that posters on FSM platforms disclose their sentiments voluntarily. Zhang et al. (2012) conducted an important experiment demonstrating that even messages without self-disclosed sentiment contain valuable information and should be incorporated into the construction of sentiment indices. However, doing so requires inferring the author's sentiment based on the content of the message itself.

This introduces a challenge: human interpretation is inherently subjective and may not always align with the author's original intent, leading to potential biases (Zhang et al. 2012).

Fortunately, artificial intelligence offers a solution. Modern text classification techniques can infer the most likely sentiment based on linguistic patterns, keyword usage, and contextual cues—reducing the influence of human judgment. In the next section, we explore the underlying principles of text classifiers and how they assign sentiment scores to messages in a more systematic and unbiased manner.

How a Text Classifier Works

A text classifier operates by applying algorithms—such as computational linguistics models or statistical learning techniques—to identify and learn distinct patterns associated with different sentiment categories (e.g., Buy, Hold, Sell) in the training dataset. This training data consists of a large pool of messages with pre-labeled sentiments provided by the original

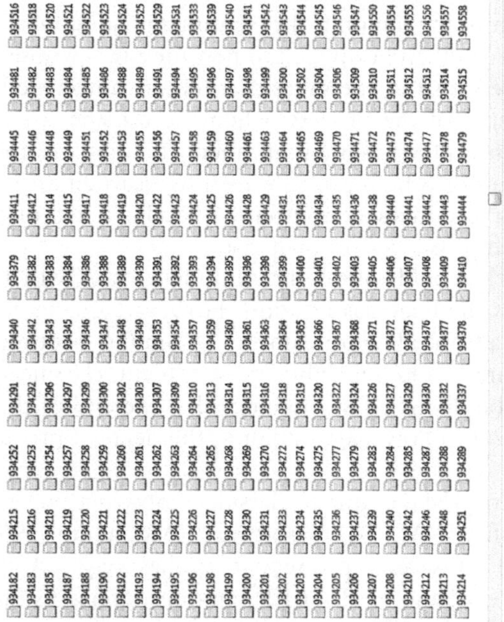

Fig. 6.2 Screen capture of my text files folder

posters. These known sentiments serve as the foundation for the classifier to "learn" the features that differentiate one sentiment class from another.

Using this labeled data, the classification algorithm constructs a model capable of distinguishing among the sentiment categories. Once the model is trained, it can then be applied to new messages whose sentiments are not self-disclosed, that is, messages that require automated inference.

In the second step of the process, when the classifier receives a new message without an explicitly stated sentiment, it compares the linguistic and structural features of the message with those learned during training. The classifier then produces an output—typically a set of probability scores, one for each possible sentiment class.

A basic approach would assign the sentiment class with the highest probability score as the final classification. However, Zhang et al. (2012) propose a more advanced algorithm for assigning sentiment, which improves the accuracy and reliability of sentiment classification. Their methodology will be discussed in more detail at the end of this chapter.

Figure 6.3 presents a flowchart outlining the detailed process of using a text classifier.

When performing data training, classifier construction, and testing, many scholars utilize RAINBOW software (McCallum 1996), which has been adopted in several prominent studies (e.g., Antweiler and Frank, 2004, 2006; Zhang et al. 2012), among others. As illustrated in Fig. 6.3, the classification setup typically requires two separate terminal computers—one functioning as the server and the other as the client.

The server computer is responsible for executing the text classification algorithm. It uses the training data to analyze incoming messages without self-disclosed sentiment. The client computer, on the other hand, sends the content of these incoming messages to the server and receives the predicted sentiment in return.

Once the sentiment is returned, the client computer translates it into a numeric score and updates the corresponding message in the Microsoft Access database, using the message number as a primary key for reference. As a result, every message in the database sample, regardless of whether it originally contained a self-disclosed sentiment, will eventually be assigned a sentiment score ranging from –3 to + 2. We keep the original sentiment scores if the messages include self-disclosed sentiments.

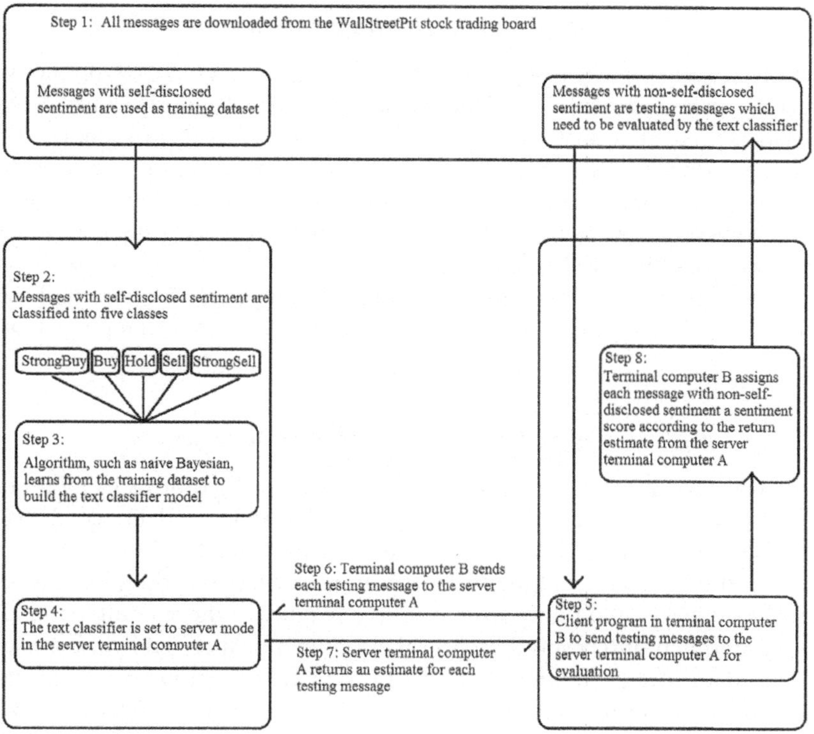

Fig. 6.3 Flowchart for using a text classifier

Issues in Constructing the Training Dataset

The effectiveness of a text classifier depends not only on the efficiency of its algorithm but also on the quality and structure of the training data. The quality of the training data is directly linked to the classifier's accuracy and reliability. If the training dataset is flawed or biased, the resulting classifier is likely to perform inaccurately.

Training data forms the foundation of the classifier. Therefore, it must be carefully curated to minimize bias and maximize informational value. The following five considerations are critical when constructing an effective training dataset:

Out-of-Sample Testing for Accuracy

Before deploying a text classifier, it is essential to evaluate its predictive performance—particularly on out-of-sample data. A poorly constructed classifier may demonstrate high in-sample accuracy (i.e., accuracy on messages drawn from the training data) but perform poorly on out-of-sample data. Since the primary use of a text classifier is to assign sentiment to new messages without self-disclosed sentiment, out-of-sample accuracy is a more relevant performance metric.

Accordingly, when assessing or comparing classifiers, greater emphasis should be placed on out-of-sample accuracy rather than in-sample performance.

Use of Self-Disclosed Sentiment Messages

Due to the lack of self-disclosed sentiment data on platforms like Yahoo! Finance before 2000, early studies such as Antweiler and Frank (2004) and Das and Chen (2003, 2007) had to rely on researchers' manual interpretation of message sentiment. However, such human coding introduces subjective bias, calling into question the reliability of the training data.[1] A good sentiment index should reflect the sentiment expressed by the poster rather than interpretations imposed by researchers. Human interpretation might introduce subjective bias, making the quality of hand-coded training data questionable.

To address this issue, Zhang et al. (2012) recommend using only messages with self-disclosed sentiment as training data. This strategy eliminates the need for manual interpretation and enhances the classifier's objectivity and power. This strategy is based on the belief that a poster's self-disclosed sentiment is consistent with the message content, since it would make little sense for a self-disclosed sentiment to contradict the meaning of the message.

Balanced Representation Across Sentiment Classes

A common issue in training data is class imbalance—where certain sentiment classes (e.g., "Strong Buy") are overrepresented compared to others (e.g., "Strong Sell"). This imbalance causes the classifier to become biased toward the majority class, compromising its ability to detect less frequent sentiments (Japkowicz and Stephen 2002; Estabrooks et al. 2004).

Zhang et al. (2012) demonstrate experimentally that class imbalance is a leading cause of classifier inefficiency. To mitigate this, the training dataset should contain a fairly equal number of messages in each sentiment category. Although it is impossible to ensure that every message conveys the same amount of information because message length and word choice vary, the relatively uniform message lengths on many FSM platforms make equal message counts per class in the training dataset a reasonable and effective solution.

Controlling for Overfitting

Another critical concern is overfitting, which occurs when the classifier memorizes the training data instead of learning generalizable patterns. This often happens when the training dataset is excessively large, even if class balance is maintained. Overfitted models may perform perfectly on the training data but fail dramatically on new messages.

To control for overfitting, researchers recommend limiting the size of the training dataset. For example, Das and Chen (2007) suggest using 350–500 messages per sentiment class, while Zhang et al. (2012) follow a similar guideline, using 500 messages per class.

Overfitting occurs when the classifier learns patterns specific to the training data rather than generalizable patterns applicable to new messages. A classifier trained to optimize in-sample performance may not generalize well, so it is important to strike a balance between training size and classifier robustness.

Exclusion of Reply Messages

The training dataset should be composed of messages that are rich in relevant information and free of excessive noise. Reply messages often contain more noise and should be excluded. Zhang et al. (2012) argue that reply and non-reply (original) messages differ significantly in structure and relevance.

Replies often respond to previous posts, agreeing, disagreeing, or elaborating, rather than making original stock recommendations. As such, replies are typically less informative or even irrelevant for sentiment classification. Including them in the training dataset can reduce classifier performance (Li and Shi 2002; Yi et al. 2003). Therefore, to enhance classifier power, only original messages should be used for training, excluding replies.

A Variety of Text Classifiers

Selecting an appropriate text classification algorithm is a crucial decision that must be made at the outset of any sentiment analysis project. Numerous classifiers exist, each employing different algorithms, and their effectiveness often depends on the specific features of the dataset and the domain of application. Across disciplines, different classifiers have proven effective for different types of data:

- In the biomedical field, Support Vector Machine (SVM hereafter) has been shown to outperform other methods in recognizing tissue samples (Furey et al. 2000).
- In object recognition, probabilistic indexing has been recognized as a promising approach (Olson 1995).
- In the realm of FSM analysis, Antweiler and Frank (2004) employ the Naïve Bayesian classifier and report comparable results when using a support vector machine.
- Takahashi et al. (2007) use the Naïve Bayesian classifier to examine the relationship between stock returns and text-based market headlines.
- Similar studies by Antweiler and Frank (2006) and Schumaker and Chen (2006, 2009) apply both Naïve Bayesian and SVM classifiers to explore how financial news affects stock market movements.
- Thomas and Sycara (2002) and Zhang and Swanson (2010) use the maximum entropy classifier in their research on FSM platforms.
- Das and Chen (2003, 2007) and Gu et al. (2007) develop their own classifiers, which incorporate variations of the Naïve Bayes approach.
- Bettman et al. (2011) use both Naïve Bayesian and SVM classifiers to test the credibility of FSM rumors related to market takeovers.
- Sabherwal et al. (2011) apply a Naïve Bayesian approach to analyze online discussions that lack accompanying fundamental news.
- Later, Sprenger et al. (2014) utilize the Naïve Bayesian classifier to study the informational value of X.com (formerly Twitter) posts related to stocks.

Although the landscape of text classification is broad, this chapter focuses on eight widely used classifiers that are particularly relevant in financial text analysis: 1. Expectation Maximization (EM); 2.Kullback–Leibler Divergence; 3. K-Nearest Neighbor (KNN); 4.Maximum Entropy; 5. Naïve Bayesian; 6. Probabilistic Indexing; 7. Support Vector Machine (SVM); 8. Term Frequency–Inverse Document Frequency (TF-IDF).

The following parameters and terminologies are adapted for demonstrating algorithms for all text classifiers: θ_j—a category or class, such as Buy, Hold or Sell; d_i —a document with self-disclosed sentiment in the training data. A training dataset that contains n number of documents can be presented as $Dn = d1, d2 \cdots dn$; d_m —a message with a sentiment class unknown and is in need of evaluation by the text classifier; x_i —a feature parameter or a key word, such as "good," "rally," "down," "pessimistic"; $\vec{x}_i$—a vector of key words, $\vec{x}_i = \{x_1, x_2, \cdots, x_n\}$; w—a weight or a weight vector, which describes the word's relative importance.

- *Expectation Maximization* (EM). An expectation maximization algorithm is an algorithm for finding maximum-likelihood estimates of parameters (θ_j) in probabilistic models, where the model depends on unobserved latent variables (Dempster et al. 1977). EM alternates between performing an expectation (E) step—which computes the expected value of the latent variables—and maximization (M) step, which computes the maximum-likelihood estimates of the parameters, given the data and setting the latent variables to their expectation.

When considering the task of finding maximum-likelihood estimates of a class θ_j from observations of training data vector $\vec{x}_i \in \Re$, which is statistically dependent on θ_j, the maximum-likelihood estimate of θ_j is $\hat{\theta}_j$ can be obtained as a solution to:

$$\hat{\theta}_j = \underset{\theta_j}{\operatorname{argmax}}\, q(\vec{x}_i|\theta_j) \tag{6.1}$$

where $q(\vec{x}_i|\theta_j)$ is the conditional density of the data $\vec{x}_i$ given the class θ_j. Unfortunately, in many cases, it is impossible to obtain a closed-form solution to the optimization problem described in Eq. 6.1. On the other hand, it may be possible to form a set of hypothetical data $\vec{y}_i \in \aleph$, related to $\vec{x}_i$ by a many-to-one relationship $h(\vec{y}_i) = \vec{x}_i$ from $\aleph \rightarrow \Re$, such that:

$$q(\vec{x}_i|\theta_j) = \int_{\aleph(\vec{x}_i)} p(\vec{y}_i|\theta_j)d\vec{y}_i \tag{6.2}$$

where $p(\vec{y}_i|\theta_j)$ is the density of $\vec{y}_i$ as a function of θ_j and $\aleph(\vec{x}_i) = \{\vec{y}_i : h(\vec{y}_i) = \vec{x}_i\}$. The two sets of data $\vec{x}_i$ and $\vec{y}_i$ are known as the incomplete data and complete data, respectively. The EM algorithm makes use of the conditional density $p(\vec{y}_i|\theta_j)$ in a two-step iterative procedure that solves the problem in Eq. 6.1. At the ith stage of the iteration, the two-step iteration is described by: (1) compute $\mathrm{E}\left[\log p(\vec{y}_i|\theta_j)|\vec{x}_i, \theta_j^i\right]$ in E-step, and (2) solve $\theta_j^{i+1} = \underset{\theta_j}{\operatorname{argmax}}\, \mathrm{E}\left[\log p(\vec{y}_i|\theta_j)|\vec{x}_i, \theta_j^i\right]$ in M-step. In the E-step, an evaluation of the conditional expectation of the function $p(\vec{y}_i|\theta_j)$, given the data $\vec{y}_i$ and the most recent estimate θ_j^i of θ_j is required.

In the M-step, the conditional expectation computed in the E-step is maximized with respect to the parameter vector θ_j. The maximizing value of θ_j is the new estimate, θ_j^{i+1} of θ_j. This estimate is then used in the E-step to produce the new conditional expectation, which is further maximized to yield the new estimate, et cetera. The procedure repeats until the algorithm converges. The last estimate of θ_j (when the algorithm converges) is taken as the final estimate for document d_m.

- *Kullback–Leibler Divergence* (KL). Kullback and Leibler (1951) studied a measure of information from a statistical point of view that involves two probability distributions, P and Q, associated with the same experiment, and identified as a discrimination function. The KL divergence, also known as relative entropy, is a measure of how different two probability distributions over the same event space are.

The Kullback-Leibler is:

$$\mathrm{KL}(P, Q) = \sum_x P(x)\log\frac{P(x)}{Q(x)} \tag{6.3}$$

for distribution of discrete variables, and

$$\mathrm{KL}(P, Q) = \int_{-\infty}^{\infty} P(x)\log\frac{P(x)}{Q(x)}dx \tag{6.4}$$

for distribution of continuous variables. The KL divergence between P and Q, can also be seen as the average number of bits that are wasted by encoding events from a distribution P with a code based on a not-quite-right distribution Q. This KL divergence is a non-symmetric information theoretic measure of distance of P from Q. The smaller the relative entropy, the more similar is the distribution of the two variables, and vice versa. We can define $\mathrm{H}(P, Q)$ as the cross-entropy of P and Q and $\mathrm{H}(P)$ as the entropy of P, so that we have:

$$\mathrm{KL}(P, Q) = -\sum_x P(x)\log Q(x) + \sum_x P(x)\log P(x) = \mathrm{H}(P, Q) - \mathrm{H}(P) \tag{6.5}$$

Since the cross-entropy is always greater than, or equal to, the entropy, which shows that the KL divergence is non-negative, we have $\mathrm{KL}(P, Q) = 0$ if and only if $P = Q$. According to the above algorithm, the KL classifier first calculates the probability distribution for each class θ_j as $P(\theta_j)$ based on the training messages D_n. Each d_i contains a vector of $\vec{x}_i$ features and stores the probability distribution for each class θ_j into a model. Secondly, for a new test document d_m, KL calculates its probability distribution, denoted as $Q(d_m)$, based on the features in that document. Finally, the classifier calculates the KL divergence as demonstrated above. The classifier picks the smallest divergence (smallest relative entropy) between the document probability distribution $Q(d_m)$ and the class probability distribution $P(\theta_j)$ and then assigns θ_j to the document d_m.

- *K-Nearest Neighbor* (KNN). The K Nearest Neighbor classifier assumes that documents that are closer in the instance space are of the same class θ_j. Therefore, unclassified documents, d_m, should belong to the same class as their nearest neighbor in the training data D_n. After all, the training data is calculated and stored in the model. A new document, d_m, is classified with the class θ_j of the nearest neighbor among all stored training documents D_n. Although several distance metrics have been proposed for nearest-neighbor algorithms, the most common metric is the Euclidean distance metric (Salzberg 1991). The Euclidean distance between two documents $d_i = \vec{x}_i = \{x_1, x_2, \cdots, x_n\}$ as a training document and $d_m = \vec{z}_i = \{z_1, z_2, \cdots, z_n\}$ as a test document on an

n dimensional space is computed as:

$$Distance(x_i, z_i) = \sqrt{\sum_{f-1}^{n} \text{diff}(f, x_i, z_i)^2} \tag{6.6}$$

where

$$diff(f, x_i, z_i) = \begin{cases} |x_f - z_f| \text{ if } f \text{ is linear} \\ 0 \text{ if } f \text{ is nominal and } x_f = z_f \\ 1 \text{ if } f \text{ is nominal and } x_f \neq z_f \end{cases} \tag{6.7}$$

$\text{diff}(f, x_i, z_i)$ denotes the difference between the values of word x_i in d_i and word z_i in d_m on feature f. The next step is to estimate the likelihood of each class by summing up the weights of the class of the K-nearest documents, as follows:

$$p(\theta_j|\vec{z}_i) \approx \sum\nolimits_{x_i \in \{\text{K-nearest document}\}} sim(\vec{z}_i, \vec{x}_i) \cdot p(\theta_j|\vec{x}_i) \tag{6.8}$$

where $sim(\vec{z}_i, \vec{x}_i)$ represents the similarity between the testing document d_m and training documents d_i by using the Euclidean distance approach. Meanwhile, $p(\theta_j|\vec{x}_i) \in \{0, 1\}$ represents the classification for the training document d_i with respect to class θ_j [$p(\theta_j|\vec{x}_i) = 1$ for Yes, and $p(\theta_j|\vec{x}_i) = 0$ for No]. Therefore, $p(\theta_j|\vec{z}_i)$ is the probability of class θ_j for testing document d_m.

- *Maximum Entropy* (ME). Maximum entropy is a method for analyzing known information from training data D_n to determine a unique epistemic probability distribution that satisfies given constraints. The principle of maximum entropy states that when nothing is known, the distribution should be as uniform as possible. Therefore, the least-biased model that encodes the given information is the one that maximizes the uncertainty measure H(p)—conditional entropy, while remaining consistent with this information. To build a normalized probability distribution model based on this training data D_n, the classifier weights the features by using them in a log-linear model:

$$p(\theta_j|d_i) = \frac{1}{Z(d_i)} \cdot \prod_{k=1}^{K} w_k^{x_k(\theta_j, d_i)} \tag{6.9}$$

$$Z(d_i) = \sum_{\theta_j} \prod_{k=1}^{K} w_k^{x_k(\theta_j, d_i)} \tag{6.10}$$

where $Z(d_i)$ is a normalization factor to ensure that $\sum_{\theta_j} p(\theta_j|d_i) = 1$. Each feature function $x_k(\theta_j, d_i)$is a binary function with the value of either one or zero:

$$x_k(\theta_j, d_i) = \begin{cases} 1, & \text{if } d_i \text{ belongs to a predefined category } \theta_j \\ 0, & \text{otherwise} \end{cases} \tag{6.11}$$

Each parameter w_k, where $w_k > 0$, corresponds to one feature x_k and can be interpreted as a "weight" for that feature. The parameters $w_1, w_2 \cdots w_k$ are found with Generalized Iterative Scaling (Darroch and Ratcliff 1972). The probability model $p(\theta_j|d_i)$ is a normalized product of those observed features. For evaluating a test document d_m , the classifier chooses a distribution p that maximizes the entropy H(p) for a test document d_m when the correct category is unknown. To maximize entropy is to maximize conditional entropy, H(p) = H $(\theta_j|d_m)$, which is subject to above constraints stated in Eqs. (6.9) and (6.10) (Ratnaparkhi 1997):

$$\mathrm{H}\left(\theta_j|d_m\right) = -\sum_{\theta_j, d_m} p(\theta_j, d_m) \cdot \log_n p(\theta_j|d_m) \tag{6.12}$$

$$\mathrm{p}^* = \mathrm{argmax}\ \mathrm{H}(\theta_j|d_m) \tag{6.13}$$

where p* is the distribution that maximizes the entropy function of H $(\theta_j\ |d_m)$ under the constraints of Eqs. (6.9) and (6.10), which makes the model match d_m's feature expectations with those observed in the training data D_n. The classifier returns a p* for each θ_j category, according to maximum entropy.

- *Naive Bayesian* (NB). The Naive Bayesian classifier is a simple probabilistic classifier. NB classifiers are based on probability models that incorporate independence assumptions (Lewis 1998 and Antweiler and Frank 2004). Given a new document d_m, the probability that

d_m belongs to sentiment category θ_j is given by Bayes rule:

$$p(\theta_j|d_m) = \frac{p(d_m|\theta_j)p(\theta_j)}{p(d_m)} \tag{6.14}$$

Based on the class-conditional independence of words, the most probable category θ_j for a document d_m can be evaluated as:

$$\theta(d_m) = \underset{\theta_j}{\operatorname{argmax}}\, p(\theta_j|d_m) = \underset{\theta_j}{\operatorname{argmax}}\, p(\theta_j) \prod_{t=1}^{n} p(x_i|\theta_j)^{n(x_i, d_m)} \tag{6.15}$$

where $n(x_i, d_m)$ is the number of occurrences of word x_i in document d_m, and the quantities $p(x_i|\theta_j)$ are usually estimated based on the training dataset D_n using Laplace's rule of succession:

$$p(x_i|\theta_j) = \frac{1 + \sum_{d_i \in \theta_j} n(x_i, d_i)}{m + \sum_{t=1}^{m} \sum_{d_i \in \theta_j} n(x_i, d_i)} \tag{6.16}$$

For a document d_m, the NB classifier calculates the highest posterior probability:
$\mathrm{p}^* = \underset{\theta_j}{\operatorname{argmax}}\, \mathrm{p}(\theta_j|d_m)$ under each category θ_j
.

- *Probabilistic Indexing* (PRIND). Probabilistic Indexing was developed by Maron and Kuhns (1960). The central idea of the PRIND model is to assign each descriptor x_i (key feature belongs to a class θ_j) in a document d_m a probability of relevance—the probability that d_m is relevant to a class θ_j, which is formulated with this descriptor.

Let us first define that for every specific class θ_j to a retrieval system, it must be transformed into a vector of key features $\vec{s}_i = \{s_1, s_2, \cdots, s_n\}$ We also assume that every wordx_i in a document can be represented as a binary vector $\vec{x}_i = \{x_1, x_2, \cdots, x_n\}$ with $x_i = 1$ if the word contains the key feature of s_i and $x_i = 0$ otherwise. The event space of this model consists of all document-class (*d*-θ) relationships between the set of all documents in the corpus and all classes to the system. Since the complete set of classes is not fully known, we assume that we have knowledge of a representative sample. A *d*-θ relationship is either relevant or irrelevant, which will be denoted by R and $\overline{R}$, respectively. The PRIND then seeks for an estimation of $P(R|\vec{x}_k, d_m)$, the probability that the document d_m is relevant to a class θ_j using feature vector$\vec{x}_k$. The higher the $P(R|\vec{x}_k, d_m)$, the higher the probability that d_m belongs to θ_j that contains $\vec{x}_k$. Three independent assumptions are possible:

$$P(\vec{x}_k) = \prod_{i=1}^{n} P(x_{k_i}) \tag{6.17}$$

$$P(\vec{x}_k|R, d_m) = \prod_{i=1}^{n} P(x_{k_i}|R, d_m) \tag{6.18}$$

$$P(\vec{x}_k|\overline{R}, d_m) = \prod_{i=1}^{n} P(x_{k_i}|\overline{R}, d_m) \tag{6.19}$$

These three assumptions relate to the distribution of descriptors x_i in the feature vector $\vec{x}_k$. Assumption 6.17 says that the distribution of the descriptors x_i in all feature vectors is independent, whereas assumptions 6.18 and 6.19 say that the distribution of the descriptors is independent only in those feature vectors where the document d_m is relevant to the corresponding request. Using assumption 6.17 and 6.18, we get the ranking equation:

$$P(R|\vec{x}_k, d_m) = P(R|d_m) \cdot \prod_{i=1}^{n} \frac{P(R|x_{k_i}, d_m)}{P(R|d_m)} \tag{6.20}$$

where $P(R|d_m)$ denotes the probability that d_m is relevant to an arbitrary class, $P(R|x_{k_i}, d_m)$ is the probability that document d_m is relevant to an arbitrary class, which contains descriptor s_i in its feature vector ($x_{k_i} = 1$) and s_i is not presented in the feature vector ($x_{k_i} = 0$). With assumption 6.19, we can have a probability formula, in the form of $O(x) = \frac{P(x)}{P(\overline{x})}$:

$$O(R|\vec{x}_k, d_m) = O(R|d_m) \cdot \prod_{i=1}^{n} \frac{O(R|x_{k_i}, d_m)}{O(R|d_m)} \tag{6.21}$$

According to Maron and Kuhns (1960), the following simplifying assumption was made implicitly:

$$\prod_{\substack{i \\ x_{k_i}=0}} P\left(x_{k_i}=0\right) \approx \prod_{\substack{i \\ x_{k_i}=0}} P\left(x_{k_i}=0 \mid R, d_m\right) \tag{6.22}$$

This equation shows that the relevance of a document with respect to a class depends only on those descriptors, which are presented in the feature vector, and not on those descriptors that the feature vector does not contain. With assumption 6.17, 6.18 and the implicit assumption Eq. 6.22, the original ranking formula of Maron and Kuhns (1960) can be written as:

$$P(R \mid \vec{x}_k, d_m) = P(R \mid d_m) \cdot \prod_{\substack{i \\ x_{k_i}=1}}^{n} \frac{P\left(R \mid x_{k_i}=1, d_m\right)}{P(R \mid d_m)} \tag{6.23}$$

Finally, replacing Eq. 6.17 by Eq. 6.19, the ranking formula yields the probability O for document d_m with respect to class features $\vec{x}_k$ as follows:

$$O(R \mid \vec{x}_k, d_m) = O(R \mid d_m) \cdot \prod_{\substack{i \\ x_{k_i}=1}}^{n} \frac{O\left(R \mid x_{k_i}=1, d_m\right)}{O(R \mid d_m)} \tag{6.24}$$

- *Support Vector Machine* (SVM). The Support Vector Machine, originally proposed by Vapnik (1995), finds a maximal marginal separating hyper-plane between two classes (class θ_j and its anti-class θ_i) of d_m. In the basic form, SVM learns linear-decision rules:

$$h(x) = sign(w \cdot x + b) = \begin{cases} +1, & if \;\; w \cdot x + b > 0 \\ -1, & otherwise \end{cases} \tag{6.25}$$

which are described by a weight vector, w, and a threshold b. Input is a sample of n number of training data: $D_n = ((x_1, y_1), (x_2, y_2), \cdots, (x_n, y_n))$, $x_i \in \Re^N$, $y_i \in \{-1, +1\}$. For a linearly separable dataset, the SVM searches the hyper-plane with maximum Euclidean distance to the closest training data. This distance is called the margin δ. For non-separable (neutral feature) training data, the amount of training error is measured using slack variables ξ_i Computing this hyper-plane is equivalent to solving the following optimization equation:

$$V(w, b, \xi) = \underset{w}{\operatorname{argmin}} \frac{1}{2}||w||^2 + C\sum_{i=1}^{n} \xi_i \tag{6.26}$$

This is subject to two constraints: $y_i(w \cdot x_i + b) \geq 1 - \xi_i$ and $\xi_i > 0$. The first constraint requires that all training data be classified correctly up to some slack ξ_i. If a training data lies on the incorrect side of the hyper-plane, the corresponding $\xi_i \cdot \geq 1$. Therefore, $\sum_{i=1}^{n} \xi_i$ is an upper bound on the number of training errors. The factor C in the optimization equation is a parameter that allows trading off training error versus model complexity. Note that the margin of the resulting hyper-plane is $\delta = \frac{1}{||w||}$. (See Burges (1998) and Joachims (2002) for solving the optimization equation).

Information gain is normally chosen to determine the weight w of document d_m's words x_i. Under a binary classification case, after solving the optimization equation by using the training data D_n, we find the hyper-plane h^*, which splits the classification system into two spaces: a certain class θ_j, such as "Buy" with a positive sign and its anti-class θ_i, such as "Sell" with a negative sign. The SVM classifier then assigns the value for d_m, where positive and negative numbers indicate whether the d_m belongs in a given class θ_j or its anti-class θ_i. We usually adopt linear kernel for the SVM classifier.

- *Term Frequency Inverse Document Frequency* (TFIDF). TFIDF evaluates the importance of a word based on the number of times the word appears in a document, but offsets that by how common the word is in all documents, Joachims (1997). The TFIDF classifier is based on the relevance feedback algorithm originally proposed by Rocchio (1971) for the vector space retrieval model. Each document d_i is represented as a vector $\overline{d} = \overline{x}_i = \{x_1, x_2, \cdots, x_n\}$, so that documents with similar content have similar vectors according to a fixed similarity metric. Each x_i for a document d_i is calculated as a combination of the statistics $\mathrm{TF}(x_i, d_i)$ and $\mathrm{DF}(x_i)$, see Salton (1991). The term frequency $\mathrm{TF}(x_i, d_i)$ is the number of times word x_i, occurs in document d_i and the document frequency $\mathrm{DF}(x_i)$ is the number of training messages in which word x_i occurs at least once. The inverse document frequency IDF(x_i) can be calculated from the document frequency:

$$\mathrm{IDF}(x_i) = \log\left[\frac{|\mathrm{D}|}{\mathrm{DF}(x_i)}\right] \tag{6.27}$$

Here, $|D|$ is the total number of training messages d_n. The inverse document frequency of a word x_i is low if it occurs in many documents and is highest if the word occurs in only one. The weight w_{x_i} is calculated as:

$$w_{x_i} = \mathrm{TF}(x_i, d_i) \cdot \mathrm{IDF}(x_i) \tag{6.28}$$

A high weight in TFIDF is reached by a high-term frequency in the given document and a low-document frequency of the term in the whole corpus of documents; the weights hence tend to filter out common terms. The Rocchio (1971) approach is commonly applied to generate the TFIDF classifier. Learning is achieved by combining document vectors into a vector $\overrightarrow{\theta_j}$ for each class θ_j. Both the normalized document vectors of the positive training data for a class θ_j as well as those of the negative training data for a class are summed up. The vector $\overrightarrow{\theta_j}$ is then calculated as a weighted difference of each:

$$\overrightarrow{\theta_j} = \left(\alpha\frac{1}{|\theta_j|}\sum_{\vec{d}\in\theta_j}\frac{\vec{d}}{\left\|\vec{d}\right\|}\right) - (\beta\frac{1}{|D-\theta_j|}\sum_{\vec{d}\in D-\theta_j}\frac{\vec{d}}{\left\|\vec{d}\right\|} \tag{6.29}$$

Following Buckley et al. (1994), $\alpha = 16$ and $\beta = 4$. θ_j is the set of training messages assigned to class j and $\left\|\vec{d}\right\|$ denotes the Euclidian length of a vector $\vec{d}$. Moreover, Rocchio (1971) requires that negative elements of the vector θ_j is set to zero. The resulting set of vectors, one for each class, constitutes the learned model, which can then be used to classify new document d_m. Again, d_m is represented as a vector $\overrightarrow{d_m}$ using the scheme described above. To classify d_m, the cosines of the vectors $\overrightarrow{\theta_j}$ with $\overrightarrow{d_m}$ are calculated. d_m is assigned to the class with which its document vector has the highest cosine:

$$\theta_{TFIDF}(d_m) = \underset{\theta_j \in \theta}{\text{argmax}}\, cos\left(\overrightarrow{\theta_j}, \overrightarrow{d_m}\right) = \underset{\theta_j \in \theta}{\text{argmax}} \frac{\overrightarrow{\theta_j}}{\left\|\overrightarrow{\theta_j}\right\|} \cdot \frac{\overrightarrow{d_m}}{\left\|\overrightarrow{d_m}\right\|} \tag{6.30}$$

so that $\theta_{TFIDF}(d_m)$ is the class to which the algorithm assigns testing messages d_m.

Class Assignment

After receiving a probability score from the text classifier for each sentiment class, how do we determine the final sentiment for a given message? The returned probabilities for each class are mutually exclusive, meaning the sum of all class probabilities equals one, and the joint probability between any two classes is zero. In a simple three-class scenario, for example, a 60% probability of Buy (coded as + 1), 30% for Hold (coded as 0), and 10% for Sell (coded as –1)—the class assignment is straightforward. The standard practice is to assign the message to the class with the highest probability estimate. In this case, the sentiment score would be + 1, since 60% > 30% > 10%.

However, classification becomes more complex when more sentiment types are involved, such as Strong Buy (+2), Buy (+1), Hold (0), Sell (−1), and Strong Sell (−2). Unlike text data in other fields, FSM includes directional sentiment classes. For example, both Buy and Strong Buy represent optimistic sentiment, while Sell and Strong Sell represent pessimistic sentiment. Due to this directional nature, a different class assignment algorithm is required, replacing the standard mutually exclusive classification approach.

This sounds tricky, but the additional rule for the probability that either Class A or B will occur is simply the sum of the unconditional probabilities for the message, P (A or B) = P (A) + P (B). The algorithm for $x_m^{i,t}$, as the sentiment score for a non-self-disclosed sentiment message assigned by a text classifier for message m associated with stock i at day t, is as follows:

$$x_m^{i,t}\begin{cases} = +2, if\, P(\text{Strong Buy or Buy}) > P(\text{Strong Sell or Sell or Hold}) and P(\text{Strong Buy }) > P(Buy) \\ = +1, if\, P(\text{Strong Buy or Buy}) > P(\text{Strong Sell or Sell or Hold}) and P(\text{Strong Buy}) < P(Buy) \\ = 0, if\, P(\text{Strong Buy or Buy}) = P(\text{Strong Sell or Sell or Short}) \geq P(\text{Hold}) \\ = 0, if\, P(\text{Hold}) \geq P(\text{Strong Buy or Buy or Strong Sell or Sell}) \\ = 0, if\, P(\text{Hold}) = P(\text{Strong Buy or Buy}) > P(\text{Strong Sell or Sell or Short }) \\ = 0, if\, P(\text{Hold}) = P(\text{Strong Sell or Sell}) > P(\text{Strong Buy or Buy}) \\ = -1, if\, P(\text{Strong Sell or Sell}) > P(\text{Strong Buy or Buy or Hold}) and P(\text{Sell }) > P(\text{Strong Sell}) \\ = -2, if\, P(\text{Strong Sell or Sell}) > P(\text{Strong Buy or Buy or Hold}) and P(\text{Sell }) < P(\text{Strong Sell}) \end{cases} \tag{6.31}$$

For example, if a message receives the following probability distribution from the text classifier—Sell: 32%, Strong Buy: 30%, Buy: 27%, Strong Sell: 6%, and Hold: 5%—the conventional mutually exclusive decision rule would assign the sentiment class with the highest individual probability ("Sell," in this case) to the message, resulting in a sentiment score of –1. However, this approach may be misleading if the goal is to determine the direction (or sign) of the message's sentiment: buy-side (optimistic), neutral, or sell-side (pessimistic).

In this example, the aggregated probabilities are as follows:

- Buy-side = P(Strong Buy) + P(Buy) = 30% + 27% = 57%
- Sell-side = P(Strong Sell) + P(Sell) = 6% + 32% = 38%
- Neutral = P(Hold) = 5%

Clearly, the buy-side sentiment dominates, as 57% exceeds the combined total of the sell-side and neutral probabilities (38% + 5% = 43%). Based on this directional analysis, the class-assignment rule first determines the dominant sentiment direction (buy-side) and then selects the sentiment class with the highest individual probability within that direction (Strong Buy: 30% > Buy: 27%).

According to the class-assignment rule proposed by Zhang et al. (2012), the correct resulting sentiment for this example should be Strong Buy, with a sentiment score of + 2, rather than Sell.

Which Text Classifier is Most Suitable for Financial Social Media Data?

Different classifiers have been shown to be effective for different data features. However, FSM applications, particularly those involving user-generated content, are unique. Unlike formal news articles or analyst reports, FSM platforms are informal, brief, often elliptical, and resemble dialogue (Admati and Pfleiderer 2001).

To compare the performance of various text classifiers, researchers typically use a confusion matrix in conjunction with Chi-square statistics. A classifier's recognition accuracy is measured by the proportion of messages correctly assigned to their original self-disclosed sentiments, the higher the match rate, the greater the accuracy. As such, messages with known, self-disclosed sentiments serve as the benchmark for evaluating classifier performance. Table 6.1 provides an illustrative example of how a confusion matrix is used to measure a classifier's accuracy.

Table 6.1 presents a sample confusion matrix based on the approach proposed by Kohavi and Provost (1998). The matrix cross-classifies actual sentiment against evaluated sentiment. Each row represents the actual self-disclosed sentiment (Buy, Hold, or Sell) posted by an author on an FSM platform. Each column shows the number of those messages classified into each category by the specific text classifier (Buy, Hold, or Sell).

The more weight concentrated along the matrix's diagonal, the less confusion the classifier experiences in assigning sentiments—and thus, the better its performance. In this example, the specific classifier achieves an average accuracy of 88.33%, calculated as (90% + 95% + 80%) / 3.

Table 6.1 An example of confusion matrix

	Classified buy	*Classified hold*	*Classified sell*	*Accuracy%*
500 Actual Buy	400	50	50	90.00
500 Actual Hold	25	450	25	95.00
500 Actual Sell	100	100	300	80.00

To determine whether one text classifier is significantly better than another, researchers apply a sequential analysis comparison. One classifier's confusion matrix is compared to another classifier's confusion matrix that has the same number of rows and columns by using the standard Chi-square statistic (Das and Chen 2003, 2007):

$$x^2_{[(n-1)^2]} = \frac{1}{n^2}\sum_{i=1}^{n^2}\frac{(S_i - I_i)^2}{I_i} \tag{6.32}$$

with degrees of freedom of $(n-1)^2$ where i is the corresponding cell in each of the classifier's confusion matrixes and n is the number of classes in the confusion matrix.

We designate the classifier with the higher accuracy in the confusion matrix as the superior model (S) and the one with lower accuracy as the inferior model (I). If the difference in performance between the two models is statistically significant, the superior model demonstrates a higher level of efficacy. Conversely, if the Chi-square test is not statistically significant, the two classifiers are considered indifferent. The superior classifier is then sequentially compared against other models. Ultimately, the classifier that consistently achieves the highest accuracy and statistical significance is selected as the most effective text classification algorithm.[2]

In the non-finance literature, many empirical studies, such as those by Berger et al. (1996), Choi et al. (1999), and Pettibone and Pon Barry (2003), report that Maximum Entropy consistently demonstrates high performance in classifying conversational discourse messages. Given that FSM posts often consist of fragmentary utterances, Maximum Entropy is considered a promising classifier with a high level of accuracy. Supporting this view, Bender et al. (2003) as well as Fernandez et al. (2005) provide empirical evidence of its effectiveness. In the finance literature, Zhang et al. (2012) find that Maximum Entropy outperforms other popular classifiers, such as Naive Bayes and Support Vector Machines, when applied to FSM data. Based on current findings, Maximum Entropy appears to be the most effective text classification algorithm among the eight introduced in this chapter.

Financial Social Media Activity Measures

Each message posted on a FSM platform is eventually assigned a sentiment score—either self-disclosed by the author or generated by a specific text classifier. With sentiment scores assigned to each individual message, we can construct an aggregate sentiment index to capture the overall mood and a disagreement index to measure the dispersion of opinions among online posters.

Below are several commonly used activity measures for a given stock i during a specific time interval t. The duration of t can vary as it may represent a minute, a day, a week, or a month. First, we introduce a set of descriptive metrics:

- Number of Messages per Stock per Period
- This represents the total number of messages related to a specific stock, posted by all users during the time interval t. For example, if 50 messages about Microsoft ("MSFT") are posted during t, this count reflects the cumulative interest in that stock across all contributors.
- Number of Replies per Stock per Period
- This is the total number of reply messages posted in response to existing discussions about a stock during time t. It excludes original messages and reflects the engagement level or follow-up interest by other investors. This is a subset of the total message count.
- Number of Readers
- This metric captures the total number of users who have viewed or read messages related to a specific stock during time t. It serves as an alternative indicator of a stock's popularity or visibility within the community.
- Number of Recommendations
- This measure indicates how many times users have recommended, liked, or endorsed a message related to a particular stock. It serves as a proxy for the perceived value or credibility of the content posted.
- Number of Unique Authors
- This refers to the number of distinct users who have posted about a stock during time t. It provides a more accurate measure of participation than the total message count, as individual users often post multiple times within the same period, and some may even use multiple accounts.

There are other, quantitative measures for posting activities:

- *Bullishness index.* Given that the total number of messages related to stock i during time t is $M_t^i = M_t^{i,BUY} + M_t^{i,SELL}$ where messages with "Hold" sentiments are ignored, Antweiler and Frank (2004) first introduce a bullishness ratio as follows:

$$B_t^i = \frac{M_t^{i,BUY} - M_t^{i,SELL}}{M_t^{i,BUY} + M_t^{i,SELL}} = \frac{R_t - 1}{R_t + 1} \tag{6.33}$$

where $M_t^{i,BUY}$ is the total number of bullish messages while $M_t^{i,SELL}$ is the total number of bearish messages related to stock i during time t. $R_t = \frac{M_t^{i,BUY}}{M_t^{i,SELL}}$ is the ratio of bullish to bearish messages. A higher B_t^i implies a stronger optimistic sentiment from online posters, and vice versa. Cook and Lu (2009) argue that "Hold" messages should not be excluded in the sentiment formula even if "Hold" is coded as zero. Zhang et al. (2022) introduce their modified bullishness ratio for stock i during time t as follows:

$$MB_t^i = \frac{M_t^{i,O} - M_t^{i,P}}{M_t^{i,O} + M_t^{i,P} + M_t^{i,N}} \tag{6.34}$$

where $M_t^{i,O}$ is the number of messages with optimistic sentiment, $M_t^{i,P}$ is the number of messages with pessimistic sentiment, and $M_t^{i,N}$ is the number of messages with neutral "Hold" sentiment. Using the ratio of bullish-to-bearish messages, $R_t^i = \frac{M_t^{i,O}}{M_t^{i,P}}$, Eq. 6.34 can be rewritten as:

$$MB_t^i = \frac{R_t^i - 1}{R_t^i + 1 + \frac{M_t^{i,N}}{M_t^{i,P}}} \tag{6.35}$$

- *Sentiment index.* Antweiler and Frank (2004) further introduce a sentiment index as:

$$B_t^{i^*} \equiv \ln\left[\frac{1 + M_t^{i,BUY}}{1 + M_t^{i,SELL}}\right] = \ln\left[\frac{2 + M_t^i(1 + B_t^i)}{2 + M_t^i(1 - B_t^i)}\right] \approx B_t^i \cdot \ln\left(1 + M_t^i\right) \tag{6.36}$$

Different from the B_t^i defined in Eq. 6.33, this $B_t^{i^*}$ considers the number of authors expressing a particular sentiment on stock *i*. Similarly, a higher $B_t^{i^*}$ implies a stronger optimistic sentiment from online posters considering the number of authors, and vice versa. If there is no message related to stock *i*, $B_t^{i^*} = 0$.

- *Agreement/Disagreement index.* Antweiler and Frank (2004) further propose a reduced form of standard deviation of sentiments as an agreement proxy. In their setup, sentiment is either Buy (+1) or Sell (−1) because Hold (0) is ignored. They also assume an equal weight (reputation) for each author. Their agreement index A_t^i is as follows:

$$A_t^i \equiv 1 - \sqrt{1 - \left(B_t^i\right)^2} \tag{6.37}$$

where B_t^i is from Eq. 6.33 and $A_t^i \in (0, 1]$. A_t^i must be a positive number and must be less or equal to one. A higher A_t^i implies a higher agreement with similar mood among authors, and vice versa. If there is no message related to stock *i*, $A_t^i = 0$.

- *Credit-weighted sentiment index.* In Eq. 6.36, Antweiler and Frank (2004) set their message sentiment as either Buy (+1) or Sell (−1) with an equal weight allocation, assuming every poster has the same credibility. If sentiment score, $x_m^{i,t}$, in message *m* during time *t* ranges from −2 to + 2 and a log of poster *k*'s credit score, $LCS_m^{k,t}$ is the message weight for message *m* during time *t*, the modified bullishness ratio stated in Eq. 6.34, $MB_t^{i^*}$ needs to be rewritten as:

$$MB_t^{i*} = \frac{\sum_{m=1}^{M_t^{i,O}} LCS_m^{k,t} \cdot x_m^{O,i,t} + \sum_{m=1}^{M_t^{i,P}} LCS_m^{k,t} \cdot x_m^{P,i,t}}{M_t^{i,O} + M_t^{i,P} + M_t^{i,N}} \tag{6.38}$$

where each $x_m^{O,i,t}$ represents an optimistic sentiment score, which could be either + 1 or + 2 while each $x_m^{P,i,t}$ represents a pessimistic sentiment score, which could be either −1 or −2. MB_t^{i*} is the modified bullishness ratio for stock *i* during time *t*. Note that $\sum_{m=1}^{M_t^{i,P}} LCS_m^{k,t} \cdot x_m^{P,i,t} \leq 0$ because optimistic credit score $LCS_m^{k,t} \geq 0$ must be none negative and pessimistic sentiment $x_m^{P,i,t} < 0$. Besides,

$\sum_{m=1}^{M_t^{i,N}} LCS_m^{k,t} \cdot x_m^{N,i,t} = 0$ is omitted in the numerator because all neutral (Hold) sentiment scores are set to zero. The denominator $M_t^{i,O} + M_t^{i,P} + M_t^{i,N}$ represents the total number of messages for stock i during time t. Neutral messages $M_t^{i,N}$ are considered in Eq. 6.38.

Antweiler and Frank (2004) construct their sentiment index by considering the number of traders expressing a particular sentiment shown in Eq. 6.36. Because they assume each message is written by a different poster, the number of messages equals the number of posters. If we use the actual number of authors, the sentiment index presented in Eq. 6.36 for stock i during time$t$ becomes:

$$SENT_t^i = MB_t^i \left[\log(1 + NPosters_t^i)\right] \tag{6.39}$$

where $NPosters_t^i$ is the number of unique posters who discuss stock i during time t and $SENT_t^i \in (-\infty, +\infty)$. A higher $SENT_t^i$ implies a stronger optimistic sentiment from online posters, considering both the number of authors and their credibility scores. When there is no author dialogue about stock i, $SENT_t^i = 0$.

- *Credit-weighted disagreement index.* Given each author's credit score, $LCS_m^{k,t}$, and that a sentiment score, $x_m^{i,t}$, ranges from –2 to + 2, a disagreement index can be written as a credit-weighted standard deviation of the sentiment scores for the stock i during time t. In this setup, neutral sentiment, Hold, is considered. Each message m's weight relative to all messages related to stock i during time t can be calculated as:

$$w_m^{i,t} = \frac{LCS_m^{k,t}}{\sum_{m=1}^{M_t^{i,A}} LCS_m^{k,t}} \tag{6.40}$$

$M_t^{i,A} = M_t^{i,O} + M_t^{i,P} + M_t^{i,N}$ is total number of messages related to stock i during time t and $\sum_{m=1}^{M_t^{i,A}} LCS_m^{k,t}$ represents the total credit scores among all k authors who discuss stock i during time t. Thus, the disagreement index is presented as follows:

$$DISG_t^i = \sqrt{\sum_{m=1}^{M_t^{i,A}} w_m^{i,t} \cdot \left(x_m^{i,t} - x_m^{-i,t}\right)} \quad (6.41)$$

where average sentiment score is $x_m^{-i,t} = \sum_{m=1}^{M_t^{i,A}} w_m^{i,t} \cdot x_m^{i,t}$ and $DISG_t^i \in (0, +\infty)$It is obvious that there is an inverse relationship between the agreement index proposed by Antweiler and Frank (2004) and the disagreement index presented in Eq. 6.41. Thus, a higher implies a lower agreement with different opinions among authors, and vice versa. If there is no message related to stock i,$DISG_t^i = 0$

Finally, how do these FSM activity measures influence stock trading? Researchers often use event study, cross-sectional regression, and time-series statistical analyses to examine the correlation and potential causality between online posting activity and actual trading behavior. The specific regression models and empirical methodologies used to explore these relationships will be discussed in detail in the following chapters.

Notes

1. Although the Yahoo! Finance discussion board now allows users to disclose their sentiment, it did not introduce this self-disclosed sentiment feature until June 2001. As a result, earlier studies faced data limitations. For instance, research using Yahoo! Finance messages from the year 2000 required scholars to manually classify, or hand code, each message to create a training dataset. Hand-classifying involves researchers reading the content of each message and assigning a sentiment score based on their own interpretation.
2. This comparison must be based on an identical testing sample and the same testing procedure. More importantly, each text classifier should be evaluated independently. Because each classifier is based on a different algorithm, its performance metrics, such as accuracy and standard error, are unaffected by the attributes of other classifiers. As long as the testing sample and evaluation method remain consistent, the order in which classifiers are tested will not affect their relative ranking.

CHAPTER 7

Patterns in Financial Social Media Posting Activities

Message-Related Patterns

To explore patterns in financial social media (FSM, hereafter) posting activities, I selected the Wall Street Pit trading platform on TheLion.com, one of the most popular stock trading platforms today. As an example, I collected real-time message data, recorded on the same day the messages were posted, from January 1, 2006, to December 31, 2010, resulting in a dataset of 1,048,575 messages. In the following sections, I analyze patterns related to messages, stocks, and posters, each from a different perspective.

Posting Pattern by Message Length

Figure 7.1 shows the distribution of messages based on their length, measured in the number of characters. As proposed by Zhang et al. (2022), message length serves as a proxy for information contained within messages. The number of characters determines the message length; the longer the message, the more information it is likely to convey. (It is worth noting that authors often include disclaimers, mottos, trading philosophies, signatures, portraits, stock charts, or emoticons. My web crawler software filters out these elements, as well as any unrecognized or irregular symbols.)

Y. Zhang, *Financial Social Media*,
https://doi.org/10.1007/978-3-032-09332-5_7

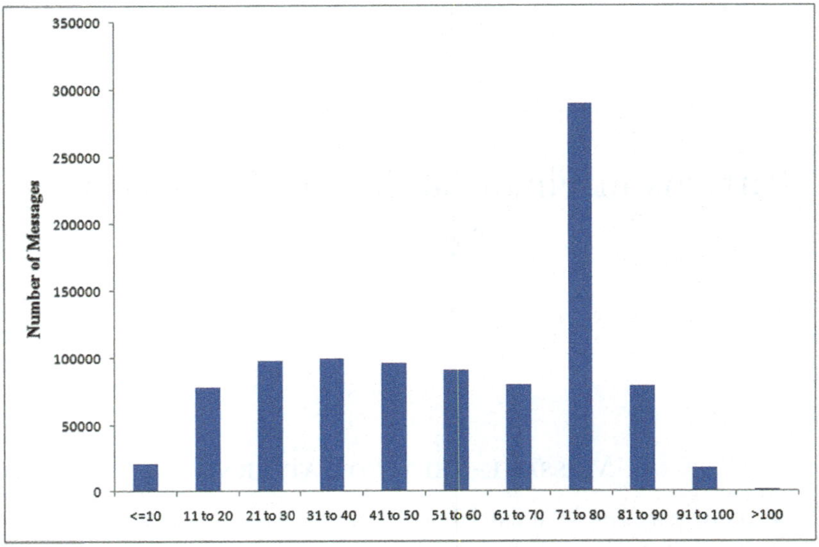

Fig. 7.1 Message length measured in number of characters

As previously mentioned, FSM messages posted by individual investors tend to be style-free, short, elliptical, and presented in a dialogue-like format. They are essentially fragmentary utterances that resemble spoken language. As expected, most messages posted on the Wall Street Pit trading platform are brief (i.e., 100 characters or fewer). In fact, most messages contain between 11 and 90 characters, with nearly 300,000 messages (30% of all messages) consisting of 71 to 80 characters.

On the Wall Street Pit trading platform, the first 80 characters of a message, serving as its title, are displayed as a hyperlink in the "Message Preview" column, allowing readers to grasp the key point at a glance. To read the full content of a message, readers must click the message preview hyperlink. Most authors avoid lengthy messages to ensure their content fits entirely within the 80-charater "Message Preview" limit. This explains why only 10% of the messages exceed 80 characters.

Posting Pattern by Hours

It has been documented that online traders tend to post very few messages outside of regular trading hours (i.e., before 9:30 a.m. or after 4:00 p.m. EST; see Antweiler and Frank 2004; Sabherwal, Sarkar, and Zhang 2008). In my sample, approximately 75% of messages were posted during market trading hours, 12% were posted before the market opened (12:00 a.m. to 9:30 a.m. EST), and 13% were posted after the market closed (4:00 p.m. to 12:00 a.m. EST).

Figure 7.2 displays the number of messages posted hour by hour. Clearly, postings proliferate when U.S. stock exchanges are open and taper off after the closing bell.

- Posting activity peaked with 142,120 messages one to two hours before noon (i.e., between 10:00 a.m. and 11:00 a.m. EST).
- The second most active posting period was the hour before the market closed (i.e., 3:00 p.m. to 4:00 p.m. EST), with 120,232 messages posted.
- The period surrounding the 9:30 a.m. opening bell (9:00 a.m. to 10:00 a.m. EST) was also active, with 117,847 messages posted.
- There were only 152 messages posted very late at night (i.e., between 11:00 p.m. and midnight).

These patterns align with previous studies that have analyzed Yahoo! Finance, Raging Bull, and other FSM platforms. The similarities suggest that online posters exhibit similar posting habits across different FSM platforms.

Posting Pattern by Day within a Week

Figure 7.3 shows the number of messages posted by day within a week. The volume of online message postings remains consistent from Monday through Friday, with Wednesday being the peak day, accounting for 217,966 messages, or 20.79% of the total. Posting volume increases steadily from Monday to Wednesday and then decreases from Wednesday to Friday. Posting activity during weekdays significantly exceeds that of the weekends, with only 16,580 messages (1.58%) posted on Saturday and 21,842 messages (2.08%) posted on Sunday. This posting pattern

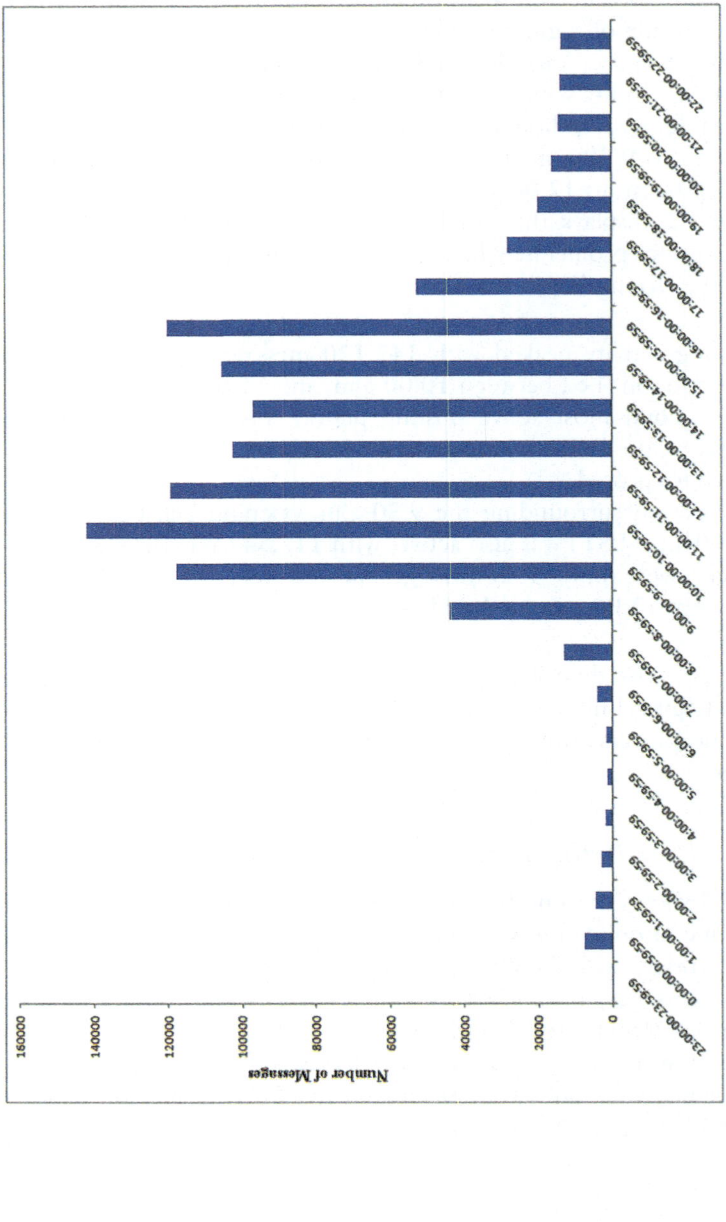

Fig. 7.2 Messages posted by hours (EST)

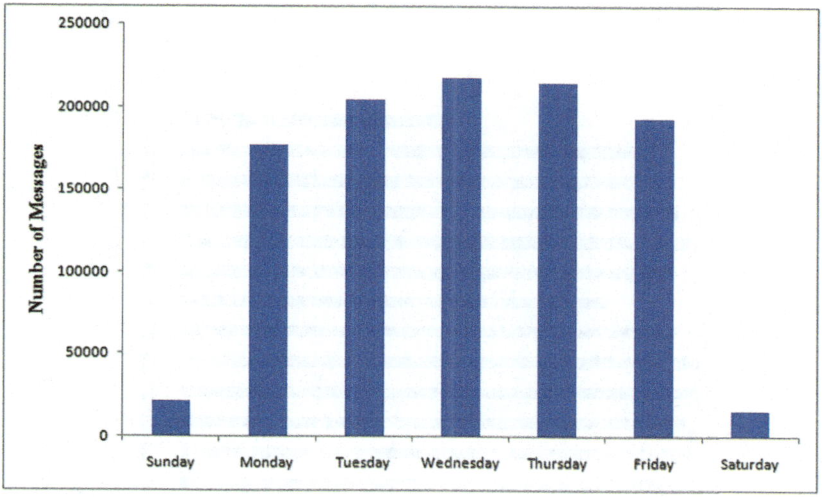

Fig. 7.3 Messages posted by day

is consistent with findings from previous studies, such as those by Sabherwal, Sarkar, and Zhang (2008) and Zhang et al. (2022).

Posting Pattern by Day within a Month

Figure 7.4 shows the number of messages posted by day within a month. Generally, message postings increase during the first five days of the month, with volume peaking in the middle of the month. Although the 25th day has the second lowest number of postings, there is otherwise little variation in daily posting activity. The reason for the sudden drop on the 25th is unclear and may be specific to this sample. The relatively small number of messages posted on the 31st (18,493) is because only seven months have 31 days.

Posting Pattern by Month

Figure 7.5 presents the number of messages posted each month from 2006 to 2010. While there is no significant difference in posting activity from month to month, a few trends do emerge. In general, posting volume:

Fig. 7.4 Messages posted by day within a month

- Peaks in October,
- Starts to drop in March,
- Reaches its lowest level in July,
- Picks up slightly in August,
- Drops significantly in November and December, and
- Is relatively lackluster in July, August, November, and December.

It is evident that posters are preoccupied with other activities during the summer months and the holiday season, which is largely consistent with patterns in stock-trading volume (Fig. 7.6).

Poster-Related Patterns

In my sample, there are a total of 3230 unique screen names, which I assume represent unique individual posters, as I do not have access to their IP addresses. Each poster carries a wealth of information, such as sentiment, credit score, and number of followers. This data is useful for identifying their rank, common characteristics, and posting habits. Let's take a closer look at who these individuals are and how they post. In this section, I present six poster-related patterns, ranging from sentiment allocation to credit score distribution.

Sentiment Self-Disclosed by Posters

Figure 7.7 shows the distribution of all messages with self-disclosed sentiments. My sample contains 125,919 such messages, with 74% expressing Strong Buy sentiments, 12% expressing Buy sentiments, 3% expressing Hold sentiments, 1% expressing Sell sentiments, 3% expressing Strong Sell sentiments, and 7% expressing Short sentiments. Strong Buy sentiments dominate the others. Overall, optimistic sentiments (Strong Buy and Buy) significantly outweigh pessimistic ones (Short, Strong Sell, and Sell). This suggests a generally bullish tone on the FSM platform, consistent with the findings of Tumarkin and Whitelaw (2001) and Tumarkin (2002), which indicate that online posters are typically bullish.

Figure 7.7 also demonstrates that posters tend to favor "strong" sentiments over "ordinary" ones. For example, there are many more Strong Buy messages than Buy messages and more Short messages than Strong Sell and Sell messages. Intuitively, when a poster chooses to express a sentiment, they may prefer using a stronger tone, see Zhang and Swanson

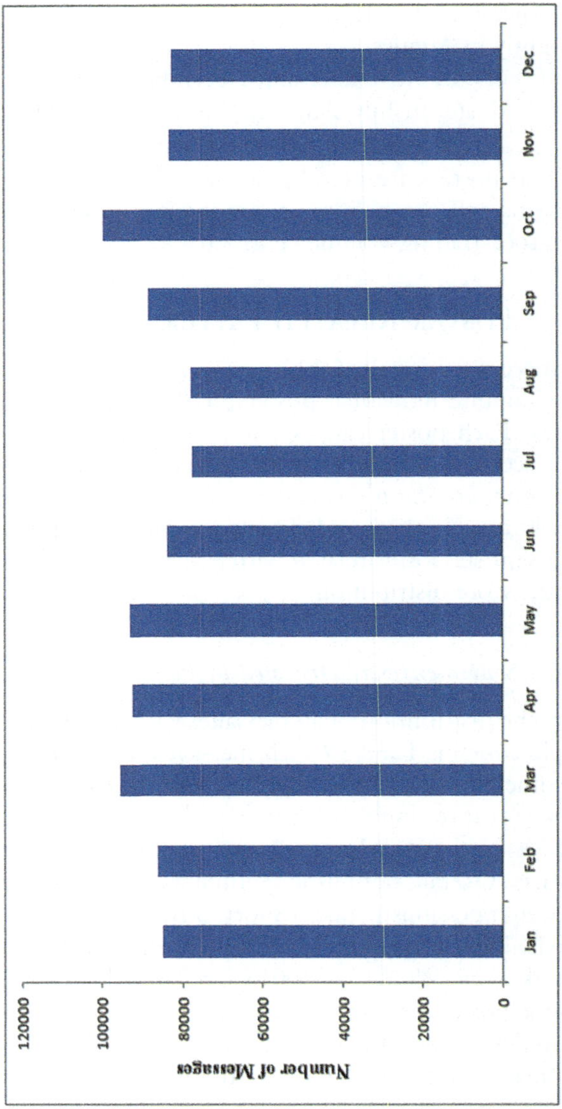

Fig. 7.5 Messages posted by month

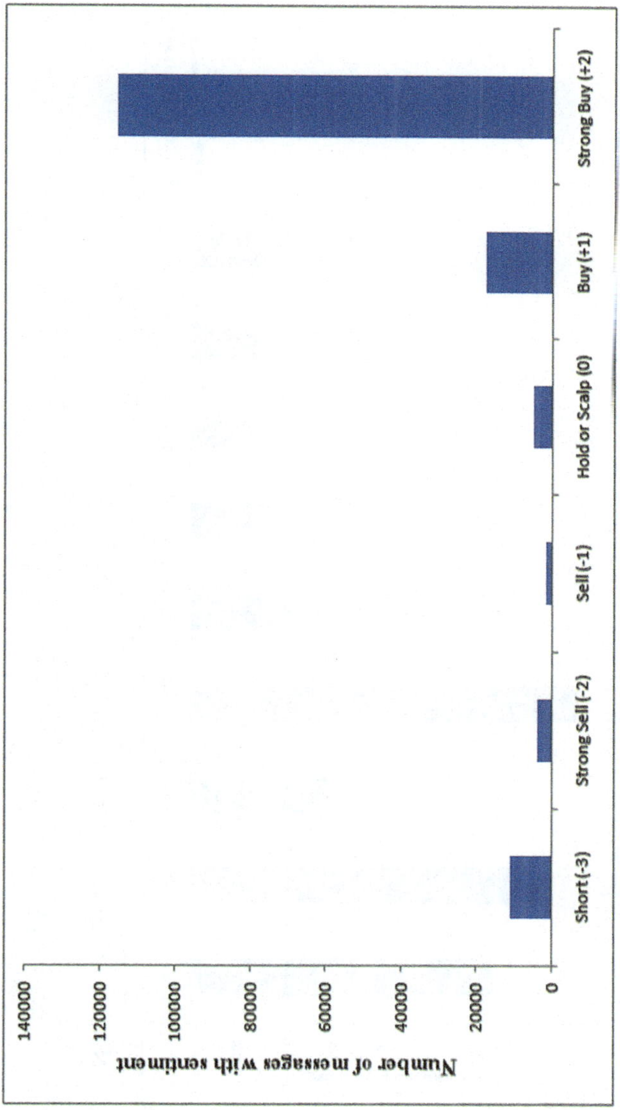

Fig. 7.6 Distribution of self-disclosed sentiment

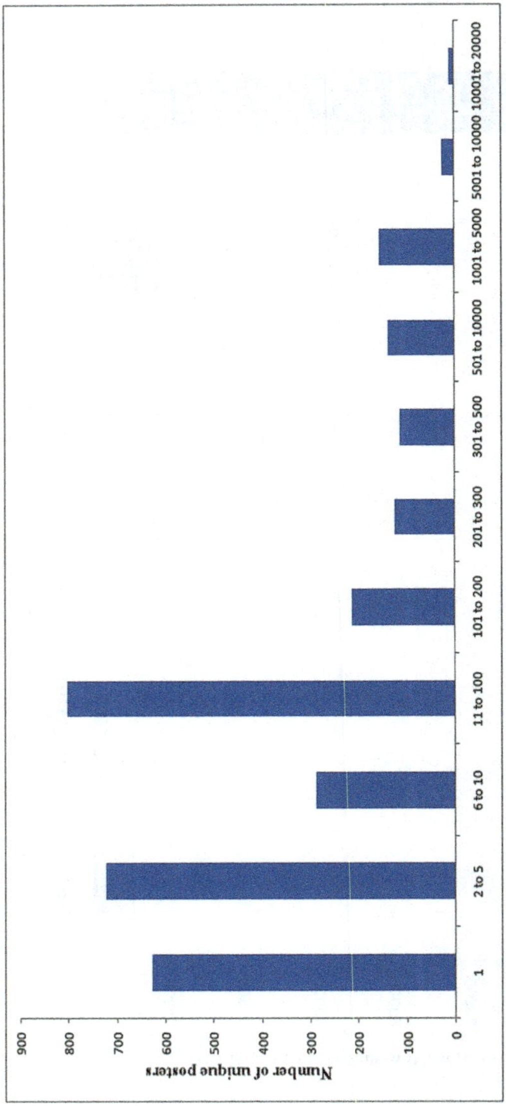

Fig. 7.7 Number of messages posted by authors

(2010). (Note that Fig. 7.7 does not include messages with sentiments assigned by the text classifier.)

Poster Posting Frequency

Figure 7.8 shows the number of messages posted by unique posters with different screen names over the entire five-year period. A few posters dominate the trading platform. For example:

- Only 11 screen names posted over 10,000 messages.
- 628 screen names posted only one message.
- 723 posters left two to five messages.
- 803 posters left 11 to 100 messages.

"Lionmaster," the moderator of the WallStreetPit platform, is an outlier in my sample. Some of Lionmaster's posts are related to platform policy and do not count as regular stock messages. Therefore, Fig. 7.8 does not include "Lionmaster," who posted over 20,000 messages between 2006 and 2010. The pattern shown in Fig. 7.8 aligns with the

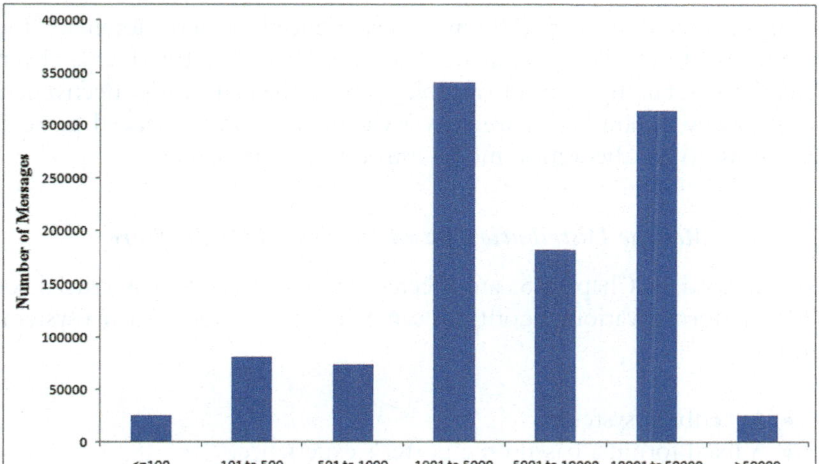

Fig. 7.8 Authors' number of postings when starting a new message

findings reported in Table II of Das, Martinez-Jerez, and Tufano (2005, page 9).

Poster's Prior Posting Experience when Leaving a Message

Because the messages were collected in real time (on the same day they were posted), I am able to report the cumulative number of messages an author had posted by the time they left a new message. This count reflects the author's cumulative activity from the time of their initial registration up to the publication of the message being analyzed. When examining the data from this perspective, the following patterns emerge:

- 82.5% of messages were posted by experienced authors with over 1000 prior messages.
- Almost 32.5% of messages were from posters with 10,000 or more prior messages.
- Only 2.5% of messages were posted by newcomers with fewer than 100 prior messages.
- Another 2.5% of messages were posted by most active authors with over 50,000 prior messages.

As illustrated in Fig. 7.9, more experienced posters dominate the trading platform. This dominance indicates that WallStreetPit has been effective in retaining its most valuable users, as the platform's effectiveness would likely diminish if it were overwhelmed by inexperienced posters, according to my theoretical model introduced in (Chapter 5).

Message Distribution Based on Poster's Credit Score

As discussed in Chapter 5, an effective reputation system is crucial for FSM platforms. Various algorithms can be used to establish such a system, including:

- A feedback system,
- A fixed formula based on a poster's experience,
- A credit score exclusively assigned by the platform administrator,
- A credit score awarded by other users on the platform.

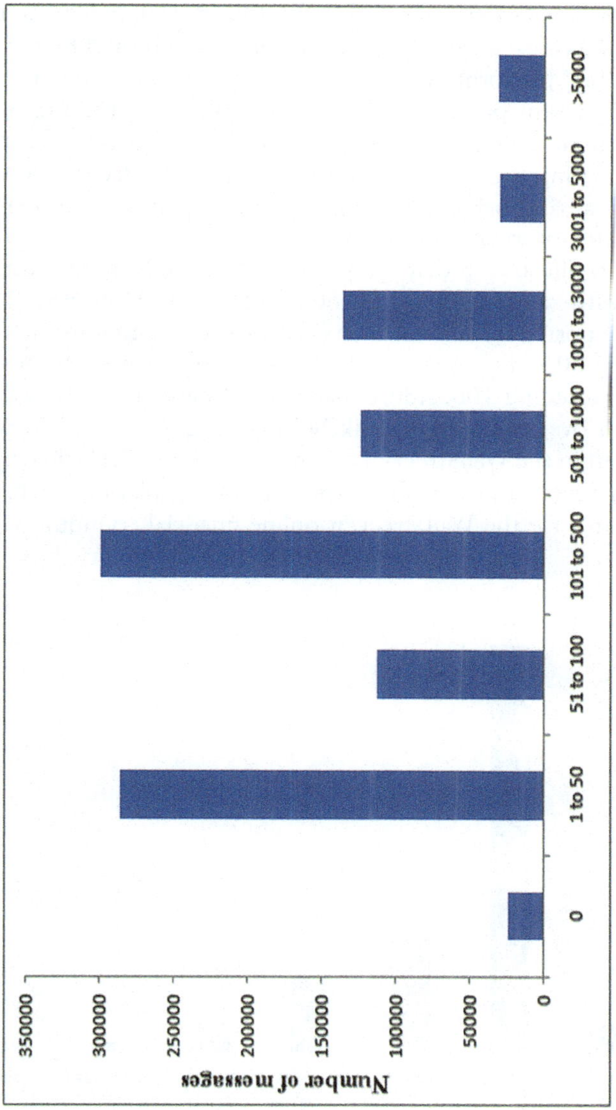

Fig. 7.9 Authors' credit scores when leaving a message

A widely adopted reputation system, employed by websites like eBay.com and Amazon.com, involves credit scores awarded by other users. WallStreetPit's reputation system follows this model, where a higher credit score indicates greater popularity for the author. On the WallStreetPit trading platform, credit scores start at zero and are never negative. This design prevents users from simply re-registering under a new account if they receive a negative score, as there is no cost associated with creating a new account. Since there is no fixed formula for earning credit, an author's credit score primarily depends on the perceived usefulness of the information they share.

Figure 7.10 illustrates that only 2% of messages were posted by newcomers with zero credit (i.e., new accounts). However, 27% of messages were posted by authors with credit scores ranging from 1 to 50. Notably, nearly 60% of messages were posted by experienced authors with credit scores exceeding 100. Additionally, 3% of messages were posted by star users with over 5000 credits, likely indicating gurus with very high reputations within the WallStreetPit community. Figure 7.10 also suggests that more experienced posters dominate the trading platform, which is a positive indicator for the WallStreetPit online financial community.

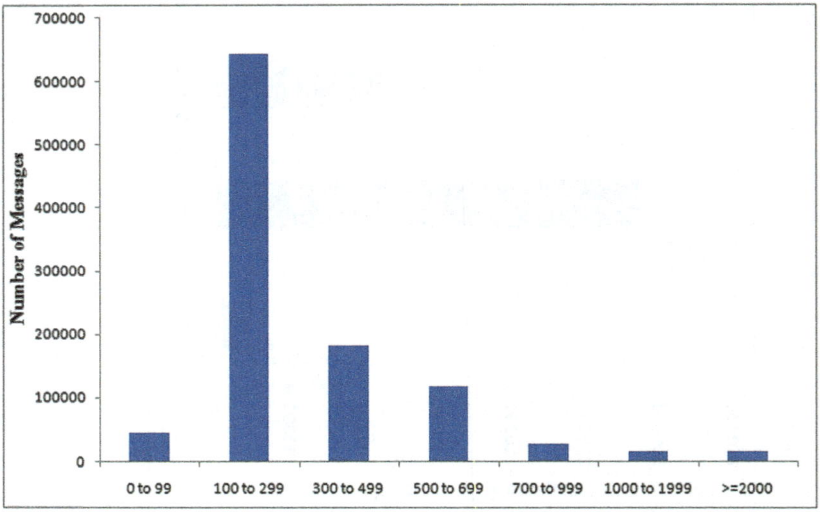

Fig. 7.10 Number of watchers when authors leave messages

Message Distribution Based on Number of Watchers

WallStreetPit allows users to add posters to their "Watch List," ensuring that all messages from those posters are highlighted for them. The trading platform also tracks the number of watchers associated with each author, providing an alternative way to measure an author's reputation. The more watchers (followers) an author has, the higher their popularity. Figure 7.11 shows the number of watchers each author had at the time they posted a new message. The patterns observed are as follows:

- 96% of messages were posted by authors with at least 100 followers.
- Only 4% of messages were posted by authors with fewer than 100 followers.
- 1.5% of messages were posted by authors with more than 2000 followers.

It is likely that authors with many watchers also have high credit scores. Although not tabulated, there is a strong positive correlation of 0.8806 (significant at the 0.01 level) between credit score and the number of watchers in my sample. Figure 7.11 suggests that most messages posted on the WallStreetPit platform were read by many users, contributing to a vibrant online community.

Reply Versus Non-reply Messages

A message is classified as a reply if it responds to an earlier post; otherwise, it is considered a non-reply or initial message. Some posters are more inclined to reply to messages, while others prefer to start new threads and seldom engage in replies. According to Zhang, Swanson, and Prombutr (2012), reply messages often differ in relevancy compared to initial messages because they typically respond to earlier posts, which can make them less relevant or even irrelevant in terms of explicit sentiment about a stock. In their study, when non-reply messages dominate, 20% are recorded as replies, while 80% are non-replies (i.e., initial messages). My sample shows a similar distribution, with 33% of messages classified as replies and 67% as initial messages. As discussed in Chapter 6, non-reply initial messages, which often contain self-disclosed sentiments, are less noisy and therefore crucial for constructing training data.

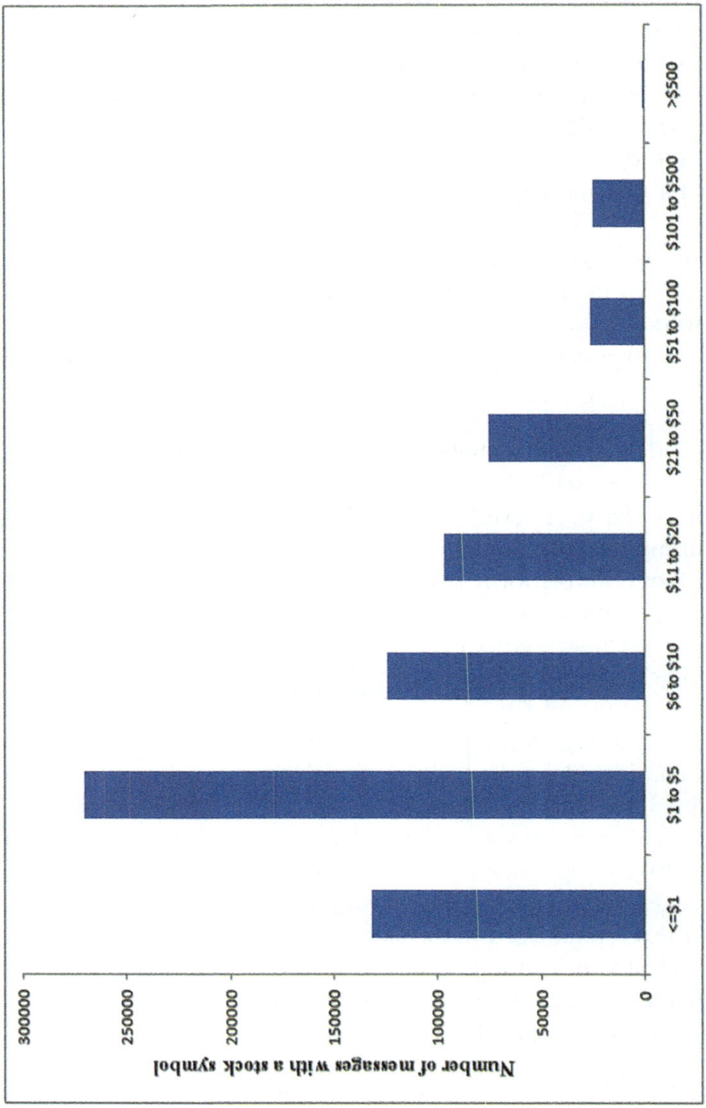

Fig. 7.11 Distribution of messages according to stock prices

Stock-Related Patterns

For practitioners and policymakers, understanding the characteristics of stocks discussed by online retail investors on FSM platforms is crucial. This knowledge helps identify which stocks are likely to be targeted by online traders and potential fraudsters. My sample includes a total of 10,277 unique stocks, encompassing both penny stocks and non-penny stocks, over the 2006 to 2010 period. The sample is comprehensive, covering over-the-counter bulletin board (OB) stocks, pink sheet (PK) stocks, funds (such as Exchange-Traded Funds, Index Funds, Bond Funds, Real Estate Investment Trusts), and common stocks. In this section, I present six stock-related patterns, ranging from price to trading volume, based on my sample.

Message Distribution Based on Stock Prices

Figure 7.12 shows the distribution of stock prices based on real-time prices at the time a stock was mentioned in a message. For messages posted after the closing bell and before the opening bell of the next trading day, the stock's closing price was recorded. Apart from equities trading for less than $1), it is evident that lower stock prices tend to attract a higher volume of associated messages.

Two factors contribute to the relatively low message volume for stocks priced under $1:

- For retail investors, an additional 0.5% of the principal value is added to the regular commission for these stocks, which increases trading costs.
- WallStreetPit is not primarily a trading platform for penny stocks; TheLion.com has a dedicated platform for penny-stock discussions.[1]

In Fig. 7.12, more than half of the messages are associated with equities trading above $1 per share but less than $5. Only 46.54% of messages pertain to stocks trading over $5 per share, and a mere 3.5% of messages are linked to stocks trading above $100 per share. This pattern aligns with the findings of Kumar and Lee (2003), who noted that individual investors tend to have a particular interest in small-cap and low-priced stocks.

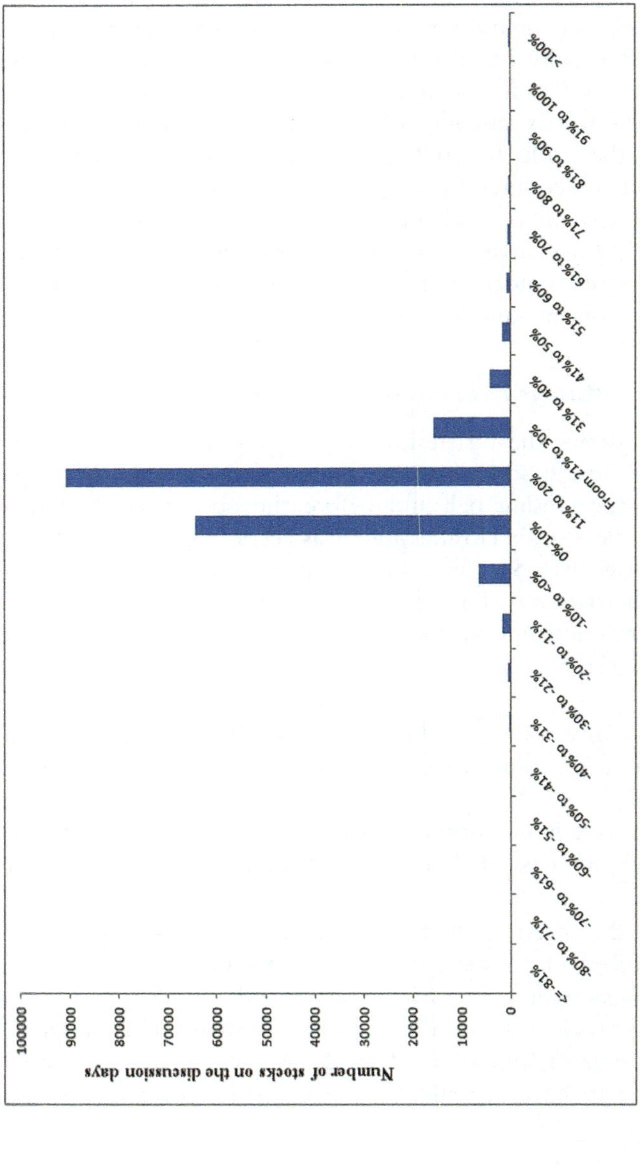

Fig. 7.12 Stock's raw return mentioned in a message

Message Distribution Based on Posting-Day Raw Return

In my sample, the average stock raw return is 6.62%, reflecting the generally optimistic tone among posters. The minimum raw return observed is −94.89%, while the maximum is 1900%. As shown in Fig. 7.13, most stocks (82.48%) discussed on the FSM platform had positive returns between 0 and 20%. Specifically, 34.22% of messages were related to stocks with returns between 0 and 10%, while 48.26% were associated with returns between 11 and 20%. Overall, raw returns are skewed toward the positive side; only 5% of messages were linked to stocks experiencing negative returns. This skew is reasonable, as online investors typically hold long positions and avoid short selling due to high costs, short-sell limitations, and the inherent risks of short selling (Odean 1999). The common understanding is that the higher a stock's return, the more attention it receives.

So, why are there significantly fewer messages related to stocks with very strong positive returns (20% and above)? One possible explanation is that a Buy-and-Hold strategy is often employed in these cases, with stocks showing modest positive returns offering more room for trading profits. As a result, posters tend to recommend stocks with moderate positive returns, showing a reluctance to hype stocks that have already seen significant gains. Figure 7.13 also supports the observation that posters are generally bullish online (see Zhang and Swanson 2010).

Message Distribution Based on the Number of Outstanding Shares

Sabherwal, Sarkar, and Zhang (2008) suggest that investors who participate in online discussions are more likely to target firms with a low number of outstanding shares. Understanding the distribution of outstanding shares for equities on the WallStreetPit trading platform is crucial for gaining insight into the psychology of posters when they recommend stocks. For comparison, I calculated the average number of outstanding shares for 9207 unique stocks in The Center for Research in Security Prices (CRSP) database from 2006 to 2010, which is 77,690,550 shares. Therefore, stocks with outstanding shares below this average are considered to have a low number of outstanding shares.

Figure 7.14 shows that approximately 41% of messages are associated with stocks that have relatively low outstanding shares (i.e., between 10 and 50 million shares). Very few messages were linked to stocks with

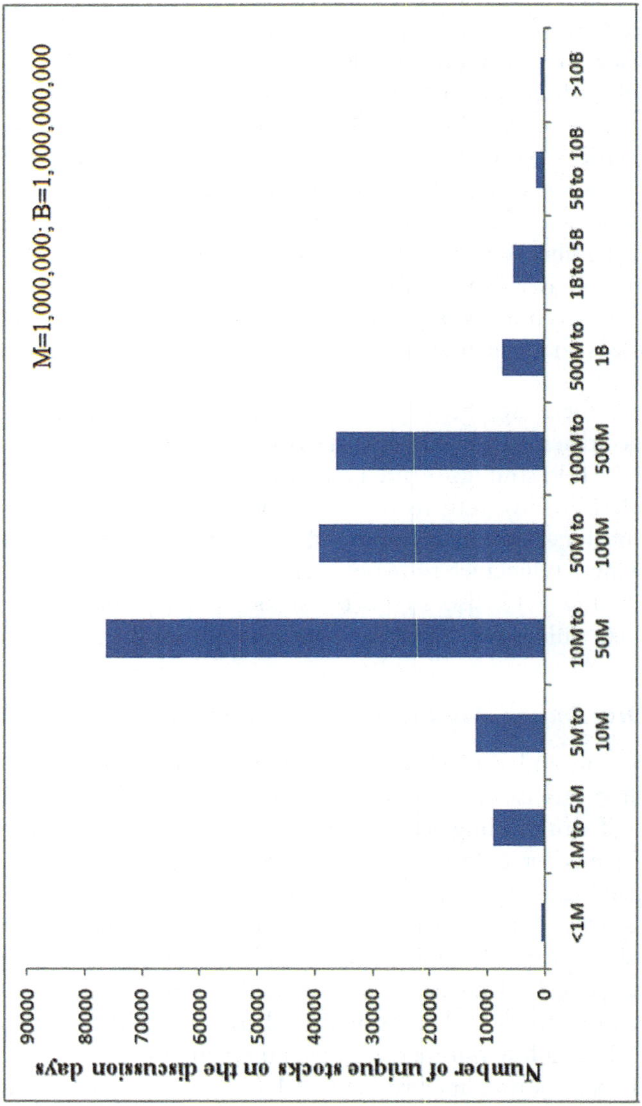

Fig. 7.13 Number of outstanding shares

outstanding shares either below 10 million or above 5 billion. Stocks with too few outstanding shares are likely unknown to online traders or suffer from low liquidity, while stocks with too many outstanding shares may be overlooked by some traders due to the challenges involved in executing a "pump-and-dump" scheme. From Fig. 7.14, I conclude that the stocks most favored by forum posters tend to have a low number of outstanding shares, between 10 million and 50 million, supporting the argument made by Sabherwal, Sarkar, and Zhang (2008).

Message Distribution Based on Market Cap

After examining the message distribution by stock price and outstanding shares, Fig. 7.15 presents the distribution of messages based on market capitalization. A stock's market cap is calculated by multiplying its trading price by its outstanding shares. In my sample, the average market cap is \$2.74 billion, with a minimum of \$540,000 and a maximum of \$323 billion. However, as shown in Fig. 7.15, only 22% of messages were associated with stocks having a market cap exceeding \$1 billion. In contrast, nearly 30% of messages were linked to stocks with a market cap between \$100 million and \$500 million, which are typically classified as small-cap stocks. Additionally, 66.11% of messages were related to stocks with a market cap ranging from \$10 million to \$500 million.

For context, the standard classification for stocks traded on U.S. exchanges during the sample period of 2006 to 2010 is as follows:

- Mega cap: over \$200 billion
- Large cap: over \$10 billion
- Mid-cap: \$2 billion to \$10 billion
- Small cap: \$250 million to \$2 billion
- Microcap: below \$250 million
- Nanocap: below \$50 million

When considering the WallStreetPit trading platform, posters favor small-cap stocks over large-cap ones. This pattern aligns with the findings of Kumar and Lee (2003), who observed that individual investors are particularly interested in low-priced, small-cap stocks, as well as Sabherwal, Sarkar, and Zhang (2008), who noted that online posters

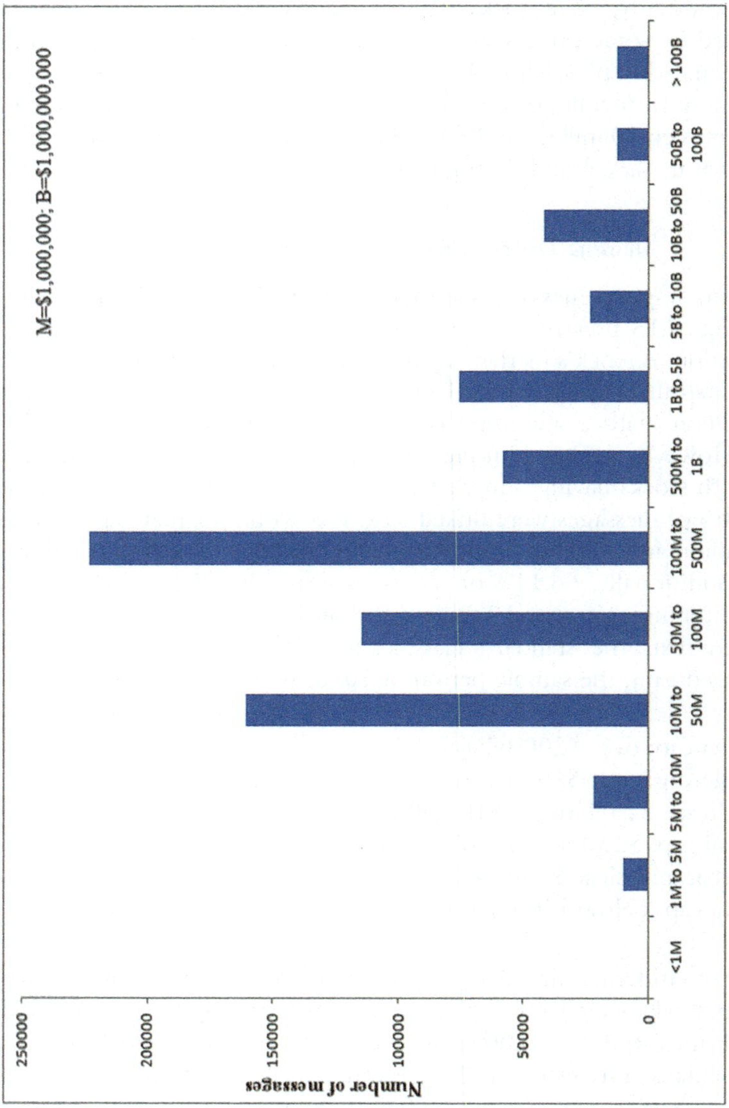

Fig. 7.14 Stock's market capitalization

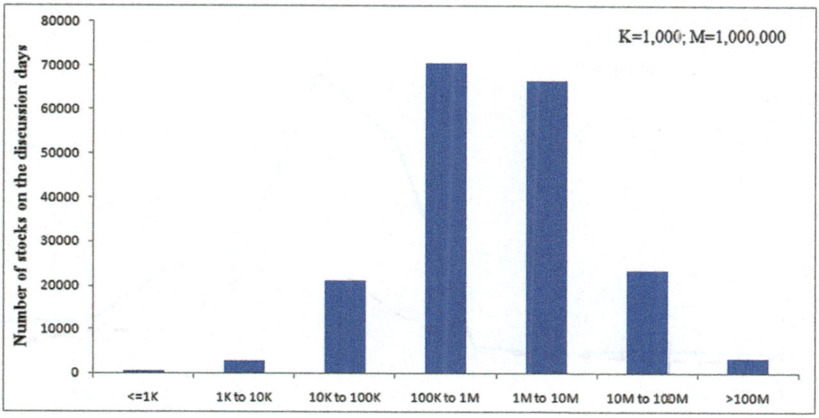

Fig. 7.15 Daily trading volume when the stock was mentioned in a message

often focus on thinly traded microcap stocks with low institutional holdings and minimal analyst coverage.

Message Distribution Based on Trading Volume

In addition to the number of outstanding shares, it is essential to examine the trading volume of stocks on the days they are mentioned in messages. Trading volume serves as an alternative measure of liquidity, complementing outstanding shares. Figure 7.16 illustrates that 37% of messages were associated with stocks experiencing low daily trading volumes, between 100,000 and one million shares, while 35% were linked to stocks with daily trading volumes ranging from 1 to 10 million shares. Consequently, only 28% of messages were associated with stocks with less than 100,000 or more than 10 million traded shares. Like outstanding shares, stocks with lower trading volumes are likely to face liquidity challenges.

Generally, stocks traded in higher volumes are perceived as more attractive to traders. However, within my sample, I discovered a significant positive correlation of 0.2649 between market capitalization and trading volume, which is statistically significant at the 0.01 level. This finding indicates that stocks with high trading volumes tend to have large market capitalizations. Given that prior research (e.g., Sabherwal, Sarkar, and

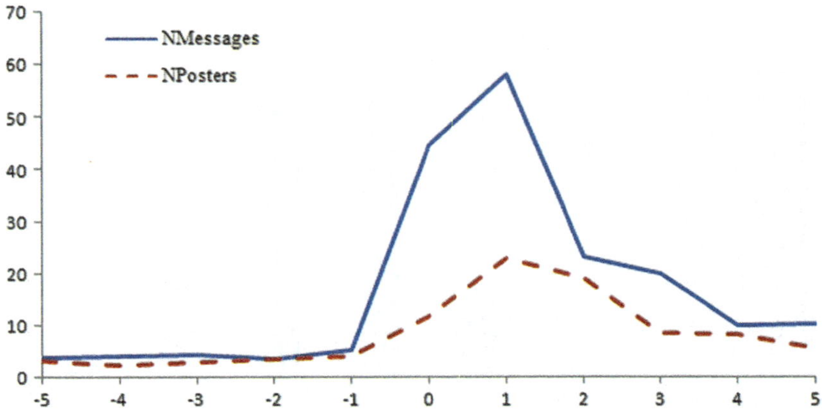

Fig. 7.16 Average numbers of messages and number of posters from t–5 to t+5

Zhang 2008) has documented that online investors tend to favor small-cap stocks, it is unsurprising that a relatively small percentage of messages were associated with stocks exhibiting very high daily trading volumes. Small-cap stocks appear to dominate the discussions in my sample.

Other Stock-Related Patterns

Firstly, since some investors prefer trading options rather than stocks, the presence of options trading for a stock may influence the likelihood of that stock being discussed on FSM platforms. To explore this, I examined the distribution of stocks with and without options trading in my sample. Although not represented visually, my findings reveal that only 12.18% of messages were associated with stocks that do not have options trading. This indicates that, based on my sample, posters on the Wall-StreetPit trading platform tend to favor discussing stocks with options trading.

Secondly, Sabherwal, Sarkar, and Zhang (2008) reported that the majority (87.40%) of the stocks in their sample were listed on the NASDAQ. My findings align with this to some extent, as 61.75% of the messages in my sample were associated with NASDAQ-listed stocks, with the remainder linked to stocks listed on other exchanges. Therefore, it appears that WallStreetPit posters prefer NASDAQ-listed stocks over those listed on other exchanges.

Online Sentiment Tends to be Bullish

To assess whether online posters' stock recommendations are free of bias, Zhang and Swanson (2010) conducted a novel experiment focused on the sentiment score of "Hold." In traditional investment analysis, a "Hold" recommendation from financial analysts suggests that the stock should perform roughly in line with market expectations. However, research has shown that portfolios based on "Hold" recommendations often yield significant negative returns, indicating that analysts' recommendations are not entirely unbiased (Asquith, Mikhail, and Au 2005; Barber, Lehavy, McNichols, and Trueman 2001).

Building on this idea, Zhang and Swanson (2010) examined whether the "Hold" sentiment expressed by online traders represents a neutral opinion or if it tends to lean towards a bullish or bearish perspective. Using a computational-linguistics approach to analyze the content of messages conveying a "Hold" sentiment, they found that these self-disclosed "Hold" sentiments were optimistic and significantly deviated from a neutral stance. Their conclusion was that online traders' "Hold" sentiments are skewed towards bullish tones rather than reflecting a neutral viewpoint.

This finding aligns with intuition, as Odean (1999) noted that many small traders adopt a buy-and-hold strategy, and it is well known that investors generally "put their money where their mouths are." Therefore, the sentiment expressed by posters online tends to align with their actual long positions, resulting in a general bias toward bullish sentiment in online discussions.

Stocks with Weak Fundamentals Are Favored by Online Posters

Research based on data from TheLion.com forum, conducted by Sabherwal, Sarkar, and Zhang (2008), revealed that the daily list of the ten most discussed stocks tends to feature companies with poor financial fundamentals. These stocks typically have low average prices, low institutional ownership, minimal professional analysis, and micro market capitalizations. Additionally, they often exhibit low book values per share, negative earnings per share, low average daily trading volumes, and a small number of shares outstanding. In summary, Sabherwal, Sarkar, and Zhang (2008) concluded that the stocks heavily discussed by online forum posters generally have weak fundamentals.

These findings are consistent with the earlier work of Wysocki (1999), who observed that online investors often target firms with poor financial metrics and thinly traded microcap stocks. Similarly, Zhang (2009) suggested that online posters frequently promote risky, overvalued stocks with weak fundamentals.

The preference for weak-fundamental stocks among online posters can be explained by the pump-and-dump manipulation pattern identified by Sabherwal, Sarkar, and Zhang (2011). They found that online traders often engage in a two-day "pump" followed by a two-day "dump" with respect to small-cap stocks that have weak fundamentals. It is well understood that stocks of firms with poor fundamentals, low institutional ownership, and minimal analyst coverage are particularly vulnerable to price manipulation schemes and securities fraud. As a result, they concluded that online social media platforms can serve as a herding tool to temporarily inflate stock prices, especially for stocks with weak fundamentals.

Posting Statistics Surrounding Discussion Days

Sabherwal, Sarkar, and Zhang (2011) report the average number of messages (NMessages), number of posters (NPosters), sentiment index, and disagreement index associated with a stock over a period of five days before (t–5) and after (t+5) the event day, t0. The event day, t0, is defined as the day when at least 30 messages are posted by at least five different posters regarding a particular stock.

In Fig. 7.17 (Panel A of Fig. 7.2 from Sabherwal, Sarkar, and Zhang 2011), we observe that from day t–5 to t–1, both NMessages and NPosters remained stable at low levels. However, there was a notable increase in the number of postings on the discussion day, t0. The number of posters (NPosters) also rose from single digit to the teens on day t0. Both NMessages and NPosters peaked on day t+1, suggesting that more people discussed the stock the day after it first gained attention. Afterward, both NMessages and NPosters began to decline, returning to their pre-discussion levels by day t+5.

In Fig. 7.18 (Panel B of Fig. 7.2 from Sabherwal, Sarkar, and Zhang 2011), sentiment increased significantly into positive territory on day

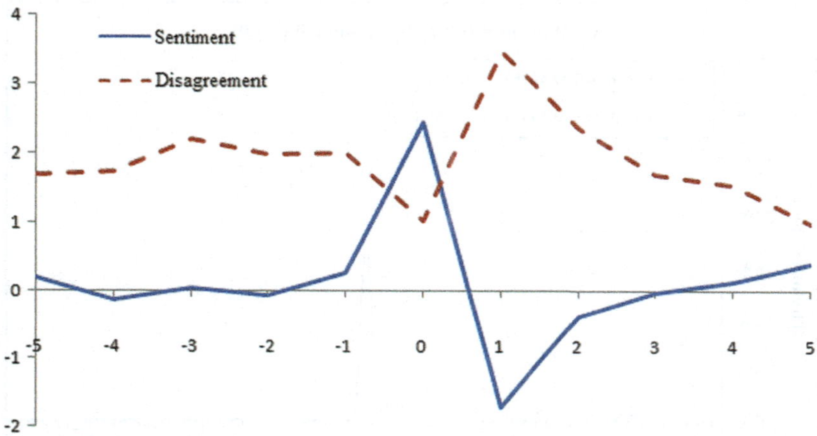

Fig. 7.17 Sentiment and disagreement indexes

t0, but quickly reversed into negative territory the following day. The sentiment index did not differ significantly from zero between t–5 and t–2. This pattern supports the two-day pump followed by a two-day dump manipulation strategy suggested by Sabherwal, Sarkar, and Zhang (2011). Disagreement remained relatively stable until day t0, when it dropped to a lower level, indicating higher consensus among posters. However, disagreement increased on day t+1, as shown by a higher disagreement score. After day t+1, disagreement gradually diminished, returning to its initial level by day t+5. The lower disagreement index on day t0, compared with the preceding days from t–4 to t–1, suggests possible herding behavior and a more unified tone among posters on the discussion day, t0.

Abnormal Return and Volume Surrounding the Discussion Day

An event study is a statistical method used to assess the impact of an event on a stock's return and trading volume. (For details on event study models and settings, refer to Sabherwal, Sarkar, and Zhang 2008, 2011.) In Fig. 7.19 (Fig. 7.2(a) in Sabherwal, Sarkar, and Zhang 2008), the mean abnormal return on day t0, represented by a solid line, is 19.35%, which is statistically significant at the 0.01 level. Additionally, there was a significant positive abnormal return of 3.81% one day before

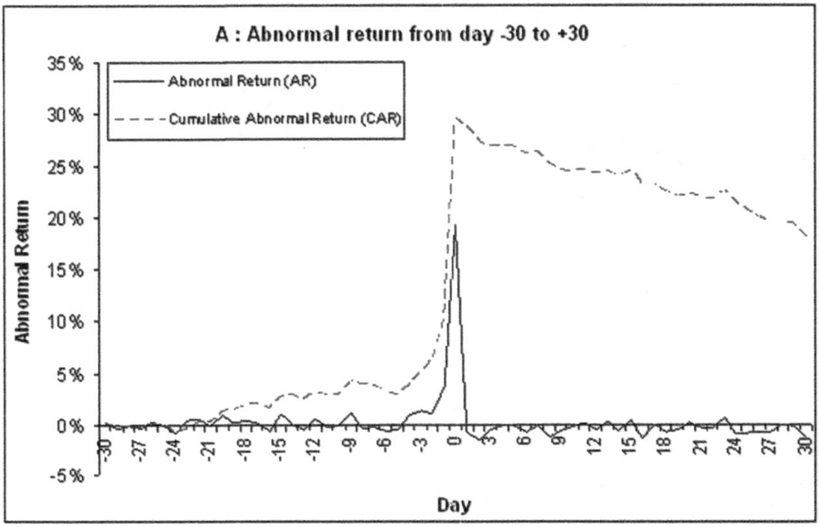

Fig. 7.18 Event study on abnormal return from t–30 to t+30

the online discussion, suggesting information leakage, rumor spread, or market anticipation. Over the first four days following day t0, there was a significant negative abnormal return, indicating a market correction (likely from contrarian trading or profit-taking) in response to the large spike on day t0. Furthermore, there was a positive cumulative abnormal return, represented by the dotted line, of about 18% during the period from t–30 to t+30, with nearly 8% of that gain occurring 30 days after the discussion day t0 (not shown in the chart).

Using the event study methodology, Sabherwal, Sarkar, and Zhang (2008) also analyzed the abnormal trading volume associated with stocks that were heavily discussed on social media platforms. The results are visually represented in Fig. 7.20 (Fig. 7.2(b) in Sabherwal, Sarkar, and Zhang 2008). Abnormal trading volume was positive a few days before day t0 and continued to remain elevated for several days after. It is evident that abnormal volume (illustrated by the solid line) surged around the discussion day, peaking on day t+3. As expected, abnormal volume subsided after day t+3 when fewer people were discussing the stock on the forum. However, the dotted line also shows the cumulative abnormal returns

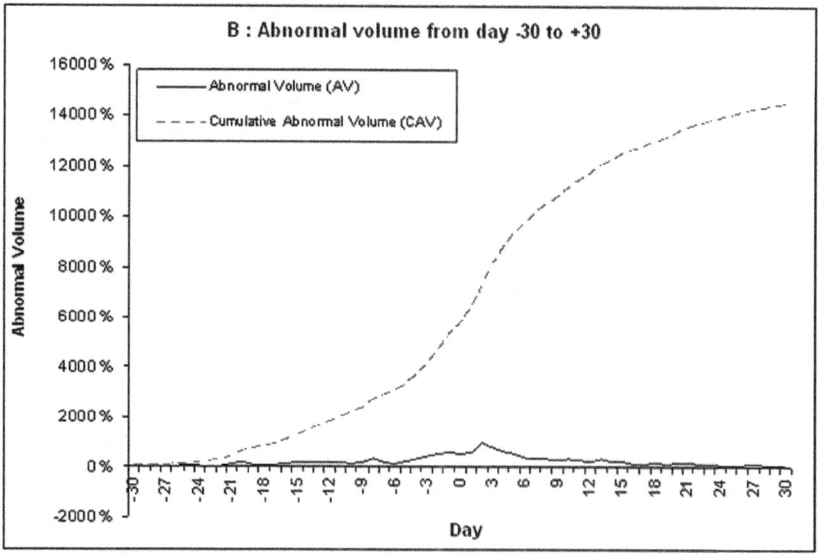

Fig. 7.19 Event study on abnormal volume from t–30 to t+30

over the t–30 to t+30 period, which continued to increase, albeit at a slower pace, due to persistent positive abnormal volumes during this time.

Using a different sample and focusing on a more condensed period (10 days surrounding the discussion day t0), Sabherwal, Sarkar, and Zhang (2011) further explored abnormal returns and volumes from t–5 to t+5. On the event day t0, the average abnormal return (AAR, hereafter) was significantly higher than on any other day within the 10-day period. As presented in Fig. 7.21 (Panel A of Fig. 7.1 in Sabherwal, Sarkar, and Zhang 2011), AAR was also significantly higher on day t–1 compared to days t–5 to t–2. DeMarzo, Vayanos, and Zwiebel (2003) suggest that online investors likely build their positions before posting messages. The event study findings from Sabherwal, Sarkar, and Zhang (2011), which show significant positive abnormal returns and volumes on day t–1, support this argument.

Figure 7.21 (Panel B of Figure 1 in Sabherwal, Sarkar, and Zhang 2011) shows that after a sharp rise in volume on day t0, heavy abnormal trading volume (AAV, hereafter) continues during days t+1 and t+2. Interestingly, as indicated in Fig. 7.21, AAR dropped significantly on these

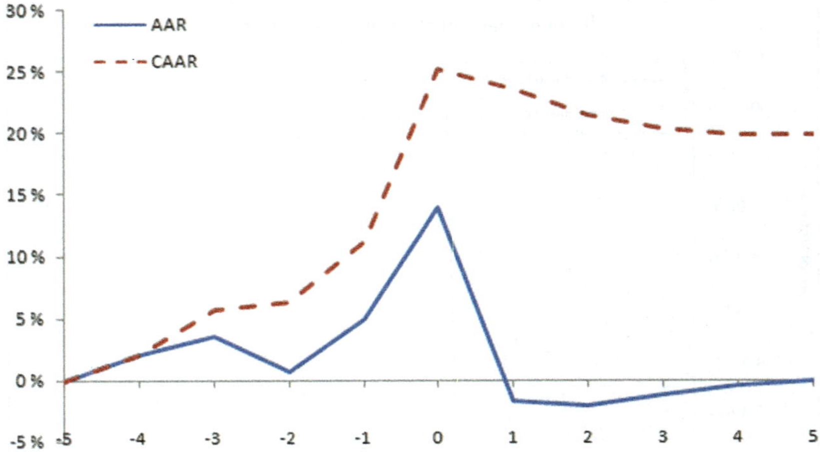

Fig. 7.20 Abnormal return from t–5 to t+5

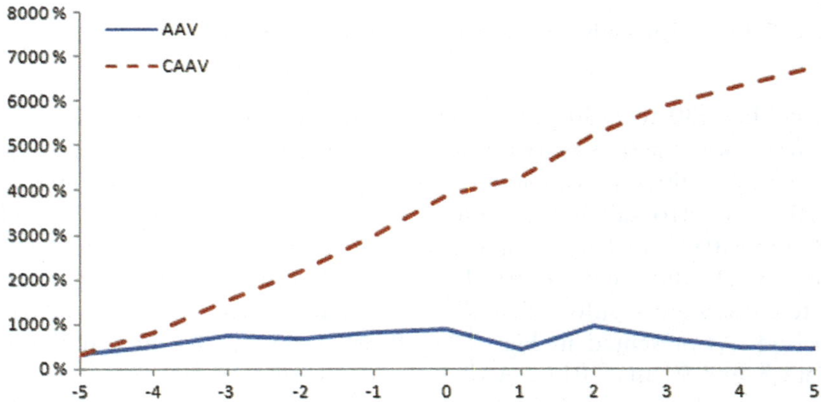

Fig. 7.21 Abnormal volume from t–5 to t+5

two days. Sabherwal, Sarkar, and Zhang (2011) argue that the post-event period on days t+1 and t+2 can be characterized as a two-day dumping phase. Trading activity on days following t+2 is associated with a smaller decline in abnormal returns, possibly due to outside traders (not social media platform users) liquidating their positions.

Note

1. Currently, WallStreetPit does not allow over-the-counter bulletin board (OB) or pink sheet (PK) stocks. OB and PK stocks are posted on a separate message board: http://thelion.com/bin/forum.cgi?tf=pinks_and_bb

CHAPTER 8

Online Talk: Does It Matter at All?

Introduction

In the preceding chapters, we explored how online discussions affect security trading, including impacts on returns, volatility, trading volume, and liquidity. Scholars have also examined whether online chatter has a meaningful influence on a company's value and reputation. If online discussions were merely noise, we would expect a decline in the number of financial social media (FSM, hereafter) platforms and participants over time. However, the proliferation of active FSM platforms and users suggests that online conversations are more than just noise (Antweiler and Frank 2004).

Understanding the effects of online discussions on security trading is crucial for practitioners, researchers, and policymakers. It sheds light on how online recommendations can shape investors' trading behavior and sentiment, ultimately influencing a firm's value. Before examining the implications in greater detail, let us first review the mathematical and statistical methodologies commonly employed by scholars to test their hypotheses.

Y. Zhang, *Financial Social Media*,
https://doi.org/10.1007/978-3-032-09332-5_8

Methodologies

Event Study

The null hypothesis in a typical event study is that on the day of the discussion, there are no significant abnormal price changes or returns (whether positive or negative) compared to the average returns before or after the discussion. Similarly, the null hypothesis for testing trading volume is that on the discussion day, there is no significant abnormal spike in trading volume relative to the average trading volume before or after the event. Empirically, an event study is conducted to estimate the daily abnormal returns and abnormal volumes for a security that is being discussed by online users.

An event study approach usually relies on estimating a benchmark model for each security using an estimation window, a period before the event occurred during which the event could not have had any effect. The study then calculates abnormal returns or volumes for an event window, which represents the period when the event is believed to influence the security price (Tumarkin and Whitelaw 2001; Tumarkin 2002).[1] These abnormal returns are indicative of the security market's reaction to the event.

To estimate the market model, researchers typically follow the standard event study methodology. This often involves using a 255-day pre-event estimation window, beginning on day $t - 300$ (where t represents the event day) and ending on $t - 46$, which is 46 trading days before the online discussion on t. If the full 255 trading days are not available, at least three trading days are required to estimate the model. Event study model coefficients are tested using the Patell (1976) Z-test or Generalized Z-test, which assesses whether average abnormal stock returns are equal to zero, assuming asymptotic normality. The abnormal return (A_{jt}) for security j on the discussion day t, using a market model, is calculated as follows:

$$A_{jt} = R_{jt} - \left(\underset{j}{\widehat{\alpha}} + \underset{j}{\widehat{\beta}} R_{mt} \right) \tag{8.1}$$

where $\widehat{\alpha}_j$ and $\widehat{\beta}_j$ are Scholes and Williams (1977) estimates of α_j and β_j, respectively, as defined by

$$\widehat{\alpha}_j = \frac{1}{255}\sum_{t=-300}^{-46} R_{jt} - \frac{1}{255}\widehat{\beta}_j\sum_{t=-300}^{-46} R_{mt} \tag{8.2}$$

where R_{jt} is the daily security return and R_{mt} is the return of a market benchmark (the S&P 500 stock market index, for example). So, we have

$$\widehat{\beta}_j = \frac{\left(\widehat{\beta}_j^{\text{Lag}} + \widehat{\beta}_j^{0} + \widehat{\beta}_j^{\text{Lead}}\right)}{1 + 2\hat{\rho}_m} \tag{8.3}$$

where $\hat{\rho}_m$ cis the estimated first-order auto correlation coefficient of the benchmark over the pre-event window $t = -300...-46$, and $\widehat{\beta}_j^{\text{Lag}}$, $\widehat{\beta}_j^{0}$ and $\widehat{\beta}_j^{\text{Lead}}$ are the ordinary least squares (OLS) model coefficients estimated from the following three models, respectively:

$$R_{jt} = \widehat{\alpha}_j^{\text{Lag}} + \widehat{\beta}_j^{\text{Lag}} R_{m,t-1} + \varepsilon_{jt}^{\text{Lag}}, \text{ where } t = -300\ldots-46, \tag{8.4}$$

$$R_{jt} = \widehat{\alpha}_j^{0} + \widehat{\beta}_j^{0} R_{mt} + \varsigma_{jt}^{0}, \text{ where } t = -300\ldots-46, \tag{8.5}$$

$$R_{jt} = \widehat{\alpha}_j^{\text{Lead}} + \widehat{\beta}_j^{\text{Lead}} R_{m,t+1} + \psi_{jt}^{\text{Lead}}, \text{ where } t = -300\ldots-46. \tag{8.6}$$

The average abnormal return (AAR, hereafter) is therefore computed as

$$\text{AAR}_t = \frac{\sum_j^N A_{jt}}{N}, \tag{8.7}$$

Here, N is the total number of securities being evaluated on day t. The cumulative average abnormal return (CAAR, hereafter) between any two days (t_1, t_2) is:

$$\text{CAAR}(t_1, t_2) = \frac{\sum_{j=1}^N \sum_{t=t_1}^{t_2} A_{jt}}{N}. \tag{8.8}$$

To compute the Patell (1976) Z statistics for each security$j$ and for each event day t, the abnormal return is standardized by the square root of its estimated forecast variance, s_{fjt}, yielding a standardized abnormal return, SA_{jt}, defined as

$$SA_{jt} = \frac{A_{jt}}{s_{fjt}} \tag{8.9}$$

where

$$s_{fjt} = \left(s_j^2 \left(1 + \frac{1}{255} + \frac{(R_{mt} - \overline{R}_m)^2}{\sum_{t=-300}^{-46} (R_{mt} - \overline{R}_m)^2} \right) \right)^{\frac{1}{2}} \tag{8.10}$$

where s_j^2 is the estimated residual variance from the Scholes and Williams (1977) market model regression:

$$s_j^2 = \frac{1}{253} \sum_{t=-300}^{-46} (A_{jt})^2 \tag{8.11}$$

where A_{jt} is the abnormal return on stock j during the estimation window with $t = -300 \ldots -46$ andR_{mt} is the return on the benchmark during the same estimation period. $\overline{R_m}$ is the mean return on market index over the same estimation period. Under the null hypothesis that CAAR $(t_1, t_2) = 0$, the Patell Z (1976) statistic equals:

$$Z_{t_1,t_2} = \frac{1}{\sqrt{N}} \sum_{j=1}^{N} Z_{t_1,t_2}^j \tag{8.12}$$

where

$$Z_{t_1,t_2}^j = \frac{1}{\sqrt{L_{t_1,t_2}^j}} \sum_{t=t_1}^{t_2} SA_{jt} \tag{8.13}$$

where $L_{t_1,t_2}^j = (t_2 - t_1 + 1)$ is the number of days over which SA_{jt} is cumulated. Average abnormal volume (AAV, hereafter) and cumulative average abnormal volume (CAAV, hereafter) are calculated in the same manner as shown in Eqs. 8.1–8.13. In a volume event study, the benchmark used is a volume index, such as the NYSE-AMEX log-transformed value-weighted volume index.

Researchers assess whether AAR and AAV are significant on the day when security j is discussed on the FSM platform. Additionally, they investigate whether the subsequent stock price performance, CAAR and CAAV, differ significantly from zero.

Contemporaneous and Predictive Regression Models

The relationship between online discussions and security trading can be analyzed using contemporaneous and predictive regression models. In a contemporaneous regression model, the dependent variables on the left-hand side (LHS) represent security trading variables, usually one variable in each model (such as return, volatility, volume, or spread), while the independent variables on the right-hand side (RHS) are measures of online posting activity (such as the number of messages, number of posters, sentiment, and disagreement). A contemporaneous model requires that both the dependent and independent variables occur within the same period, such as on the same day. The contemporaneous relationship between message board activity and stock trading can be tested with the following regression model:

$$Y_t^i = \beta_0 + \beta_1 X_t^i + \beta_2 \text{Control}_t + \beta_3 Y_{t-1}^i + \varepsilon_t \tag{8.14}$$

where Υ represents one of the security trading variables. Note that each stock trading variable should be tested in a separate regression, keeping the same RHS variables. β_0 is the intercept, representing the value when all independent variables are zero. The vector X contains posting activity variables. β_1 represents the vector of coefficients for each of these posting activity variables. The vector Control includes control variables, such as a size dummy, holiday dummy, and listing-exchange dummy, with β_2 being the vector of coefficients for these control variables. A one-period lagged dependent variable Υ_{t-1} is also included to control for one-period autocorrelation, with β_3 representing its coefficient. Finally, ε is the residual of the regression model, representing the variation in Υ not explained by the independent variables. The smaller the ε, the better the model fits.

For testing the one-day predictive ability of online discussions, Antweiler and Frank (2004) propose time-sequencing tests. These involve introducing a lead time, where the dependent variable and control variables are shifted by one trading day relative to the independent variables.

This can be expressed as:

$$Y_{t+1}^{i} = \beta_0 + \beta_1 X_t^i + \beta_2 \text{Control}_{t+1} + \beta_3 Y_t^i + \varepsilon_{t+1} \tag{8.15}$$

Similarly, researchers can test the predictive ability of online discussions on trading activities for any subsequent day.

Dummy Variables and Interaction Terms

It is essential to discuss the use of dummy control variables in regression models. The literature includes several dummy control variables, each serving a specific purpose. For instance, because retail investors often favor NASDAQ-listed stocks, scholars include a variable, "Listing," which is a dummy variable controlling for NASDAQ-listed stocks. Thus, Eq. 8.14 becomes:

$$Y_t^j = \theta_0 + \theta_1 X_t^j + \theta_2 \text{Listing} + \theta_3 Y_{t-1}^j + \mu_t \tag{8.16}$$

where "*Listing*" is a binary variable where Listing = 1 indicates NASDAQ-listed stocks and Listing = 0 indicates otherwise. For example, let us define Y_t^j as the stock trading volume for stock j on day t; the coefficient θ_2 on the dummy variable Listing captures the difference in average trading volume between NASDAQ-listed and non-NASDAQ-listed stocks. When testing the influence of X_t^j on Y_t^j conditional on Listing, an additional interaction term can be introduced:

$$Y_t^j = \theta_0 + \theta_1 X_t^j + \theta_2 \text{Listing} + \theta_3 X_t^j * \text{Listing} + \theta_4 Y_{t-1}^j + \mu_t \tag{8.17}$$

where $X_t^j *$Listing is an interaction term (or a vector of interaction terms) between exogenous variable X_t^j and dummy variable Listing so that coefficients $\theta_1 + \theta_3$ depict the average impact on Y_t^j by X_t^j when stocks are listed on the NASDAQ exchange with Listing = 1. On the other hand, θ_1 alone depicts the average impact on Y_t^i by X_t^i when stocks are listed outside the NASDAQ exchange with Listing = 0. Each of the following dummy variables can be tested similarly:

- Option Dummy: Since some investors prefer trading options over stocks, a dummy variable "Option" is included, where Option = 1 indicates stocks with option trading and Option = 0 indicates otherwise.

- Special Trading Days: Special trading days, such as those before or after a weekend or major holiday when traders are generally less active, are controlled for using dummy variables. Additionally, the third Friday of the month is normally an options expiry day, which may lead to increased online discussions. Dummy variables for these special days are included as controls.
- News Dummy: A dummy variable "News" is included to control for the occurrence of significant market news. News = 1 indicates days with substantial market news, and News = 0 indicates otherwise. Market news includes events like stock splits, mergers, management changes, new product introductions, earnings announcements, and analyst recommendations.
- Size Dummy: When testing the asymmetric effects of financial social media, a "Size" dummy variable is included. Size = 1 indicates small-cap stocks, and Size = 0 indicates otherwise.
- Crisis Dummy: The 2008–2009 global financial crisis may have influenced the frequency and volume of message postings. To control for this, a "Crisis" dummy variable is introduced to capture any shifts in message-posting activities before and after the crisis. Crisis = 1 indicates the period before the crisis, and Crisis = 0 indicates the period after the crisis.
- Industry Dummies: Media coverage may be biased toward certain industries, and traders may have specific interests in industries such as telecommunications or pharmaceuticals. To control for these preferences, industry dummy variables are used. For instance, Sabherwal et al. (2011) employ six industry dummy variables (D1–D6), covering consumer goods, financials, healthcare, industrial goods, services, and technology. Basic materials serve as the reference industry, acting as the base group in the regression. Interaction terms between the exogenous variables and these dummy variables are often included, like the approach used in Eq. 8.17.

Empirical Evidence

If online discussions did not impact security trading, there would be no significant changes in security trading activity on days with heavy posting activity, especially when no other market news is present. Consequently, the null hypothesis in most FSM event studies is that there is no abnormal return and/or volume on the day a security is mentioned on an FSM platform. However, empirical evidence often rejects this null hypothesis in favor of the alternative: that online discussions do indeed matter. Several academic studies provide evidence that online discussions induce abnormal returns and trading volumes, particularly on the days when these discussions occur (event days).

Tumarkin and Whitelaw (2001), for example, conducted an event study based on 181,633 messages collected from Raging Bull between April 17, 1999, and February 18, 2000. They examined industry-adjusted returns and abnormal volumes around days with abnormal message board activity. They found that on event days, stocks receiving both strong- and weak-positive signals experienced statistically significant, positive industry-adjusted returns. Conversely, stocks that attracted negative opinions on event days showed insignificant, negative industry-adjusted returns. Moreover, on the event day (t) and the following day ($t + 1$), trading volumes spiked, with the most significant volume increases occurring in stocks experiencing strongly positive changes in weighted opinion. Based on these results, they concluded that abnormal financial social media activity coincides with abnormal stock returns and trading volumes.

Hallett (2007) also explored message board takeover rumors by analyzing 431 rumors disseminated between January 2003 and December 2006. His findings revealed that these rumors generated significant positive abnormal returns and trading volumes on the days the rumors circulated.

Sabherwal et al. (2008) downloaded over 160,000 messages from TheLion.com, covering the period from July 18, 2005, to July 18, 2006, to study the effect of financial social media. Unlike previous research, they focused on the most actively discussed stocks to determine whether these online discussions contained useful information or were merely noise. Their research showed that online posters favored thinly traded, micro-cap stocks with low institutional holdings and limited analyst coverage. An event study revealed that stocks ranked among the 10 most discussed stocks on any given day experienced significant abnormal positive returns and trading volumes on that day.

In a follow-up study, Sabherwal et al. (2011) investigated pump-and-dump schemes involving heavily discussed stocks using real-time data from TheLion.com over the same period. Their event study demonstrated that on days with heavy online discussions, both average abnormal returns and volumes were significantly higher, even in the absence of market news. The results supported the hypothesis that stocks initially experience positive abnormal returns when pumped on message boards, followed by significant negative abnormal returns when the stocks are presumably dumped.

Clarkson et al. (2006) conducted an event study on 189 takeover rumors posted on HotCopper IDS (hotcopper.com.au) between May 1999 and March 2000. They found evidence of abnormal returns and trading volumes on the days the rumors were posted and on the preceding days. Interestingly, their intraday analysis revealed significant returns and trading volumes during the 10-minute posting intervals and abnormal trading volumes during the 10-minute intervals immediately preceding them.

Bettman et al. (2011) used an event study method to examine takeover rumors on the Yahoo! Finance message board between January 2003 and December 2008. Their results indicated that message board takeover rumors led to significant abnormal returns and trading volumes, specifically generating significant positive abnormal returns compared to market portfolios. They concluded that the release of takeover rumors on financial social media can have a significant impact on shareholder wealth.

Lastly, Zhang et al. (2022) explored the asymmetric effects of financial social media by controlling for firm size and news occurrence. Their event study revealed a significantly strong and positive market reaction for small-cap stocks on days when they were discussed in online forums, regardless of media coverage. In fact, there was an even greater market response to online discussions when no media coverage was present. Conversely, large-cap stocks generated a much smaller market reaction on discussion days, especially when accompanied by concurrent media coverage. Interestingly, no market reaction was detected for large-cap stocks on discussion days when no media coverage was present.

Impact on Firm Value (Stock Returns)

While event studies generally suggest that online discussions can induce abnormal returns and trading volumes, researchers often design contemporaneous and lead-lag regression models to explore the extent and direction of the influence that online discussions have on stock returns. Among the various measures of online activity, researchers are particularly interested in how factors such as the number of postings, the number of authors, the average message length, poster sentiment, poster disagreement, and poster bullishness affect stock returns. Below, I summarize several key academic studies that examine the impact of online discussions on stock returns.

Using data from the Yahoo! Finance and Motley Fool message boards in 1998, Wysocki (1998) provided early evidence that changes in the daily number of messages are associated with daily changes in stock returns. Additionally, he found that overnight message postings have predictive power for changes in stock returns on the following day. In further research, Wysocki (2000) demonstrated that message-posting activity is associated with trading activity and that this relationship appears to reflect legitimate information rather than random noise.

Antweiler and Frank (2004) examined over 1.5 million messages posted on Yahoo! Finance and Raging Bull, focusing on 45 companies within the Dow Jones Industrial Average and the Dow Jones Internet Index. They investigated whether the information contained in Internet financial social media impacts stock returns. Their findings revealed useful information in these discussions. Through penal regression analysis with fixed effects, they reported a significantly negative contemporaneous correlation between the number of messages and stock returns. A time-sequencing test further showed that a positive shock in message board postings predicts negative stock returns on the next day ($t + 1$) after the stock is discussed on day (t). However, they concluded that although the impact of message board postings on stock returns is statistically significant, it is economically small once transaction costs are considered.

Antweiler and Frank's (2004) sample consisted primarily of large-cap stocks, leaving the impact of online discussions on smaller stocks unclear. Sabherwal et al. (2008) sought to address this gap by investigating whether online postings influence stock returns for thinly traded, micro-cap stocks. They found that the number of messages posted about a stock on a given day was positively related to the stock's abnormal return on that day, and it also positively predicted abnormal returns for the following day. This finding contrasts with Antweiler and Frank's (2004) conclusion, where they reported a negative correlation between the number of messages and stock returns on day (t) and day ($t + 1$). The discrepancy likely stems from the different samples used, which involved firms of varying sizes.

In subsequent work, Sabherwal et al. (2011) argued that poster sentiment is a critical predictor of trading-related activities, particularly stock returns. In a sample of 64 fringe stocks comprising approximately 12,000 messages, they found that investors' credit-weighted sentiments outweighed other message-posting parameters (such as the number of messages and disagreement) in explaining stock returns. Specifically, they found that online traders' credit-weighted sentiment indexes were positively associated with contemporaneous returns but negatively predicted next-day returns $(t + 1)$ and returns on the day after that $(t + 2)$. Higher sentiment was correlated with higher returns on the discussion day (t), but it predicted lower returns over the next two trading days. Similarly, Das et al. (2005) also found that sentiment changes gradually and are positively related to stock returns.

Although most studies generally agree that online discussions are not mere noise, researchers hold differing views on whether message board activities can predict future stock returns. Zhang et al. (2022) argued that these discrepancies stem from whether researchers used self-selected or board-generated samples in prior studies. To address these inconsistencies, they analyzed 1,058,366 valid messages downloaded from WallStreetPit from January 1, 2006, to December 31, 2011. They examined the asymmetric effects of financial social media across different categories (small- versus large-cap stocks, and news versus non-news events). Their findings indicate that message board activity, measured by the number of postings, sentiment, disagreement, and average message length, affects stock returns, particularly on the discussion day. The effect was more pronounced for small-cap stocks with concurrent news coverage. In the absence of market news, online discussions only influenced current and future returns for small-cap stocks, with no impact on large-cap stocks. Additionally, Oh and Sheng (2011) provided further evidence that stock microblog sentiments have predictive power for both simple and market-adjusted stock returns.

Impact on Trading Volume

Is higher posting volume associated with increased trading volume? Can today's posting volume predict tomorrow's trading activity? And do other FSM metrics, such as sentiment and disagreement, explain trading volume? To address these questions, researchers often design time-series and cross-sectional regression analyses, typically starting with the null hypothesis that online discussions have no impact on current or future stock trading volume.

A key issue researchers have explored is the measurement of trading volume. Various proxies for stock trading volume are used in the literature, including:

- Total trading volume,
- Number of trades,
- Proportion of small or large trades, and
- Turnover ratio.

Some argue that the number of small trades is a better proxy for total trading volume, as online retail investors, who are more likely to be influenced by posting activity, are often behind these trades. Others prefer to use total trading volume or the total number of trades. Findings often differ based on the measure employed. Below is a summary of the literature on the relationship between online discussions and trading volume.

Using daily message-posting activity linked to 100 companies on Yahoo! Finance message boards during 1997 and 1998, Wysocki (1998) examined the relationship between stock market activity and daily changes in message-posting volume. He documented that changes in daily message board posting volume are associated with daily changes in stock trading volume. Moreover, overnight message-posting volume was found to predict changes in the next day's stock trading volume. These findings were further confirmed by empirical tests using Motley Fool data in Wysocki (2000). Tumarkin and Whitelaw (2001), who studied Internet service stocks, found that on days with abnormally high posting activity, changes in online investor opinion were correlated with contemporaneous stock trading volume but did not predict future trading volume. Tumarkin (2002) reported similar findings.

Antweiler and Frank (2004) argued that message boards can be helpful in predicting trading volume. For example, disagreement among posters is often associated with increased trading volume, and the poster sentiment measured by a bullishness index also exhibits some predictive ability. However, Antweiler and Frank (2004) noted that smaller traders may wish to discuss purchases they have already made, implying that small-size trades can actually drive poster sentiment rather than the reverse. Importantly, they found that greater disagreement on a given day predicts lower trading volume on the following day, all else being equal.

Using language-processing algorithms, Das et al. (2005) analyzed the intensity and dispersion of sentiment in over 170,000 messages posted about four stocks: AMZN, DAL, GMGC, and GWRX. They examined the determinants of sentiment levels and disagreement among posters and found a close relationship between sentiment, posting activity, stock returns, and trading volume. They suggested that sentiment is positively related to current trading volume.

Zhang (2009) proposed that recommending stocks with high average trading volume is favored by online traders because higher trading volume implies greater liquidity, which helps build a strong reputation in the online community. Sabherwal et al. (2011) reported that online traders prefer non-financial stocks with low prices, high trading volumes, small floats, and low price-to-book ratios. Focusing on these types of stocks, they found that the stronger the poster sentiment, the higher the proportion of small-size trades on the same day. Additionally, the proportion of small-size trades was greater for stocks with a higher number of messages posted on the same day. In terms of predictive ability, they found that stronger sentiment significantly predicted a greater number of small trades over the next one to two days.

Zhang et al. (2022) examined the impact of online discussions on the turnover ratio, defined as the number of small-size trades divided by the total number of trades on a given day. They found that higher disagreement among posters and a greater number of postings increased the turnover ratio for large stocks. However, sentiment and message length had no significant impact when stock-related news was concurrently covered in the media. For small stocks, both disagreement and posting volume had a more pronounced positive effect on the turnover ratio. Higher online sentiment for small stocks also led to a higher turnover. In the absence of concurrent media coverage, more message postings induced higher turnover for small stocks, while for large stocks, no financial social media measure significantly impacted current or future turnover ratios.

Impact on Return Volatility

It has been shown that trading volume is positively correlated with volatility (Jones et al. 1994). As discussed earlier, online discussions not only influence trading volume contemporaneously but also predict subsequent day trading volume, particularly for small-cap stocks. Online discussions are therefore expected to affect return volatility.

Like volume, several measures of volatility are used to test the relationship between online discussions and return volatility. The most widely used volatility measures include:

- Intraday return volatility,
- Share price volatility,
- Volatility derived from option prices,
- Volume-weighted volatility of trade prices,
- Realized volatility based on 15-minute intraday returns, and
- Standard deviation of midpoints of bid-ask quotes.

In addition to conventional regression analyses, scholars have also conducted time-series causality tests to determine whether online discussions cause volatility or if volatility leads to online discussions. Studying the impact of FSM activities on volatility is crucial, as changes in volatility can affect a firm's cost of capital, management strategies, investor relations, investment policies, and mergers and acquisitions.

The following is a summary of significant studies that address the relationship between online discussions and return volatility:

Antweiler and Frank (2004) found that the number of messages posted online helps predict realized volatility, though the effect of bullishness and disagreement on realized volatility is weak. In a contemporaneous framework, they found that both the number of messages and the bullishness index positively correlate with realized volatility, while higher disagreement is associated with lower realized volatility. Further time-sequencing tests suggest that only the number of messages can predict realized volatility, indicating that the causality runs from message postings to trading volatility. However, they conclude that the level of message-posting activity is correlated with volatility, but the direction of causation ultimately runs from volatility to day trading. On the other hand, Koski et al. (2004) found the opposite result regarding causality, using messages collected from the same sites for stocks within the NASDAQ-100 Index. They concluded that financial social media information increases current stock return volatility but does not contribute to predicting stock returns in any fundamental way.

Sabherwal et al. (2008) focused on thinly traded micro-cap stocks with low institutional holdings and low analyst coverage. They found that the number of postings does not affect intraday return volatility. Using a larger sample and a sentiment index measure, Sabherwal et al. (2011) suggested using the absolute value of the sentiment index, as both optimistic and pessimistic sentiments could increase volatility. They found that absolute sentiment among posters is negatively related to contemporaneous and subsequent two-day intraday volatility. Lower volatility on days $t0$, $t + 1$, and $t + 2$ suggests possible herding behavior among online traders when strong sentiment (either optimistic or pessimistic) is present. Interestingly, aside from absolute sentiment, the number of messages and disagreement index were found to be uncorrelated with volatility on any day.

Bird and Thapa (2010) studied component stocks in the Ordinaries Index (comprised of the 500 largest companies listed on the Australian Stock Exchange [ASX]). They found that in the presence of unscheduled company news, high contemporaneous message board activity increases trading volatility. Using HotCopper message board data from 2004 to 2008, Thapa (2013) further found that while message boards do not contribute to stock returns or liquidity, they do increase share price volatility. Thapa presented evidence that message board activity increases volatility in the short term, and that the number of unique user participants in online discussions is positively related to changes in volatility.

Finally, Zhang et al. (2022) examined the effects of online discussions on volatility by splitting their sample by firm size and media news appearances. For large stocks with concurrent news in the media, they found that both sentiment and the number of messages significantly and positively explained contemporaneous and next-day volume-weighted volatility, while disagreement and message length had no impact. For small stocks with media news, only sentiment had a significant impact on volatility, with other measures such as disagreement, number of messages, and message length showing no effect. They concluded that higher sentiment induces greater contemporaneous and future volatility, regardless of firm size or the presence of media news, while other measures of online discussions had no significant impact on volatility on any given day.

Impact on Bid-Ask Spread

The bid-ask spread, also known as the standardized bid-ask spread, is a traditional measure of liquidity. It is defined as the ratio of a stock's average bid-ask spread (the difference between the ask price and the bid price at a given time) to its mean ask price. A narrower bid-ask spread indicates higher liquidity, which is generally preferred by investors. Trading volume also reflects aspects of liquidity, as higher trading volume implies greater liquidity. Consequently, there is a negative relationship between the bid-ask spread and trading volume. Any model that examines the relationship between online discussions and the bid-ask spread should include trading volume as a control variable (Amihud and Mendelson 1986). Below is a summary of some research findings on the relationship between online discussions and the bid-ask spread.

Antweiler and Frank (2004) conducted a contemporaneous regression analysis and found that a bullishness index significantly increases the bid-ask spread, while an agreement index reduces it. The number of messages posted has no impact on the bid-ask spread. In their lead-lag experiments, they further discovered that a more positive bullish tone among posters and a higher degree of agreement significantly predict a higher bid-ask spread on the following day, whereas the number of messages remains non-predictive. However, none of these online discussion measures can predict the bid-ask spread two days after the initial discussion.

Hallett (2007) studied 431 message board takeover rumors disseminated via Raging Bull and Yahoo! Finance between January 2003 and December 2006. He found that while these rumors generate significant positive abnormal returns and trading volumes, they do not significantly affect the bid-ask spreads, which serve as a proxy for the inherent aggregate risk of the rumored target firms. Bettman et al. (2011) reported similar results, extending the data sample to cover the period from January 2003 to December 2008.

Using a contemporaneous bid-ask spread regression, Sabherwal et al. (2011) showed that absolute sentiment is not significantly related to the bid-ask spread. However, the coefficients for absolute sentiment, disagreement, and the number of messages are all negative, suggesting that higher levels of these variables tend to reduce the bid-ask spread, indicating greater trading liquidity. The bid-ask spread is strongly and positively related to the previous day's lagged bid-ask spread, suggesting autocorrelation in this variable.

From a different perspective, Lerman (2020) found that greater accounting-related online discussions during earnings announcements are associated with a reduction in the bid-ask spread. She concluded that either increased investor attention to accounting information or the message board discussion itself may reduce information asymmetry during information releases. Additionally, Zhang et al. (2014) reported that, in the presence of news on discussion days, there is no significant difference in the average standardized spread between small and large stocks. Sentiment, disagreement, and the number of messages all significantly reduce standardized bid-ask spreads for large stocks, implying higher liquidity. For small stocks, however, only the number of messages has a significant negative impact on the spread, meaning that more messages correspond to higher liquidity.

Interestingly, they found that the bid-ask spread was narrower on the first trading day after a weekend or holiday, indicating higher liquidity when people are generally less focused on trading. They also observed that the spread tended to narrow when the stock market was rising. Nonetheless, regardless of stock size, posting activities on the discussion day generally do not significantly affect the bid-ask spread over the next one or two trading days. For small stocks without news on discussion days, more message postings, higher sentiment, and greater disagreement among posters all contribute to a significantly narrower spread. The average message length does not significantly affect the bid-ask spread. Surprisingly, the impact of online discussions on the bid-ask spread fades over the following one to two days. For large stocks, online discussions appear to have no significant impact on the bid-ask spread, either contemporaneously or predictively.

Impact on Firm's Reputation

The literature review above shows that online discussions are not mere noise; rather, they contain valuable information that can influence various security trading metrics, including return, volatility, volume, and spread. Given this, it is worth considering whether online discussions can also affect a firm's reputation. A firm's reputation is an intangible asset and challenging to measure. Below are several research papers that address reputation issues related to FSM.

Wysocki (1999) suggests that message-posting activity is linked to a company's information environment. He argues that firms should view their financial social media as a "barometer of investors' demands for information." An abnormal surge in online discussions could indicate investor discontent and signal a need to fill the information gap. Wysocki (1999) further demonstrates that financial social media can enable a small group of individuals to disproportionately influence "public opinion" about a firm through online discussions. This was the first paper to suggest that individual opinions posted online can shape public perceptions of a firm's reputation.

Felton and Kim (2002) conducted an experiment to determine whether online discussions convey information about a firm's reputation and value. They examined the Yahoo! Finance message board for Enron, which collapsed in 2001, at a time when most Wall Street analysts were strongly optimistic about its common stock. By analyzing 129 posts from Enron's message board, they showed that the fall of Enron was not without warning online. Their findings suggest that companies and regulators should pay closer attention to anonymous employee postings on message boards, as online discussions can sometimes be early indicators of a firm's reputation before news is substantiated in the mass media.

Another issue affecting a firm's reputation is the potential for rumormongers to spread negative messages online in an attempt to defame a firm and drive down its stock price. Many of these individuals, often referred to as "bashers," are found to be short sellers (Wysocki 1999). A common tactic used by bashers is to spread negative rumors about a company on message boards while expressing strong pessimistic sentiments. It is believed that bashers often engage in this behavior after taking short positions.

Through an in-class experiment with 110 MBA students, Pleis (2009) concluded that only negative postings influence investors' decisions. Negative messages posted online may result from short sellers attempting to drive down stock prices or from individuals upset with the company. Consequently, negative online discussions can have an inverse impact on a firm's reputation and value, as they tend to influence investors toward selling.

In a study focused on corporate governance, Carson and Felton (2004) emphasized the importance of Internet message boards on corporate reputations. They explained how negative commentary on message boards and online stock manipulation, such as "pump and dump" schemes, can harm the value of target firms. Detractors may include unhappy employees, unions, dissatisfied customers, or angry shareholders.

Nevertheless, message boards are powerful platforms due to their transparency, allowing a single voice to reach large and diverse audiences. Carson and Felton (2004) pointed out that message boards can even help certain information go viral. Therefore, corporations should closely monitor what is being said about them online by anonymous posters, as a single rumor can quickly spread and significantly alter a firm's reputation.

Miscellaneous Issues on financial social media Research

In addition to the major topics discussed above, there are several ancillary considerations that warrant attention. These issues remain inconclusive and will require further research. Wysocki (1999) was the first to report that changes in overnight posting activity contain valuable information, noting that increases in overnight posting volume generally indicate a positive change in stock prices. Barber and Odean (2001) and Litan and Rivlin (2001) also demonstrate that Internet message boards are changing the way investors invest, trade, and acquire information. Since then, numerous studies have explored whether the information contained on message boards can explain and predict future stock trading.

Predictive Ability of Online Discussions

In the early stages of FSM research, many scholars argued that online discussions were merely noise with little predictive power. Bagnoli et al. (1999) were among the first to criticize the credibility of information on message boards, highlighting the presence of bias and unfounded rumors. Tumarkin and Whitelaw (2001) found that on days with abnormally high posting activity, changes in online investor sentiment were correlated with contemporaneous stock trading volume but did not predict future trading volume. Similar findings were reported by Tumarkin (2002). Although Das et al. (2005) observed that posting activity was associated with same-period stock returns, they found that sentiment among posters did not predict returns. Koski et al. (2004) suggested that while message board information increased stock return volatility, it did not fundamentally predict stock returns.

With the evolution of Internet technology and the exponential growth of Internet users, the effect of FSM has become more pronounced. Later studies have suggested that online discussions do matter and significantly influence not only contemporaneous but also future stock trading. This view is supported by researchers such as Clarkson et al. (2006), Sabherwal et al. (2011), Bettman et al. (2011), Oh and Sheng (2011), and Zhang et al. (2012). Given that the sample stocks in these studies vary, especially in terms of firm size, it is possible that the inconsistent results are due to differences in sample selection.

The Endogeneity Problem

In statistics, endogeneity occurs when there is a loop of causality between the independent and dependent variables in a model. The relationship between online discussions and stock trading activities is sometimes ambiguous. Several studies have found that causality may flow more from market trading activities to online discussions rather than the other way around. Tumarkin and Whitelaw (2001) and Tumarkin (2002) concluded that it is unclear whether message board activity causes abnormal stock returns or is merely a response to them. Das et al. (2005) reported that sentiment does not predict returns, concluding that returns drive sentiment. Koski et al. (2004) suggested that market volatility generates message board postings rather than postings producing volatility.

However, Wysocki (1999) proposed that messages posted on financial social media can influence public opinion about a firm. Antweiler and Frank (2004) also suggested that the causality for volatility may flow from message boards to the market. Gu et al. (2006) argued that informed posters on financial social media possess information not fully incorporated into market prices, thereby allowing message board sentiment to predict stock returns. Sabherwal et al. (2011) found that when there is no market news, online traders' sentiments cause positive contemporaneous returns and negatively predict the next day's returns. Clarkson et al. (2006) and Bettman et al. (2011) documented that online rumors cause significant abnormal returns and trading volumes. Bird and Thapa (2010) observed that unscheduled company news combined with contemporaneous message board activity causes positive return drifts, while high message board activity increases trading volatility. Oh and Sheng (2011) revealed that stock microblog sentiments have predictive power for both simple and market-adjusted stock returns.

Since these studies use different samples and statistical models, it is possible that the endogeneity problem arises from factors such as measurement error, autoregression with autocorrelated errors, simultaneity, or omitted variables. Further discussion on future research in this field is covered in the last chapter.

Note

1. Some researchers apply a post-event window to their Event studies. Cowan et al. (1990) suggest a post-event window to mitigate any bias induced by the pre-event price momentum.

CHAPTER 9

Trading Strategies Based on Financial Social Media Information

Introduction

In general, a trading strategy is a predetermined plan designed to achieve positive returns by taking long and/or short positions in markets. Such strategies may be based on the type of security, the trading horizon, budget constraints, and/or the purpose of the trade. Common trading strategies include, but are not limited to, mean reversion, short-term momentum, long-term trends, zero-cost arbitrage, event-driven approaches, and continuous high-frequency trading. Financial social media (FSM hereafter) platforms, as unique virtual venues where investors exchange opinions and comments, offer a wealth of information that can be leveraged to develop profitable trading strategies.

The influence of FSM discussions on securities trading is undeniable. As explored in previous chapters, variables such as message volume, sentiment, disagreement, and message length have measurable impacts on returns, volatility, trading volume, and bid-ask spreads. Consequently, numerous trading strategies can be developed based on the information available on FSM platforms.

Practitioners are increasingly utilizing FSM information to enhance their trading capabilities. As mentioned in Chapter 1, Derwent Capital Markets launched a hedge fund in 2012 with $40 million under management, employing a strategy based on signals derived from Twitter

Y. Zhang, *Financial Social Media*,
https://doi.org/10.1007/978-3-032-09332-5_9

(now X.com). In May 2013, Cayman Atlantic, an investment management firm, began using real-time social media data to identify profitable trading opportunities. Bloomberg introduced a feature in 2013 that delivers a stream of relevant Twitter messages to its clients, followed later that year by Reuters, which launched its investing tool LikeFolio.com to scan social media feeds for mentions of trending stocks.

Research also supports the value of social media in trading. Karabulut (2013) found that Facebook's Gross National Happiness (GNH) index could predict changes in both daily returns and trading volume in the U.S. equity market. Heimer and Simon (2012) provided empirical evidence of the spread of active foreign exchange trading strategies within a network of retail traders on a Facebook-style social networking website. Oh and Sheng (2011) demonstrated that sentiments extracted from stock microblogs on StockTwits.com have predictive power for both simple and market-adjusted stock returns. Additionally, several online services, such as PredictWallStreet.com, MarketWatch.com, SocialPicks.com, Stockpkr.com, and TheTradeXchange.com, have begun aggregating stock sentiments from social media channels and sharing this information with investors, brokerages, and other financial intermediaries.

Both practitioners and researchers clearly recognize the value of social media information for developing trading strategies and enhancing trading profits.

Pump-and-Dump Strategy

As mentioned earlier, the SEC alleged in September 2000 that a 15-year-old used an online FSM platform to manipulate stock prices and then unloaded his positions in a classic pump-and-dump operation. There have been several similar cases involving pump-and-dump schemes on FSM platforms. According to Jiang et al. (2005), a pump-and-dump strategy occurs when online traders post messages designed to improve their positions at the expense of other investors. Sabherwal et al. (2011) conclude that a typical pump-and-dump scheme involves an influencer with a high reputation, many followers (e.g., readers), and a long position in a target stock. This influential agent may either work alone or collaborate with other superior authors online, via email, or through text messages. The target stock is likely a small-cap stock with weak financials and low institutional ownership since such stocks are easier to manipulate (see Khwaja and Mian 2005; Aggarwal and Wu 2006). After establishing a long position, the influencer pumps the stock on the platform through messages with strong bullish tones.

Due to the poster's reputation and strong sentiment, followers are likely to herd and trade based on the influencer's opinions, driving the price upward. In this context, the influencer can be considered a well-informed trader, while the followers are less informed. Uninformed traders who are not subscribed to the platform, such as chartists and momentum traders, may also take positions as they observe the price movement. Within a day or two, the price may overshoot, allowing the influencer to reverse his or her long position and sell the stock before the herds do so. As a result, both the influencer and the followers profit at the expense of uninformed traders.

Theoretically, influencers could execute the opposite dump-and-pump strategy by using a short position followed by a buy-to-cover transaction. However, Odean (1999) shows that 99 percent of small investors take long positions and do not sell short due to high costs, short-sell limitations, and the high risk associated with short selling. Antweiler and Frank (2004) also document that current institutions make it much easier for small traders to hold long positions than short positions. Therefore, it is easier to attract more followers using long positions. For more details on the theoretical model of the pump-and-dump strategy, see Van Bommel (2003).

Empirically, Sabherwal et al. (2011) investigate online traders' pump-and-dump strategies by focusing on TheLion.com stock-trading board. They make two significant findings. First, they observe a significant positive abnormal return on the day a stock is heavily discussed by posters, as well as on the preceding day. There are also significant negative abnormal returns over the next two days. These abnormal returns suggest a two-day pump followed by a two-day dump pattern among online traders. However, there are no long-term economic effects, as the stock price reverts to the pre-pump level within a few days. Second, online traders prefer non-financial stocks with low prices, high trading volume, small float, and low price-to-book ratios. Due to sample selection, Sabherwal et al. (2011) focused on micro-capitalization stocks, and the above findings might not apply to large-cap stocks. In fact, Zhang et al. (2022) reported that online discussions do not significantly impact large-cap stocks, implying that FSM pump-and-dump strategies might only work on micro- to small-cap stocks with weak fundamentals.

It is important to note that I am not promoting the pump-and-dump strategy, which typically violates securities laws according to the SEC. Instead, understanding the mechanism of pump-and-dump schemes helps us identify and avoid them. After all, pump-and-dump is considered a "strategy" by certain traders who utilize FSM information to trade.

Contrarian Trading Strategy

Although online traders seldom take short positions (due to the short-sell restrictions discussed earlier), a significant price drop caused by profit-taking (or dump activity) offers contrarian traders an opportunity to make a profit. Sabherwal et al. (2011) suggested that the significant price drop during the dumping period signals potential opportunities for certain traders (e.g., arbitrageurs and contrarian traders) who are willing to take opposite positions in reaction to FSM activity. They also found that poster sentiment significantly and negatively predicts volatility over the next couple of days and significantly positively predicts small-trade volume on those days. They concluded that online sentiment is an important predictor of trading-related activities. For any investor who engages in volatility plays using options or volatility-tracking funds, the days immediately following a security being heavily discussed by online posters are golden opportunities to profit.

Zhang et al. (2012) further documented a negative correlation between poster sentiment and subsequent stock returns. In other words, there is a significant price reversion in the days following heavy discussion of a stock on an FSM platform. Consequently, they advised investors not to chase highly discussed and overly optimistic stocks on FSM platforms. However, their findings imply contrarian trading opportunities based on FSM information from previous days. In fact, because sentiment negatively predicts future returns, a long position trading opportunity exists for contrarian traders if the sentiment was bearish on the previous trading day.

Logically, a contrarian trading strategy is a natural counter to the pump-and-dump scheme. If a stock price surges solely due to online touts without any substantial market news, there is a strong likelihood that it will quickly revert to its previous level. In such cases, a contrarian trading strategy using a short position is warranted. Additionally, contrarian trading opportunities are implied by event study results in the literature. For example, Sabherwal et al. (2011) recorded that within about 30 days after a stock was "pumped" without market news, the price reverts back to its pre-event level. They concluded that online touts are short-lived due to the lack of fundamental news and have no long-term economic impacts on stock prices or a firm's value. Thus, a contrarian strategy might be effective for up to 30 trading days after a significant "pump" by online posters. According to Sabherwal et al. (2011) findings, a 15.33 percent average abnormal return can be realized using a contrarian strategy over the 30-day post-event period.

Long–Short Hedging Strategy

An important trading strategy based on FSM platforms was investigated by Gu et al. (2006). They challenged the notion that online discussions are merely noise, suggesting instead that there are informed posters on FSM platforms whose insights are not fully reflected in market prices. Based on this observation, they proposed that an implementable trading strategy could be developed to exploit the information available on these platforms. Specifically, they argued that a trading strategy utilizing investor sentiment can be formulated by analyzing the historical performance of online posters.

Although it is difficult to directly identify informed investors on a platform, they can be recognized by evaluating their historical performance and sentiment forecasting accuracy. Gu et al. (2006) introduced a method where a weight is assigned to each message based on the poster's historical forecasting accuracy. They then used a weighted-average approach to aggregate all sentiments related to a particular stock on a given day. Their empirical results revealed that the forecasting-accuracy-weighted average sentiment index has significant predictive power over future one-day, one-week, and even one-month subsequent stock returns.

Given these findings, Gu et al. (2006) suggested two implementable trading strategies. The first is a long-short, zero-cost strategy that involves taking long positions in stocks with positive aggregate sentiment while simultaneously shorting the market index. The second strategy is also a long-short, zero-cost approach, but it involves going long on the market index while shorting stocks with negative aggregate sentiment. According to their study, these combined strategies, using a weighted average of aggregated sentiment, yielded a 0.66 percent positive return over one week and a 2.10 percent positive return over one month.

Furthermore, the authors proposed a refined strategy by limiting the information aggregation to posters who have demonstrated forecasting ability beyond random guessing, using a threshold measure. This refined strategy produced even higher trading profits, with a 1.45 percent positive return for a one-week holding period and 4.03 percent for one month. These profits were both statistically and economically significant, even after accounting for transaction costs.

A related study by Liu et al. (2006) also explored a trading strategy based on frameworks developed from Yahoo! Finance platform information. Unlike other studies, they introduced a novel approach that focuses on identifying the most historically accurate posters and analyzing their sentiments in a completely automated fashion. They found that implementable strategies based on this extracted information could achieve statistically significant returns, even after adjusting for market effects and commission rates.

Event-Trading Strategy

Event trading involves buying or selling a security when news is released. This strategy is driven by market-moving events such as financial analyst reports, changes in the federal funds rate, reports of unexpected GDP growth, updates on the unemployment rate, and corporate earnings surprises. Traders can achieve significant profits if they understand and anticipate how other traders or the broader market will react to such news.

Although information from FSM platforms is not traditionally classified as "news," profitable event-trading strategies can be developed based on rumors, online discussions, posting activities, and poster sentiments. To determine whether event trading is feasible, one must first conduct an event study to assess how information from FSM platforms impacts security prices—in other words, how the market reacts to online discussions. Conventional event study methodology is presented in Chapter 8.

Using daily forum discussion data from TheLion.com during the 2005–2006 timeframe, Sabherwal et al. (2008) conducted an event study to estimate daily abnormal returns on stocks mentioned in discussions. They considered a stock's appearance on TheLion.com's list of the Top 10 most discussed stocks as the "news" event. Their empirical findings indicated that, on the day a stock becomes one of the Top 10 most discussed stocks, it experiences an average abnormal return of 19.35

percent. This is both statistically and economically significant, regardless of transaction costs. However, on each of the first four days after the discussion day, there is a significant negative abnormal return (–0.71 percent, –1.48 percent, –0.38 percent, and –0.08 percent, respectively), suggesting a market correction following the event-day spike. Additionally, the stock price drops by 11.35 percent over the 29 days following the initial discussion.

Given that an appearance on the Top 10 list, coupled with a price spike, qualifies as an event, a profitable event-trading strategy can be constructed based on the findings of Sabherwal et al. (2008). Specifically, stocks that appear on TheLion.com's Top 10 list and experience a significant price spike would be expected to have negative returns in the subsequent days. On average, an event-trading strategy involving short positions at the end of the event day would yield 2.56 percent abnormal returns over a four-day holding period. If new stocks appear on the Top 10 list each day, this strategy could be executed continuously, resulting in an annualized return of 399 percent, compounded daily over 252 trading days per year. Transaction costs are unlikely to negate such substantial returns.

It is important to note that the Top 10 lists analyzed by Sabherwal et al. (2008) included stocks influenced by market news. In other words, a stock's heavy discussion on platforms may have been triggered by market news on that day. When significant news is associated with a stock, market activity is likely to drive platform activity rather than the reverse. Since Sabherwal et al. (2008) did not control market news, their findings are confounded by the presence of stocks with related news.

To address this limitation, Sabherwal et al. (2011) conducted an event study focused specifically on online discussions that occurred without corresponding news in mainstream media. The adjusted sample revealed a smaller, but still statistically significant, 13.93 percent abnormal return on the event day. However, the subsequent four trading days saw larger, significant negative abnormal returns: –1.65 percent, –2.06 percent, –1.19 percent, and –0.46 percent, respectively. Thus, a refined event-trading strategy involving short positions on stocks at the end of the event day (t0), when no related news appears in mainstream media, would yield a 5.36 percent abnormal return over a four-day holding period on average. Again, this strategy can be executed continuously, potentially resulting in an astounding annualized return of 2762.77 percent, compounded daily over 252 trading days per year. Transaction costs are unlikely to erode such substantial profits.

Using a larger sample from TheLion.com, Zhang et al. (2022) further divided the event study samples into two groups based on large-cap and small-cap stocks without related news in mainstream media. The small-cap stocks experienced a significant 23.97 percent abnormal return on the event day, followed by four days of negative abnormal returns of –1.95 percent, –0.81 percent, –0.82 percent, and –0.05 percent, respectively. In contrast, large-cap stocks without market news showed no significant abnormal returns on any day. In summary, an event-trading strategy based on FSM discussions is both feasible and profitable. More importantly, event traders should focus on small-cap stocks and pay close attention to the absence of news during periods of heightened online discussion.

Momentum or Trend-Trading Strategy

In finance, a trend-trading strategy assumes that once a security's price begins moving in one direction, the trend will continue for some time. The goal for trend traders is to enter a trade near the start of the trend and exit shortly after it ends. Momentum trading strategies are similar to trend trading but focus more on the size and strength of the price movement, in addition to the direction. Momentum traders seek stocks that are moving significantly in one direction on high volume and aim to capitalize on this momentum to generate profit. They are typically short-term traders or day traders who require rapid execution to seize these opportunities. Momentum traders may hold their positions for a few minutes, several hours, or even throughout the entire trading day, depending on how quickly and strongly the stock moves and when it changes direction. Momentum trading is not suitable for mid- to long-term investors who hold positions for more than a day.

For example, one or more influential posters may strongly recommend (or tout) a particular stock with an explicit self-disclosed sentiment—Strong Buy. Without any market news other than online discussions, the stock may begin to surge, potentially far above its intrinsic value or the target price set by analysts. (It is worth noting that posters often tout stocks with weak fundamentals, low institutional holdings, and thin float.) The price rises significantly, largely because many momentum traders (off-platform traders and uninformed momentum traders) are trying to profit from the uptrend, driving the price even higher.

Inexperienced individual traders are advised not to adopt a momentum trading strategy based on online discussion information, as they could easily fall victim to a pump-and-dump scheme. Zhang et al. (2012) documented a negative correlation between poster sentiment and subsequent-day stock returns, warning investors not to follow highly discussed and overly optimistic stocks on a given day.

Here is what typically happens to inexperienced traders: An influx of strong sentiments from one or more posters causes the stock price to spike. Meanwhile, FSM platforms continue to receive more bullish opinions, with claims such as the stock will double or even triple in the near future. Initially, the inexperienced investor tries to exercise self-control and wait. However, as the stock price climbs higher, they can no longer resist and decide to buy in, hoping to make a profit. Shortly after, the stock begins to retrace, rapidly losing value. Frustrated and angry, the inexperienced investor sells the stock. Hours later, they notice that after the pullback, the stock rises again. Frustrated once more, they wonder how to ride the momentum train to secure a profit.

The reality is that when an online discussion breaks out, the targeted stock typically becomes very volatile. The stock price tends to swing significantly from the moment the discussion begins, with this volatility potentially lasting for several hours. During this time, momentum traders attempt to profit by making rapid trades based on the stock's fluctuating price. Even experienced traders need prompt and precise execution to seize these fleeting opportunities. The difference between a gain and a loss can come down to a matter of seconds. For experienced momentum traders, a delay of seconds to minutes is unacceptable.

In an intraday study using 15-minute intervals, Antweiler and Frank (2004, Appendix 2) reported a significant negative relationship between the number of messages and the number of words in a message during the first minute and stock returns 15 minutes later. In other words, the more online chatter about a stock within a given minute, the lower the stock price 15 minutes later. Using 24-hour intervals, they also found a significant negative relationship between the number of messages and the number of words in a message on day t and stock returns on the next day, t + 1. Interestingly, the relationship reversed itself two days later. From this empirical evidence, we learn that a stock's price can swing significantly under the influence of online discussions within a trading day and can change direction rapidly in a matter of minutes. On a longer interval basis, a stock's price also tends to reverse its direction each day. While a momentum trading strategy is executable, it requires sophisticated trading skills and caution due to the rapid alternation of price movements over short periods.

Continuous Trading Strategy Based on Financial Social Media Feeds

In 2013, several financial services firms, including Bloomberg, Reuters, PredictWallStreet, MarketWatch, SocialPicks, StockTwits, Stockpkr, and TheTradeXchange, began gathering stock sentiments from FSM platforms and offering trading signals to both institutional and retail traders. For example, TheTradeXchange charges users $29 per month to access aggregated social media feeds in real time. Researchers have demonstrated that such a strategy is both feasible and economically significant. With the exponential growth of online traders and FSM participants, the development of trading strategies based on these feeds has become a tangible and potentially lucrative opportunity.

In academic literature, Antweiler and Frank (2004) measured poster sentiment on Raging Bull and Yahoo! Finance using a naïve Bayesian text classifier and found that FSM platforms are highly informative. Their research revealed that poster bullishness sentiment is positively and significantly associated with both current and future stock returns, suggesting that a trading strategy can be formed based on poster sentiment over short (15-minute) or longer (24-hour) intervals.

Das and Chen (2007) analyzed data from Yahoo! Finance using statistical and natural language processing techniques to extract the emotive content of messages and classify posts as bearish, bullish, or neutral. They reported that the time-series and cross-sectional aggregation of message sentiment can enhance the quality of the sentiment index. Furthermore, they found that sentiment aggregated across stocks tracks the Morgan Stanley High-Tech Index (MSH) returns, indicating that a feasible MSH index fund trading strategy can be implemented based on aggregated FSM sentiments.

Clarkson et al. (2006) examined market reactions to online takeover rumors on the HotCopper Internet Discussion Site (IDS). Over both daily and intraday 10-minute intervals, they found consistent results showing that the posting of takeover rumors on IDS is highly correlated with abnormal stock returns and trading volume. Later, Bettman et al. (2011) studied FSM takeover rumors on Yahoo! Finance and found that these rumors generate significant positive abnormal returns and trading volumes. They concluded that online rumors present an economically exploitable trading opportunity for investors. Collectively, these findings suggest that continuous trading strategies based on online sentiments or rumors are viable and can be effectively developed.

FSM platforms serve as valuable venues for traders to gauge other traders' sentiments. Platforms like Yahoo! Finance, Raging Bull, The Motley Fool, Reddit, TheLion.com, and Silicon Investor are popular among online traders for sharing opinions. Institutional investors, such as hedge funds and investment banks, frequently engage in high-frequency trading (HFT), which is sometimes informed by extensive FSM information. Many high-frequency trading algorithms are programmed to execute trades within milliseconds based on trading signals such as aggregated and quantified sentiments. Numerous studies have already documented that FSM platforms convey valuable information to traders and that sentiments expressed on these platforms can explain, and more importantly, predict subsequent stock-trading activities. As a result, continuous trading strategies based on FSM feeds appear to be entirely feasible.

Volatility Play

Volatility is essentially the risk aspect of the market. Since 2009, market volatility has been securitized, allowing traders to directly buy and sell volatility-related securities. To understand this concept, we must first discuss the VIX, the Chicago Board Options Exchange (CBOE) Market Volatility Index. This "fear index" is a popular measure of the implied volatility of S&P 500 index options. Although it is not possible to invest directly in the CBOE VIX, there are various volatility-related tradable securities such as VXX, VXZ, VIXS, VIXY, and VIXM. These securities are based on the VIX and enable traders to speculate on future market volatility. Traders buy and sell these securities as their perceptions of future market risk change. When they anticipate a significant increase in market volatility, they invest in these volatility-related instruments. Additionally, VIX futures contracts and exchange-listed VIX options are available for trading.

Although there is limited documentation on volatility plays based on FSM information, this topic deserves attention in this book. In Chapter 8, we explored how FSM activities influence current and future return volatility. For example, Antweiler and Frank (2004) found that the number of messages on a FSM platform helps predict realized volatility, and that day trading activity correlates with volatility. Koski et al. (2004) observed that FSM information increases current stock return volatility, with causality running from platform posting activity to stock trading. Sabherwal et al. (2008) found that absolute sentiment among posters is negatively related to contemporaneous and the next two days' intraday volatility. Bird and Thapa (2010) reported that when unscheduled company news coincides with high online posting activity, trading volatility increases. Thapa (2013) further provided evidence that FSM activity increases short-term volatility and that the number of unique participants in online discussions is positively related to changes in volatility. Lastly, Zhang et al. (2022) found that for large stocks with corresponding news in the media, sentiment, and message volume have significant and positive explanatory power on current and future volume-weighted volatility. For small stocks with media coverage, poster sentiment has an even stronger and more significant positive impact on volatility. Without market news, they concluded that higher sentiment leads to more contemporaneous and future volatility, regardless of firm size and news arrival. In summary, FSM information significantly impacts both contemporaneous and future stock return volatility.

For example, if the number of messages or sentiment on a FSM platform positively predicts market volatility the following day, a trading strategy can be devised based on the market-wide aggregate level of FSM information and using volatility-related securities. A high level of posting activity would imply higher market volatility the next day, so a long position on VXX today could yield positive returns tomorrow. Similar logic can be applied to correlating the aggregate level of sentiment or disagreement with VIX-related securities. Although this has not been extensively studied on an individual stock level, a possible trading strategy is attainable if the stock has option trading available. If a trader anticipates future volatility of a stock based on FSM information, they could take advantage of a straddle position in options to capture trading gains. For example, an investor might take a long straddle position if they expect the security to be highly volatile but are uncertain about the direction of its price movement. Conversely, a short straddle, a riskier non directional options trading strategy, can also be employed when future volatility is predictable.

Trading Strategies Based on Other Financial Social Media

Message boards were the original FSM for online investors. These online bulletin boards provided a space for traders to discuss and debate various stock-related topics, and they remain important building blocks of today's FSM landscape. However, with the rise of other social media platforms, the question arises: Can these other forms of social media also be used to construct trading strategies? Several studies have examined trading strategies based on various social media sources, including blogs, YouTube videos, and Google's Search Volume Index (SVI). Many of these strategies have been shown to be executable and profitable. Below, I discuss several important papers that have successfully tested trading strategies based on information from these alternative social media sources.

Zhang and Skiena (2010) conducted a comprehensive study on how a company's reported media exposure (i.e., blog and news frequency) and sentiment anticipate or reflect stock returns and trading volumes. They concluded that media data is highly informative and proposed a market-neutral stock-trading strategy based entirely on sentiment data from published blog or news sources. Specifically, their strategy ranks companies by their reported sentiment each day and involves taking long positions in stocks with positive sentiment and short positions in stocks with negative sentiment. They found that this strategy consistently provides favorable returns with low uncertainty, before accounting for transaction costs and timing issues.

Da et al. (2011) introduced a novel measure of investor attention using search frequency data from Google's SVI. They demonstrated that SVI effectively captures the attention of retail investors and found that an increase in SVI predicts higher stock prices over the next two weeks, followed by a price reversal within the year. Although they did not explicitly test a trading strategy based on SVI, the predictive ability of SVI suggests its application in trading. For example, a long-short, zero-cost strategy could be employed with either a two-week or one-year holding period. Specifically, one could go long on stocks with high SVI change and short stocks with low SVI change, holding these positions for two weeks. For a longer-term strategy, one could reverse this approach after two weeks, shorting stocks with originally high SVI change and going long on those with low SVI change, holding the positions for the remainder of the year. Both strategies can be executed continuously.

Karabulut (2013) utilized Facebook's Gross National Happiness (GNH) index as a novel and direct measure of investor sentiment. Using vector autoregressive models, Karabulut examined the relationship between GNH and daily stock market activity, finding that GNH can predict statistically significant and economically meaningful changes in aggregate market returns. Specifically, a one-standard deviation increase in GNH predicts a 0.1286 percent increase in market returns the following day. However, like Da et al. (2011), Karabulut found that the influence of GNH on market returns is temporary and reversed during the following trading week. Accordingly, two continuous trading strategies are available. First, a long (short) position in U.S. market index funds can be taken when GNH is higher (lower) on day t0, with the position held until the end of the next trading day (t + 1). Second, a reverse trade at the end of day t + 1 can further boost gains by shorting the previous long position and going long on the previous short position, holding this new position for one week. Both strategies can be executed continuously.

Bollen et al. (2010) investigated whether sentiment derived from large-scale Twitter feeds is correlated with or predictive of the Dow Jones Industrial Average (DJIA) over time. Their results indicate that Twitter mood can predict the stock market three to four trading days in advance, with an accuracy of 87.6 percent in predicting daily up and down movements in the DJIA. They concluded that incorporating public mood states from Twitter into trading strategies could yield significant profits. For instance, a long position in a DJIA exchange-traded fund (ETF) could result in significant profits three to four trading days later if Twitter sentiment is positive.

A related study by Rao and Srivastava (2012) found a high positive correlation between stock prices and Twitter sentiment, showing that Twitter discussions greatly impact short-term stock price movements. Later, Sprenger et al. (2014) found that Twitter contains valuable information not yet fully reflected in market indicators. They reported that increased bullishness on Twitter can serve as a proxy for positive investor sentiment, which is associated with rising stock prices. Additionally, the volume of tweets about a stock predicts its next-day trading volume. In summary, tweets affect both current and future stock-trading activities, indicating that trading strategies based on Twitter feeds hold significant potential.

CHAPTER 10

Legal Issues Associated with Financial Social Media Posting

Introduction

It is crucial to understand that there is no such thing as "absolute privacy" on the Internet. When posting online, you are not fully anonymous; it doesn't take much effort for a web operator to trace the source of messages and identify your IP address and other digital footprints. However, web operators are not typically obligated to share that information, so in most cases, your identity remains concealed, and your "online speech" is protected by the First Amendment. This protection generally means that others do not have the right to uncover the identities of anonymous posters.

However, in cases involving illegal activities, web operators often cooperate with the legal system and may disclose personal information of users to law enforcement. Regulatory bodies like the SEC and other law enforcement agencies regularly monitor financial social media (FSM hereafter) platforms. Securities laws prohibit the posting of messages intended to manipulate stock prices. The SEC, through legal actions, can obtain the identities of anonymous posters and, with sufficient evidence, can charge them with fraud for stock manipulation.

Since the SEC's first Internet Securities Fraud Sweep in 1998, numerous lawsuits have been filed against FSM posters. In this chapter, I will highlight several well-known examples and discuss the issues

Y. Zhang, *Financial Social Media*,
https://doi.org/10.1007/978-3-032-09332-5_10

surrounding free speech, anonymity in cyberspace, and the vital role the SEC plays in preventing online securities fraud.

Ten Famous Lawsuits Related to Financial Social Media Posting

Online securities fraud involves manipulating the price of a security by disseminating false information and subsequently trading the security to make a profit. This practice is illegal under both federal and state laws. Regulators such as the SEC and FTC closely monitor FSM platforms to prevent investment scams and protect investor interests.

Here are ten notable cases related to FSM securities fraud:

- Case 1: SEC v. Jonathan G. Lebed[1]

In the late 1990s, 15-year-old Jonathan G. Lebed from northern New Jersey executed a successful pump-and-dump scheme using the Internet. Lebed purchased large quantities of low-priced penny stocks and then hyped them on FSM platforms under false names. As stock prices rose due to increased buying from his "followers," Lebed sold his shares for a profit, leaving other investors to incur losses. The SEC took notice and filed a civil suit against him in September 2000 for securities manipulation. Lebed settled by paying a fraction of his gains without admitting wrongdoing.

- Case 2: FTC v. Whole Foods[2]

John Mackey, CEO of Whole Foods Market, used the alias "rahodeb" on the Yahoo! Finance discussion board, an anagram of his wife's name Deborah, to post anonymous criticisms of Wild Oats Markets. He predicted the company's bankruptcy and questioned the stock's value. Shortly after, Whole Foods announced its acquisition of Wild Oats in February 2007 for about $565 million, or $18.50 per share. The FTC challenged the acquisition, alleging Mr. Mackey used anonymous posts to lower Wild Oats' price for a cheaper acquisition. After an extensive legal battle, a federal appeals court approved the deal. Whole Foods amended its code of conduct to prohibit senior executives from posting about the company on unsanctioned forums.

- Case 3: SEC v. Yun Soo Oh Park[3]

Yun Soo Oh Park, also known as "Tokyo Joe," was an Internet stock-trading "guru" who ran a stock-tipping website and private chat room. Claiming to be a "financial advisor," he charged subscribers a monthly fee. In August 1999, Park hyped Information Management Associates (IMA) in his chat room, predicting it would rise to $14. The stock briefly reached that level but later declined significantly. Park made substantial illegal profits from this manipulation. The SEC fined him in March 2001 for front-running his picks and required him to forfeit over $400,000 in illegal gains and pay a penalty, along with agreeing to an antifraud injunction

- Case 4: Clifton G. Swiger v. Allegheny Energy, Inc. and Others[4]

In 2003, Allegheny Energy, Inc. discovered a damaging anonymous post about the company on Yahoo! Finance, believed to be by an employee. The company filed a "John Doe" lawsuit for "breach of duty of loyalty" and sought an emergency motion to stop further postings.[5] They subpoenaed Yahoo! to identify the poster, revealing Clifton G. Swiger, an engineering technician. Allegheny dropped the lawsuit after learning his identity, but Swiger was later fired for violating company policies. Swiger sued Allegheny in 2008 on various claims, including abuse of process and wrongful discharge.

- Case 5: SEC v. Christopher P. Hastings[6]

In 2000, the SEC charged Christopher P. Hastings, using the screen name "Stockpicks1," for promoting stocks through an email newsletter, his website, and FSM platforms. Hastings falsely inflated his track record, claiming a 410 percent increase in stock values after his recommendations. He sold his personal holdings at inflated prices, netting approximately $70,309 in profits. Hastings, a school bus mechanic with no securities industry experience, agreed to disgorge $70,309 plus interest, with a reduced penalty due to his inability to pay

- Case 6: SEC v. George Charles Pappas[7]

In 2000, the SEC charged George Charles Pappas and his companies—Wellness Universe Corporation and Synpan Corporation—with issuing misleading press releases to manipulate stocks. Between mid-December 1999 and early February 2000, Pappas caused his companies to issue false press releases to inflate stock prices, allowing him to sell shares at these inflated prices. The SEC ordered Pappas to disgorge $1,128,572.24 in ill-gotten gains, pay a $75,000 civil penalty, and imposed bars on his participation in future securities offerings.

- Case 7: SEC v. Aziz Golshani and Others[8]

On December 15, 1999, the SEC alleged that Aziz Golshani, along with Melamed and Derzakharian, manipulated the market for NEI Webworld, Inc. by creating false demand through deceptive Internet messages. The stock price soared from under a dollar to $15.50, enabling them to make a nearly $350,000 profit. The SEC obtained preliminary orders to freeze their assets and restrain further violations. Later, the SEC amended its complaint to include additional manipulations, leading to further charges against Golshani and Melamed.

- Case 8: SEC v. Jason A. Greig and Liberty Capital Group, Inc.[9]

In 1998, the SEC alleged that Jason A. Greig and Liberty Capital Group, Inc. distributed information on micro-cap companies without disclosing compensation received from those companies. From April 1996 to April 1998, Greig and Liberty published information on around 20 companies, receiving nearly $1.2 million in cash and stock. The SEC alleged that they failed to disclose the existence of compensation agreements.

- Case 9: SEC v. David A. Wood, Jr. and ICS Communications, Inc.[10]

Since April 1997, David A. Wood, Jr. and ICS Communications, Inc. managed an investor relations program for a company under consulting agreements. Wood published messages on the SiliconInvestor (www.siliconinvestor.com) platform and paid others to promote the company, receiving $10,000 and at least 610,000 shares of stock. He did not disclose this compensation in his messages. Wood also set up a company website, ran advertisements, and sent promotional emails without adequate disclosure of compensation.

- Case 10: SEC v. Eugene B. Martineau[11]

From December 1996 to May 1997, Eugene B. Martineau made over 60 postings on SiliconInvestor regarding a company traded on the over-the-counter Bulletin Board. Martineau praised the company's stock without disclosing that he held a 24-month option to buy 5000 shares at $1.50 per share. As the stock price rose to $9 per share, Martineau's promotion led to significant personal gains. The SEC charged him for failing to reveal his financial interest in the stock.

These cases illustrate the legal risks associated with FSM postings and highlight the importance of regulatory oversight in preventing and addressing online securities fraud.

Freedom of Speech, Securities Fraud, and Anonymity in Cyberspace

In the United States, freedom of speech is protected by the First Amendment, as well as state and federal laws. The U.S. Supreme Court extends these constitutional protections to materials published on the Internet, equating them with traditional media such as books, magazines, films, and spoken expression. An individual's decision to remain anonymous is considered "an aspect of the freedom of speech protected by the First Amendment," meaning that online speech is afforded the same protections as offline speech.

However, freedom of speech is not without limitations. The Supreme Court has recognized several categories of speech that are excluded from protection and has allowed governments to impose reasonable restrictions on the time, place, or manner of speech. Among these exceptions is online securities fraud. Securities fraud involves deceptive practices that mislead investors, resulting in financial losses and violations of securities laws. According to the SEC, online securities fraud manifests in several ways:

- Online Investment Newsletters: These newsletters offer seemingly unbiased information about companies for free. The authors of these newsletters may then sell shares they previously acquired at lower prices when hype-driven buying inflates the stock price. This practice, known as scalping, may not be adequately addressed by conflict-of-interest disclosures included in the newsletter.
- Financial Social Media Platform: Fraudulent messages posted on FSM platforms can manipulate stock prices by spreading false information, often as part of a pump-and-dump scheme. Another related scheme is short selling, where fraudsters disseminate misleading information to cause a stock price to drop, then buy the stock at the lower price and wait for the stock to recover before selling it for a profit.
- Email Spam: Fraudulent schemes can also be conducted through spam emails. These can include pump-and-dump or scalping schemes, like those seen on FSM platforms.
- Phishing: This involves acquiring sensitive information (such as usernames, passwords, credit card information, and ultimately money) by pretending to be a trustworthy entity in electronic communications.

Regarding online libel or defamation, an individual targeted by anonymous attacks often files a lawsuit against a "John Doe" defendant, seeking to uncover the anonymous person's identity. This process typically involves subpoenaing the Internet service provider or website operator. Courts, however, frequently dismiss such lawsuits or refuse to unmask the anonymous critic. Additionally, a California law, which took effect on January 1, 2009, allows anonymous Internet speakers whose identities are sought by a subpoena in California, based on a lawsuit filed in another state, to challenge the subpoena and recover attorney fees if they are successful.

In cases involving FSM, anonymous posts may merely reflect the opinions of investors or potential investors about a company or its management. These cases are challenging to prosecute because messages in FSM platforms are often framed as opinions, which are protected by the First Amendment. It is also unlikely that laws will be enacted to compel anonymous posters or web operators to disclose identities, as such requirements have been deemed unconstitutional by the Supreme Court.

When online securities fraud is evident and harmful to investors, the SEC acts. The SEC typically brings civil actions against individuals for violating securities laws. During investigations, the SEC may subpoena web operators and/or Internet service providers to obtain and reveal the identities of the fraudulent posters. In most cases, these entities cooperate with the SEC's requests.[12] The SEC works closely with law enforcement agencies to ensure that fraudsters are brought to justice.

Thus, while U.S. law does not specifically guarantee the right to anonymity, this right is generally protected under the First Amendment.

The Role of the SEC in Monitoring Online Securities Fraud

The Securities and Exchange Commission (SEC) serves as a key regulator in the financial markets, with a mission to protect investors, ensure fair, orderly, and efficient markets, and facilitate capital formation. To achieve these goals, the SEC requires public companies to disclose "meaningful financial and other information to the public," enabling investors to make informed decisions about buying, selling, or holding securities.

In addition to overseeing public companies, the SEC regulates participants in the securities industry, including brokers, dealers, financial advisers, and mutual funds. The SEC has the authority to bring civil suits against individuals or companies that violate securities laws. Its responsibilities include interpreting federal securities laws, issuing new rules, amending existing ones, overseeing inspections of securities firms, brokers, investment advisers, and ratings agencies, maintaining private regulatory organizations in securities, accounting, and auditing, and coordinating U.S. securities regulation with federal, state, and international authorities.[13]

The SEC's functions are organized into five divisions and 23 offices, all headquartered in Washington, D.C. These divisions are:

- Division of Corporation Finance: Assists in overseeing corporate disclosure of significant information to the investing public.
- Division of Trading and Markets: Ensures the maintenance of fair, orderly, and efficient markets.

- Division of Investment Management: Focuses on investor protection and capital formation through regulation of the $128 trillion (as of 2024) investment management industry.
- Division of Economic and Risk Analysis: Integrates economic analysis and data analytics into the SEC's work to protect investors and maintain market efficiency.
- Division of Enforcement: Responsible for recommending and prosecuting investigations into securities law violations. This division works closely with other law enforcement agencies, including the FBI, both domestically and internationally.

In monitoring securities fraud, the Division of Enforcement gathers evidence from various sources, such as market surveillance activities, investor tips, complaints, self-regulatory organizations, and media reports. Investigations are conducted privately, with the SEC staff interviewing witnesses, examining brokerage records, reviewing trading data, and using other investigative methods. With a formal order of investigation, the staff can subpoena witnesses to testify and produce documents. The findings are then presented to the commission, which decides whether to file a case or bring an administrative action. Many cases are settled without going to trial.

Common violations that may trigger SEC investigations include:

- Misrepresentation or omission of significant information about securities.
- Market manipulation.
- Theft of customer funds or securities.
- Breach of the broker-dealer's duty to treat customers fairly.
- Insider trading (trading on material, nonpublic information).
- Selling unregistered securities.

The SEC defines Internet securities fraud as involving pump-and-dump schemes where false or fraudulent information is spread through chat rooms, forums, message boards, or email to manipulate the price of thinly traded stocks or shell company stocks. Once the price increases, the fraudsters sell their holdings for substantial profits before the stock price falls back to its normal level, leaving unsuspecting buyers to incur losses.

While the First Amendment protects the right to express opinions about stocks and companies on FSM platforms, it does not shield those who intentionally disseminate false or fraudulent information for financial gain. Such activities violate securities laws and are subject to SEC investigation.

Use of Disclosure and/or Disclaimer

In legal terms, a disclaimer is a statement that denies responsibility, aiming to prevent civil liability arising from specific actions or omissions. When encountering stock recommendations and picks on FSM platforms, it's common to see disclaimers like the one I use with my account "yingzhang" on TheLion.com[14]:

Disclaimer: I posted this message for your casual reading only. The message(s) above are neither investment advice nor suggestions to buy or sell any securities at any time. The accuracy, completeness, or timeliness of the information posted here is not guaranteed by me. There may be delays, omissions, or inaccuracies in the information. The message postings here are 100% free and intended solely for casual and entertaining reading. I am not a registered investment advisor in any capacity; please do not request investment advice from me. By the time you read this post, I may have already bought any of the securities mentioned above before posting. I may also sell all the mentioned securities within minutes or retain some for day trading and/or short-term investing. The decision to buy or sell any security listed above is made purely at your own risk. Please consult a licensed broker before trading. You are 100% responsible for your own trades and actions. Please conduct your own research before trading.

The primary goal of using a disclaimer and/or disclosure is to protect against potential legal action from entities like the SEC and FTC. However, the effectiveness of a disclaimer in achieving this protection is debatable. Can a disclaimer truly shield someone from liability if they disseminate false or fraudulent information about a stock on an FSM platform? Clearly, it cannot. Securities fraud would flourish if one paragraph of disclaimer could ward off any securities fraud charge.

The SEC has clarified that a mere disclaimer is insufficient for shielding issuers from responsibility for information provided to investors, whether through hyperlinks or otherwise. As stated in their interpretation on the use of electronic media:

> We do not view a disclaimer alone as sufficient to insulate an issuer from responsibility for information that it makes available to investors whether through a hyperlink or otherwise. To conclude otherwise would permit unscrupulous issuers to make false or misleading statements available to investors without fear of liability as long as the information is accompanied by a disclaimer.[15]

Some posters use disclaimers while claiming to be stock gurus, star traders, financial advisors, or winners of stock-picking contests. Others may highlight that their recommendations are based on thorough research or proprietary models. The SEC warns that FSM platforms are frequently used by fraudsters who excessively promote certain firms, sometimes by pretending to offer "insider" information. Posters who claim to be unbiased investors may be hired promoters, and those asserting thorough research may be stock manipulators without genuine analysis. Investors must exercise extreme caution when considering investment advice from others, particularly from FSM platforms.

How to Spot Financial Social Media Manipulators

FSM platforms are filled with diverse content, including stock recommendations, corporate news, and personal opinions. While some information can be valuable, distinguishing reliable sources from those meant to deceive can be challenging. Stock manipulators are prevalent on nearly all FSM platforms, particularly penny stock forums, where they exploit the ease of pumping and dumping thinly traded stocks.

Identifying stock manipulators is essential for online traders. The anonymity of the Internet should prompt skepticism about the information shared, especially from unfamiliar or newly created aliases. If information originates from an anonymous and unknown poster, it warrants caution. Conduct thorough research and due diligence before making trading decisions.

Here are several ways to recognize FSM manipulators:

- Anonymous Posting: Manipulators often post anonymously. If you notice multiple posts about the same stock with similar tones and timings but from different posters, it is likely that manipulators are using multiple accounts to create a pump-and-dump scenario.
- Excessive Optimism: Manipulators tend to exhibit overly bullish sentiments and make unrealistic stock price predictions. Comparing

their predictions with those of established financial analysts can reveal their excessive optimism.

- Strong Sentiments: Manipulators frequently use emphatic language, such as "Strong Buy" during a pump phase and "Strong Sell" or "Short" when they are selling short. They rarely use moderate or nuanced tones.
- Repetitive Messaging: Manipulators often post the same inflammatory language across multiple platforms. This repetition indicates their desperation to influence the stock's price.
- Lack of Concrete Data: Manipulators typically fail to support their recommendations with verifiable numbers. When they do provide figures, they should be cross-checked with reliable sources to ensure they are not fabricated. Manipulators often disparage those who disagree with their predictions.
- Inconsistent Engagement: Manipulators often promote a stock aggressively while its price is rising but will cease discussions once they have sold their shares. They may re-engage only if they seek to manipulate the stock again in the future.

Although there is no foolproof method for identifying manipulators due to the inherent anonymity of the Internet, recognizing these patterns can significantly improve your ability to spot them. With experience, you can develop an intuitive sense for distinguishing between genuine and manipulative posters on the Internet.

How to Avoid Financial Social Media Scams

While much of the information on FSM platforms is useful and beneficial to investors and the public, some messages are misleading or even fraudulent. Many popular platforms contain deceptive posts from unscrupulous individuals who aim to manipulate stock prices for personal gain through pump-and-dump schemes. These fraudsters often claim to reveal insider information about a company, announce new products, or disclose lucrative contracts. A single poster can create the illusion of widespread interest in a small, thinly traded stock by posting multiple messages under different aliases. These individuals frequently claim in disclaimers that they have conducted due diligence before sharing information, making it difficult for others to verify their credibility, especially since most FSM platforms allow users to remain anonymous.

To avoid falling victim to such scams, it is crucial to approach information on FSM platforms with caution and skepticism. Never make an investment decision based solely on what you read, particularly if the recommendation involves a small, thinly traded company that you are unfamiliar with. Before acting on any small stocks, thoroughly investigate the company and verify all information. Conduct additional research and review all available accounting statements and SEC filings.

Richard H. Walker, former SEC Director of Enforcement, once highlighted the dangers of online fraud, stating:

What used to require a network of professional promoters and brokers, banks of telephones, and months to accomplish can now be done in minutes by a single person using the Internet and a home computer. Thinly traded microcap stocks are particularly susceptible to online manipulations. That is why the SEC has made this area one of our highest enforcement priorities. Ultimately, however, the best way for investors to protect themselves against all forms of Internet fraud, including pump-and-dump schemes, is to do their homework and to be highly skeptical of information they receive from strangers on Internet websites, message boards, and chat rooms.[16]

Many people believe that the performance of penny stocks is driven primarily by speculation. These stocks often lack liquidity, making them prime targets for fraudulent investors to manipulate prices. The SEC itself, in Schedule 15G, warns: *Investors in penny stocks should be prepared for the possibility that they may lose their entire investment.*[17] Fraudsters frequently implement pump-and-dump schemes with small, thinly traded companies online because it is easier to manipulate a stock when little or no information is available about the company.

The SEC provides the following advice to investors to help avoid potential online scams:

- Consider the Source: When you encounter an offer on the Internet, assume it is a scam until you can prove its legitimacy through your own research. Remember, those touting the stock may be insiders of the company or paid promoters who stand to profit if you trade.
- Find Out Where the Stock Trades: Many of the smallest and most thinly traded stocks cannot meet the listing requirements of NASDAQ or a national exchange like the New York Stock Exchange. Instead, they trade in the "over-the-counter" market and are quoted via OTC systems such as the OTC Bulletin Board or Pink Sheets.

Stocks traded in the OTC market are generally the most risky and susceptible to manipulation.

- Independently Verify Claims: It is easy for a company or its promoters to make grandiose claims about new product developments, lucrative contracts, or the company's financial health. Before investing, ensure that you have independently verified these claims.
- Research the Opportunity: Always request and carefully read the prospectus or current financial statements. Check the SEC's EDGAR database to see if the investment is registered. Some smaller companies may not have to register their offerings with the SEC, so always check with your state securities regulator as well.
- Watch Out for High-Pressure Pitches: Beware of promoters who pressure you to buy before you have time to think about and fully investigate the so-called opportunity. Do not fall for the claim that you will lose out on a "once-in-a-lifetime" chance to make big money if you do not act quickly.
- Always Be Skeptical: Whenever someone you do not know offers you a hot stock tip, ask yourself: Why me? Why is this stranger giving me this tip? How might they benefit if I trade?

The FBI also provides valuable tips to protect yourself from Internet investment fraud:

- Do Not Judge a Person or Company by Their Website: Flashy websites can be set up quickly.
- Do Not Invest in Anything You Are Not Absolutely Certain About: Research the investment and company to ensure they are legitimate.
- Check Out Other Websites Regarding This Person or Company.
- Be Cautious When Responding to Special Investment Offers, especially those received through unsolicited emails.
- Be Wary of Dealing with Individuals or Companies from Outside Your Country.
- Inquire About All Terms and Conditions.

Finally, I must emphasize the importance of being skeptical about stock tips shared on FSM platforms. As Nancy M. Smith, Director of the SEC's Office of Investor Education and Assistance, advised: "Never, ever, make an investment based solely on what you read in an online newsletter or Internet bulletin board, especially if the investment involves a small, thinly traded company that isn't well known. Assume that the information about these companies is not trustworthy unless you can prove otherwise through your own independent research."

How to Report Securities Fraud

Reporting securities fraud to the SEC is a straightforward process. Simply visit the SEC's website and submit a complaint through their online form.[18]

The Dodd-Frank Wall Street Reform and Consumer Protection Act, enacted on July 21, 2010, authorizes the SEC to provide financial rewards to eligible whistleblowers. If your information leads to an SEC action resulting in monetary sanctions exceeding $1,000,000, you may qualify for a monetary award.

If you prefer to remain anonymous but still wish to be considered for a reward, you must be represented by an attorney and provide their contact information. For more details on this program, including how to submit a tip and the requirements for anonymity, visit the SEC's whistleblower web page.[19]

Notes

1. www.sec.gov/news/press/2000–135.txt
2. www.ftc.gov/opa/2007/06/wholefoods.shtm
3. http://www.sec.gov/news/headlines/tokyojoe2.htm
4. http://www.gpo.gov/fdsys/pkg/USCOURTS-paed-2_05-cv-05725/content-detail.html
5. "John Doe" is used as a placeholder name for a party whose identity is unknown or must be withheld in a legal action, case, or discussion.
6. http://www.sec.gov/litigation/litreleases/lr16684.htm
7. http://www.sec.gov/litigation/litreleases/lr16439.htm
8. http://www.sec.gov/litigation/litreleases/lr16620.htm
9. http://www.sec.gov/litigation/litreleases/lr15953.txt
10. sec.gov/files/litigation/admin/3-9768.txt
11. http://www.sec.gov/litigation/admin/33-7885.htm

12. For example, Yahoo collects personal information when you register. Yahoo also automatically receives and records information from your computer and browser, including your IP address, Yahoo cookie data, software and hardware details, and the pages you request.
13. For more detailed information about the SEC, visit http://www.sec.gov.
14. http://www.thelion.com/bin/forum.cgi?tf=yingzhangtradingboard&msg=11&cmd=r&t=
15. http://www.sec.gov/rules/interp/34-42728.htm
16. https://www.sec.gov/news/press/2000-124.txt
17. http://www.sec.gov/divisions/marketreg/bdguide.htm
18. https://www.sec.gov/submit-tip-or-complaint
19. http://www.sec.gov/about/offices/owb/reg-21f.pdf

CHAPTER 11

Whisperers Versus Analysts and Implications for Market Efficiency

Market Efficiency

Before comparing stock opinions on financial social media (FSM hereafter) with financial analyst recommendations, it's essential to understand the concept of market efficiency and how these different sources of information impact the Efficient Market Hypothesis (EMH). Financial markets are generally believed to efficiently reflect available information in security prices. According to Fama (1970), if a market is efficient, information spreads very quickly, if not instantly, and is incorporated into security prices without delay. Consequently, neither technical analysis (the study of past stock price patterns to predict future prices) nor fundamental analysis (the study of financial information to identify mispriced stocks) would enable an investor to achieve abnormal returns greater than those obtained from holding a randomly selected, well-diversified portfolio of securities, *ceteris paribus*.

In essence, an "efficient market" implies that it is impossible for an investor to outperform a well-diversified market portfolio because all available information is already reflected in stock prices. Investors who subscribe to this view typically adopt passive investment strategies, holding index funds that track overall market performance. Conversely, those who reject this view tend to pursue an active investment strategy, seeking to identify and hold mispriced securities to surpass the market portfolio returns.

Y. Zhang, *Financial Social Media*,
https://doi.org/10.1007/978-3-032-09332-5_11

Market efficiency refers to the extent to which stock prices reflect all available and relevant information. But how efficient are the U.S. financial markets in practice? Investors and academics have diverse views on the efficiency of U.S. stock markets, which is reflected in the weak, semi-strong, and strong-forms of the Efficient Market Hypothesis (EMH):

- Weak-Form of EMH: This form assumes that current prices reflect all information contained in past prices, suggesting that charts and technical analysis based solely on past prices would not be useful in identifying mispriced (i.e., overvalued or undervalued) stocks. Share prices exhibit no serial dependencies, meaning that asset prices follow no predictable patterns. Therefore, future price movements are determined entirely by information not contained in the current price series, implying that prices follow a random walk. The weak-form of EMH asserts that superior returns (i.e., higher than the market portfolio) cannot be achieved using technical analysis.
- Semi-Strong Form of EMH: This form assumes that current prices reflect not only past prices but also all public information, including financial statements and news reports. As a result, public information is rapidly incorporated into prices and investors cannot consistently outperform the market using publicly available information. Only private information may allow investors to earn abnormal returns. The semi-strong form of EMH incorporates the weak-form and concludes that superior returns cannot be achieved using either technical or fundamental analysis based on known information.
- Strong-Form of EMH: This form assumes that current prices reflect all information, both public and private, and that no investor can consistently identify mispriced stocks. The strong-form of EMH incorporates the semi-strong and weak-forms and implies a perfect market, concluding that abnormal returns are impossible to achieve consistently, regardless of the method used. In the U.S. financial markets, strong-form efficiency is unlikely in practice because insiders possess private information that is not immediately reflected in market prices. However, if insiders were to disseminate private information through FSM platforms, it could challenge the assumptions underlying the strong-form of EMH (Carson and Felton, 2004).

The theoretical framework of EMH has motivated a large body of empirical research designed to test whether financial markets behave consistently with its predictions. Next, we discuss conventional empirical tests for the EMH in the context of the U.S. financial markets:

- Tests of the Weak-Form of EMH: Common empirical tests include autocorrelation tests (where returns are not significantly correlated over time) and runs tests (where stock price changes are independent over time). Researchers also investigate whether there are any long-lasting patterns in security prices based on historical data that could lead to significant abnormal returns.
- Tests of the Semi-Strong Form of EMH: The primary empirical test is an event study, as discussed in previous chapters. An event study analyzes security prices before and after an event (e.g., corporate news, earnings announcements, and upgrade/downgrade news) to determine whether an investor can achieve above-average returns by trading on news of the event. Since the semi-strong form of EMH posits that superior returns cannot be achieved using technical or fundamental analysis, researchers also explore the possibility of return forecasting using cross-sectional and time-series analyses based on current and historical information.
- Tests of the Strong-Form of EMH: To empirically test the strong-form of EMH, researchers focus on groups of investors with excess information (e.g., company insiders, exchange specialists, financial analysts, and institutional money managers). They examine whether such informed agents consistently outperform the overall market benchmark. If they do, empirical evidence rejects the strong-form of EMH.

In financial literature, numerous studies suggest that the weak and semi-strong forms of EMH are widely accepted, as long-lasting patterns in security prices are nonexistent, and trading on news announcements does not yield abnormal returns on average. However, evidence regarding the strong-form of EMH is mixed. On the one hand, institutional money managers, such as those managing mutual funds and pensions, typically do not consistently outperform the market benchmark, supporting the strong-form of EMH. On the other hand, financial analysts' advice often triggers price movements in equities, and their recommendations can help investors achieve above-average returns, which challenges the strong-form of EMH. Thus, the evidence for the strong-form of EMH is inconclusive.

The implications of FSM for market efficiency are similarly mixed. Early research on FSM, such as Tumarkin and Whitelaw (2001), found that online posting activity did not predict industry-adjusted returns or abnormal trading volume. Tumarkin (2002) further showed that abnormal online posting activity does not predict future stock price movements over a one-day or five-day window. He also reported statistically insignificant changes in value after event days. This evidence supports the semi-strong form of EMH.

However, some scholars argue that the market is inefficient due to the predictive power of FSM information. In Chapter 9, I mentioned that a trading strategy using a poster's historical performance as a weight to aggregate information from FSM is not only feasible but also profitable. The semi-strong form of EMH suggests that public information should be fully incorporated into security prices, and current or historical information should have no predictive power over future stock movements. However, several studies (e.g., Gu, Konana, Liu, Rajagopalan, and Ghosh (2006)) provide evidence that information available on FSM platforms has not been fully incorporated into stock prices. Liu, Gu, Konana, and Ghosh (2006) also explored trading strategies based on the posters' historical performances and sentiments from Yahoo! Finance discussion board, suggesting that informed investors are active on FSM platforms but that their information is not fully reflected in market prices. This evidence presents a challenge to the semi-strong form of EMH in the U.S. market.

Stock Recommendations from Financial Analysts

Today, stock recommendations and picks are readily available and free on FSM, though the quality of this information can sometimes be questionable. Recommendations can be found on FSM platforms, Facebook groups, X.com (formerly Twitter), Google Plus communities, and a multitude of free stock-picking websites. Before this era, stock picks were shared through methods such as email, instant messages, and chat rooms. In addition to these free resources, there is still a substantial amount of paid information provided by financial analysts from various securities research firms.

Securities research professionals, commonly known as financial analysts, develop and communicate insights regarding the value, risk, and volatility of covered securities. Their goal is to assist investors in making decisions about whether to buy, hold, sell, avoid a security, or use financial derivatives to hedge potential risks. To gather their information, financial analysts review periodic financial statements of companies and their competitors, participate in or listen to management conference calls, read industry news, analyze trading history and industry information databases, interview managers and customers of issuers, conduct statistical analyses, and perform independent research.

Historically, securities research was very expensive for retail investors to obtain and was typically purchased by institutional investors. However, thanks to advances in computing and the Internet, retail investors now have online access to these research reports at a reasonable price. Securities research is provided by investment banks (e.g., Goldman Sachs and Morgan Stanley) as well as various third-party independent securities research firms, such as Valueline.com and Valuengine.com, often referred to as sell-side analysts. Below is a partial list of commonly cited firms that provide professional analysts' stock recommendations.[1]

First Call Consensus Recommendation[2]

The First Call Consensus Recommendation is provided by Thomson Reuters, using information gathered from third-party independent research contributors. For each security with a consensus recommendation, the number of contributors is also provided alongside the recommendation. The Thomson Reuters standardized recommendation scale is as follows: 1—Strong Buy; 2—Buy; 3—Hold; 4—Underperform; 5—Sell. Each contributor aligns their individual recommendation with the Thomson Reuters First Call five-point scale. First Call delivers consensus recommendations and timely earnings forecast data across nine critical data measures for more than 5000 U.S. stocks.

Investor's Business Daily[3]

Investor's Business Daily (IBD hereafter) is a daily newspaper designed for investors who want to manage their investments in publicly traded securities such as stocks, bonds, and mutual funds. The newspaper offers a variety of tools to gain pertinent information about the stock market, including news reports, earnings reports, and tables. The stock rating system designed and used by IBD is a valuable tool for investors to research and track publicly traded companies. IBD's SmartSelect composite rating uses a scale from 1 to 99. Stocks that earn a 99 are considered to have the best overall strength in terms of investment potential, indicating the highest potential for a fair return on investment soon.

Morningstar[4]

Morningstar, an independent investment research provider, offers a comprehensive range of products and services for individual investors, financial advisors, asset managers, and retirement plan providers and sponsors. Morningstar provides data on numerous investment offerings, such as stocks, mutual funds, and similar vehicles, along with real-time global market data on millions of equities, indexes, futures, options, commodities, precious metals, foreign exchange markets, and Treasury markets. Morningstar also offers investment management services through its registered investment advisor subsidiaries and created the Morningstar Rating, which rates each covered security from five stars (best) to one star (worst).

Standard & Poor's[5]

Standard & Poor's stock reports are updated weekly and include price-volume charts, statistical measures, fundamental analytics, analysts' estimates and projections, industry outlooks, and the latest company news. Standard & Poor's also has a five-tiered stock ranking system known as STARS (Stock Appreciation Ranking System), which ranges from five stars (Strong Buy) to one star (Strong Sell). The STARS system measures the short-term (6- to 12-month) appreciation potential of stocks. STARS performance is compared to the S&P 500 for U.S. stocks. Unlike many other security research firms, this ranking system is based on the final analysis of S&P analysts. Besides the STARS system, Standard & Poor's also provides S&P Earnings & Dividend and S&P Fair Value Rank for each covered stock, with approximately 1500 individual stocks regularly covered.

Thomson Reuters "StarMine"[6]

StarMine, a division of Thomson Reuters, focuses primarily on building quantitative factor models for institutional investors. StarMine's equity analytics and research management tools help investment firms worldwide generate abnormal returns and process equity information more efficiently. Their performance scoring helps investors predict trends in analyst sentiment, anticipate surprises, evaluate financial statements for earnings quality, and more. The five-scale Equity Summary Score and associated sentiment ratings by StarMine are categorized as very bearish, bearish, neutral, bullish, and very bullish. An Equity Summary Score is only provided for stocks with ratings from four or more third-party independent research providers. These ratings reflect relative (not absolutely forecasted) performance among the 1500 largest stocks by market capitalization.

Value Line[7]

Valueline.com is an independent investment research and financial publishing firm. Each week, Value Line ranks 1700 stocks according to their prospects for the upcoming year, based on its proprietary ranking system. Value Line is best known for publishing the Value Line Investment Survey (VLIS), a stock analysis newsletter that is updated and announced online at 8:00 a.m. EST every Monday.[8] The company provides stock recommendations, primarily reflected in its timeliness rank (ranging from 1, the lowest, to 5, the highest), through its website Valuel ine.com. Besides timeliness, Value Line also provides technical and safety ranks for each covered stock. Additionally, Value Line offers research surveys for small- and mid-cap stocks alongside the 1700 large-cap stocks.

ValuEngine[9]

ValuEngine, a stock valuation and forecasting service founded by finance academics, utilizes quantitative techniques and analysis to develop the ValuEngine stock valuation models and econometric models for forecasting stock price movement. ValuEngine's main products include Val uEngine.com (for individual investors) and ValuEngine Institutional (VEI), a software package for equity fund managers and other financial professionals. ValuEngine's stock recommendations are based on the proprietary ValuEngine one-year forecast return model output for each covered equity. A stock is rated Strong Buy, Buy, Hold, Sell, or Strong Sell based on the forecast of its one-year return.

Wright Quality Rating[10]

The Wright Quality Rating measures the overall investment quality of a company. Wright Quality Ratings are based on a variety of individual measures, grouped into four principal components: (1) investment acceptance, (2) financial strength, (3) profitability and stability, and (4) growth. The ratings are derived from established principles using five to six years of corporate records and other investment data. Ratings consist of three letters and a number, where each letter reflects a composite, qualitative measurement of various individual standards: A = Outstanding; B = Excellent; C = Good; D = Fair; L = Limited; N = Not Rated. The number component of the quality rating is a composite measurement of annual corporate growth, based on earnings and modified by growth rates of equity, dividends, and sales per common share. The highest quality rating assigned by Wright is AAA20.

Zacks Investment Research[11]

Zacks Investment Research conducts independent research and shares its profitable discoveries with investors. Zacks provides data and tools for both individual and institutional investors to make informed investment decisions. Len Zacks, the company's founder, developed a mathematical ranking system to harness the power of earnings estimates. The Zacks Rank rates stocks in terms of their expected price performance over the next three to six months. The ranking system uses a quantitative model based on trends in estimate revisions and earnings per share surprises. Stocks are ranked from one to five, with one being the best rank (Strong Buy) and five being the worst (Strong Sell). Zacks allows individual investors to take advantage of trends in earnings estimate revisions and benefit from the power of institutional investors.

Measure of Analyst Consensus, Security Recommendation Accuracy, and Earnings Forecast Accuracy

Measure of Analyst Recommendations

Like the online sentiment ratings provided by posters, which range from "Strong Buy" to "Short", financial analysts use either sentiment rankings or quantified sentiment scores when recommending securities. For example, Zacks employs a sentiment ranking system that ranges from Strong Buy to Strong Sell, while Value Line uses a sentiment score scale from one to five. Beyond the standard five-point scales, you may also encounter three-point scales (Buy/Outperform, Hold/Indifferent, Sell/Underperform) and four-point scales (Excellent, Good, Fair, Bad). Most ranking systems include at least three distinct opinions: positive, neutral, and negative. Consequently, services like First Call and StarMine (both owned by Thomson Reuters) can convert analyst sentiments into a five-point scale ranking system via third-party independent research providers.

To aggregate and quantify analyst sentiments, practitioners and scholars often use either mean or median sentiment scores. A mean sentiment is the average of all sentiments provided by multiple analysts for a particular security during the same period. For example, if a stock is rated by four analysts, with one giving a Strong Buy (coded as 1), one giving an Outperform (coded as 1), one giving a Fair rating (coded as 2), and one giving a Hold (coded as 3), First Call would calculate the mean sentiment as $(1+1+2+3)/4 = 1.75$. This score falls between Buy and Strong Buy, assuming one is the best and five is the worst. In this system, the optimal score is 1, indicating a Strong Buy.

Another widely accepted method is to examine the median sentiment, especially when pooling data from many financial analysts. For instance, if a stock is followed by five analysts who give sentiment ratings of 1, 1, 3, 4, and 4, the median sentiment would be 3. In the same scenario, the sentiment score would be 2.6 if the mean sentiment is applied.

This approach allows for a more comprehensive understanding of overall analyst consensus, enabling investors to make informed decisions based on aggregated expert opinions.

Measure of Security Recommendation Accuracy

To evaluate the accuracy of analyst sentiments, we need a method to test these sentiments after they have been coded into scores and aggregated into either mean or median values. Analyst sentiment reflects the general prevailing attitude of financial analysts towards the future price movement of a security. For instance, if analysts anticipate an upward price movement or a positive return for a stock, the sentiment is considered bullish or optimistic. Conversely, if the sentiment is bearish or pessimistic, analysts expect a downward price movement or negative returns. Essentially, sentiment represents an opinion about a security's future price or expected return.

One straightforward method to measure the accuracy of a security recommendation is by comparing a known return at the current time (t) to a past recommendation made before it (t-1). It is important to note that it is impossible to compare a current recommendation to a future return because future returns are not yet available. According to Depken and Zhang (2010), a metric called "RIGHT0" equals one if the sentiment matches the security returns on the same day the sentiment was announced, and zero otherwise. RIGHT0 = 1 indicates that the sentiment was accurate because the same-day security return aligns with the sentiment. For example, if the average sentiment among analysts was "Buy" on day t0 and the stock return after the sentiment announcement was positive on day t0, then RIGHT0 = 1. In other words, the sentiment matches the security returns on day t0. Similarly, "RIGHT5" means that the sentiment matches the security returns over the first five trading days after the sentiment was made available. This approach allows for the measurement of the accuracy of a security recommendation over any subsequent time span.

In the FSM literature, Zhang, Swanson, and Prombutr (2010) proposed a similar measure for the accuracy of a poster's sentiment. In particular, they proposed an accuracy measure "A," which is a binary function determining whether the poster's sentiment is in the same direction as the same-day stock return:

$$A \begin{cases} = 1,\ if\ \dfrac{x_m^{i,t}}{R_t^i} > 0\ or\ x_m^{i,t} = R_t^i = 0 \\ = 0,\ otherwise \end{cases} \qquad 11.1$$

where $x_m^{i,t}$ is the sentiment score of an online message, *m*, associated with stock *i* at day *t*. $x_m^{i,t} = -2$ if the sentiment is Strong Sell or Short, $= -1$ if it is Sell, $= 0$ if it is Hold, $= +1$ if it is Buy, and $= +2$ if it is Strong Buy. R_t^i is the stock *i*'s raw return at day *t*. Therefore, the average accuracy for *K* number of messages, disclosed by multiple posters, $\overline{A}$ is measured as: $\overline{A} = \sum_{k=1}^{K} A_k/K$.

Measure of Earnings Forecast Accuracy

When discussing financial analysts and market efficiency, it is essential to address the measure of earnings forecast accuracy. Beyond providing security recommendations, one of the most critical tasks of financial analysts is offering earnings forecasts. These forecasts are directly linked to a firm's value, as they provide insights into expected future performance. Recommendations, on the other hand, reflect analysts' opinions of a stock's value relative to its current price.

There are two approaches in the literature to measuring the accuracy of analyst's earnings forecasts. Most often, scholars calculate the standardized unexpected earnings (SUE). SUE is a means of comparing earnings surprise to the company's track record of earnings surprises. That is SUE is the earnings surprise at a given time divided by the standard deviation of earnings surprises measured over some historic period, such as in the previous quarter *Q*:

$$\mathrm{SUE_Q} = \frac{A_Q - F_Q}{STD_Q} \quad 11.2$$

where SUE_Q is quarter *Q*'s SUE; A_Q is quarter *Q*'s actual earnings per share (EPS) reported by the firm; F_Q is quarter Q consensus EPS, forecasted by financial analysts in the previous quarter Q_{t-1}; and STD_Q is quarter Q's standard deviation of earnings estimates among multiple analysts. STD_Q is a numerical expression of how much earnings estimates deviate from the mean expected EPS. The numerator measures the discrepancy between the actual EPS announced by the firm and the estimated mean or median EPS given by analysts.

The sign of SUE is determined by the sign of the numerator. Therefore, the greater the positive SUE, the greater the positive earnings surprise above the earnings estimate; the smaller the negative SUE, the greater the negative earnings surprise below the earnings estimate. If the actual earnings per share equals the consensus earnings estimate, there is no earnings surprise and SUE = 0. The only drawback of Eq. 11.2, when all analysts hold the same EPS estimate (this is very rare), is that the denominator becomes *zero* and SUE is undefined.

As an alternative, we can divide the numerator in Eq. 11.2 by the stock's closing trading price ten trading days before the EPS was released in Quarter Q (see Philbrick and Ricks 1991):

$$ES_Q = \frac{AE_Q - EF_Q}{P_{t-10}} \quad 11.3$$

where ES_Q is the most recent price-deflated earnings surprise for the stock in quarter Q, AE_Q is the actual EPS reported for quarter Q, EF_Q is the analysts' one quarter ahead mean or median forecast of EPS for quarter Q, and P_{t-10} is the stock's closing price ten trading days before its EPS was officially released by the company in quarter Q. Equation 11.1 to 11.3 will help you understand the subsequent materials in this chapter.

When Whisperers Talk, Who Listens?

There is little doubt that many investors, especially online traders, pay close attention to the opinions of whisperers when trading securities. Whisper is an individual providing unofficial or non-institutional financial commentary. Both individual and institutional investors, including certain hedge funds and investment banks, often base their trading decisions on information disclosed by these whisperers. The question arises: Do financial analysts also pay attention to these online discussions?

Fortunately, evidence from surveys, interviews, and academic literature suggests that financial analysts do indeed pay some level of attention to what whisperers are saying online. For instance, Carson and Felton (2004) reported that a general partner at Rocker Management, a $600 million hedge fund, actively builds relationships with platform posters in hopes of gathering useful information.

In another case cited by Carson and Felton (2004), a Warburg Dillon Read analyst admitted to regularly monitoring FSM platforms. The analyst stated, "At the end of the day, I'm not going to put a buy, sell, or hold recommendation based on a bulletin board posting, but looking at and monitoring boards is something a prudent analyst has to do."

Furthermore, Thomson Reuters incorporated X.com and StockTwits into its Eikon data platform to help finance professionals identify trends in security trading. Danielle Tierney, an analyst with Aite Group, emphasized, "The ability to incorporate social media into the analytics toolkit is becoming an increasingly frequent demand from today's generation of traders. Such functionality is no longer just a value add; it is well on its way to becoming an important part of many quantitative strategies. The real differentiator is usability, or how this data is then harnessed to present financial professionals with an easily digestible picture of market trends."[12]

A research study by Bagnoli, Clement, Crawley, and Watts (2010) explored whether financial analysts who respond to investor sentiment issue more or less profitable stock recommendations than their peers. Their findings revealed that analysts tend to issue more favorable stock recommendations when recent and future investor sentiment is bullish, and vice versa. Additionally, the study showed that analysts who consider investor sentiment tend to issue less profitable stock recommendations than their peers. However, analysts following stocks most sensitive to investor sentiment and recent sentiment trends often provide more profitable recommendations than their peers. In conclusion, the study supports the idea that some analysts may base their recommendations partially on whisperers' sentiments, which do not always directly reflect company fundamentals.

Whisperers Versus Analysts: Whose Information Is more Accurate?

A substantial body of research demonstrates that financial analysts' opinions significantly influence stock price movements, and their trading recommendations often help investors achieve above-average returns. For instance, Womack (1996) analyzed new buy and sell recommendations from analysts at major U.S. brokerage firms, showing that these recommendations lead to significant initial and subsequent price reactions. This suggests that analysts possess market timing and stock-picking abilities. Similarly, Jegadeesh, Kim, Krische, and Lee (2004) found that changes in analysts' consensus recommendations serve as robust predictors of returns, containing information not available from other predictive variables.

Jegadeesh and Kim (2006) extended their analysis to the G7 countries, finding that stock prices react significantly to recommendation revisions in all countries except Italy. In the United States, they observed the largest price reactions around recommendation revisions and the most significant post-revision price drift, suggesting that U.S. analysts' recommendations are particularly effective in identifying mispriced stocks compared to their foreign counterparts.

Later, Loh and Stulz (2011) showed that only 12 percent of recommendation changes lead to significant market reactions. The impact of these changes is most pronounced when they come from well-known or influential analysts, deviate from consensus, are accompanied by earnings forecasts, and target growth stocks, small-cap firms, or companies with high institutional ownership or forecast dispersion. Overall, there is broad agreement among scholars that financial analysts possess insights into firm values and price trends, making their recommendations valuable to investors.

But how useful is the information provided by whisperers? Das, Martinez-Jerez, and Tufano (2005) interviewed Glenn R., a prolific poster on Yahoo! Finance's Amazon.com discussion board. Glenn argued that professional analysts often overlook key details about firms, and he used online discussion boards to test his analyses. Although Glenn did not believe he or other active platform users had proprietary or insider information, he emphasized that they had the time, experience, and inclination to thoroughly analyze Amazon's fundamental data. He noted that much of Amazon's corporate information was buried in footnotes and required considerable effort to extract, which he believed many analysts missed.

Hirschey, Richardson, and Scholz (2000a, 2000b) provided evidence of market responses to stock recommendations on The Motley Fool's discussion platform. In their study published in the *Financial Analysts Journal*, they demonstrated that buy recommendations on The Motley Fool moved prices and increased trading volumes, particularly for small-cap growth stocks. A subsequent study in the *Financial Review* found that these recommendations led to significant price increases (or decreases) on the announcement day, highlighting herd-like behavior among Internet investors. They concluded that Motley Fool's advice was more influential than traditional media recommendations.

In a seminal study, Bagnoli, Beneish, and Watts (1999) compared First Call analyst earnings forecasts to unofficial whispers. They found that whispers were more accurate proxies for market expectations than analysts' forecasts and that trading strategies based on the relationship between whispers and First Call forecasts could earn abnormal returns. This suggests that whispers contain valuable information not captured by analyst forecasts. Similarly, Zaima and Harjoto (2005) compared analysts' forecast errors to those of whisperers and found that the market reacted more strongly to whisperers' forecast errors, especially when there was a conflict between the two.

Chen, De, Hu, and Hwang (2013) validated the predictive power of crowd-sourced research by examining stock market opinion blogs on Seeking Alpha. They documented that the tone of these blogs predicted stock returns and earnings surprises, providing insights beyond what was available in Wall Street analyst reports and financial news articles. While it is difficult to assert that Seeking Alpha contributors are consistently better than highly paid Wall Street analysts, the findings suggest that Seeking Alpha sentiment offers additional insights.

However, not all researchers support the value of whisperers' information. Dewally (2003), writing in the *Financial Analysts Journal*, rejected the informational value of whisperers' recommendations. Analyzing stock recommendations from major online discussion groups, Dewally found that these recommendations were overwhelmingly bullish, followed sharp price increases, and did not elicit significant market reactions. His findings suggest that these recommendations lack new information and do not add value.

In conclusion, while a direct statistical comparison between analysts and whisperers remains to be conducted, the available evidence suggests that both groups can provide valuable insights. Some analysts do listen to whisperers as a supplementary source of information, and in some cases, whisperers' earnings forecasts may be more accurate than those of analysts. Therefore, certain whisperers' opinions can be valuable, useful, and beneficial to investors.

Trading Profits Based on Whisperer or Analyst Recommendations

The semi-strong form of the Efficient Market Hypothesis (EMH) suggests that investors cannot consistently achieve returns above the market average by trading on new information, including security recommendation announcements. Event studies are often employed to test whether investors can earn above-average returns by trading on recommendations from whisperers or analysts when such recommendations are made public. Any statistically and economically significant trading profits would challenge the semi-strong form of the EMH.

In the FSM literature, substantial evidence supports the significant investment value of sentiments expressed by whisperers online. For example, Sabherwal, Sarkar, and Zhang (2008) conducted an event study to estimate daily abnormal returns on stocks mentioned in online discussions. Their empirical findings revealed that on the day a stock was among the top 10 most discussed, it experienced an average abnormal return of 19.35 percent, which is statistically and economically significant at any level of transaction cost. Further, Sabherwal, Sarkar, and Zhang (2011) performed another event study focusing on online discussions that had no corresponding coverage in mainstream media. Even in this constrained sample, they found a smaller yet still statistically significant abnormal return of 13.93 percent on the event day, again significant at any transaction cost level.

Later, Zhang et al. (2022) reported significant abnormal returns in small-cap stocks without news. Focusing on small-cap stocks without news, they observed a 23.97 percent positive and significant abnormal return on the event day. The only group where no significant abnormal return was observed on the event day was large-cap stocks without news. In summary, investors can achieve significant abnormal returns by trading on the sentiments of whisperers as expressed on FSM platforms.

In the financial analyst literature, considerable evidence also shows that analyst recommendations add value for investors. Womack (1996) found that buy recommendations lead to a mean post-event drift of 2.4 percent, though this effect is short-lived. In contrast, sell recommendations result in a larger negative drift of –9.1 percent, extending for six months. He concluded that analysts possess market timing and stock-picking abilities. Barber, Lehavy, McNichols, and Trueman (2001) documented that purchasing stocks with the most favorable analyst consensus recommendations, using a daily rebalanced strategy after recommendation changes, could yield annual abnormal gross returns exceeding 4 percent. Green (2006) further demonstrated that early access to analysts' stock recommendations increases investment value for brokerage firm clients. Specifically, a strategy of purchasing (or short selling) stocks that have been upgraded (or downgraded) yields an average two-day return of 1.02 percent (1.50 percent) after accounting for transaction costs. Additionally, a calendar-based strategy produces positive abnormal daily returns of over 0.1 percent, roughly 30 percent annualized. Green concluded that brokerage firm clients benefit from the informational advantage provided by analysts' recommendation changes. Importantly, financial analysts' stock-picking abilities are not simply a matter of luck. Michaely, Womack, and Kent L. Womack (1999) showed that analysts whose recommendation revisions yielded the highest excess returns in the past continued to outperform in the future and vice versa. In sum, financial analysts add significant value for investors, with their stock-picking abilities and earnings forecasting skills being both exceptional and consistent. Together, the evidence suggests that profitable trading strategies based on either whisperers' or analysts' recommendations challenge the semi-strong form of the EMH.

However, profitable trading strategies based on whisper information appear feasible only at the aggregate level. In other words, following whisperers' recommendations for a single security or a small group of securities generally does not guarantee a profit. Extreme stock price predictions for a single security, especially when made by only a few posters, could indicate a pump-and-dump scheme or another form of market manipulation. It is both unwise and risky to trade a security solely based on the opinions of a few whisperers. Research typically focuses on broad sets of observations rather than single securities; research findings are consistently drawn from a broad set of observations.

This is where the "wisdom of crowds" comes into play. The aggregate information provided by whisperers represents the opinions of many investors regarding a stock, a sector, or the entire market. Aggregated sentiment reflects the average opinion of many investors, making it valuable information. This is the rationale behind hedge funds' event-trading strategies that utilize Internet information. To the best of my knowledge, no hedge fund or investment company would ever base a trading strategy on the opinion of a single analyst, let alone an unknown whisperer on the Internet.

Notes

1. There are also many security research firms that provide financial analysts' recommendations on fixed-income securities, foreign currencies, and commodities among other financial assets.
2. www.thomsonreuters.com
3. www.investors.com
4. www.morningstar.com
5. www.spoutlookonline.com
6. www.starmine.com
7. www.valueline.com

8. Ranks are announced online at 8:00 a.m. EST on Tuesday if Monday is a public holiday.
9. www.valuengine.com
10. www.wisi.com
11. www.zacks.com
12. http://thomsonreuters.com/press-releases/022014/Thomson-Reuters-Adds-Unique-Twitter-and-News-Sentiment-Analysis-to-Thomson-Reuters-Eikon

CHAPTER 12

Alternative Information on the Internet

Finding Free Information

The Internet offers a vast array of channels providing free information on securities trading and investment. Some of this information is legitimate and useful, while other information can be misleading or even deceptive. It is essential to exercise caution when exploring these resources.

Instant Messenger (IM) and Short Message Service (SMS)

If you need to communicate with other traders during trading hours, instant messaging (IM) software can be an ideal solution. IM is a form of online chat that enables real-time text transmission over the Internet. Various IM software platforms allow you to exchange messages with other traders on your contact list, and many of these services are free of charge (e.g., WhatsApp, Telegram, and Discord). There is also software like Trillian that integrates multiple IM services into a single platform.

Short Message Service (SMS) is another text messaging service that caters to investors in a similar way. Unlike IM, which requires the installation of software and often connects users who are already acquainted, SMS can be used more broadly. To send or receive trading information via IM, you typically need to be a member of a chat group, a contributor to a trading team, or a subscriber to a stock alert service. IM is a convenient tool for communicating with brokers and fellow traders and has become

Y. Zhang, *Financial Social Media*,
https://doi.org/10.1007/978-3-032-09332-5_12

part of many traders' daily routines. However, it is advisable to keep your contact list short to avoid interruptions from unwanted chatters during trading.

Here are two examples of IM and SMS services used by traders:

- IMTrader: This platform turns instant messages into instant stock trades.[1]
- ICE Chat: This IM platform is designed for traders and brokers in the commodity and equity derivatives markets. By combining IM, automation, and data integration, ICE Chat streamlines market communications, enabling faster trading decisions. ICE Chat is available as a value-added feature of WebICE.[2]

Research by Saavedra, Hagerty, and Uzzi (2011) found that traders who "sync up" using IM tend to generate higher profits, as IM facilitates a more organic and faster exchange of information compared to other channels. The study revealed that as IM volume increases, trading volume also rises, suggesting that the collective wisdom emerging from these communications can help traders make more informed decisions. This synchronous trading, enabled by IM, allows traders to observe and respond to market movements more quickly.

A Brokerage Firm's Chat Room

In Chapter 2, I discuss public chat rooms, which typically require no registration and allow traders to freely exchange ideas (e.g., Activetrader via FinancialChat.com). However, there is a special type of semipublic chat room operated by online discount brokerage firms (e.g., E-Trade and Charles Schwab), where traders can obtain "free" information and share opinions. These chat rooms differ from traditional public chat rooms in that only customers of the brokerage firm are eligible to use them. As a result, the information is not entirely free; users must meet a minimum deposit requirement to become a customer of the brokerage firm.

In early 1998, E-Trade launched the first broker-operated, real-time chat room for its customers. Although investors might promote or discuss stocks as in other chat rooms, this platform is moderated by E-Trade to ensure that users are not attempting to manipulate securities. Additionally, only stocks traded on major stock exchanges are discussed, and investors are prohibited from discussing small, thinly traded penny stocks. Unlike a regular chat room, E-Trade requires all participating investors to provide their real names and addresses in advance and to sign a contract agreeing not to use the chat room to manipulate stocks. E-Trade also publishes a disclaimer stating that it is not responsible for views expressed in the chat room and keeps records of all messages sent.

In 1999, TD Ameritrade (currently under Charles Schwab) introduced its trader's lounge via Thinkorswim software, which serves as a semipublic chat room for its customers. This chat room allows customers and other investors to exchange ideas and information about stocks and investing topics in general. On the Thinkorswim.com platform, you can see a list of available chat rooms and join any real-time discussion by double-clicking the "Trader's Lounge." In each chat room, a list of other users' aliases is also displayed. However, unlike E-Trade, TD Ameritrade does not require users to disclose their real names in the chat room.

Email

Many stock-picking websites request your email address and subsequently send stock recommendations via email. These emails may contain stock tips and investment advice, but they may also include unsolicited messages from unknown senders promoting "hot" stocks. These unsolicited emails are commonly referred to as spam.

Most people receive unwanted spam daily. According to Commtouch, an international email security firm, of the 347 billion email messages sent daily in 2025, 46 percent, or about 160 billion, were spam. Of these spam emails, approximately 2.5 percent, or 4.3 billion per day, were related to stock scams. Scholars, practitioners, and regulators generally view all investment-related spam as security scams. While most stocks recommended via spam are real U.S. penny stocks, they are extremely risky and have little investment value.

Frieder and Zittrain (2007) conducted a survey of 75,000 unsolicited emails sent between January 2004 and July 2005. They concluded that spammers could make an average return of 4.29 percent using this method, while recipients who acted on the spam typically lost nearly 5.5 percent of their original investment within two days. Another study by Böhme and Holz (2006) revealed a similar effect, showing that stocks targeted by spam are almost always penny stocks—thinly traded, difficult or impossible to short, not listed on major exchanges, and priced under $5 per share.

On the days of mass emailing, Nelson, Price, and Rountree (2013) reported significantly higher returns and trading volume for the stocks featured in these messages. These emails often include optimistic target price projections, bundled with seemingly credible information quoted from previous company press releases. Hanke and Hauser (2006) indicated that spammers typically acquire the stock before sending the messages and liquidate their positions on the day the emails are sent.

This type of spam email is illegal because it violates Section 17(b) of the Securities Act of 1933, which prohibits promoting stocks for compensation without disclosing the payment received.[3] Section 17(b) states:

> It shall be unlawful for any person, by the use of any means or instruments of transportation or communication in interstate commerce or by the use of the mails, to publish, give publicity to, or circulate any notice, circular, advertisement, newspaper, article, letter, investment service, or communication which, though not purporting to offer a security for sale, describes such security for a consideration received or to be received, directly or indirectly, from an issuer, underwriter, or dealer, without fully disclosing the receipt, whether past or prospective, of such consideration and the amount thereof.

In 2007, the SEC launched "Operation Spamalot," which suspended trading for ten days in 35 Pink Sheet companies that had been promoted in spam email campaigns.[4] In one case cited by the SEC, shares of Apparel Manufacturing Associates Inc. (APPM) closed at six cents on a trading volume of 3500 shares on December 15, 2006. After a weekend spam campaign, trading on the following Monday reached 484,568 shares, and the stock climbed to over 19 cents a share—an increase of over 300 percent. Two days later, on December 20, 2006, it hit 45 cents a share. By December 27, 2006, Apparel Manufacturing's stock price had returned to 10 cents on a volume of 65,350 shares.

Because scammers can operate from anywhere, it is difficult to trace these scams back to the perpetrators. Sometimes, they further victimize individuals by hacking into their email accounts and sending pump-and-dump securities messages from those accounts. To avoid email scams, it is strongly advised not to trade stocks recommended via email.

Financial Blogs

Financial blogs are ubiquitous on the Internet, offering a platform where anyone can share their thoughts on investments. Websites like Blogger.com and MySpace.com make it easy to start a blog, often at no cost. Consequently, we see a wide range of financial blogs, from those maintained by financial professionals (e.g., Motley Fool[5] and FreeRealTime[6]) to contributions from individual investors (e.g., SeekingAlpha.com). Like the work of professionals, many smaller blogs attract attention and discussion among investors. Some blogs are written by renowned economists (e.g., Dr. Paul Krugman[7]), others by famous investors (e.g., Jim Cramer), while some are less well-known (e.g., blog.stocktradersalmanac.com).

The content posted on financial blogs is generally opinion, protected under the First Amendment. Bloggers are not considered solicitors or scammers urging readers to trade based on their recommendations. Instead, they typically offer sentiments and suggestions regarding various stocks, leaving the final trading decisions to their readers.

Jim Cramer, a former hedge fund manager, launched the television show "Mad Money" on CNBC on March 14, 2005. The show focuses on investments and speculation, particularly with publicly traded stocks, and presents itself more as entertainment than as a news broadcast.[8] Cramer also runs a website, "Cramer's Mad Money," where he provides daily updates and stock picks, dividing them into "buy" and "sell" categories, with around ten recommended stocks in each group per day. He consistently includes a disclaimer at the bottom of each post.[9]

Neumann and Kenny (2007) studied stock recommendations made on Jim Cramer's "Mad Money" program, finding statistical evidence of market responses to both his buy and sell opinions. They suggested that while professional investors might exploit buy picks with a contrarian strategy, individuals with limited funds should be cautious about short-term trading based on the show's suggestions. Keasler and McNeil (2008) also researched "Mad Money" and documented significant market reactions to Cramer's stock recommendations, especially for small-cap stocks. However, they found that returns following buy recommendations often reversed and there was no evidence of positive, longer-term abnormal returns. They cautioned investors against following stock recommendations announced in the mass media, particularly on the "Mad Money" blog.

The Motley Fool website has also garnered significant investor attention. Hirschey, Richardson, and Scholz (2000a) were the first to document that Motley Fool's buy (sell) recommendations, announced via its website, generated significant positive (negative) stock returns on announcement days. They concluded that Motley Fool's online announcements are more impactful than second-hand buy-sell recommendations published in traditional print and electronic media.

Oh and Sheng (2011) studied microblog sentiments to determine their predictive power on future stock price movements. Their research analyzed 72,221 blog postings covering 1909 stock tickers and 3874 distinct authors. They found that stock microblog sentiments have predictive power for both simple and market-adjusted returns, with predictive accuracy consistent with the underreaction hypothesis observed in behavioral finance. In summary, many stock blogs do possess predictive power regarding future stock price movements.

SeekingAlpha.com, one of the largest investment-related social media websites in the United States, allows individual investors, rather than journalists or analysts, to contribute posts and publish their own articles.[10] Chen, De, Hu, and Hwang (2013) found that Seeking Alpha articles and comments were predictive of future stock prices and earnings surprises across all time frames studied, from one month to three years.

Social Networks: Facebook

Facebook, an online social networking service, is currently one of the most popular social media platforms. It allows users to share thoughts, pictures, videos, and comments; make new friends; send instant messages; and join groups based on common interests. Among the millions of user groups, many focus on stock trading or investment (e.g., Morpheus Trading Group, The Adam Mesh Trading Group, Top Stock Picks, and Stock Market Investment Tips). Users can join these groups for free and keep track of real-time discussions via their news feeds.

Facebook offers several features that may facilitate securities trading and investment decision-making. Like a financial social media (FSM hereafter) platform, Facebook discussion groups display entire threads of online conversations, typically arranged from newest to oldest. Membership in these groups is generally free, and users can easily follow posts. Facebook also shows how many users "Like" a group and are actively discussing it. Unlike most FSM platforms, Facebook highlights top comments and recent activity under each topic, making it easier for users to engage in discussions, comment, and share information. Group members frequently share their sentiments, discuss trades, offer forecasts, comment on posts, and answer questions—information that can be highly beneficial to investors.

Karabulut (2013) studied Facebook's Gross National Happiness (GNH) as a direct measure of investor sentiment. He found that GNH could predict changes in both daily returns and trading volume in the U.S. stock market. Specifically, he documented that a one standard deviation increase in GNH predicts a 0.1123 percent rise in market returns the following day. However, while GNH has strong predictive power, its positive influence on market returns is temporary and fully reverses in the following trading weeks. Nonetheless, higher GNH consistently predicts increases in future trading volume.

Another study by Heimer and Simon (2012) did not directly use data from Facebook but instead focused on a Facebook-style social networking website. They collected detailed trading records and communications from over 5500 traders and concluded that, within the trading community, individual investors are more likely to initiate communication with others who have higher returns. They also found that investors increase their trading intensity upon hearing about these good returns.

Today, many financial websites (e.g., MarketWatch.com), brokerage firms (e.g., Scottrade), and even investment banks (e.g., J.P. Morgan) maintain their official Facebook pages to facilitate customer communication. Many websites also feature a "Like" button, enabling users to endorse and recommend the site to their friends on Facebook. For example, when using the stock-trading simulator on Investopedia.com, users can log in via Facebook, allowing their trading records, holding positions, and portfolio performance to be shared on their Facebook pages.

Microblogs: X.Com (Formerly Twitter)

X.com is an online social networking and microblogging service that enables users to send and read "tweets," which are text messages limited to 280 characters. Registered users can both read and post tweets, while unregistered users are limited to reading them. As of 2025, X.com ranked among the ten most visited websites globally, according to similarweb. com, and it has been described as the short message service of the Internet.[11]

Like Facebook, X.com allows users to create discussion groups and track online conversations. To follow a discussion, users simply click the "Follow" button for the groups they wish to join. Numerous discussion groups on X.com focus on securities trading and investment (e.g., Guru Algo Trading, Stock Tips Network, and Stock Investment Tip). By following these groups, investors can access free trading tips, hot stock picks, and market trend information.

On April 2, 2013, the SEC issued guidelines allowing companies to use social media sites like Facebook and X.com to share company announcements. This guidance followed an investigation into Netflix CEO Reed Hastings, who posted monthly viewership results on his Facebook page in July 2013, instead of through an SEC filing or traditional news release. U.S. companies are now permitted to post earnings on X.com or update their status on Facebook, if investors have been informed in advance where to find this information. However, company communications via social media could violate the fair disclosure rule known as Regulation FD if investors are not properly notified about where the information will be posted.[12]

X.com has become a game changer for commodities traders seeking an edge. For example, farmers now use X.com to discuss harvests and shortages, providing traders with real-time updates on the supply and demand of certain commodities. This method offers a faster alternative to traditional telephone surveys or field trips. A London hedge fund, Derwent Capital, uses X.com to make investment decisions based on real-time tweets. With millions of tweets generated daily, the fund applies quantitative models to sift through this data and identify sentiment trends that may serve as leading indicators of stock movements several days later.[13] Derwent Capital is believed to be the first fund to incorporate real-time mood analysis as a key component of its investment-decision process.

Mao, Counts, and Bollen (2011) reported that Twitter Investor Sentiment, measured by the frequency of financial terms on Twitter over the previous one to two days, significantly predicts daily market returns. Bollen, Mao, and Zeng (2011) further discovered that the collective mood on Twitter, as measured by millions of random daily tweets, could predict with 86.7 percent accuracy the movement of the Dow Jones Industrial Average up to four days in advance. Zhang, Fuehres, and Gloor

(2011) also used tweets to forecast financial market movements, focusing on gold and crude oil prices, currency exchange rates, and the stock market. They concluded that information on Twitter is correlated with, and even predictive of, financial market movements.

Evangelopoulos, Magro, and Sidorova (2012) analyzed Twitter posts related to 18 Fortune 500 companies using latent semantic analysis to extract key themes and concepts. They suggested that Twitter can serve as a macro informer for stock markets. In addition, Sprenger, Tumasjan, Sandner, and Welpe (2014) reported that tweet sentiment correlates with stock returns, tweet volume with trading volume, and tweet disagreement with volatility. They concluded that users providing above-average investment advice are retweeted more frequently and have more followers.

Google's Search Volume Index

Another effective method to gauge investor sentiment and market trends is by utilizing Google's Search Volume Index (SVI). Google provides public access to the SVI of search terms through its product, Google Trends.[14] Google Trends is a public web tool that shows how frequently a particular search term is entered relative to the total search volume across various regions of the world and in multiple languages. It also allows users to refine search results by region and time.

For example, if you type in "TSLA," the SVI will display the level of interest in Tesla Motors' common shares, along with related corporate news presented in a time-series format. This information helps you understand how often and intensely people are paying attention to Tesla's stock. Additionally, SVI allows for the comparison of search volumes for multiple keywords. For instance, you can compare the attention given to "Toyota," "Honda," and "Ford" over a specific period. Google Trends also enables users to narrow down SVI results to specific regions, making it possible to track market trends at a global, national, state, or even city level.[15]

A particularly useful feature is the "Forecast" option, which, when checked, displays a dotted line predicting how popular the search term is expected to be in the near future. This can help investors anticipate future market trends. Furthermore, SVI data can be downloaded for free into Excel for further analysis. Numerous research papers have employed SVI as a proxy for investor sentiment, and ongoing academic research is exploring whether Google searches can predict future stock price performance.

Da, Engelberg, and Gao (2009) were among the first to use SVI to predict firm-revenue surprises, earnings surprises, and earnings announcement returns. They found that SVI for a firm's products serves as a valuable leading indicator of the firm's future cash flow, revealing that market value is not fully incorporated into prices before earnings announcements. In a subsequent study, Da, Engelberg, and Gao (2011) used SVI to measure retail investor attention, finding that SVI captures investor attention in a timelier manner than traditional, indirect methods such as news and advertising expenses.

Interestingly, their research showed that an increase in SVI predicts higher stock prices over the next two weeks, followed by an eventual price reversal within a year. They also found that SVI contributes to the large first-day returns and long-run underperformance of IPO stocks. The authors suggested that a trading strategy based on SVI could outperform the stock market by up to 10 percent per year. Building on their earlier work, Da, Engelberg, and Gao (2014) developed the Financial and Economic Attitudes Revealed by Search (FEARS) index, a new measure of investor sentiment based on SVI. They concluded that the FEARS index predicts short-term return reversals, temporary increases in volatility, and mutual fund money flows in and out of equity and bond funds.

Bank, Larch, and Peter (2011) also suggested that an increase in SVI is associated with a rise in trading activity and stock liquidity. Their research demonstrated that an increase in search volume correlates with temporarily higher future returns. Mao, Counts, and Bollen (2011) supported the view that weekly Google Insight Search volumes related to financial queries have predictive power. Similarly, Drake, Roulstone, and Thornock (2012) found that abnormal increases in SVI occur about two weeks before an earnings announcement, spike sharply at the announcement, and remain elevated for a period afterward. They concluded that information diffusion does not happen instantaneously with the release of earnings information but instead spreads out over a period surrounding the announcement.

Video-Sharing Website: YouTube

YouTube is a video-sharing platform currently owned by Alphabet Inc. that allows users to upload, view, and share videos. In addition to its primary function as a video repository, YouTube offers social features such as user profiles and the ability to comment on videos. Content on YouTube is uploaded by individuals, corporations, and various organizations, and many users engage in video blogging to share their opinions, similar to how they might write on a blog.

Beyond educational and training videos on how to trade securities, YouTube hosts a vast array of videos created by investors that feature daily stock picks, trading tips, and market trend analyses. For example, Zacks Investment News regularly uploads videos in which analysts share their value stock picks on a weekly basis.[16] The Motley Fool provides daily trading advice, market analysis, and recommendations on stocks to watch or buy for the long term via their YouTube channel.[17] Peter Schiff, an American financial commentator, frequently broadcasts his insights on the economy and stock market through his YouTube channel.[18]

YouTube also allows users to post comments under each video, share videos, and, if registered, add videos to playlists within their Google accounts to share with others in the Google Plus community. Each video comes with statistics such as the number of views since its debut and daily views over time. In 2008, YouTube introduced a text sentiment analysis feature based on users' comments. Comments are categorized as "Good" or "Poor," which helps users gauge the overall viewer sentiment toward a video. Additionally, users can vote on a video by clicking "Thumbs Up" or "Thumbs Down."

In the realm of investment-related videos, the number of views may serve as a popularity or sentiment index, while the like/dislike ratio can be an indicator of investor mood. Scholars are actively researching how information from YouTube can aid investors. O'Donnell, Gibson, Milliken, and Singer (2008) found that different demographic groups, such as women and men, community members and nonmembers, and lurkers and posters, react differently to user-generated online videos. Their research provides insights into how aggregated information from YouTube can be used to weigh each viewer's opinion. Hill and Ready-Campbell (2011) argued that online, user-generated content, including YouTube videos, can be used to automatically generate accurate predictions about the future performance of stocks. In addition, Cao, Liang, and Ni (2012) suggested that investor sentiment could potentially be measured by analyzing the "Good" and "Poor" comments on YouTube.

In addition to YouTube, X.com had introduced a video-sharing application called Vine, which was a mobile app that allowed users to create and post short video clips with a maximum length of seven seconds. These clips could be shared via Vine's social network and other platforms. Vine was shut down in 2017 but it is currently being revived as a new platform called diVine. Facebook also provides users with the capability to upload and edit their videos. Current popular video-sharing applications include TikTok and Instagram Reels.

Short videos are a powerful communication tool—they are effective at reaching target audiences, can be produced inexpensively, and are compatible with computers and many mobile devices. This is why video has become the preferred format for many people seeking to share information.

In conclusion, video-sharing websites offer a wealth of useful and free information that can be valuable to investors.

Online Trading Simulation

A stock-trading simulator is an online or mobile application that replicates various features of real financial markets, such as the stock market, bond market, cryptocurrency market, and options market. Participants can practice trading securities without incurring any real financial risk by using virtual money, a process often referred to as "paper trading." Trading simulations allow investors to test investment strategies and trading philosophies in a risk-free environment and are frequently used for educational purposes. For example, the online trading and investment simulator, known as OTIS, enables students to apply concepts of investing and portfolio management in a hands-on learning environment, working with real-world trading data without risking any actual money. This experience provides invaluable practice. Other popular online trading simulators include Investopedia,[19] Mocktrading,[20] Marketwatch,[21] Stocktrak,[22] and Tradestation,[23] among others. Participating in these simulation games offers a significant opportunity to acquire trading knowledge and experience.

For instance, anyone can register for free with Investopedia and join existing trading games or create a new one. When designing a new game, the creator can set the starting cash amount, up to $1 million, and choose whether to make the game private or public. In a public game, anyone can see and join the game freely. For a private game, the creator must invite participants and provide them with a password. Once you join a game, you can view other players' current rankings, cumulative returns, portfolio holdings, transaction records, and performance histories. Thousands of games are readily available to play on Investopedia.com.

There are many skilled traders on Investopedia, and it's beneficial to observe how others are performing in the market and what securities they hold. Other traders' picks and strategies can provide valuable insights, and if a strategy proves successful in the simulation, it is likely to work in real-life trading since the simulation is based on real market data.

On Investopedia, users are limited to trading stocks, stock options, and cryptocurrencies due to the absence of market data for other types of securities. Therefore, trading in fixed-income securities, currencies, commodities, futures, forward contracts, and other financial assets is not available on this platform. However, specialized online trading simulators are available for different types of assets. For example, the Mocktrading.com simulator allows users to trade commodities, while the Tradestation.com simulator supports currency trading.

Public Financial Websites

The Internet has made obtaining financial information cheaper, quicker, and more efficient. In addition to the nine methods discussed above for gathering free information using technology, it is essential to briefly mention a traditional source of financial data, public financial websites. Before the advent of the Internet, investors relied on newspapers, magazines, television programs, brokers, direct contact with company representatives, and discussions with other investors to gather information. Today, investors can access real-time market news, security trading prices, trading volumes, financial statements, analyst recommendations, retail investor sentiments, and other investment-related information online.

For example, the Yahoo! Finance website offers investors a wealth of free information. For nearly every publicly traded company, you can find real-time stock quotes, stock option quotes, historical prices, interactive charts with technical analysis indicators, corporate news, SEC filings, analyst coverage, financial ratios, and accounting statements. Even after the market closes, Yahoo! Finance provides access to off-hour trading activities at no cost. The platform offers free information not only for equities but also for fixed income, derivatives, commodities, currencies, and other types of financial assets. Additionally, Yahoo! Finance covers markets outside of the United States, including those in Asia, Europe, and South America.

Another valuable resource is Google Finance, which provides similar free information to investors. Google Finance also offers sector summaries, allowing investors to gauge the performance of various sectors by showing how many stocks are up or down within a sector.[24] The platform includes a stock screener, enabling users to filter stocks based on specific criteria such as market capitalization, price-earnings ratios, dividend yield, and 52-week price changes. A unique feature of Google Finance is "My Portfolio," which allows users to add stocks and funds to track their performance over time.

Google Domestic Trends is another tool that monitors Internet traffic within specific sectors of the economy, such as automotive, business and industrial, durable goods, and real estate. Changes in search volume within a sector can offer unique economic insights. Users can access individual trend indexes, which measure relative query volumes, and compare them to the total number of Google searches. This feature enables investors to monitor sector-specific investor attention, aiding in informed investment decisions. Google Finance provides market information for the United States, Hong Kong, Canada, China, and the United Kingdom.

Numerous other financial websites also provide free financial information, including Bloomberg, CNBC, CNNMoney, Financial Times, Investors, MarketWatch, Morningstar, Reuters, MSN Money, TheStreet, and The Wall Street Journal. Major financial news is typically shared across these platforms, with most sites featuring embedded Facebook and X.com buttons that redirect users to their respective social media pages.

Financial Social Media Platforms outside the United States

FSM platforms exist in many different languages (e.g., Chinese, Dutch, English, German, Japanese, Korean, Russian, and Spanish). Most of these platforms share similar functions and structures to those in the United States, and it is possible for the same poster to express identical content in different languages across various platforms (e.g., posting the same message on both U.S. and UK FSM platforms).

Below are examples of FSM platforms serving China, South Korea, Japan, and the United Kingdom. International scholars closely monitor these platforms to study how they impact securities trading and financial markets in foreign countries.

- JRJ Forum is one of the most popular FSM platforms in China and is operated by China Finance Online Co., a publicly traded company listed on NASDAQ in the form of an American Depositary Receipt (ADR). Other popular online stock platforms in China include Sina, Sohu, Eastmoney, and Ruoshui. Huang, Qiu, and Wu (2012) used the guba.eastmoney.com stock forum to investigate local bias and found that individual investors pay more attention to stocks of local companies, supporting the investor-attention local bias theory.
- Naver.com is a widely used FSM community in South Korea. Park, Konana, Gu, Kumar, and Raghunathan (2013) studied how information from the Naver.com stock forum influences investors' trading decisions and investment performance. They concluded that participation in FSM platforms increases investors' propensity to make investment mistakes, which is likely detrimental to their investment outcomes.
- Several FSM platforms cater to Japanese stocks and funds. For example, messages.yahoo.co.jp is an FSM platform hosted by Yahoo, primarily used by investors in Japan. Matsuo, Ohsawa, and Ishizuka (2002) found an abundance of useful information posted on the site. Another notable forum is an FSM platform for EWJ, an iShares MSCI Japan ETF fund that tracks the investment results of the MSCI Japan Index, which consists of stocks traded primarily on the Tokyo Stock Exchange.
- The "Shares and Stock Markets" forum on thisismoney.co.uk allows UK investors to discuss markets, share price movements, and trading strategies.[25] Users can read, reply to, and start new messages in this forum, as well as search messages within specific timeframes. Another popular stock forum in the United Kingdom is the Interactive Investor website.[26] This platform is the United Kingdom's leading community of security traders and investors, uniquely enabling its millions of users to trade and invest directly from the platform while sharing their thoughts in discussion forums. The structure of these two platforms is quite like those in the United States, such as Yahoo! Finance and TheLion.com.

FSM platforms can be found in many other countries, such as the Iraqi Dinar Discussion Board, Shareswatch Australia, and the Istanbul Stock Exchange Discussion. Wherever there is a stock market, there is likely to be an FSM platform. The cost of building, running, and maintaining a platform is relatively low, while the demand for such platforms remains strong. After all, investors need a virtual space to discuss trades, share opinions, and voice concerns.

Platforms for a Variety of Financial Assets

Below are examples of online platforms that focus on financial assets other than common stocks:

Penny Stocks

A stock is considered a "penny stock" if its share price is below $5. According to the SEC, short selling is not allowed on penny stocks. These stocks are typically not listed on major stock exchanges; instead, they are traded via over-the-counter exchanges or pink sheets. The transaction cost of trading penny stocks is generally higher than for non-penny stocks, and trading in penny stocks is riskier. There are many platforms dedicated to discussions about penny stocks.[27]

Exchange-Traded Funds (ETFs)

An exchange-traded fund (ETF) is an investment fund that is traded on stock exchanges. An ETF holds assets such as stocks, commodities, currencies, or bonds and trades close to its net asset value throughout the trading day. ETFs generally track an equity index, bond index, commodity, or currencies but trade like a stock on an exchange. Unlike mutual funds, whose prices change only once a day after the closing bell, ETFs experience price changes throughout the day as they are bought and sold. ETFs are attractive because of their low costs, tax efficiency, and stock-like features, making ETF-related platforms popular.[28]

Fixed-Income Securities

A fixed-income security is a legally binding agreement between a borrower and a lender that specifies fixed terms. Unlike variable-income securities (e.g., common stocks), where dividends vary over time, the payments of a fixed-income security are known in advance. The maturity date is fixed and predetermined. There are various types of fixed-income securities, such as Treasury securities, corporate bonds, municipal bonds, commercial papers, and certificates of deposit (CDs), and there are numerous discussion platforms for these types of securities.[29]

Treasury Securities

U.S. Treasury securities are government debts issued by the U.S. Department of the Treasury through the Bureau of the Public Debt. Treasury securities are the debt financing instruments of the U.S. federal government. There are four types of marketable Treasury securities: Treasury bills, Treasury notes, Treasury bonds, and Treasury Inflation-Protected Securities (TIPS). All are considered fixed-income securities and are generally safer than corporate bonds. Online discussions about Treasury securities can be found on the Elite Trader.[30]

Currency

Currency is a type of financial asset backed by the issuer, typically a country's federal government. Currency serves as a medium of exchange, a store of wealth, and a standard of value. As one of the major financial markets, the foreign exchange market is a global, decentralized (over-the-counter) market for trading different currencies. The main participants in this market are large international banks. In a typical foreign exchange transaction, a party purchases some quantity of one currency by paying some quantity of another currency. Online discussions on currency trading can be found on websites like Babypips.com.[31]

Commodities

A commodity is a marketable item produced to satisfy wants or needs, such as gold, wheat, petroleum, and sugar. Commodities are interchangeable with other commodities of the same type. Unlike financial assets, commodities are real assets, most often used as inputs in the production of other goods and services. When traded on an exchange, such as the Chicago Mercantile Exchange (CME), commodities must meet specified minimum standards, known as basis grades. IG is a popular platform for discussing commodity trading.[32]

Options

An option is a type of financial derivative representing a contractual agreement between two parties: the writer who sells the contract and the holder who buys it. The contract gives the buyer the right, but not the obligation, to buy or sell a financial asset at an agreed-upon price during a certain period. Options can be based on an underlying security price, index level, commodity price, or other benchmarks. Risk-seeking traders use options to speculate (a riskier practice compared to trading stocks or bonds), while hedgers use options to reduce the risk of holding an asset. Online discussions about option trading are not scarce.[33]

Futures and Forward Contracts

A futures contract, another type of financial derivative, is a standardized contract between two parties to buy or sell a specified asset of standardized quantity and quality at an agreed-upon price, with delivery and payment occurring on a specified future date. The specified asset could be a financial asset (e.g., stock) or a real asset (e.g., commodity). These contracts are negotiated at a futures exchange, such as the Chicago Board Options Exchange, which acts as an intermediary between the two parties. Futures contracts are exchange-traded and, therefore, standardized. Forward contracts, on the other hand, are private agreements between two parties and are not as rigid in their terms and conditions. Online discussion platforms are available for both futures and forward contracts.[34]

Cryptocurrency

Cryptocurrencies are digital assets that use cryptographic protocols and blockchain technology to secure transactions and maintain decentralization. Unlike fiat currencies issued by central banks, cryptocurrencies are typically managed by decentralized networks of computers, making them resistant to centralized control or monetary policy changes. Bitcoin, launched in 2009, is the most well-known cryptocurrency, but the market now includes thousands of others such as Ethereum, Binance Coin, Solana, and Cardano. Depending on their design, these assets may serve as stores of value, mediums of exchange, or platforms for decentralized applications.

Cryptocurrency trading differs from traditional financial markets in several ways. Markets operate around the clock, every day of the year, without fixed trading hours. Price volatility is significantly higher, with large daily price movements common. The investor base is dominated by retail participants from around the world, which fuels rapid shifts in sentiment and momentum-driven trading.

Given the fast pace and complexity of the market, traders often rely on FSM platforms and online forums for timely information and sentiment analysis. CryptoCompare offers discussion platforms, live pricing, analytics, and portfolio tools. Bitcointalk, founded by Bitcoin's pseudonymous creator Satoshi Nakamoto, remains an active platform for technical discussions, market news, and token launches. Reddit's r/CryptoCurrency, with over six million members, provides a space for community-driven debates on token releases, security concerns, trading strategies, and regulatory updates. These platforms influence market behavior by shaping opinions and spreading information in real time, making cryptocurrency-focused FSM one of the most active and rapidly evolving segments of the digital investment space.

Notes

1. https://im-markets.com/
2. www.ice.com
3. https://www.sec.gov/about/laws/sa33.pdf
4. https://www.sec.gov/news/press/2007/2007–34.htm
5. caps.fool.com
6. www.freerealtime.com
7. https://www.nytimes.com/column/paul-krugman
8. https://www.cnbc.com/mad-money/
9. Jim Cramer's disclaimer is "Always do your own research as these are recommendations and I make no guarantees. No one cares about your money more than you do!"
10. http://seekingalpha.com
11. https://www.similarweb.com/website/x.com/#overview
12. Regulation FD, or Regulation Fair Disclosure, prevents the selective disclosure of information by publicly traded companies and other issuers. It requires that when an issuer discloses nonpublic information to certain individuals or entities (e.g., securities market professionals, stock analysts, or holders of the issuer's securities

who may trade based on the information), the issuer must make that information public. The rule aims to promote full and fair disclosure.

13. www.statisticsbrain.com reports 58 million tweets per day on January 1, 2014.
14. http://www.google.com/trends
15. By default, the search starts with the whole world.
16. http://www.youtube.com/user/ZacksInvestmentNews
17. http://www.youtube.com/user/TheMotleyFool
18. http://www.youtube.com/user/SchiffReport
19. www.investopedia.com/simulator
20. www2.mocktrading.com
21. http://www.marketwatch.com/game/
22. http://www.stocktrak.com/
23. https://www.tradestation.com/platforms-and-tools/simulated-trading/
24. The ten sectors are: energy, basic materials, industrials, cyclical consumer goods and services, noncyclical consumer goods and services, financials, health care, technology, telecommunications services, and utilities.
25. http://boards.thisismoney.co.uk/shares-stock-markets/
26. http://www.iii.co.uk/
27. http://thelion.com/bin/forum.cgi?tf=pinks_and_bb
28. http://investorshub.advfn.com/boards/boards.aspx?cat_id=140
29. https://discussion.fool.com/c/investing-strategies/bonds-fixed-income-investments/42
30. https://www.elitetrader.com/et/forums/fixed-income.87/
31. http://forums.babypips.com/
32. https://community.ig.com/forums/forum/30-commodities/
33. http://thelion.com/bin/forum.cgi?tf=writing_options
34. https://www.reddit.com/r/FuturesTrading/

CHAPTER 13

Implications of Financial Social Media

Introduction

Millions of users visit financial social media (FSM, hereafter) platforms daily, contributing their thoughts to the global online financial community. These platforms have far-reaching impacts on various aspects of the financial market. They have become hotspots for individual investors, provided institutional investors with new ways to gather information and trade, prompted businesses to rethink corporate governance and investor relations, and captured the attention of researchers exploring the significance of online discussions. Below is a detailed discussion of the implications of FSM platforms for each party.

Implications for Individual Investors

Gathering Information

Investors today demand more efficient and faster channels for information, increasingly turning to the Internet. FSM platforms are invaluable for those seeking insights from peer investors about specific stocks and the broader market. In the past, investors relied on traditional media, such as newsletters, magazines, corporate earnings announcements, and analyst reports, to gather information. However, in today's fast-paced and ever-changing market, much of the information from traditional sources is often outdated and adds little value.

Y. Zhang, *Financial Social Media*,
https://doi.org/10.1007/978-3-032-09332-5_13

FSM platforms attract millions of users daily, including traders, hedgers, arbitrageurs, economists, corporate employees, executives, regulators, investment experts, and enthusiasts. Market news headlines are quickly disseminated and discussed on these online financial communities, and some messages may contain unverified or privately sourced information not reported elsewhere. Participation in these communities not only allows investors to quickly access public information but also provides a new channel for acquiring private information.

Sharing Thoughts

FSM platforms enable users not only to read others' posts but also to contribute their own opinions on stocks, financial markets, and the economy. Users can post new messages, comment on existing ones, and reply to others, creating a dynamic exchange of ideas. Many online traders enjoy sharing their experiences and sometimes even disclose their current trading positions, enriching the information available on these platforms. This abundance of information attracts more users, creating a virtuous cycle of participation and data sharing.

Active Learning

Members of online financial communities gain significant benefits from free and timely access to both public and privately shared information, while steadily improving their investing and trading skills. What may begin as casual exchanges often develops into an interactive learning environment, where participants assess the expertise of others through visible indicators of credibility. For example, on TheLion.com, higher credit scores signal greater experience and reliability. Users with strong reputations often share well-researched insights, respond to questions, and offer detailed reviews or commentary, helping to elevate the overall quality of discussion and knowledge within the community.

FSM platforms are particularly valuable for beginners, offering a venue to explore opinions on securities and markets while accumulating trading and investment knowledge at little to no cost. Scholars have documented that less-skilled traders benefit from following more experienced traders, allowing them to improve their trading skills over time, learn from one another, and achieve trading profits that often exceed those of the average retail investor.

Trading Strategy

The primary reason investors participate in online discussions is to enhance their trading profits. By gauging investor consensus on stock price movements and market trends, investors can make informed decisions. The rapid dissemination of information via FSM platforms enables investors to quickly identify which stocks are popular and generating interest (e.g., on TheLion.com, users can track "Top Stock Discussions," "Most Active Forums," and "Most Stock Searches" in real-time). Some messages include the authors' self-disclosed sentiments, and readers can often infer the authors' moods from their writing. This makes FSM platforms a useful tool for sensing overall investor sentiment. Additionally, message volume is a key indicator, with high posting volumes signaling strong investor interest or attention.

In conclusion, the information available on FSM platforms empowers individual investors to make better and more timely trading decisions.

Implications for Financial Institutions

Trading Strategy on an Aggregate Level

Unlike individual investors, who often focus on information about specific stocks, institutional investors tend to concentrate on market-wide or aggregate-level information. By analyzing data from FSM platforms, it is possible to construct a retail investor sentiment index at an aggregate level. This is important because not all messages contain explicit self-disclosed sentiments, and it is impractical for institutional traders to read each message's content. Therefore, practitioners often rely on artificial intelligence tools, such as text classifiers, to process and analyze the data. Similarly, indices for overall disagreement and total posting volume can be developed to inform trading strategies for institutional investors.

Several data providers, including Dataminr, Gnip, and DataSift, supply feeds from X.com (formerly Twitter) and other platforms to hedge funds and asset managers, enabling them to refine their investment strategies. At the same time, these firms contribute to the development of market-wide retail investor sentiment indexes.

Feedback from Clients

As mentioned earlier, some online discount brokerage firms, such as E*TRADE and Charles Schwab, operate semipublic discussion platforms. These platforms offer a win-win situation for both traders and the hosting firms. Traders gain access to "free" information and can share their opinions, while the hosting firms receive valuable feedback from their clients. Access to these platforms is typically restricted to clients of the brokerage firms. Often, these firms create separate discussion platforms specifically for feedback on the functionality of the platforms, the structure of the broker's website, and the quality of the online discount broker's services. Questions posted on these platforms are quickly addressed by customer service agents, often via live chat. This interaction helps brokerage firms better understand their clients' needs and improve their services.

Conveying Information

It is not uncommon to find paid surrogate posters working for financial institutions on many FSM platforms. These agents usually disclose their affiliation in their usernames (e.g., "AgentforBOA" or "JPMSurrogate") and include customer service phone numbers in their user profiles, allowing others to verify their identities. Surrogate posters are more commonly found on private platforms than on public ones, mainly due to credibility concerns in public platforms.

These agents often share news, promote financial products, and announce new services. For example, an agent might post about the date of an IPO underwritten by their firm or the launch of a new ETF. Such information is typically released through multiple channels at the same time, with discussion platforms serving as an additional venue for disclosure.

For most financial institutions, FSM platforms provide an opportunity to build stronger customer relationships and reach a wider audience of potential clients.

Advertising

According to a report by TheLion.com, there were over 46 billion messages, blogs, tweets, and Facebook posts on the Internet in early 2025. Financial institutions have taken advantage of this trend through targeted advertising. It is common to see their ads on FSM platforms—for example, E*TRADE ads on InvestorVillage.com, Charles Schwab and Wells Fargo Advisors ads on InvestorHub.com. Since FSM platforms are typically free to use, users are generally not bothered by the presence of ads. (Private discussion platforms, which generate most of their revenue through membership fees rather than ads, tend to feature far fewer advertisements.)

With the exponential growth of FSM usage, we can expect to see even more ads from financial institutions in the future.

Implications for Businesses

Disseminating Information

On April 2, 2013, the SEC issued guidance permitting companies to use FSM platforms like Facebook and X.com to communicate company announcements. U.S. companies can now post corporate announcements on X.com or update their status on Facebook, if investors have been informed in advance where to find this information. Corporate press releases often include earnings announcements, future business plans, dividend policies, new products, contract announcements, and changes in corporate structure and governance. We can expect to see this type of corporate news increasingly shared on FSM platforms. For example, each publicly traded company has a dedicated FSM platform on Yahoo! Finance, offering an excellent venue for disseminating news—again, if investors know where to look.

Business Promotion

Businesses today recognize the importance of social media and the benefits it brings to the economy. They understand that when people discuss them on online platforms, whether those individuals are current shareholders or customers, it reflects genuine interest. This presents a valuable opportunity for outreach. We can expect companies to advertise on their dedicated FSM platforms soon. These platforms are ideal online venues for promoting services and products, as well as attracting new customers and investors.

Investor Relations

Investor relations is a strategic management responsibility that integrates finance, communication, marketing, and securities law compliance to facilitate effective two-way communication between a company, the financial community, and other stakeholders. This ultimately helps ensure fair valuation of a company's securities. Traditionally, investor relations have been conducted through meetings, websites, newsletters, phone calls, and emails. However, it would also be feasible and cost-effective for companies to use FSM platforms to support their investor relations initiatives. In many companies, public relations and legal teams already monitor FSM platforms closely, attempting to manage the information published about the company. As a result, many companies diligently monitor these platforms and participate in online discussions to "set the record straight" and engage in damage control. Companies should view FSM platforms as indicators of investor demand for information.

Corporate Governance

Corporate governance refers to the system by which corporations are directed and controlled. The governance structure specifies the distribution of rights and responsibilities among different participants within the corporation and establishes specific rules and procedures for making decisions on corporate affairs. Today, current and former employees, company representatives, and shareholders often communicate anonymously on FSM platforms, rather than merely reacting to official corporate announcements. For instance, Allegheny Energy, Inc. discovered a defamatory post against their company on the Yahoo! Finance, authored by an anonymous user later identified as Clifton G. Swiger, an engineering technician who had worked for Allegheny Energy Service for 16 years. Risks to corporate governance stem not only from external posters but also from internal leadership. In another example, John Mackey, the CEO of Whole Foods Market, anonymously criticized Wild Oats Markets on FSM platforms to push down their stock price, enabling Whole Foods Market to acquire it at a lower cost. After this scandal, the Whole Foods Market amended its code of business conduct to prohibit senior executives and directors from posting messages about the company, its competitors, or vendors on unsanctioned FSM platforms.

Consequently, corporations need to closely monitor discussions on FSM platforms, identify who is participating, and develop new policies to address challenges as technologies continue to evolve.

Implications for Regulators

Insider Information

Regulators are closely monitoring FSM platforms for potential leaks of insider information. Insider information refers to private details about a publicly traded firm that could provide a financial advantage if used to trade the company's stock. It is not only employees but sometimes even chief executives who might post insider information online. Other platform users can then exploit this information for trading purposes. Company communications made through social media channels could potentially violate the fair disclosure rule known as Regulation FD.

Any disclosure of nonpublic information to a select group of investors that results in illegal trading constitutes a violation of securities law. Even though fake "insider" information made available to the public does not violate Regulation FD, it still qualifies as securities fraud, specifically when used to manipulate market prices through fraudulent news.

Undisclosed Compensation for Stock Promotion

Given the vast number of investors using FSM platforms daily, these platforms are ideal for promoting stocks. However, the SEC explicitly states that failing to disclose compensation for touting stocks on the Internet, including on FSM platforms, violates securities law. Many posters are paid to promote one or several securities through social media. Direct compensation can include cash or securities payments, while indirect compensation might involve stock options or contingent payments if the stock price rises. Regardless of the form of payment, securities law requires paid agents to fully disclose their compensation, usually at the end of their messages. Additionally, federal securities laws mandate that public statements disclose the sources, amounts, and types of funding behind promotions. Many fraudsters fail to do so, misleading investors into believing they are receiving independent advice. Even if the information shared by paid agents is genuine, it still violates securities law if the promoter fails to disclose the existence of compensation.

Pump-and-Dump Scheme

While some information posted on FSM platforms is legitimate, other content may be fraudulent. Fraudsters sometimes exploit online discussions to execute pump-and-dump schemes, particularly targeting vulnerable microcap companies. They often use aliases to post messages urging investors to buy or sell stocks based on supposedly "insider" information, which is often false or misleading. To maximize their trading profits, fraudsters may risk using fabricated news, despite knowing it is illegal. For example, they might create press releases that exaggerate or lie about a company's sales, acquisitions, revenue projections, products, or services, coupled with explicit trading sentiments, and disseminate them under various aliases via FSM platforms. Pump-and-dump schemes typically involve lesser-known microcap companies due to the lack of market information about these firms. Many microcap companies do not file reports with the SEC, have weak fundamentals, minimal institutional holdings, thin trading volumes, and are not covered by financial analysts. With sufficient evidence of securities fraud, regulators can prosecute and incarcerate these fraudsters.

A New Channel to Disclose Information

On April 2, 2013, the SEC issued guidelines allowing companies to use social media sites, including FSM platforms, to communicate company announcements. This decision followed an investigation into Netflix's CEO, Reed Hastings, who in July 2013 posted monthly viewership results on his Facebook page instead of filing with the SEC or issuing a traditional news release. U.S. companies can now post corporate announcements on any social media site, if investors are informed in advance where to look for the information. Although many companies have not yet replaced traditional media with social media for official news dissemination, this trend is likely to grow in the future.

Implications for Financial Markets

Market Efficiency

Market efficiency refers to the extent to which stock prices reflect all available and relevant information. In the early 2000s, initial research indicated that activities on FSM platforms did not predict industry-adjusted returns or abnormal trading volumes. However, the influence of online discussions has grown significantly over time. Scholars have begun to observe tangible market impacts stemming from information shared on FSM platforms, leading to the belief that these platforms contribute to improving market efficiency overall. The primary benefit for investors is the ability to receive and share information quickly and freely, allowing them to react to news more swiftly. This, in turn, enables more accurate trades, with reduced instances of overreaction and mispricing.

Predicting Market Movement

Recent empirical evidence supports the notion that sentiments derived from FSM platforms possess predictive power regarding both simple and market-adjusted stock returns. Additionally, the aggregated sentiment of posters on these platforms has shown significant predictive power over the future movements of the stock market. As previously mentioned, FSM platforms provide valuable information for traders, and the sentiments expressed therein can serve as predictors of trading activities. Consequently, trading strategies based on FSM platform data have proven to be viable. Institutional investors, such as hedge funds, have already developed successful trading strategies using social media data. Some researchers have found that the volume of messages on these platforms can help predict future trading volatility, while others have discovered that poster sentiment can predict future small-trade volumes. Thus, trading strategies involving volatility-dependent financial derivatives may be formulated based on FSM activity.

At this point, growing evidence suggests that FSM activity can predict future market movements, including returns, trading volume, and volatility. However, these predictions are generally more significant at the aggregate level rather than the individual firm level. This suggests that trading strategies based on FSM information are more viable and profitable when applied to a large basket of securities rather than a select few.

Higher Risk Due to Herding

Herding behavior among traders is a growing concern, as it can lead to increased market volatility. Herding is a term in behavioral finance that describes situations in which individuals make similar investment decisions simultaneously, largely because others are doing the same. When herding occurs on a large scale, volatility tends to rise, which increases the risk (or uncertainty) for investors.

Many scholars have identified severe herding patterns associated with stocks that are frequently discussed on FSM platforms. These herding activities often involve stocks highlighted in online discussions, and scholars have cautioned that FSM platforms can serve as mechanisms for herding. This behavior can temporarily increase stock prices before the trend reverses, resulting in higher-than-normal trading volumes and excess volatility. A consequence of herding is that online investors may overreact to market news or rumors, whether positive or negative, causing stock prices to move further away from their fundamental values. However, the increased trading volume can also lead to higher liquidity and a narrower bid-ask spread, which can potentially reduce trading costs for investors.

Illegal Activities

Illegal activities on FSM platforms primarily involve securities fraud, a deceptive practice that induces investors to make trading decisions based on false information, often resulting in financial losses and violations of securities laws. Previously, I discussed various forms of online securities fraud, including selling fraudulent or unregistered securities to unsophisticated investors, attacking a company's reputation without justification, recommending stocks without disclosing compensation, and participating in pump-and-dump schemes. These fraudulent activities have numerous negative consequences, including financial losses for investors, diminished investor confidence, increased burdens on regulators, taxpayer costs, damage to corporate reputations, disruption of trading order, and impediments to market efficiency and fairness. Despite these risks, FSM platforms offer more benefits than drawbacks, and securities fraud can be monitored and mitigated through appropriate legislation and regulation.

Implications for Researchers

The recent surge in FSM platform usage has attracted the attention of researchers, highlighting the growing interest in Internet-based stock trading. Studies on FSM platforms date back to the late 1990s when both researchers and investors sought to explain abnormal, Internet-driven stock performances that were not accounted for by classical finance theories. Since then, researchers have been exploring various questions to determine the real impact of FSM platforms.

Noise or Useful Information?

The most fundamental question is whether online discussions are merely noise or if they contain valuable information. Evidence increasingly suggests that online talk is indeed significant and provides useful insights for investors. There are several empirical approaches to examining this. Initially, researchers found a correlation between same-day posting volume and contemporaneous stock returns. Subsequent studies have continued to investigate whether posting volume has predictive power. However, many findings suggest that posting volume either fails to predict future stock returns or does so only weakly. Researchers have also explored poster sentiment and disagreement as potential predictors of future stock-trading activities. Fortunately, several recent studies conclude that FSM sentiment and disagreement are important indicators of future trading behavior. In summary, empirical evidence clearly refutes the notion that online discussions are merely noise.

Does the Market React to Online Talk?

A key area of FSM platform research involves determining whether the market responds to online discussions. The event study methodology is commonly used to assess market reactions to specific events, such as online conversations. Specifically, an event study measures the impact of online discussions on stock returns and trading volume on days when messages are posted. Early event studies often reveal a significant market response on days with heavy online discussion. For example, stock returns tend to be higher on days with active online chatter, with positive returns correlating with optimistic sentiments and negative returns with pessimistic ones. Additionally, trading volume often increases on these days, indicating a market response to online talk.

However, there are two challenges. First, online traders tend to focus on smaller stocks, which may skew the results. Researchers have noted that large-cap stocks may not exhibit the same market response to online discussions as small-cap stocks do. Second, market reactions to material news might overshadow the impact of online talk. In such cases, online discussions may intensify following significant market news, leading to potentially misleading event study results if not properly controlled.

Researchers have begun examining asymmetric market reactions to different categories of stocks while controlling for the presence of market news. Preliminary evidence suggests that when event studies are free from external news contamination, the market responds to FSM posting activity, especially for microcap stocks. Findings also show a significant positive reaction on heavy discussion days for small stocks, regardless of whether news is present. In contrast, large stocks exhibit only a modest market reaction on discussion days with news and no significant reaction on days without news.

A Rise in Herding?

FSM platforms can be viewed as virtual financial communities where individuals discuss stocks and trading strategies, quickly absorbing others' opinions and decisions. Researchers are keen to determine whether FSM platforms can serve as herding mechanisms, potentially driving stock prices up or down in pump-and-dump schemes. Herding behavior is characterized by irrational decision-making that is not based on independent fundamental analysis. It can lead to large, unjustified buy-ins or sell-offs, often driven by minimal fundamental data and reinforced by social media.

When multiple posters (possibly including numerous aliases used by the same individual) express a similar sentiment about a stock, it can create the impression that this reflects the majority view among online investors. Consequently, investors may follow the general sentiment and trade accordingly, especially on platforms frequented by inexperienced traders.

Given this, it is plausible that FSM platforms could be exploited by manipulators to conduct pump-and-dump schemes. Recent studies have indeed found strong herding behavior among online investors when there is a consensus on an FSM platform. Therefore, researchers argue that FSM platforms can effectively serve as herding mechanisms for stock manipulation.

Biased Self-Disclosed Sentiment?

Most online posters are believed to be individual traders, and it is well-documented that individual investors generally hold long positions (buy-and-hold) and rarely engage in short selling due to high costs, limitations on short selling, the inherent risks, and the relative ease with which financial institutions facilitate long positions. Additionally, online traders typically post on FSM platforms when they already have positions in a particular stock, leading to the assumption that discussions are generally biased toward long positions. This bias is reflected in the prevalence of bullish sentiments over bearish ones, as well as the stronger language used to express positive views (e.g., "Strong Buy" versus "Buy").

Financial analysts, in contrast, are expected to provide more objective opinions based on thorough analysis and due diligence. The question arises: Do online posters exhibit similar objectivity? Researchers have investigated this by analyzing "Hold" (neutral) sentiments posted by day traders. Their findings suggest that even "Hold" sentiments are not free from bias and tend to reflect a buy-side inclination, likely due to the predominance of long positions among day traders. This suggests that online posters' sentiments are often biased toward their existing trading positions. Although this issue has not been fully explored, it is reasonable to infer that bullish sentiments are more subjective, while bearish sentiments are relatively more objective.

Implications for Educators

Beyond investors, institutions, and regulators, FSM platforms also have important implications for education and academic research. The rise of FSM has significant implications for educators, particularly those teaching finance, economics, communication, and related fields. As social media continues to shape the landscape of financial markets, it is essential that educators understand these changes and adapt their teaching methods accordingly.

Integrating Social Media into Financial Education

FSM platforms, such as TheLion, Stocktwits, and Reddit, have become key sources of information and discussion for investors. Educators need to incorporate these platforms into their curricula to provide students with a comprehensive understanding of modern financial markets. By analyzing real-time discussions and trends, students can learn how social media influences market sentiment, trading behavior, and stock prices. Case studies based on social media-driven market events, like the GameStop short squeeze, can help illustrate the practical impact of these platforms on financial markets.

Teaching Critical Evaluation of Information

One of the biggest challenges in the age of FSM is the sheer volume of information, much of which can be biased, misleading, or outright false. Educators must emphasize the importance of critical thinking and the ability to discern reliable information from noise. This includes teaching students how to verify sources, assess the credibility of online posts, and recognize the potential for manipulation, such as pump-and-dump schemes or biased sentiment from individuals with vested interests.

Ethics in Financial Communication

With the increasing influence of social media on financial markets, there is a growing need for ethical considerations in financial communication. Educators should address the ethical responsibilities of individuals and institutions when discussing financial information online. This includes the importance of transparency, the risks of spreading misinformation, and the potential consequences of unethical behavior, both for individuals and the market. Discussions on the legal implications, such as the SEC regulations on insider trading and market manipulation, are also crucial.

Preparing Students for a Social Media-Driven Financial World

As future professionals, students must be prepared to navigate a financial landscape increasingly shaped by social media. This includes understanding how to leverage social media for market research, investor relations, and personal branding. Educators can provide practical training in using social media tools and analytics to track market trends, gauge investor sentiment, and communicate effectively with a broad audience. Courses should also cover the potential risks and challenges of social media, such as the spread of misinformation and the impact of viral trends on market stability.

Research Opportunities in Financial Social Media

The evolving nature of FSM presents numerous opportunities for academic research. Educators should encourage students to explore this field, whether through empirical studies on the impact of social media on market efficiency, sentiment analysis of online discussions, or the role of social media in shaping investor behavior. By fostering a research-oriented mindset, educators can help students contribute to the growing body of knowledge in this area and develop a deeper understanding of the complex interactions between social media and financial markets.

Lifelong Learning and Adaptation

Given the rapid pace of technological change, it is crucial for educators to instill a mindset of lifelong learning in their students. The tools and platforms that dominate FSM today may evolve or be replaced by new technologies. Educators should emphasize the importance of staying current with industry trends, continuously updating skills, and being adaptable in a dynamic environment. This will ensure that students remain relevant and effective in their future careers.

By addressing these implications, educators can better prepare their students for the challenges and opportunities presented by the integration of social media into financial markets. As FSM continues to evolve, so must the approaches and strategies used in financial education.

CHAPTER 14

GameStop and Other Meme Stocks' Short Squeeze Frenzy

Introduction

In early 2021, financial markets witnessed an extraordinary event that rattled Wall Street and drew global attention. A community of retail traders on the Reddit platform WallStreetBets (WSB hereafter) collectively participated in an aggressive wave of buying that propelled GameStop (GME) shares from roughly $20 to nearly $400 within weeks. This surge triggered one of the most dramatic short squeezes in Wall Street history, blindsiding professional hedge funds and igniting widespread debate over the shifting balance of power in contemporary trading.

While GameStop was the focal point, the frenzy soon expanded to other stocks such as AMC Entertainment, BlackBerry, Nokia, and Bed Bath & Beyond, which were heavily shorted by hedge funds. Online retail investors, energized by a sense of rebellion and empowerment, viewed this as an opportunity to challenge institutional dominance, turning the movement into a symbolic clash between everyday investors and Wall Street. It was about more than just profits; it was a cultural moment fueled by viral Internet memes and social media-driven populism.

This phenomenon was enabled by popular commission-free trading platforms like Robinhood, which allowed retail traders to buy shares and options in large volumes, triggering a massive short squeeze. Hedge funds with significant short positions were forced to cover their bets, pushing prices even higher and resulting in billions of dollars in losses. Media

Y. Zhang, *Financial Social Media*,
https://doi.org/10.1007/978-3-032-09332-5_14

coverage only added fuel to the fire, drawing in more traders and further intensifying the volatility.

Social media platforms such as Reddit, X.com (formerly Twitter), and Discord played a central role in organizing and amplifying the movement. Traders exchanged strategies, celebrated their gains, and urged others to hold their positions despite sharp price fluctuations, using rallying cries like "diamond hands" and "to the moon." What began as a niche conversation quickly evolved into a global phenomenon, attracting participants from diverse backgrounds. The situation escalated significantly that Robinhood and other platforms restricted trading on certain stocks, sparking accusations of unfair market intervention. This led to widespread public protest and Congressional hearings, as well as calls for stricter regulatory oversight. The episode raised important questions about the fairness of the financial system, the role of technology, and the balance of power between retail investors and large institutions.

This chapter will discuss the causes and consequences of the GameStop short squeeze, the rise of other meme stocks, and the crucial role financial social media (FSM hereafter) and the options market played in these events. It will also explore the broader implications for financial markets, regulations, and the future of retail trading as the fallout from this extraordinary episode continues to unfold.

WallStreetBets: The Epicenter of the Meme Stock Frenzy

WSB, a subreddit known for high-risk trading, became the center of the meme stock movement. Meme stocks are equities that see a surge in volume not due to company performance, but due to social media hype and community coordination. For years, WSB attracted traders willing to take bold risks, often betting on volatile stocks and options. By late 2020, WSB's user base exploded, fueled by interest in heavily shorted stocks like GameStop. One user, Keith Gill (known as "Roaring Kitty" on the Internet), posted a detailed analysis of GameStop, arguing it was undervalued and primed for a short squeeze. A short squeeze happens when a stock's price rises sharply, forcing short-sellers to buy back shares, pushing prices even higher. Gill's posts resonated with the community, and momentum built around GameStop.

As GameStop's stock price surged in early 2021, WSB's enthusiasm grew. The stock's rise, fueled by retail investors, soon captured mainstream attention. GameStop became a "meme stock," driven more by online excitement than traditional financial metrics. But for many WSB users, the rally wasn't just about making money, it was a symbolic fight against Wall Street institutions, particularly hedge funds that had shorted GameStop heavily.

GameStop's stock skyrocketed from under $20 to over $400, and WSB users celebrated each milestone with memes and stories of financial triumph. The movement gave retail investors a sense of empowerment, temporarily shaking Wall Street. However, as quickly as the stock soared, it fell just as fast, leaving many latecomers with significant losses. Despite this, the impact of the GameStop incident on retail trading and financial markets was undeniable.

This event represents one episode in Reddit's growing influence on the financial world. In 2024, Reddit went public under the ticker RDDT, opening at $47 per share and reaching a valuation of $8 billion. The IPO marked Reddit's emergence as a major player in both social media and finance. Reddit's success continues to hinge on its community, and the platform remains influential in shaping retail investing, including newer areas like cryptocurrencies. WSB, still a driving force within Reddit, continues to play a significant role in influencing markets, making it an FSM platform to watch as the world of retail trading evolves.

The Mechanics of Short Selling and Short Squeezes

Short selling is a trading strategy that allows investors to profit from declining stock prices. It involves borrowing shares, selling them at the current market price, and later repurchasing them at a lower price to return to the lender. The profit comes from the difference between the selling price and the lower repurchase price, essentially selling high first and then buying back low.

For example, if an investor shorts a stock at $100, selling 100 shares for $10,000, and the price later drops to $80, they can repurchase the shares for $8000, making a $2000 profit. However, if the stock rises instead, short-sellers can face unlimited losses, since they must buy back the shares at the market price, no matter how high it goes. If the stock rises to $150, for instance, they would lose $5000.

A short squeeze happens when a heavily shorted stock unexpectedly rises, forcing short-sellers to buy shares to minimize losses. Their buying activity pushes the stock price even higher, creating a cycle of rising prices and forced buybacks. The January 2021 GameStop short squeeze provides a clear example. Heavily shorted by hedge funds, more than 100% of GameStop's shares were sold short. When retail investors on FSM platforms like WSB began buying the stock on a massive scale, the price soared from $20 to nearly $500, triggering panic among short-sellers, such as Melvin Capital, who rushed to cover their positions, amplifying the price surge. Short squeezes illustrate how market dynamics can create extreme volatility, catching short-sellers off guard and resulting in significant losses. While short selling can be profitable, its risks, especially in cases like GameStop, make it a highly speculative and dangerous strategy.

Gamma Squeezes: The Role of Options Trading

A key factor in the GameStop incident was the use of call options, which give investors the right to buy a stock at a set price before a specific expiration date. When the stock price rises above this strike price, the option becomes profitable. As retail traders purchased large volumes of call options for GameStop, market makers who sold these options had to hedge their exposure by buying shares of the stock. This increased demand for shares pushed the stock price even higher, triggering what is known as a gamma squeeze.

A gamma squeeze occurs when the rapid buying by market makers, who must buy shares to cover their positions as more options move "in the money," drives the stock price up further. This creates a feedback loop where rising prices lead to more hedging, which in turn drives prices even higher.

In the GameStop case, the gamma squeeze amplified the price surge caused by the short squeeze. As more call options became profitable, market makers had to buy more shares, fueling the stock's dramatic rise. This dynamic, where options trading significantly impacts stock prices, shows how online retail investors can influence large-scale price movements through concentrated buying.

The interaction between call options and stock prices in the GameStop event illustrates the powerful role options trading can play in amplifying volatility. Online retail investors, by buying large amounts of call options, forced market makers into a cycle of stock buying that intensified the price surge. This episode underscores how options markets can shape stock movements, particularly when driven by coordinated retail action.

The Fallout for Hedge Funds

The 2021 GameStop short squeeze sent shockwaves through the hedge fund industry, leading to significant losses for firms heavily betting against the stock. Hedge funds were blindsided by the sudden price surge, driven by online retail investors from FSM platforms like Reddit's WSB. One of the most affected was Melvin Capital, which had taken a large short position in GameStop. As the stock skyrocketed, Melvin faced over $6 billion in losses and needed a $2.75 billion bailout from Citadel and Point72 to stay afloat. Despite the bailout, the firm's reputation took a severe hit.

Melvin Capital was not alone. Other hedge funds that had shorted GameStop, AMC, and similar stocks also suffered significant losses. Collectively, the hedge fund industry suffered losses exceeding $20 billion. This event forced many firms to rethink their risk management practices, highlighting the dangers of short selling, especially when market forces are driven by unpredictable retail actions.

Short selling itself is a risky strategy. Hedge funds borrow shares and sell them, hoping to buy them back later at a lower price to turn a profit. However, when a stock's price rises instead of falling, the potential losses are theoretically limitless. This is what happened during the GameStop squeeze—retail investors piled into the stock, sending its price soaring and forcing hedge funds to buy back shares at a much higher cost.

The GameStop situation revealed that many hedge funds had underestimated the influence of online retail investors and FSM. Hedge funds, convinced that GameStop was a solid short bet due to its business struggles, failed to account for the power of collective action from online retail investors. When the stock price surged, hedge funds were forced into a short squeeze, leading to devastating financial losses. In response, many hedge funds began revising their strategies. Some reduced their short positions, diversified their portfolios, or avoided heavily shorted stocks altogether. Others implemented stricter risk management protocols to prevent future losses from similar events.

The GameStop incident also sparked a broader debate about the ethics of short selling and market manipulation. Many retail traders viewed their participation as a form of financial justice, seeing it as a chance to profit while hedge funds incurred losses. The squeeze highlighted growing concerns about market fairness, with some accusing hedge funds of manipulating stock prices for their benefit.

While the short squeeze empowered many online retail investors, it also resulted in substantial losses for those who bought at the peak. This sparked concerns about whether retail participants fully grasped the risks of meme stock trading and whether the excitement was leading inexperienced traders to incur significant losses.

The hedge fund losses also prompted calls for stricter regulation. Some lawmakers pushed for closer oversight of short-selling practices and more protections for online retail investors. The GameStop event was a wake-up call for both hedge funds and retail traders, emphasizing the need for caution and stronger risk management in an increasingly volatile market.

The Broader Meme Stock Movement: AMC, Nokia, and beyond

While GameStop dominated headlines during the meme stock frenzy, it wasn't the only company targeted by retail traders. Stocks like AMC, BlackBerry, Nokia, Bed Bath & Beyond, and Koss Corporation saw similar speculative surges, driven largely by sentiment and FSM coordination. These companies, largely overlooked by institutional investors, became hot targets for a short period.

For instance, BlackBerry, once a leader in smartphones, had shifted its focus to cybersecurity. Despite this, online retail investors driven by fond memories of the brand pushed its stock price up more than 250 percent in January 2021. As with GameStop, the spike was unsustainable, and those who bought in at the peak faced steep losses when prices corrected.

Nokia and Bed Bath & Beyond experienced similar surges, despite no fundamental changes in their businesses. These price increases were driven by coordinated buying rather than market fundamentals, offering quick profits for some but leaving others exposed to potential long-term losses when the hype faded.

The meme stock phenomenon had a significant impact on market dynamics, raising questions about the power balance between online retail investors and institutional investors, and the role of FSM platforms like Reddit in coordinating mass buying. It also sparked debates about transparency in trading and the ability of traditional markets to handle such volatility.

AMC Entertainment quickly became another focal point. Its stock jumped from under $5 in early January 2021 to over $20 by the end of the month. Like GameStop, AMC was hit hard by the pandemic in 2020, making it attractive to short-sellers. Online retail investors, many with sentimental ties to the cinema chain, saw an opportunity to support the company and trigger a short squeeze.

Other stocks, like Sundial Growers (SNDL), also saw retail-driven surges. Many of these companies had high short interest, and brands like Nokia and BlackBerry carried sentimental appeal. While not all these stocks reached the levels of GameStop or AMC, the movement highlighted the disruptive potential of retail traders.

The meme stock craze became more than just a financial event. It showcased how collective retail actions could disrupt traditional stock market norms and demonstrated the growing influence of grassroots movements on market dynamics.

The Robinhood Controversy: Market Manipulation or Risk Management?

In early 2021, Robinhood, a popular brokerage app, found itself at the center of controversy when it restricted trading in GameStop, AMC, and other meme stocks during their price surges. On January 28, 2021, the platform, along with others, limited users from buying more shares of these volatile stocks while still allowing sales. This decision outraged retail traders, who saw it as favoring institutional investors.

Robinhood stated that it was compelled to act due to requirements imposed by the clearinghouse. To process trades, clearinghouses demand brokerage firms hold a certain amount of capital to manage risks during periods of extreme volatility. According to Robinhood's CEO, Vlad Tenev, the spike in demand for meme stocks pushed the company close to violating these requirements, leaving no choice but to restrict trading. He argued that without these measures, the platform's stability could have been compromised, worsening market turmoil. However, online retail investors saw it differently. Many believed Robinhood's move protected hedge funds that had shorted these stocks, accusing the platform of abandoning its mission to democratize finance. Conspiracy theories circulated, claiming that Citadel, one of Robinhood's financial backers and a major market maker, pressured the platform to halt trading to protect institutional interests.

The backlash was swift. Furious users flooded social media, lawsuits were filed, and public figures, including lawmakers, called for investigations into whether Robinhood's relationships with Wall Street influenced its actions. Critics argued that allowing only sales created an imbalance, artificially suppressing stock prices and disadvantaging online retail investors. Robinhood defended the decision as necessary risk management to avoid a potential platform collapse.

In the aftermath, Tenev testified before Congress, explaining that Robinhood had to deposit over $3 billion with clearinghouses to support the surge in meme stock trading. He denied any outside influence, including from Citadel, and emphasized that the decision was purely about stabilizing the platform, not protecting hedge funds. Skepticism lingered, as the hearings highlighted potential conflicts of interest in Robinhood's business model. Under a system called "payment for order flow," Robinhood receives payments from market makers like Citadel for routing trades through them, raising concerns about whether these relationships affected Robinhood's decisions. The controversy dealt a blow to Robinhood's image as a champion of retail investors and sparked multiple class-action lawsuits from traders who claimed the restrictions caused financial losses. It also reignited debates over market transparency, retail investor protection, and the fairness of the financial system, with some arguing that hedge funds still hold an unfair advantage.

While Robinhood has continued to grow and attract new users, the events of January 2021 left a lasting mark on its reputation, highlighting the delicate balance between technology, finance, and regulation in modern financial markets.

The Long-Term Performance of Meme Stocks

The dramatic rise of meme stocks like GameStop and AMC captured the financial world's attention in early 2021. However, after the short squeeze frenzy faded, the long-term performance of these stocks became a point of focus. Online retail investors, largely driven by social media, propelled stock prices to astonishing highs, with GameStop briefly surpassing $400, but these gains were not sustained. Meme stocks have since seen significant volatility, with GameStop, AMC, and others undergoing sharp corrections from their peaks. Though prices remained higher than pre-surge levels, their unpredictable movements revealed the speculative nature of these rallies, posing risks to investors holding these stocks long-term.

A key issue with meme stocks is the disconnect between stock prices and company fundamentals. Retail-driven rallies were sparked by factors like short interest and social media buzz, rather than by improvements in the underlying businesses. For example, GameStop, despite efforts to transition to e-commerce, still faces industry headwinds in the form of declining physical game sales. Similarly, AMC, while benefiting from post-pandemic theater reopening and attempts to diversify with initiatives like accepting cryptocurrency, is burdened with debt and struggling against the rise of streaming platforms.

The meme stock phenomenon challenges traditional investment theory, which holds that stock prices should reflect a company's intrinsic value. In these cases, online retail investors disrupted market norms, pushing prices beyond what professional analysts would consider reasonable. The question remains whether such rallies are sustainable without corresponding improvements in the companies' business models. For many investors, the speculative nature of meme stocks has resulted in a high-risk, high-reward scenario. Early traders who capitalized on the short squeeze profited, but those who bought near the peaks often faced significant losses. Many were driven by a fear of missing out (FOMO), rather than confidence in the companies' long-term potential. Concerns have also emerged about possible manipulation of online retail investors by more sophisticated market participants. Some analysts believe that institutional traders may have taken advantage of meme stock volatility, profiting by selling before price corrections and leaving less experienced retail investors holding inflated stocks. The extreme price movements in meme stocks have sparked discussions about regulatory oversight and the influence of FSM on stock prices. The SEC and other regulators have investigated whether these rallies indicate market manipulation or expose gaps in protections for retail traders.

In conclusion, while meme stocks like GameStop and AMC altered retail investing and generated profits for some, their long-term performance reveals a more complex picture. These stocks have proven to be volatile and speculative, often disconnected from traditional measures of value, leaving many retail traders with losses. The future of meme stocks will likely hinge on whether the companies behind them can successfully adapt to changing market conditions.

Regulatory Responses: The Future of Retail Trading and Market Oversight

The GameStop event sparked widespread reflection on how financial markets are structured, regulated, and how retail investors participate in them. The ability of retail traders, coordinated through FSM platforms, to exert significant influence on stock prices shook traditional views on market behavior. This event highlighted several areas of concern regarding market fairness, transparency, and the systems underpinning retail trading.

A central issue that emerged was the role of payment for order flow (PFOF hereafter). This practice involves retail brokers directing customers' trade orders to certain market makers in exchange for a fee. While PFOF is legal and common in the financial world, critics argue it creates conflicts of interest. Brokers may be motivated to route orders to market makers who offer them the highest payment, potentially at the expense of their clients getting the best execution on their trades. During the meme stock frenzy, attention was drawn to the relationship between Robinhood, a popular retail trading platform, and Citadel, a market maker. Many online retail investors believed Robinhood's decision to restrict trading was influenced by its financial ties to Citadel, raising concerns about the transparency and fairness of these arrangements.

In the wake of these concerns, there have been calls for reform. Lawmakers and regulators, including Gary Gensler, chairman of the SEC, have signaled that they are reviewing the implications of PFOF. Potential changes may include stricter rules on the practice or even the banning of PFOF altogether, along with measures to ensure greater transparency between retail brokers and the market makers they partner with.

Beyond PFOF, the incident also reignited debates around short selling. Short selling is a legitimate strategy in financial markets, helping with price discovery and market efficiency. However, the massive losses suffered by hedge funds that were shorting GameStop led some to question whether the risks of shorting are adequately controlled. In response, certain hedge funds have reduced their short positions, while regulators have considered reforms aimed at increasing disclosure requirements for short-sellers, potentially giving retail traders more insight into which stocks have large short interests. These changes are aimed at preventing the kind of extreme volatility seen during the meme stock craze.

Another area of regulatory focus has been the risks tied to options trading, particularly among retail investors. The increased accessibility of options trading platforms like Robinhood allowed many inexperienced investors to trade complex financial instruments, sometimes without fully understanding the risks involved. The popularity of call options during the GameStop frenzy, which contributed to a gamma squeeze, underscored the dangers of unregulated options activity. Some regulators have suggested that platforms may need to implement stronger safeguards to protect investors from significant financial losses tied to options trading. Discussions include introducing more stringent checks to ensure that traders are aware of the potential risks and providing greater transparency in the options market to prevent unforeseen price surges.

In addition to these specific market practices, the GameStop incident also prompted broader questions about market manipulation and FSM's role in stock trading. The phenomenon where traders band together to drive stock prices, often based on sentiment rather than company fundamentals, challenged the traditional understanding of efficient markets. While some regulators worry about the potential for manipulation in these scenarios, others argue that the involvement of online retail investors represents a democratization of markets, where everyday investors have more say in price movements. Going forward, regulators may need to strike a balance between encouraging retail participation and ensuring that markets remain fair and transparent for all participants.

In sum, the GameStop incident has led to an ongoing reevaluation of key financial practices and raised important questions about the future of retail trading. How regulators respond will likely shape the landscape of financial markets for years to come, influencing how individual traders, institutional players, and platforms operate.

Final Thoughts: A Turning Point in Retail Trading

The GameStop short squeeze and the wider meme stock frenzy of early 2021 became a critical moment in financial history, redefining the relationship between online retail investors and the broader financial markets. For many participants, this was seen as a revolutionary act of financial activism, a rare opportunity for retail investors to challenge the dominance of large hedge funds and institutional investors who had, until then, maintained significant power in the market. By coordinating through FSM platforms like Reddit's WSB, retail traders aimed to reverse what they saw as unfair practices, namely the excessive shorting of stocks by institutions that profited from the downfall of companies.

In essence, the meme stock rally was about collective action. Online retail investors, who traditionally lacked the capital and influence to move markets, realized that they could make a significant impact by working together. This was not just about making quick profits, though that was certainly a motivator for many. It was also about sending a message that Main Street could fight back against Wall Street's elite, exposing weaknesses in the system. The rally was driven by a mix of speculation, frustration, and a desire to level the playing field in what was perceived as a rigged financial game.

However, the fallout from the meme stock frenzy has also highlighted the inherent risks of speculative trading, particularly for those who lack experience. Many retail traders who entered the fray at the height of the short squeeze found themselves on the losing end when the bubble burst and prices of stocks like GameStop and AMC plunged. These individuals, motivated by the excitement of seeing stocks soar in value, often failed to grasp the complexities of short squeezes or the volatility that can accompany such rapid price movements. For some, this translated into significant financial losses, especially those who were caught up in the FOMO mentality.

The aftermath of the meme stock rally, though quieter, is no less important. It has prompted regulatory bodies and lawmakers to take a closer look at the dynamics of retail trading platforms and the role of FSM in influencing markets. Platforms like Robinhood came under intense scrutiny for their role in restricting trades at critical moments, sparking accusations of protecting institutional interests over those of online retail investors. These events have led to ongoing discussions about market fairness, regulatory oversight, and the potential conflicts of interest between retail brokers (such as Robinhood and E*TRADE) and the financial institutions that back them.

Moreover, this period also marked a paradigm shift in how financial markets can be influenced by public sentiment. Unlike previous decades, where market movements were dominated by economic fundamentals and institutional decision-making, the meme stock incident showed that FSM trends and viral content can significantly impact stock prices. Equipped with free trading apps and driven by viral online posts, retail investors were able to create short-term disruptions in markets traditionally dominated by professionals. This raised new questions about whether financial markets, long seen as efficient and rational, can now be swayed by mass sentiment more than by underlying value.

As the dust settles, one of the lingering questions is: What does this mean for the future of retail trading? The meme stock episode has left an indelible mark, reminding everyone of the power of retail traders in a digitized financial landscape. Whether this newfound influence will lead to lasting structural changes in markets or simply remain a unique event in financial history is unclear. Many analysts and market commentators are already predicting a rise in regulation as governments and regulatory bodies like the SEC grapple with the implications of retail-driven market volatility.

In the long term, this event has also spurred debates about market transparency. Retail investors, who have historically lacked the resources and data that institutional investors enjoy, may now be calling for better access to information and market tools. If retail traders are to continue playing a significant role in financial markets, it may require not only education but also the creation of a more equitable system—one that addresses the imbalance between institutional and individual investors.

Ultimately, the GameStop short squeeze was emblematic of much larger societal trends. It reflected the democratization of finance, where barriers to entry in stock trading have been lowered, allowing anyone with a smartphone to participate in markets. It showcased the enormous power of FSM, which enabled retail traders to coordinate and rally around specific stocks. And finally, it demonstrated the growing discontent among individuals who feel left out of traditional financial systems, turning to unconventional methods to make their voices heard.

As we move forward, the lessons from the meme stock incident will likely shape the future of both market regulation and retail investing. Whether this results in a more inclusive and transparent financial system or simply introduces new complexities and risks remains to be seen. Nonetheless, it's clear that the events of 2021 will be studied for years to come, serving as a powerful reminder of how quickly financial markets can change when new players enter the field with new tools and motivations.

Academic Perspectives on the GameStop Short Squeeze

The GameStop short squeeze is widely recognized as a unique and revolutionary moment in financial history. It demonstrated the power of retail investors, interacting through FSM platforms like Reddit's WSB, to challenge traditional market players like hedge funds. Scholars have analyzed this phenomenon from several angles, including the role of FSM, collective online retail investor behavior, and its impact on market efficiency.

FSM platforms, particularly Reddit, played a pivotal role in driving the meme stock frenzy. Researchers have noted how online communities empowered individual investors to share information, speculate on stock movements, and even challenge institutional investors. Welch (2022) highlighted the influence of platforms like Robinhood on retail investor behavior. He argued that while Robinhood traders can exhibit some collective intelligence, their behavior during the GameStop event often resembled herd mentality, driven by emotions and speculative fervor rather than fundamentals.

Narratives played a central role in the GameStop frenzy. Shiller (2021), in his book Narrative Economics, discussed how stories can influence economic behavior, particularly in the stock market. The GameStop incident is a vivid example of narrative economics at work, where the story of retail investors versus Wall Street captured the public's imagination and drove participation in the short squeeze.

The GameStop short squeeze has provided fertile ground for academic inquiry across multiple disciplines. Whether from the lens of behavioral finance, market microstructure, or regulatory policy, scholars agree that the incident represents a watershed moment in financial history, reshaping how we understand the dynamics between retail investors, institutional players, and the role of social media in financial markets.

CHAPTER 15

How Metaverse Will Change Financial Social Media

Introduction

The rise of Metaverse represents a transformative shift in how individuals and organizations interact in the digital world. As an immersive, three-dimensional virtual space, Metaverse extends beyond the traditional social media landscape, offering a more dynamic, interactive, and participatory environment. Unlike conventional financial social media (FSM hereafter) platforms, where financial discussions occur through static posts, videos, and live streams, Metaverse enables users to engage in real-time, lifelike interactions within virtual financial hubs, simulated trading floors, and decentralized communities. This transformation holds profound implications for FSM, potentially redefining how financial information is shared, analyzed, and acted upon.

One of the most significant ways Metaverse will impact FSM is by fostering deeper engagement between investors, influencers, and financial institutions. Rather than just reading tweets or watching YouTube videos about market trends, users will be able to enter virtual environments to attend live financial seminars, join real-time trading simulations, and speak directly with industry experts from anywhere in the world. Virtual reality (VR) and augmented reality (AR) will make these experiences more engaging by offering interactive learning and hands-on investment simulations, bringing financial education to a wider audience.

Y. Zhang, *Financial Social Media*,
https://doi.org/10.1007/978-3-032-09332-5_15

Furthermore, the integration of decentralized finance (DeFi hereafter) within Metaverse will amplify the shift toward peer-to-peer financial interactions. Blockchain technology and tokenized assets will empower users to trade, lend, and invest directly within virtual ecosystems, bypassing traditional financial intermediaries. This new paradigm could democratize access to financial markets, providing opportunities for individuals across the globe to participate in economic activities without the constraints of centralized banking systems. However, it also raises critical questions regarding security, regulation, and financial transparency, as the decentralized nature of Metaverse financial platforms challenges existing legal frameworks.

Despite its immense potential, the convergence of Metaverse and FSM is not without challenges. Issues such as cybersecurity risks, misinformation, regulatory uncertainty, and digital identity verification will play a crucial role in determining the success and sustainability of financial activities in virtual spaces. As financial transactions and discussions become more immersive, ensuring user protection against fraud, data breaches, and financial manipulation will be paramount.

This chapter explores the evolving landscape of FSM within Metaverse, addressing both its transformative potential and the challenges that must be navigated. It examines the emergence of virtual financial communities, the role of DeFi in reshaping digital transactions, the impact of interactive trading simulations on investor behavior, the expansion of financial literacy through immersive experiences, and the regulatory frameworks that will shape the future of financial engagement in virtual environments. By understanding these dynamics, we can anticipate how FSM will evolve in the coming years, paving the way for a new era of financial communication and innovation.

Metaverse as a New Medium for Financial Social Interaction

Traditional FSM platforms such as X.com (formerly Twitter), Reddit, and specialized stock message boards and trading boards have long served as spaces where traders, investors, and financial enthusiasts share insights, discuss trends, and collaborate on investment strategies. These platforms have broadened access to financial discussions, allowing online retail investors to engage with market trends in real time, participate in viral stock movements, and gain exposure to diverse financial perspectives.

However, these interactions remain largely confined to two-dimensional interfaces, where discussions take place through text, images, and videos. While these platforms have successfully facilitated information exchange, they lack the depth, immediacy, and engagement of in-person financial discussions.

Metaverse introduces a spatial, immersive dimension that revolutionizes the way financial conversations take place. Users can interact within virtual environments such as financial districts, trading floors, or even simulations of Wall Street, where avatars can move freely, communicate via voice, and analyze live financial data projected into their surroundings. These interactions closely mimic real-world financial hubs, creating a more engaging and intuitive way to process complex financial information.

Virtual Financial Communities

FSM in Metaverse will extend beyond traditional forums and message boards to create vibrant, interactive financial communities. Instead of posting on subreddits or browsing investment tweets, users can step into digital environments where financial discussions unfold in real-time, fostering more dynamic and nuanced exchanges. These virtual communities may take various forms, including:

- Virtual Stock Exchanges: Spaces where traders gather to watch real-time price movements, conduct technical analysis, and share insights through voice discussions. These exchanges can feature immersive dashboards that allow users to change stock charts in three dimensions, test trading strategies in simulation mode, or receive AI-generated market summaries.
- Trading Lounges and Clubs: Private or public spaces where investors with shared interests such as cryptocurrency, real estate investing, or day trading gather to exchange ideas, discuss investment strategies, and collectively analyze market data. These environments can be tailored with tools like interactive financial models, algorithmic back-testing stations, and peer-led investment workshops.
- Financial Conferences and Panels: Events hosted in Metaverse where industry leaders, financial influencers, and economists discuss macroeconomic trends, market forecasts, and new financial technologies. Attendees can participate in Q&A sessions, visit virtual

booths showcasing fintech innovations, and network with others in a more engaging way than traditional webinars or live-streamed conferences.

- Metaverse Investment Clubs and DAOs: Groups of investors who come together to make collective investment decisions using Decentralized Autonomous Organizations (DAOs hereafter). These clubs can pool funds, vote on investment strategies, and execute trades through smart contracts, all within a fully immersive and transparent environment.

Unlike traditional online financial communities, which are often asynchronous and text-based, these Metaverse-based hubs enable real-time, voice-driven discussions that feel more natural and dynamic. Investors can engage in debates, host live strategy sessions, or even walk through financial graphs in 3D, making complex data more comprehensible and actionable.

A key advantage of these virtual financial communities is their ability to break geographical barriers. Investors from different parts of the world can interact seamlessly without the constraints of time zones or physical location. This fosters a more inclusive and globally connected financial ecosystem, where diverse perspectives converge in a shared space, facilitating knowledge exchange and collaboration on an unprecedented scale.

Enhanced Networking and Collaboration

Networking has always been a critical component of financial success, whether for individual investors seeking mentorship or professionals looking to build strategic partnerships. Metaverse redefines financial networking by enabling avatar-based interactions that capture the nuances of real-world engagements, such as body language, spatial awareness, and dynamic data visualization.

Investment firms, hedge funds, and trading companies can establish virtual headquarters where they host potential clients, conduct market briefings, and offer financial advisory services. These digital offices could feature:

- 3D Portfolio Walkthroughs: Clients can explore their investment portfolios in an interactive format, visualizing asset performance over time, comparing different investment scenarios, and engaging with data-driven simulations.
- Immersive Market Briefings: Instead of static PowerPoint presentations, financial analysts can present market insights through interactive data models, allowing clients to manipulate variables, test economic scenarios, and understand the implications of financial trends more clearly.
- Personalized Financial Planning: Advisors can guide clients through custom-built investment strategies, using AI-driven recommendations and virtual whiteboards to outline risk factors, diversification strategies, and projected returns.

These interactions go beyond traditional Zoom meetings or webinar-style consultations, offering a more engaging and informative client experience that fosters deeper trust and understanding.

Financial professionals, including traders, analysts, and portfolio managers, can use Metaverse as a collaborative space to enhance decision-making and market responsiveness. Some key use cases include:

- Virtual War Rooms for Traders: Investment teams can gather in real-time to analyze market trends, execute trades, and respond to financial news as it breaks. With live charts, AI-generated sentiment analysis, and interactive economic indicators, these war rooms create an optimal environment for split-second decision-making.
- Augmented Reality Data Visualization: Financial analysts can present reports with AR-enhanced charts that attendees can manipulate and dissect together. For example, a hedge fund manager reviewing a company's earnings report can pull up interactive financial statements, overlay economic indicators, and compare historical performance within a fully immersive space.
- Investor Presentations and Fundraising: Startups and fintech companies seeking investment can pitch their ideas in virtual boardrooms, using 3D models and immersive demonstrations to showcase their vision. Investors can engage in due diligence in real-time, interacting with financial projections and company roadmaps in a more intuitive manner than traditional pitch decks.

Independent financial influencers, educators, and content creators can leverage Metaverse to build more engaging and interactive audiences. Instead of hosting pre-recorded courses or live webinars on conventional platforms, they can conduct fully immersive learning experiences, where participants:

- Engage with financial models to understand stock market trends, economic cycles, or investment strategies.
- Participate in role-playing investment scenarios, where they act as fund managers, making real-time trading decisions based on simulated economic events.
- Network with other attendees in an interactive classroom setting, creating a more engaging alternative to passive content consumption.

The inclusion of AI-driven financial assistants further enhances these experiences. AI-powered virtual advisors can offer personalized market insights, recommend educational materials based on user preferences, and even assist in networking by suggesting relevant connections.

In sum, the transition from traditional FSM to an immersive Metaverse-driven ecosystem will fundamentally change how investors, professionals, and financial influencers engage with one another. By merging real-time collaboration, data-rich environments, and spatial interactivity, Metaverse offers an unparalleled medium for financial discourse.

The implications are vast: financial decision-making will become more informed through hands-on simulations, networking will become more intuitive and dynamic, and financial literacy will reach new heights through immersive educational experiences. While challenges such as security risks, misinformation, and regulatory concerns must be addressed, the potential for innovation far outweighs the obstacles. As Metaverse continues to evolve, FSM will transform into a deeply interactive, community-driven ecosystem that fosters collaboration, inclusivity, and greater financial empowerment.

Trading Simulations and Financial Education in Metaverse

One of the most compelling applications of Metaverse in FSM is its ability to revolutionize financial education and trading simulations. Traditional financial education often relies on static content such as books, online courses, and lectures that may not fully capture the complexities of real-world investing. Even interactive financial platforms, such as paper trading accounts and investment simulators, lack the immersion needed to replicate the fast-paced, high-stakes nature of financial markets.

Metaverse introduces an entirely new paradigm by creating real-time, interactive, and experiential learning environments that bridge the gap between theoretical knowledge and practical application. Through virtual stock exchanges, AI-driven simulations, and interactive trading experiences, both novice and experienced traders can refine their skills in an engaging and risk-free setting.

Interactive Trading and Investing

Gamification has already proven to be a powerful force in financial education, as seen with platforms like Robinhood, which employs game-like mechanics to make investing more engaging, and eToro, which introduces social trading elements to encourage knowledge sharing. However, these platforms are still confined to traditional digital interfaces. Metaverse can take gamification to an entirely new level by bringing financial markets to life in immersive, real-time environments.

Imagine a virtual trading floor, where users step into a fully simulated stock exchange. Here, participants can:

- Execute trades in a live market simulation, complete with stock price movements, order books, and economic indicators.
- Engage in trading competitions, where users test their investment strategies in simulated environments that mimic real-world market conditions.
- Practice risk management techniques, experiencing firsthand how different levels of leverage and asset allocation impact portfolio performance.

- Train in crisis scenarios, where users navigate market crashes, inflationary periods, and black swan events to understand how economic shifts influence financial decisions.

AI-driven financial simulations further enhance this experience by allowing users to replay historical market events and analyze their outcomes. For example, traders could step into a simulation of the 2008 financial crisis, observing how different asset classes responded to the collapse of Lehman Brothers. They could then adjust investment strategies, testing whether alternative approaches such as shorting specific assets or reallocating into commodities might have reduced losses.

Additionally, virtual trading platforms in Metaverse can introduce dynamic, AI-powered market conditions, where traders respond to breaking news, central bank decisions, and geopolitical events in real-time. These adaptive learning experiences can help investors develop the emotional resilience and strategic discipline required to navigate volatile markets.

By making trading more interactive and immersive, Metaverse provides a safe yet realistic environment for individuals to develop financial acumen before deploying real capital in live markets.

Interactive Financial Courses and Workshops

Metaverse has the potential to redefine financial education, moving beyond traditional lecture-based learning to fully immersive, hands-on experiences. Universities, financial institutions, and independent educators can create virtual campuses and financial training centers where students engage in experiential learning.

Instead of passive learning through textbooks and slideshows, students in Metaverse can:

- Interact with economic models, manipulating variables such as inflation rates, interest rates, and GDP growth to observe their effects on financial markets.
- Walk through stock market trends in a fully immersive space, observing how companies, sectors, and asset classes react to economic cycles.

- Collaborate on investment case studies, where teams of students analyze corporate earnings reports, assess risk factors, and present trading strategies to virtual instructors.

For example, an economics professor could host a live simulation of the Federal Reserve's interest rate decision, allowing students to act as policymakers, traders, and analysts. As decisions are made, participants could observe their impact on bond yields, stock prices, and currency markets in real time, reinforcing key economic principles through direct experience.

AI-driven financial assistants can personalize learning experiences by analyzing each student's progress and tailoring content accordingly. For instance:

- A beginner in investing might start with basic portfolio management exercises, gradually progressing to advanced trading strategies as they demonstrate proficiency.
- An AI tutor could provide instant feedback on trading decisions, explaining why a certain strategy succeeded or failed based on historical market data.
- Personalized courses could adapt in real-time, offering additional exercises on risk management, derivatives trading, or behavioral finance based on student performance.

Metaverse also enables live, interactive financial workshops, where participants engage in real-time discussions with investment professionals, economists, and financial influencers. Unlike traditional webinars, where interaction is limited to chat boxes and Q&A sessions, Metaverse workshops offer:

- Breakout rooms for investment discussions, where attendees form small groups to analyze stock market trends or debate financial strategies.
- Hands-on learning with virtual financial tools, such as AR-enhanced stock charts and predictive modeling software.
- One-on-one mentoring from industry experts, allowing students and professionals to receive tailored advice and career guidance.

Financial institutions could even host exclusive training programs for employees in corporate finance, portfolio management, and algorithmic trading, leveraging Metaverse to create realistic financial work environments that replicate the high-pressure decision-making of real markets.

Democratizing Financial Education: Making Investing Accessible to all

One of the most transformative aspects of Metaverse is its ability to democratize financial education, making high-quality investing knowledge accessible to a global audience.

- Financial education no longer needs to be limited to elite universities or expensive training programs. Anyone with a Metaverse-capable device can access world-class investment training.
- Underrepresented communities and developing economies can benefit from virtual financial literacy programs, helping to bridge knowledge gaps and empowering individuals to make informed financial decisions.
- Microlearning experiences can be integrated into everyday digital interactions, allowing users to pick up investing concepts in small, digestible lessons while navigating virtual spaces.

For example, a new investor from a developing country might step into a Metaverse-based financial literacy hub, where they can:

- Learn about the basics of stock markets, personal finance, and wealth building through interactive experiences.
- Participate in real-time trading challenges with peers worldwide.
- Access mentorship programs led by experienced investors, who provide guidance on investment principles and risk management strategies.

In sum, by combining real-time simulations, AI-driven learning, gamified trading environments, and immersive financial workshops, Metaverse may significantly reshape financial education and investing practices. This evolution will:

- Provide a safer, risk-free space for new investors to develop confidence and competence.
- Offer realistic and dynamic trading simulations, preparing participants for the fast-paced nature of financial markets.
- Democratize financial knowledge, making investment education more accessible and engaging for a global audience.
- Enhance collaboration among students, professionals, and mentors through interactive, experiential learning.

As FSM integrates more deeply into Metaverse, education will become more than just reading about markets. It will be an interactive, dynamic, and engaging experience that fosters better decision-making, improves financial literacy, and supports smarter investing for all.

Integration of Decentralized Finance (DeFi) and Digital Assets

The rise of DeFi and blockchain technology aligns naturally with Metaverse's decentralized, user-driven ecosystem. Traditional financial systems rely on centralized entities such as banks, exchanges, and regulators to facilitate transactions and maintain trust. However, DeFi introduces a trustless financial infrastructure where transactions occur directly between participants through smart contracts, which are self-executing agreements that run on blockchain networks.

As FSM evolves within Metaverse, new decentralized financial ecosystems will emerge, enabling users to participate in peer-to-peer trading, lending, and investing in an interactive, immersive environment. Whether through virtual asset exchanges, Non-Fungible Token (NFT hereafter)-based financial products, or smart contract-driven financial services, Metaverse has the potential to transform how individuals and organizations engage with digital assets and decentralized markets.

Virtual Asset Trading and NFTs

One of the most significant financial developments in Metaverse is the rise of virtual asset trading, particularly in the form of NFTs. While NFTs have been primarily associated with digital art, collectibles, and gaming assets, they are increasingly being integrated into financial products, investment vehicles, and tokenized real-world assets (RWA).

In a Metaverse-driven FSM landscape, users could perform several activities, including:

- Showcase and trade digital portfolios in virtual financial districts, where NFTs represent ownership of assets such as virtual real estate, in-game items, and blockchain-based financial instruments.
- Engage in peer-to-peer NFT trading with real-time price discovery and liquidity pools, enabling frictionless asset exchanges without intermediaries.
- Access exclusive financial content or investment opportunities by holding specific NFT-based memberships, unlocking premium research, educational resources, or private investment groups.

Beyond simple asset trading, Metaverse could enable fractional ownership of high-value NFTs, allowing multiple users to invest in a single asset. For instance, instead of purchasing an entire digital property, investors could buy fractionalized shares, earning passive income from virtual rentals, advertising, or other monetization methods.

The role of NFTs in Metaverse extends beyond digital collectibles. They can also function as tokenized representations of real-world financial products, enabling seamless ownership transfers and broader access to traditionally illiquid assets. For example:

- Tokenized real estate: Physical properties could be represented as NFTs, allowing users to invest in real estate without the complexities of traditional property ownership. Investors could trade fractions of buildings, participate in rental income distributions, or even engage in Metaverse-based real estate transactions backed by real-world deeds.
- Blockchain-based company shares: Traditional stocks could be digitized as security tokens, providing transparent, blockchain-verified ownership while enabling seamless cross-border trading and settlement.
- NFT-backed commodities and derivatives: precious metals, energy assets, and other commodities could be tokenized and traded within

Metaverse, providing enhanced liquidity, reduced transaction costs, and direct ownership transfers without intermediaries.

The introduction of these tokenized financial instruments would create an entirely new layer of financial engagement, where users interact with digitized assets in real-time, within fully immersive environments.

DeFi Lending, Borrowing, and Smart Contracts

DeFi has already disrupted traditional finance by providing open, permissionless financial services that eliminate the need for banks and financial institutions. By integrating these DeFi protocols into Metaverse, users can access a new realm of financial opportunities directly from their virtual environments.

In Metaverse, users will be able to collateralize their virtual assets such as NFTs, tokenized real estate, or digital currencies to secure loans and liquidity without having to sell their holdings. This introduces a completely new financial model, where:

- Virtual assets serve as collateral: Users can pledge valuable digital assets in exchange for stablecoins or other liquid cryptocurrencies, providing instant capital without liquidating their investments.
- Interest rates are dynamically determined: Borrowing rates could be influenced by real-time market demand, smart contract algorithms, and on-chain credit scoring, enabling a more efficient capital allocation system.
- Cross-Metaverse lending pools emerge: Decentralized lending platforms could establish Metaverse-specific liquidity pools, where users from different virtual worlds provide liquidity and earn yield by lending assets to other participants.

This virtual-first financial system would enable entrepreneurs, traders, and investors to access liquidity seamlessly, fueling the growth of decentralized businesses, Metaverse-based economies, and blockchain-native financial institutions.

Smart contracts are a fundamental building block of DeFi, allowing for automated, trustless financial agreements without intermediaries. Within Metaverse, smart contract-driven services could include:

- Automated lending and borrowing: Instead of relying on banks, users could interact directly with smart contracts that manage loan issuance, repayments, and collateral liquidation.
- Decentralized insurance protocols: Smart contract-based insurance could cover digital assets, virtual real estate, and even Metaverse-based businesses, providing decentralized risk management solutions.
- Trustless escrow services: Users engaging in high-value transactions, such as real estate purchases, tokenized securities trading, or digital business acquisitions, could use smart contract escrow services to ensure secure and transparent asset transfers.

The integration of AI-powered financial advisors could further enhance this ecosystem. AI-driven smart contracts could:

- Optimize investment strategies based on real-time market data.
- Detect fraudulent activities and prevent malicious transactions within decentralized financial ecosystems.
- Provide financial recommendations tailored to users' individual risk profiles, investment goals, and trading histories.

By embedding DeFi infrastructure and smart contracts into Metaverse, FSM will transform into a fully decentralized, intelligent, and user-driven ecosystem, enabling seamless financial interactions without reliance on traditional financial intermediaries.

The Future of Financial Social Media in a Decentralized Metaverse

The convergence of DeFi, NFTs, and smart contract automation within Metaverse will create a new financial paradigm where users interact, trade, and invest in a decentralized, immersive environment. This evolution will:

- Eliminate traditional barriers to financial participation, allowing users worldwide to access lending, investing, and asset trading without the need for a centralized financial institution.
- Foster transparency and security, as blockchain technology ensures that all transactions, asset ownership records, and financial agreements remain immutable and verifiable.

- Empower individuals to take control of their financial futures, with AI-driven tools and smart contracts automating complex financial decisions.

As FSM shifts toward a Metaverse-based, DeFi-integrated future, we can expect a dramatic transformation in how financial information is shared, how investment decisions are made, and how users interact with financial markets. The transition from traditional banking systems to decentralized, community-driven financial ecosystems will democratize access to wealth-building opportunities, making financial empowerment accessible to a broader global audience.

Challenges and Risks in the Financial Metaverse

While Metaverse presents unprecedented opportunities for FSM, it also introduces significant challenges that must be addressed to ensure security, legitimacy, and sustainability in this rapidly evolving digital domain. As immersive financial ecosystems develop, risks such as cybersecurity threats, regulatory uncertainty, and financial misinformation could undermine user trust and market stability. To fully realize Metaverse's potential, platforms, regulators, and users must collaborate to establish robust security measures, transparent financial practices, and effective oversight mechanisms.

Security and Fraud Prevention

Cybersecurity will be one of the most critical challenges facing FSM in Metaverse. With financial transactions occurring in decentralized, immersive environments, users will become prime targets for cybercriminals seeking to exploit vulnerabilities in digital wallets, smart contracts, and virtual interactions. New types of scams and fraud will emerge, requiring innovative security solutions.

As financial activity shifts to virtual environments, traditional cybersecurity risks will evolve into more complex and sophisticated threats, including:

- Avatar Impersonation Scams: Fraudsters could hijack or mimic user avatars to impersonate trusted financial advisors, investment firms, or even friends and family, persuading users to make fraudulent transactions.

- Malicious Smart Contracts: Cybercriminals may develop smart contracts with hidden vulnerabilities, allowing them to drain funds, execute unauthorized transactions, or trap investors in unfair agreements.
- Phishing in Virtual Worlds: Hackers could create fake virtual financial institutions or exchanges, luring users into depositing funds in fraudulent schemes. They may also employ social engineering tactics to steal private keys and wallet access credentials.
- Virtual Real Estate and NFT Fraud: As digital land and assets grow in value, scams involving fake property deeds, counterfeit NFTs, and fraudulent Metaverse real estate investments will become more prevalent.

To mitigate these risks, Metaverse financial platforms must adopt comprehensive security frameworks, incorporating:

- Biometric Authentication: Identity verification through facial recognition, fingerprint scanning, or retina detection could prevent unauthorized access to financial accounts and wallets.
- Decentralized Identity Verification: Blockchain-based identity systems could enable users to securely verify their credentials without relying on centralized databases vulnerable to hacks.
- AI-Powered Fraud Detection: Machine learning algorithms could analyze transaction patterns, detect anomalies, and flag potentially fraudulent activities in real-time.
- Multi-Signature Wallets and Smart Contract Audits: Implementing multi-signature authentication and regular third-party audits of smart contracts would help prevent unauthorized transactions and security breaches.
- Financial Literacy and Awareness Programs: Educating users about common scams, phishing tactics, and best practices for securing digital assets will be crucial in building a safer financial Metaverse.

By proactively integrating advanced cybersecurity measures and fostering user awareness, Metaverse platforms can create a more secure and resilient financial ecosystem.

Regulatory Considerations

As financial transactions increasingly take place in decentralized, borderless virtual worlds, global regulators will face significant challenges in monitoring, taxing, and enforcing financial laws. Ensuring compliance with data privacy, anti-money laundering (AML hereafter), and investor protection regulations will be essential to prevent fraud, tax evasion, and illicit financial activities.

One of the biggest hurdles in Metaverse finance is the lack of clear jurisdictional oversight. Some of the pressing regulatory questions include:

- Who has the authority to regulate financial transactions in Metaverse? Should regulation fall under the jurisdiction of the country where the user resides, the country where Metaverse platform is registered, or a new global regulatory body?
- How will virtual asset taxation work? If an investor buys and sells digital securities or tokenized real estate in a virtual economy, which government has the right to impose capital gains taxes?
- How will AML and Know Your Customer (KYC hereafter) regulations be enforced? Given the anonymous and decentralized nature of many blockchain-based transactions, how will governments ensure that financial activities comply with AML and KYC laws?

Without clear international agreements, financial activities in Metaverse may become a regulatory gray area, leading to potential exploitation, tax evasion, and legal conflicts.

To address these challenges, regulators will need to:

- Develop international cooperative agreements that create harmonized financial regulations for virtual transactions.
- Implement blockchain-based compliance tools that allow governments to monitor suspicious financial activities while preserving user privacy.
- Require financial platforms to adhere to KYC and AML standards, ensuring legitimate financial activities while mitigating illicit transactions.

- Create tax reporting frameworks tailored for virtual assets, NFTs, and digital securities, clarifying how gains from Metaverse-based financial activities should be reported and taxed.

The lack of clear regulations could hinder the growth of legitimate financial services in Metaverse, while over-regulation could suppress innovation. Striking the right balance will be crucial for building a sustainable, secure, and legally compliant financial ecosystem.

Combatting Financial Misinformation

Social media has long been a breeding ground for financial misinformation, and Metaverse could amplify this issue to an unprecedented level. Hyper-realistic virtual settings, deepfake technology, and immersive financial simulations could make fraudulent investment schemes more convincing than ever.

In Metaverse, fraudulent financial influencers could exploit immersive environments to mislead investors in ways that traditional social media cannot. Potential risks include:

- Virtual Ponzi Schemes: Fraudsters could create lavish virtual headquarters to simulate legitimacy, persuading users to invest in nonexistent or unsustainable financial products.
- Deepfake Impersonations: AI-generated deepfake avatars could be used to mimic real financial experts, spreading false investment advice to manipulate markets.
- Manipulative Market Coordination: Virtual financial communities could facilitate pump-and-dump schemes, where coordinated groups artificially inflate the price of assets before selling at a profit, leaving other investors at a loss.

Meanwhile, to counteract financial misinformation, Metaverse platforms must integrate:

- Blockchain-Based Reputation Scores: Like current FSM platforms, such as TheLion.com, users could have on-chain verifiable credentials linked to past financial activities and reviews, helping to distinguish reputable financial advisors from bad actors.

- AI-Driven Fact-Checking Systems: Machine learning tools could analyze and flag misleading financial claims, providing real-time verification of investment advice.
- Decentralized Financial Advisory Services: A DAO (Decentralized Autonomous Organization) model could be used to create transparent, community-driven investment guidance, reducing reliance on unverified influencers.
- Financial Education Initiatives: Platforms should prioritize user education, ensuring that investors understand risk factors, speculative investments, and the dangers of financial misinformation.

As FSM evolves within Metaverse, regulating financial content and ensuring information accuracy will be essential in preventing market manipulation and protecting investors.

Balancing Innovation with Risk Management

While Metaverse has the potential to revolutionize financial engagement, unaddressed risks could undermine user trust and hinder adoption. By proactively addressing security vulnerabilities, regulatory gaps, and misinformation challenges, FSM in Metaverse can evolve into a more secure, transparent, and sustainable ecosystem.

Through collaborative efforts between technology developers, financial regulators, cybersecurity experts, and the investment community, Metaverse can become a transformative yet responsible financial landscape, empowering users while safeguarding against exploitation, fraud, and regulatory chaos.

The Future of Financial Social Media in Metaverse

As technology advances and the adoption of Metaverse grows, the landscape of FSM will undergo a profound transformation. The convergence of VR, AI, DeFi, and blockchain will reshape the way individuals and institutions interact with financial information, trade digital assets, and engage in investment communities.

Over the next decade, Metaverse is poised to introduce new paradigms of financial engagement, enabling users to experience immersive, real-time financial interactions that go far beyond traditional FSM platforms. Some of the key developments that will define this future include the rise of virtual financial influencers, AI-driven financial advisors, institutional adoption, and decentralized financial communities.

The Rise of Virtual Financial Influencers

Today's financial influencers leverage platforms like YouTube, X.com, TikTok, and Instagram to share market insights, investment strategies, and financial education with their audiences. In Metaverse, however, financial influencers will evolve into fully immersive entities, creating dynamic, real-time financial environments where users can interact with market data in ways never before possible. Virtual financial influencers will be able to:

- Host live trading sessions inside interactive virtual stock exchanges, where users can experience real-time market movements, analyze technical indicators in 3D, and place simulated or real trades within immersive environments.
- Conduct virtual financial seminars and workshops using VR-based classrooms and AI-generated financial simulations, allowing users to practice investment strategies and understand financial risk through realistic, scenario-based training.
- Create AI-driven avatars that engage with followers 24/7, providing on-demand financial insights, market updates, and investment guidance through interactive, AI-powered discussions.

Additionally, deep fake and AI-generated influencer technology will enable the creation of hyper-realistic financial experts, some modeled after real investors, while others may be entirely virtual AI-powered financial analysts. Ethical concerns regarding misinformation, trust, and regulatory oversight will need to be addressed to ensure the credibility of these virtual influencers.

AI-Driven Financial Advisors and Virtual Investment Assistants

As artificial intelligence advances, AI-powered financial advisors will become integral components of Metaverse. These digital assistants will offer personalized investment strategies, real-time market analysis, and portfolio optimization within fully immersive virtual settings. AI-driven financial advisors have the following features:

- Real-Time Market Monitoring: AI advisors will continuously analyze real-time financial data, tracking stock movements, economic indicators, and market sentiment to generate instant investment recommendations.
- Customized Portfolio Strategies: Users will be able to input risk tolerance, investment goals, and financial preferences, allowing AI-driven advisors to generate optimized portfolio allocations tailored to their individual needs.
- Interactive Risk Simulation: AI-driven virtual advisors will enable users to simulate potential portfolio outcomes under various market conditions, helping them make more informed investment decisions.
- Conversational AI Interfaces: These AI-driven advisors could appear as holographic avatars, guiding users through investment strategies, tax planning, and financial literacy lessons in a way that feels as natural as speaking with a human expert.

AI-driven advisors have the potential to democratize financial advice, making high-quality, personalized investment guidance accessible to a global audience without the need for traditional financial intermediaries. However, ensuring the transparency and ethical integrity of AI-generated advice will be crucial in maintaining investor confidence.

Seamless Integration of Traditional Financial Institutions

As FSM expands into Metaverse, traditional banks, investment firms, and trading platforms will seek to establish a strong presence within virtual spaces. The transition from physical financial services to digital financial hubs will redefine how users engage with financial institutions. The following developments illustrate the emergence of virtual financial institutions:

- Virtual Bank Branches and Investment Offices: Major banks could create fully functional digital branches, enabling customers to consult with AI or human financial advisors, apply for loans, and conduct transactions entirely within immersive Metaverse environments.
- Interactive Financial Conferences and Networking Events: Large investment firms may host Metaverse-based financial summits, bringing together investors, policymakers, and industry leaders for panel discussions, market outlook presentations, and networking sessions.
- Institutional Trading Floors in Metaverse: Investment banks and hedge funds could operate virtual trading floors, where traders monitor market data, execute trades, and interact with AI-driven analytics tools in real time.

Traditional financial institutions may also explore tokenization of real-world assets, enabling stocks, bonds, real estate, and commodities to be traded as blockchain-based digital assets within Metaverse. This transformation could greatly enhance liquidity, efficiency, and accessibility in financial markets by allowing fractional ownership of high-value assets without the need for intermediaries.

Development of Decentralized Financial Communities

Metaverse provides a rich environment for the expansion of DeFi communities, where users can engage in peer-to-peer trading, lending, and governance through blockchain-based ecosystems. A self-governing financial ecosystem should include the following features:

- Decentralized Autonomous Organizations (DAOs): DeFi communities can be structured as DAOs, enabling users to collectively manage financial assets, vote on investment decisions, and participate in community-driven financial initiatives.
- Smart Contract Based Financial Agreements: Automated smart contracts allow users to conduct transparent, trustless financial transactions, reducing reliance on centralized financial intermediaries.

- Community-Driven Investment Pools: Users can pool funds to crowdfund new projects, participate in decentralized hedge funds, or invest in blockchain-based real estate ventures.

While DeFi and blockchain governance models offer greater transparency and autonomy, they also carry risks related to regulatory compliance, security vulnerabilities, and investor protection. Future progress will require finding the right balance between financial decentralization and regulatory oversight to ensure sustainability and trust in Metaverse-based financial communities.

The Evolution of Financial Social Media in Metaverse

As FSM evolves in Metaverse, we can expect:

- Hyper-Personalized Financial Ecosystems: AI-driven systems will customize financial experiences based on user behavior, risk preferences, and investment goals, making FSM more tailored than ever before.
- Decentralized and Democratized Finance: The traditional control over access to financial knowledge and investment opportunities will continue to diminish as blockchain powered financial communities empower users to engage in autonomous financial decision-making.
- The Intersection of Virtual and Physical Economies: Metaverse economy and real-world financial markets will become increasingly interconnected, with tokenized assets, digital currencies, and virtual real estate playing significant roles in the broader financial landscape.

Final Thoughts

Metaverse is not just a technological trend, it is a paradigm shift with the potential to reshape the way we engage with financial markets, investment strategies, and economic communities. As FSM transitions into fully immersive virtual environments, the opportunities for education, collaboration, and financial empowerment will expand exponentially.

However, this transformation will not be without its challenges. Security, regulatory adaptation, and financial ethics must evolve in parallel with technological advancements to ensure that Metaverse remains a safe, transparent, and sustainable financial ecosystem.

In the coming years, FSM in Metaverse will move from concept to reality, redefining the financial industry and creating a new frontier of digital finance that is more inclusive, innovative, and interactive than anything we have seen before. Those who embrace this evolution while remaining mindful of its risks will be at the forefront of a transformative shift in global financial engagement.

CHAPTER 16

How Artificial Intelligence Will Affect Financial Social Media

Introduction

The integration of Artificial Intelligence (AI hereafter) into financial social media (FSM hereafter) is fundamentally transforming the way people consume, analyze, and act on financial information. From AI-powered chatbots and automated news aggregators to sophisticated sentiment analysis tools and algorithmic trading signals, AI is reshaping user interactions, enhancing efficiency, and democratizing access to financial insights. FSM platforms have long played a crucial role in shaping market sentiment, with discussions, rumors, and breaking news influencing asset prices and investor behavior. Now, AI is amplifying this impact by processing vast amounts of financial data in real time, identifying trends, and delivering hyper-personalized content to users based on their preferences and investment behaviors.

AI-driven tools are enabling retail investors and financial professionals to make more informed decisions by offering features such as predictive analytics, risk assessment models, and AI-generated market commentary. Advanced machine learning models can sift through millions of posts, news articles, earnings reports, and macroeconomic indicators to extract meaningful patterns, providing traders and investors with a competitive edge. Platforms like X.com (formerly Twitter), Reddit, and specialized financial communities such as StockTwits and Seeking Alpha are leveraging AI to improve user engagement, filter out noise, and surface

Y. Zhang, *Financial Social Media*,
https://doi.org/10.1007/978-3-032-09332-5_16

high-quality discussions. AI is also enhancing customer support and portfolio management through robo-advisors and virtual assistants, making financial guidance more accessible to a broader audience.

However, the rise of AI in FSM is not without significant risks. The ability of AI to generate and distribute information at an unprecedented scale has given rise to a new wave of misinformation, market manipulation tactics, and algorithmic distortions. Deepfake financial influencers, AI-generated articles, and bot-driven sentiment manipulation campaigns pose serious threats to market integrity. Pump-and-dump schemes, once orchestrated manually, are now being automated by AI, making them more sophisticated and harder to detect. Furthermore, the opacity of AI models raises concerns about biased recommendations, ethical implications, and potential conflicts of interest in financial advice generated by AI systems.

Regulators, platform operators, and market participants face the challenge of balancing AI's vast potential with the need for ethical standards, transparency, and security in FSM. Addressing these challenges will require a combination of robust regulatory frameworks, AI-driven content moderation, and digital literacy initiatives to help users differentiate between credible financial insights and deceptive content.

As AI continues to evolve, its influence on FSM will only grow, shaping the way investors interact, trade, and make decisions. This chapter explores the many dimensions of AI's impact in this domain, highlighting its benefits, identifying the risks it poses, and discussing the measures necessary to create a trustworthy AI-enhanced financial ecosystem.

AI-Powered Chatbots: Revolutionizing User Engagement

On FSM platforms, users can interact not only with other human participants but also with chatbots designed to enhance the experience. These chatbots provide reliable market updates and answer questions related to trading and investing, offering quick, accessible support to both novice and experienced investors. AI-powered chatbots are transforming FSM by fundamentally changing how users access and engage with financial information. These intelligent virtual assistants use Natural Language Processing (NLP hereafter), machine learning, and big data analytics to interact with users in real time, providing instant, accurate, and contextually relevant responses. By automating financial guidance, simplifying complex investment concepts, and improving accessibility, AI chatbots are making FSM more interactive, efficient, and user-friendly.

Their applications extend far beyond answering basic inquiries. AI chatbots can serve as personal financial assistants, providing tailored market insights, risk assessments, and even trade execution assistance. Whether an investor is looking for information on stock trends, cryptocurrency fluctuations, or portfolio diversification strategies, AI-driven chatbots can process vast amounts of historical and real-time financial data within seconds to deliver personalized responses. Their ability to interact 24/7 without fatigue makes them an indispensable tool for investors seeking continuous support.

Real-Time Financial Guidance

One of the most significant advantages of AI chatbots in FSM is their ability to offer real-time investment guidance. Traditional financial advisory services often require scheduled consultations and come with high fees, limiting accessibility for retail investors. AI chatbots eliminate these barriers by offering instant insights based on market conditions, historical trends, and individual user preferences.

Many advanced chatbots integrate with financial platforms and brokerage accounts, allowing users to receive investment suggestions tailored to their portfolios. They analyze risk tolerance, diversification strategies, and asset performance, providing actionable recommendations. Some AI chatbots even use sentiment analysis to track market mood by scanning social media discussions and financial news, giving users an edge in understanding market sentiment.

Several financial platforms have begun integrating AI-powered chatbots into portfolio management and investment guidance. The Commonwealth Bank of Australia, through its partnership with OpenAI, is developing AI tools to provide clients with personalized financial advice. Google Finance recently added a conversational AI chatbot to deliver real-time market data and contextual investment insights. Startups like Mezzi offer AI-driven personal finance assistants that analyze user portfolios and recommend tailored strategies. These advancements highlight the growing role of AI in enhancing accessibility, personalization, and efficiency in financial decision-making.[1]

Enhanced Accessibility for Novice Investors

AI-powered chatbots are also playing a crucial role in breaking down barriers for novice investors. Many individuals interested in investing hesitate due to a lack of financial literacy and the overwhelming complexity of financial markets. AI chatbots help bridge this gap by providing clear, simplified explanations of investment principles, stock market terminologies, and trading strategies.

For instance, a user with no prior knowledge of cryptocurrency can interact with an AI chatbot to understand the basics of blockchain technology, market volatility, and risk factors associated with digital assets. Through interactive conversations, chatbots guide users through investment fundamentals in an engaging and approachable manner, making financial markets more inclusive for a broader audience.

Scalability and Cost Efficiency

For financial institutions, fintech startups, and independent financial influencers, AI chatbots offer a scalable and cost-efficient solution for engaging with large audiences. Traditional customer service and financial advisory teams can only handle a limited number of queries at a time, often leading to delays and increased operational costs. AI chatbots, on the other hand, can manage thousands of user inquiries simultaneously, ensuring that each user receives prompt responses without human intervention.

This scalability is particularly valuable for social media-based financial communities, where real-time engagement is critical. A financial influencer with a large following can deploy an AI chatbot to answer common questions, provide stock market updates, and even generate insights based on real-time market data. Similarly, financial firms can use AI-driven virtual assistants to enhance customer experience, improve client engagement, and reduce operational expenses.

In sum, AI-powered chatbots are revolutionizing user engagement in FSM by making investment insights more accessible, personalized, and scalable. Their ability to provide real-time financial guidance, simplify complex financial concepts, and handle large volumes of queries has positioned them as invaluable tools for both novice and experienced investors. However, ensuring the accuracy, security, and ethical use of AI chatbots will be crucial in maintaining trust and reliability in the financial ecosystem. As technology continues to evolve, AI-driven virtual assistants will likely play an even more significant role in shaping the future of financial decision-making and social media engagement.

The Dark Side of AI: Fake Content and Misinformation

While AI can enhance financial decision-making and user engagement, it also has a darker side that threatens market integrity and investor trust. Malicious actors are increasingly exploiting AI tools to generate fake financial news, manipulate stock prices, and impersonate trusted financial experts. The rapid evolution of AI-driven content creation, including deepfake videos, AI-generated text, and social media bots, has made it easier than ever to spread misinformation at an unprecedented scale.

The financial world is particularly vulnerable to AI-driven deception because market movements are heavily influenced by sentiment, speculation, and breaking news. False or misleading financial information can lead to panic selling, artificial price inflation, and significant monetary losses for unsuspecting investors. As AI-generated content becomes more sophisticated, distinguishing between legitimate financial insights and fabricated narratives is becoming increasingly difficult. This section explores three major ways AI is being misused to spread financial misinformation.

AI-Generated Fake News

One of the most concerning aspects of AI's misuse in FSM is the ability to generate convincing fake news about market events, company earnings, and macroeconomic developments. AI-powered text generation models, such as GPT-based tools, can produce highly realistic news articles, social media posts, and market reports that appear credible to the average reader.

These fabricated stories can manipulate investor sentiment, create panic, or drive artificial market fluctuations. False news about mergers, regulatory changes, or corporate scandals can spread rapidly across FSM platforms, influencing trading activity before the truth is uncovered. Unlike traditional market rumors, which could be traced to human sources, AI-generated news can be mass-produced and distributed in real time, making it significantly harder to track and debunk.

Recent real-world incidents show that AI-generated misinformation is becoming a significant threat to financial stability. In China, regulators have launched crackdowns on AI-driven fake stock market news to protect investors and maintain market integrity. In the United Kingdom, researchers found that fabricated AI content, such as false claims about bank insolvency, could spark panic by manipulating public sentiment. Meanwhile, advances in deepfake technology now enable the creation of highly realistic impersonations of financial executives, increasing the risk of fraud, reputational damage, and unauthorized transactions.[2]

Impersonation of Financial Experts

Another alarming development is the rise of AI-driven impersonation, where AI tools clone voices, create realistic deepfake videos, and mimic writing styles to impersonate trusted financial influencers, analysts, and executives. Scammers use these techniques to establish credibility and persuade investors to follow fraudulent advice or invest in scams.

AI-generated deepfakes can create deepfake videos showing well-known financial experts seemingly endorsing specific stocks, cryptocurrencies, or investment strategies. Similarly, AI-powered bots can generate fake social media accounts that post content indistinguishable from real financial professionals. These impersonation tactics make it difficult for users to distinguish between authentic financial advice and AI-fabricated deception.

Recent real-world cases highlight the growing danger of deepfake technology in financial scams. Fraudsters have impersonated high-profile figures such as Elon Musk, Justin Trudeau, and well-known media personalities including Martin Lewis, Zoe Ball, and Ben Fogle to promote fraudulent cryptocurrency or investment schemes. In one incident, a deepfake video of Elon Musk appeared on YouTube endorsing a bogus cryptocurrency project, leading to significant investor losses before it was exposed as fake. In another case, a man lost his $12,000 life savings after believing a deepfake video of Justin Trudeau promoting a crypto exchange. Similar tactics have been used in the United Kingdom, where fake celebrity endorsements were linked to scams that collectively defrauded savers of more than $35 million. These incidents demonstrate how convincingly AI-generated media can be used to manipulate investor trust, spread misinformation rapidly across social platforms, and cause substantial financial harm before the deception is uncovered.

AI-Driven Pump-and-Dump Schemes

Pump-and-dump schemes, a long-standing form of financial fraud, have become more sophisticated with AI. Traditionally, these schemes involved groups of traders artificially inflating the price of a stock or cryptocurrency through coordinated hype before selling their holdings at a profit, leaving late investors with worthless assets. AI has taken this manipulation to new levels by automating the process and making it more difficult to detect.

AI-powered bots can flood FSM platforms with coordinated posts, creating the illusion of organic investor interest in a particular asset. These bots can generate thousands of positive comments, fake testimonials, and AI-written news articles within minutes, artificially boosting the perceived demand for a stock or cryptocurrency. By the time real investors buy in, the orchestrators of the scheme have already sold their holdings, causing the asset price to collapse and leaving unsuspecting traders with heavy losses.

Regulators have warned that fraudsters are increasingly using AI to mass-produce convincing social media posts, online articles, and chatroom messages to promote low-value stocks or cryptocurrency schemes. These AI-generated campaigns can create the illusion of widespread investor enthusiasm, luring unsuspecting traders to buy in. Once prices are artificially inflated, the perpetrators sell their holdings for a profit, causing the asset's value to collapse. Authorities have noted that the scale, speed, and realism enabled by AI make these pump-and-dump schemes more sophisticated and harder to detect than traditional methods, posing heightened risks for retail investors.[3]

In sum, the dark side of AI in FSM poses significant threats to investor trust, market stability, and overall financial integrity. AI-generated fake news, deepfake impersonations, and AI-driven pump-and-dump schemes are reshaping how financial misinformation spreads, making it more difficult to detect and mitigate. As AI technology advances, the financial community must remain vigilant, adopting proactive measures to identify and combat AI-generated fraud. Strengthening regulatory oversight, improving AI detection mechanisms, and promoting investor awareness will be crucial in maintaining a secure and trustworthy financial landscape.

Detecting and Mitigating AI-Generated Threats

As AI-generated threats continue to evolve in FSM, detecting and mitigating these risks has become a critical priority for platforms, regulators, and investors. The growing sophistication of AI-generated fake news, deepfake impersonations, and automated market manipulation requires a multi-layered approach that combines technology, regulatory oversight, and user awareness. Addressing these challenges effectively involves leveraging advanced AI detection tools, implementing stringent verification systems, and educating users about potential threats.

This section explores key strategies to identify and counteract AI-driven financial misinformation, ensuring a safer and more trustworthy digital financial landscape.

Advanced Detection Algorithms

AI-generated threats are often designed to mimic organic user behavior, making them difficult to detect using traditional moderation methods. However, FSM platforms can deploy AI-driven detection algorithms trained to recognize patterns associated with fake content and malicious activities. These models can analyze large volumes of data in real-time, identifying anomalies that suggest coordinated disinformation campaigns or AI-generated fraud.

Key indicators used in AI-driven threat detection include:

- Unusual posting frequencies: AI-powered bots often post at an abnormally high rate, spamming financial discussions with misleading or promotional content.
- Repetitive language patterns: Many AI-generated posts share strikingly similar phrasing, grammar, and structure, which can signal automated content creation.
- Anomalous spikes in engagement metrics: Suspicious surges in likes, shares, and comments, especially on posts promoting specific stocks or cryptocurrencies, may indicate coordinated bot activity.
- Cross-platform activity synchronization: AI-driven misinformation campaigns often operate across multiple social media platforms simultaneously, amplifying their reach before detection mechanisms catch on.

Several social media platforms such as Facebook and TikTok have begun implementing AI-powered moderation systems to combat the spread of harmful or manipulative content.[4] These systems use tools like NLP and behavioral analysis to detect suspicious activity, including coordinated campaigns to influence public opinion or promote fraudulent schemes. While these efforts are not yet widely documented in the context of FSM, they demonstrate how advanced AI moderation can be used to identify and remove misleading posts, suspend malicious accounts, and reduce the risk of large-scale manipulation. The success of these approaches on mainstream platforms suggests a clear opportunity to adapt similar safeguards to protect investors in online financial communities.[5]

Verification Systems for Financial Experts

One of the most effective ways to combat AI-driven impersonation scams is by implementing mandatory verification systems for financial influencers, analysts, and investment advisors. Since AI can now generate highly realistic deepfakes and clone writing styles, ensuring that financial content originates from verified sources is essential for maintaining trust in FSM.

FSM platforms can introduce:

- Identity verification: Financial influencers and experts should be required to provide government-issued IDs and professional credentials to confirm their legitimacy.
- Knowledge assessments: To prevent misinformation, verified financial content creators could be required to pass an industry-specific assessment before being granted a certification badge.
- Blockchain-based verification: Decentralized verification methods using blockchain technology could enhance transparency by ensuring that credentials cannot be forged or tampered with.

LinkedIn has implemented a verification system for financial professionals, ensuring that only licensed advisors and certified analysts can claim expertise in their profiles. Expanding such verification measures to other FSM platforms such as X.com, Reddit, and YouTube could significantly reduce impersonation risks and improve content credibility.[6]

AI-Powered Fact-Checking and Content Authentication

To counteract AI-generated fake news and financial misinformation, FSM platforms can integrate AI-powered fact-checking tools that verify the authenticity of financial claims before they gain traction. These systems can cross-reference user-generated content with reputable financial news sources, regulatory filings, and real-time market data to flag inconsistencies or potential falsehoods.

Some potential applications include:

- Automated credibility scores: AI can assess the credibility of financial posts by analyzing source references, factual consistency, and expert verification.
- Deepfake detection models: Machine learning models trained to detect AI-generated images and videos can help identify and remove deepfake impersonations of financial experts.
- Warning labels for high-risk content: When posts exhibit signs of manipulation, FSM platforms can issue automated warnings, alerting users to exercise caution.

Google has invested in AI-powered fact-checking tools that analyze financial news articles for accuracy. By implementing similar systems within FSM platforms, users could be warned when engaging with content that lacks credible sourcing or shows signs of AI fabrication.[7]

User Education and Awareness

While technological solutions play a vital role in detecting AI-generated threats, empowering users with knowledge is equally crucial. Many investors, especially retail traders, may not be aware of how AI-generated misinformation operates or how to identify fraudulent financial content.

Educational initiatives should focus on:

- Recognizing red flags: Users should be trained to spot warning signs of AI-generated misinformation, such as overly optimistic investment claims, exaggerated profit guarantees, and suspicious endorsements from unverified accounts.
- Cross-checking information: Investors should be encouraged to verify financial news and recommendations by consulting trusted

sources such as official financial news websites, regulatory agencies, and licensed financial professionals.

- Understanding AI-generated content risks: FSM platforms can launch awareness campaigns to inform users about deepfake technology, AI-driven bot networks, and misinformation tactics commonly used in financial fraud.

Major financial institutions and regulatory bodies, such as the U.S. Securities and Exchange Commission (SEC) and the Financial Conduct Authority (FCA), have started issuing public advisories on the risks of AI-generated scams. By expanding these efforts and integrating educational modules into FSM platforms, users can develop better digital literacy skills to protect themselves from deceptive AI content.[8]

In sum, as AI-generated threats become more advanced, FSM platforms, regulators, and users must adopt comprehensive strategies to detect and mitigate misinformation. By deploying AI-powered detection tools, implementing verification systems, promoting user education, and strengthening regulatory measures, the financial community can safeguard against AI-driven fraud and manipulation. The future of FSM depends on a collective effort to ensure that AI is used responsibly, maintaining trust and integrity in online financial discussions.

Ethical Implications and Regulatory Challenges

As AI continues to shape FSM, it brings a host of ethical dilemmas and regulatory complexities. While AI-driven advancements enhance user engagement, investment decision-making, and financial accessibility, they also introduce challenges related to transparency, accountability, and potential misuse. Regulators and industry leaders face the delicate task of fostering innovation while implementing safeguards to protect investors from AI-driven misinformation, manipulation, and fraud.

This section explores the ethical considerations and regulatory challenges associated with AI in FSM, highlighting the need for responsible AI deployment and global cooperation.

Balancing Innovation and Oversight

AI is revolutionizing FSM by providing users with real-time insights, predictive analytics, and personalized financial recommendations.

However, excessive or restrictive regulation could hinder the development and adoption of beneficial AI technologies. Striking the right balance between innovation and oversight requires a collaborative approach involving financial institutions, technology companies, regulators, and industry stakeholders.

Key considerations include:

- Encouraging responsible AI innovation: Regulation should support the ethical development of AI while ensuring it does not become a tool for fraud, misinformation, or market manipulation.
- Avoiding over-regulation: Excessive restrictions could deter AI-driven advancements that benefit investors, such as automated financial planning tools, AI-powered risk assessment models, and intelligent market analysis bots.
- Ensuring consumer protection: AI regulations must prioritize transparency, fairness, and accountability to protect retail investors from misleading or biased AI-generated content.

The SEC has expressed concerns about AI's role in financial markets, particularly in algorithmic trading and AI-powered financial advisory services. To address these risks, the SEC is exploring regulatory frameworks that encourage AI-driven financial innovations while preventing market manipulation and conflicts of interest.[9]

Accountability for AI Systems

One of the most complex ethical and regulatory challenges surrounding AI in FSM is determining accountability. When AI-powered tools generate financial recommendations or influence investment decisions, who bears responsibility for the outcomes?

Key accountability concerns include:

- Liability for AI-generated investment advice: If an AI chatbot provides misleading financial guidance that results in losses, should the responsibility lie with the platform, the AI developer, or the user?
- Algorithmic biases and fairness: AI systems trained on biased data may produce recommendations that disproportionately favor certain

assets or investment strategies. Ensuring fairness and transparency in AI decision-making is a critical ethical challenge.

- Misuse of AI-driven automation: Malicious actors can exploit AI tools to manipulate market sentiment or spread disinformation. Holding perpetrators accountable requires robust regulatory enforcement mechanisms.

Global Harmonization of AI Standards

FSM operates across borders, making it essential to establish international standards for AI governance. Without global regulatory alignment, discrepancies in AI oversight could create loopholes that allow unethical AI practices to flourish in jurisdictions with weaker regulations.

Key challenges in global AI regulation include:

- Regulatory inconsistencies: Different countries have varying approaches to AI governance, leading to a fragmented regulatory landscape that complicates enforcement.
- Cross-border fraud and manipulation: AI-generated financial scams and market manipulation tactics can quickly spread across multiple jurisdictions, requiring coordinated regulatory responses.
- Standardizing AI ethics frameworks: Establishing universally accepted ethical guidelines for AI in FSM is crucial for ensuring transparency, accountability, and investor protection.

Ethical Considerations in AI Transparency and Bias Mitigation

AI systems are only as reliable as the data the data on which they are trained. Ethical concerns arise when AI algorithms unintentionally reinforce biases, provide opaque recommendations, or prioritize profit-driven motives over investor well-being.

To ensure ethical AI deployment, FSM platforms should:

- Promote algorithmic transparency: Users should be informed about how AI-driven financial recommendations are generated, including the data sources and methodologies used.

- Address biases in AI models: AI developers must regularly audit training datasets to eliminate biases that could lead to skewed investment recommendations.
- Implement explainable AI (XAI) principles: AI systems should provide clear explanations for their predictions, allowing users to understand the reasoning behind financial insights.

Several studies, including Navarro et al. (2021) and Mavrogiorgos et al. (2024), have shown that AI-powered credit scoring algorithms can exhibit biases against certain demographic groups due to historical biases in financial data. Such biases raise ethical concerns about fairness and equal access in AI-driven financial decision-making, emphasizing the need for regulatory oversight in AI model development.

Strengthening Regulatory Enforcement and Compliance

As AI adoption in FSM grows, regulatory agencies must strengthen enforcement mechanisms to ensure compliance with ethical AI practices. Key measures include:

- Developing AI-specific financial regulations: Governments should establish tailored regulations addressing AI-driven investment advice, algorithmic trading, and automated financial decision-making.
- Enhancing AI audit and monitoring systems: Regulatory bodies should conduct regular audits of AI-powered financial platforms to detect potential risks and biases.
- Encouraging self-regulation among industry players: Financial institutions and FSM platforms should proactively adopt ethical AI guidelines and best practices.

The U.S. Financial Industry Regulatory Authority (FINRA) has begun monitoring AI-driven financial platforms to ensure compliance with fair trading practices and investor protection standards. Similar initiatives worldwide could help create a more ethical and transparent AI-driven financial ecosystem.[10]

In sum, the ethical and regulatory challenges of AI in FSM require a balanced approach that fosters innovation while protecting investors from misinformation, bias, and manipulation. By implementing transparent AI systems, holding AI developers and platforms accountable, promoting global regulatory alignment, and strengthening ethical AI practices, the financial industry can harness AI's potential responsibly. As AI technologies continue to evolve, ongoing collaboration between regulators, financial institutions, and technology providers will be crucial in shaping an ethical and well-regulated AI-driven financial ecosystem.

Final Thoughts

AI is fundamentally reshaping FSM, driving innovation while simultaneously introducing new risks. AI-powered tools have revolutionized how users access financial information, engage with investment communities, and make informed decisions. From AI-powered chatbots providing personalized financial guidance to advanced algorithms detecting market trends in real time, the integration of AI has democratized financial knowledge, making it more accessible to a broader audience. However, these advancements come with significant ethical, regulatory, and security challenges that must be addressed to ensure the integrity of FSM.

The benefits of AI in FSM are undeniable. AI-driven automation enhances user experiences, streamlines financial analysis, and enables scalability for financial influencers, institutions, and content creators. By breaking down complex financial concepts into digestible insights, AI has empowered novice investors and improved decision-making for experienced traders. Additionally, AI's ability to analyze vast datasets within seconds has introduced predictive analytics that help investors navigate volatile markets more effectively.

Despite these advantages, AI also presents substantial risks. The proliferation of AI-generated fake news, deepfake financial experts, and AI-driven pump-and-dump schemes has raised concerns about misinformation and fraud. Malicious actors can manipulate AI algorithms to spread deceptive financial narratives, artificially inflate stock or cryptocurrency prices, and exploit unsuspecting investors. The rapid dissemination of AI-generated misinformation threatens investor trust, market stability, and the credibility of FSM as a whole.

To mitigate these threats, a comprehensive approach is necessary, combining technological innovation, ethical AI development, and strong regulatory frameworks. FSM platforms must implement advanced AI detection algorithms to identify and prevent the spread of fake content, while mandatory verification systems for financial experts can help combat impersonation. Moreover, educating users about the risks of AI-generated misinformation will play a crucial role in fostering a more discerning and informed investor base.

Regulators face the challenge of balancing innovation and oversight, ensuring that AI-driven advancements continue to enhance financial engagement without enabling unethical practices. Governments and financial watchdogs must collaborate globally to establish harmonized AI standards, preventing regulatory loopholes that allow AI-driven fraud to thrive in unregulated markets. Additionally, platforms must prioritize AI transparency and accountability, ensuring that AI-powered financial tools operate ethically and without bias.

As AI continues to evolve, its impact on FSM will only grow. The key to navigating this transformation lies in responsible AI adoption, using its potential to enhance financial engagement while protecting against its risks. If industry leaders, regulators, and financial platforms work together to establish ethical AI practices, improve detection mechanisms, and enforce responsible AI usage, the FSM landscape can thrive as a dynamic, engaging, and trustworthy ecosystem.

By embracing AI responsibly, stakeholders can promote informed decision-making, strengthen investor confidence, and uphold market integrity, ensuring that AI serves as a force for positive transformation rather than a tool for manipulation. The future of AI in FSM will be defined by how well these challenges are addressed, making it imperative for all participants to prioritize transparency, security, and ethical responsibility in the AI-driven financial revolution.

Notes

1. https://www.sfchronicle.com/personal-finance/article/ai-financial-adviser-artificial-intelligence-20343063.php
2. https://www.reuters.com/world/china/china-crack-down-stock-market-fake-news-ai-spurs-misinformation-says-state-media-2025-03-15/
3. https://www.securities.nd.gov/news/investor-alert-artificial-intelligence-ai-and-investment-fraud
4. https://www.wired.com/story/facebook-says-new-ai-identify-more-problems-faster/

5. https://www.reuters.com/technology/bytedance-cuts-over-700-jobs-malaysia-shift-towards-ai-moderation-sources-say-2024-10-11/
6. https://www.wired.com/story/linkedin-verification-clear/
7. https://newsinitiative.withgoogle.com/resources/trainings/google-fact-check-tools/
8. https://www.nasaa.org/70780/nasaa-investor-alert-artificial-intelligence-and-investment-fraud
9. https://www.sec.gov/newsroom/speeches-statements/uyeda-ai-roundtable-032725
10. https://www.finra.org/rules-guidance/notices/24-09

CHAPTER 17

How Financial Social Media Affects Corporate Value and Governance

Introduction

Financial social media (FSM hereafter) has transformed how stakeholders perceive and interact with corporations. FSM platforms like TheLion, Seeking Alpha, X.com (formerly Twitter), Reddit, and StockTwits allow investors, analysts, and the public to share opinions and sentiments that influence corporate image, market value, and the accountability mechanisms that shape corporate governance.

Unlike traditional financial news outlets, FSM operates in real time, providing an unfiltered and immediate dialogue. This creates opportunities for companies to engage directly with stakeholders, but also introduces risks, such as the rapid spread of rumors and misinformation. The transparency enabled by these platforms allows stakeholders to scrutinize corporate actions more closely, reshaping traditional power dynamics in financial markets and amplifying the influence of retail investors, as demonstrated by the 2021 GameStop short squeeze.

FSM has also blurred the lines between professional and personal opinions. Influential figures, including CEOs such as Elon Musk, use these platforms to engage directly with audiences, fostering authenticity but introducing risks such as regulatory compliance and market volatility.

This chapter examines impact of FSM on corporate image, market value, and the accountability mechanisms that shape corporate governance. It provides strategies for navigating this dynamic environment,

Y. Zhang, *Financial Social Media*,
https://doi.org/10.1007/978-3-032-09332-5_17

emphasizing proactive engagement, sentiment analysis, and crisis management as important tools for navigating this environment.

Impact on Corporate Image

In the contemporary digital information environment, FSM has become a powerful force in shaping corporate image. Unlike traditional media channels, platforms like X.com, Reddit, and TheLion allow instant and widespread communication, where a single post or comment can influence public perception on an unprecedented scale. Companies must now navigate an environment where their reputations are not only shaped by their actions but also by the narratives amplified by millions of users worldwide.

Historically, corporate image was managed primarily through controlled press releases, advertising campaigns, and public relations efforts. These traditional approaches allowed organizations to frame their messages carefully, ensuring consistency and alignment with brand objectives. However, the rise of FSM has upended this model. Public perception is now more democratized, as individuals can amplify their voices and spark large-scale discussions. This shift presents both opportunities and challenges for companies aiming to maintain a positive reputation.

Positive sentiment on FSM can significantly enhance a corporation's image. For instance, Tesla has benefited greatly from enthusiastic online communities, where advocates frequently praise the company's innovative technologies and environmental initiatives. This groundswell of support not only bolsters customer loyalty but also fosters confidence among investors. Tesla's ability to leverage these platforms as a marketing and engagement tool has contributed to its perception as a forward-thinking and dynamic company.

Conversely, negative sentiment can rapidly damage a company's image. A well-documented example is the Wells Fargo scandal involving the creation of unauthorized customer accounts. The backlash on FSM platforms was swift and severe, with hashtags like #BoycottWellsFargo trending for weeks. This online outrage translated into tangible consequences, including customer losses, regulatory fines, and a prolonged period of reputation rebuilding.

Another critical aspect of FSM is its role in spreading rumors and misinformation. A single unverified message or post can trigger panic among investors and stakeholders. In addition, influencers and opinion leaders also play a significant role in shaping corporate image. Endorsements or criticisms from prominent figures can have outsized effects. A notable example is Elon Musk, whose tweets have frequently moved markets, for better or worse. On the positive side, his enthusiastic promotion of Tesla and other ventures has rallied supporters and boosted brand visibility. On the downside, controversial statements have occasionally sparked backlash, highlighting the double-edged nature of influencer-driven content.

Moreover, FSM has a global reach that compounds its impact. Localized incidents, such as labor disputes or environmental controversies, can quickly escalate into international discussions. For example, reports of poor working conditions at the Rana Plaza factory in Bangladesh on April 24, 2013, gained traction on social media, sparking a global outcry and calls for boycotts. The incident demonstrated how issues that were once confined to local markets can now affect global corporate reputations.

To navigate these complexities, companies must adopt proactive strategies for managing their corporate image on FSM. Advanced analytics tools can help monitor sentiment trends, identify emerging risks, and gauge the effectiveness of engagement efforts. Additionally, transparent and authentic communication is crucial for addressing criticism and building trust with stakeholders. Companies that successfully leverage FSM as a tool for engagement, rather than merely a threat to be managed, are better positioned to align their image with their strategic goals.

In summary, FSM has transformed the way corporate image is built and maintained. While it offers unprecedented opportunities for engagement and visibility, it also exposes companies to heightened risks. By adopting proactive and adaptive strategies, organizations can harness the power of FSM to shape their reputations positively and mitigate potential harm.

The Role of Viral Content

The nature of FSM makes it fertile ground for viral content, which can dramatically influence corporate reputation and market dynamics. Viral posts, hashtags, or videos often achieve widespread visibility within hours, creating significant opportunities and risks for companies.

Viral content typically gains traction due to its emotional impact, novelty, or shock value. In the financial context, this includes unexpected announcements, bold claims, or even rumors. A prime example is the 2021 GameStop short squeeze, driven by the Reddit community r/WallStreetBets. Posts highlighting the opportunity to counter institutional short-sellers gained massive traction, leading to a dramatic surge in GameStop's stock price and widespread media coverage. The incident showcased how retail investors can collectively influence markets through the viral spread of information.

Positive viral content can significantly enhance a company's reputation. Campaigns that align with social values, for instance, often resonate deeply with audiences. Patagonia, the American retailer of outdoor clothing and gear, frequently sees its sustainability initiatives go viral, reinforcing its image as an ethical and environmentally conscious brand. Similarly, companies that engage in philanthropy or community-building efforts often find their initiatives amplified through FSM, boosting goodwill among consumers and investors.

However, the flip side of viral content is its potential to escalate negative events into full-blown crises. The 2017 United Airlines incident, where a passenger was forcibly removed from an overbooked flight, is a case in point. Video footage of the event went viral on platforms like X.com and Facebook, sparking global outrage. The ensuing backlash included calls for boycotts, a sharp drop in the company's stock price, and lasting reputational damage.

Influencers further amplify the impact of viral content. A single tweet or post from a high-profile individual can dramatically alter public perceptions. Elon Musk's infamous tweet about taking Tesla private at $420 per share exemplifies this dynamic. While the tweet generated significant buzz, it also led to regulatory scrutiny and legal challenges. This highlights the need for caution and strategic planning when engaging with influential voices on FSM.

Meme culture adds another layer of complexity to the viral content phenomenon. Memes often distill complex issues into humorous or provocative formats, making them highly shareable. The GameStop saga, for example, was propelled in part by memes celebrating the retail investor movement and mocking institutional players. This cultural element underscores the unpredictable nature of FSM and its ability to shape narratives in unconventional ways.

To manage the risks and harness the benefits of viral content, companies should invest in robust monitoring tools and develop agile response strategies. Engaging positively with trending topics, collaborating with credible influencers, and addressing negative content transparently are essential tactics. By understanding the dynamics of viral content, organizations can position themselves to thrive in the ever-evolving FSM landscape.

Real-Time Crisis Management

The speed and reach of FSM make real-time crisis management an essential capability for modern organizations. Crises that might have unfolded over days or weeks in the past can now escalate within minutes, requiring swift and strategic responses to mitigate damage.

One of the most illustrative examples of real-time crisis management is Starbucks' response to a 2018 incident in which two Black men were arrested at a Philadelphia location while waiting for a friend. The incident, captured on video, quickly went viral, sparking widespread outrage and accusations of racial bias. Recognizing the gravity of the situation, Starbucks issued a public apology, closed more than 8000 stores for racial bias training, and committed to ongoing efforts to address systemic inequities. This proactive approach minimized long-term reputational damage and demonstrated the importance of addressing viral issues directly.

Crises on FSM often follow a predictable trajectory: an initial event sparks outrage or concern, which is then amplified by shares, comments, and media coverage. Early detection is critical for effective management. Advanced tools that monitor FSM activity can help identify potential crises in their early stages, allowing companies to respond before they spiral out of control.

Transparency and accountability are key components of successful crisis management. Nike's 2018 campaign featuring Colin Kaepernick, which sparked polarized reactions, serves as an instructive example. Despite the initial backlash, including calls for boycotts, Nike's unwavering support for the campaign's message ultimately resonated with its core audience, boosting sales and reinforcing its brand identity. This case highlights the value of aligning crisis responses with organizational values.[1]

Proactive crisis management requires preparation. Companies should establish dedicated crisis management teams comprising representatives from public relations, legal, social media, and senior leadership. Developing crisis protocols with predefined response frameworks can also streamline decision-making during high-pressure situations. Additionally, leveraging official FSM channels to disseminate accurate information and counter misinformation is crucial for maintaining control over the narrative.

Empathy plays a critical role in effective crisis responses. Genuine expressions of concern and a commitment to corrective action can foster goodwill and rebuild trust. When Target faced backlash for a controversial product launch, the company's heartfelt apology and efforts to address customer concerns helped to diffuse tensions and restore confidence.

By adopting a proactive and empathetic approach to crisis management, organizations can not only weather the storm but also strengthen stakeholders' relationships and enhance their long-term resilience.

Influence on Corporate Value

FSM platforms like TheLion, Seeking Alpha, StockTwits, and Reddit have democratized access to market information, enabling individual investors to influence stock prices alongside institutional players. This democratization creates a feedback loop in which online sentiment impacts stock prices, which in turn fuels further discussion on FSM.

FSM often serves as an early indicator of shifts in investor sentiment. During the 2021 GameStop short squeeze, for example, discussions on r/WallStreetBets led to a dramatic increase in trading volume, driving the stock price from under $20 to over $400. This event disrupted traditional market dynamics and underscored the power of collective action among retail investors.

Positive sentiment on FSM can attract investors and drive stock prices higher, even in the absence of fundamental changes. Companies with strong online followings, such as Tesla, often experience increased demand for their shares due to the enthusiasm generated by their supporters. On the flip side, negative sentiment can trigger panic selling, eroding corporate value and creating volatility.

Long-term valuation is also influenced by FSM-driven narratives. Persistent negative sentiment can deter institutional investors and damage consumer confidence. Boeing's reputation suffered significantly after the 737 Max crashes, as FSM amplified scrutiny and criticism. This prolonged period of negative sentiment contributed to a decline in Boeing's stock value, highlighting the long-term impact of reputational issues on financial performance.

Prominent voices on FSM, such as Elon Musk and Cathie Wood, wield considerable influence over corporate value. Musk's tweets about

Tesla and cryptocurrencies have frequently moved markets, while Wood's investment insights often attract significant attention and drive trading activity. Hedge funds and institutional investors increasingly incorporate FSM sentiment into their trading strategies, leveraging tools like natural language processing to identify emerging trends.

In conclusion, the interplay between FSM and corporate value is profound and multifaceted. By understanding and engaging with these dynamics, companies can better position themselves to capitalize on opportunities and mitigate risks in an increasingly interconnected market environment.

Transformation of Investor Relations

FSM has revolutionized investor relations, enabling direct and real-time interactions between companies and stakeholders. This shift has fundamentally redefined how corporations manage their public image and engage with investors in a more dynamic and transparent environment.

FSM platforms such as X.com, TheLion, and StockTwits grant companies unfiltered access to diverse audiences, allowing precise control over narratives. These channels enable firms to share timely updates on earnings, strategies, and milestones, fostering transparency and trust. Additionally, FSM facilitates swift responses to shareholder concerns, curbing the spread of misinformation and enhancing inclusivity, especially for retail investors.

For instance, Apple exemplifies the strategic use of FSM, leveraging platforms like X.com and Instagram to generate anticipation for product launches. Through teasers, behind-the-scenes content, and engaging visuals, the company captivates both consumers and investors, creating a synergistic effect that amplifies brand visibility and fosters positive market sentiment. This strategy often leads to increased media coverage and favorable analyst commentary, benefiting short-term stock performance.

While FSM offers immense opportunities for communication, it also presents challenges:

- Regulatory Compliance: Companies must balance the imperative for transparency with the need to comply with regulations governing material information disclosure.

- Reputational Risks: The open nature of FSM exposes firms to potential misinformation and adverse narratives that can escalate quickly.

To address these challenges, companies are increasingly adopting proactive strategies such as sentiment analysis tools and structured engagement protocols to ensure effective communication and alignment with investor expectations.

Challenges in Real-Time Communication

The immediacy of FSM has revolutionized corporate communication but also introduces unique risks. Real-time interaction requires precision, speed, and consistency, as missteps such as poorly worded posts or delayed responses can quickly escalate into reputational crises, undermining investor confidence and damaging market perception.

Unlike traditional media, FSM platforms amplify mistakes through their viral nature, forcing companies to balance rapid responses with meticulous messaging. Even a minor error can have long-lasting effects on credibility.

A stark example is Boeing's response during the 737 MAX grounding crisis. The company's delayed and inconsistent messaging on social media exacerbated stakeholder frustration, creating a perception of opacity and evasiveness. Investors, deprived of clear updates on safety and regulatory measures, lost confidence, contributing to prolonged stock declines and reputational damage.

To manage real-time communication effectively, companies should adopt:

- Crisis Management Plans: Implement pre-approved templates and response strategies to minimize delays.
- Centralized Oversight: Ensure consistent messaging across platforms, even under pressure.
- Proactive Engagement: Monitor social sentiment and address emerging concerns transparently to prevent escalation.

By leveraging these strategies, firms can mitigate risks while capitalizing on FSM's speed and reach to maintain trust and resilience in volatile environments.

Managing Misinformation and Strategic Response in the Digital Era

The rapid dissemination of misinformation on FSM presents significant challenges for companies, particularly in industries where valuation is highly sensitive to market sentiment. False narratives, whether deliberate, accidental, or based on misinformation, can spread almost instantly, damaging reputation, eroding investor confidence, and destabilizing markets. Unlike traditional media, the largely unregulated nature of FSM allows unverified claims to gain traction quickly, underscoring the need for vigilant oversight and swift intervention.

To succeed in this environment, companies must combine proactive misinformation management with broader strategic integration of FSM into corporate decision-making. Effective practices include:

- Active Monitoring and Analytics: Continuously track conversations, sentiment, and emerging risks with advanced tools to detect false narratives or crises early.
- Direct and Transparent Communication: Deliver authoritative responses through FSM platforms, using clear data and, when appropriate, video statements from leadership to reinforce credibility.
- Data-Driven Rebuttals: Counter misinformation with verifiable evidence, ensuring stakeholders have access to reliable information.
- Preemptive Education: Share regular operational and financial updates to create an informed community less vulnerable to rumors.
- Specialized Response Teams: Establish dedicated crisis communication teams trained to address sensitive issues with speed, accuracy, and professionalism.
- Integrated Crisis Protocols: Embed FSM strategies within broader corporate crisis management plans for consistency and seamless execution under pressure.

By prioritizing transparency, preparedness, and responsiveness, companies not only mitigate the risks of misinformation but also strengthen stakeholder relationships and maintain a competitive edge in an increasingly digital marketplace.

Implications for Corporate Governance

FSM has significantly influenced corporate governance by amplifying stakeholder demands for transparency and accountability. Boards and executives now operate in a digital landscape where public opinion can directly shape corporate policies.

FSM heightens scrutiny, with stakeholders increasingly demanding accessible information on executive compensation, labor practices, environmental impact, and social responsibility. These platforms amplify collective voices, influencing boardroom decisions.

In January 2014, iconic activist investor Carl Icahn leveraged X.com to directly address Apple's leadership. He publicly revealed that his stake in Apple had exceeded $3 billion and urged the company to significantly increase its stock buyback program. In one tweet, he emphasized that the Apple board was "doing a great disservice" to shareholders by not enhancing its buyback plan. This social media campaign coincided with Apple's share price climbing nearly 5 percent in less than two hours, demonstrating the platform's powerful influence. Icahn's tweets showcased the power of social platforms in reshaping shareholder activism and putting immediate pressure on corporate governance. This example underscores FSM's potential to drive governance reforms and highlights the importance of open communication with stakeholders.[2]

Moreover, FSM has elevated Environmental, Social, and Governance (ESG hereafter) issues as central to corporate governance. FSM platforms facilitate rapid dissemination of perceived shortcomings, prompting debates and requiring immediate action.

To navigate the influence of FSM, companies should:

- Proactively Engage: Use FSM platforms to understand stakeholder concerns and demonstrate responsiveness.
- Embed Transparency: Ensure clarity in operations and communications to preempt criticism.
- Strengthen ESG Efforts: Prioritize measurable ESG initiatives to align with stakeholder expectations and build trust.

By leveraging these strategies, corporations can harness FSM's potential to foster stronger stakeholder relationships, enhance governance practices, and drive sustainable growth.

Leveraging Sentiment Analysis

Understanding public opinion on FSM is essential for effective corporate strategy in the digital age. Sentiment analysis, powered by natural language processing (NLP) and machine learning, enables companies to evaluate the tone and mood of online discussions about their brand, industry, or competitors. These insights help anticipate risks, seize opportunities, and make data-driven decisions that strengthen stakeholder trust.

Sentiment analysis is invaluable for detecting emerging concerns, evaluating the impact of corporate announcements, and assessing overall brand perception. These insights enable companies to refine communication strategies, proactively address issues, and foster stronger stakeholder relationships.

For example, in January 2021, after rising criticism on X.com and Reddit about a planned privacy policy update, WhatsApp issued clarifications, published detailed FAQs, and delayed the rollout while pledging clearer communication about what data is and is not shared. The company's blog post and multiple news reports document the steps it took to calm users and outline privacy feature messaging.

The effective use of sentiment analysis offers several benefits:

- Early Warning System: Detecting sentiment shifts allows companies to address potential risks before they escalate.
- Informed Decision-Making: Insights guide strategic decisions, such as refining products, tailoring marketing campaigns, or adjusting corporate messaging.
- Competitive Edge: Monitoring competitor sentiment enables firms to exploit weaknesses or replicate successful strategies.

However, the value of sentiment analysis lies in timely action. Delayed responses can render even the most accurate analysis ineffective in preventing reputational harm. Integrating sentiment analysis into corporate decision-making aligns business strategies with stakeholder expectations, fostering trust and driving long-term value in a fast-evolving social media landscape.

Financial Social Media and Initial Public Offerings (IPOs)

FSM sentiment plays a pivotal role in shaping the success of IPOs. FSM platforms like X.com, Seeking Alpha, Reddit, and StockTwits are essential for generating visibility and influencing investor perceptions. For companies preparing for an IPO, FSM has introduced a new layer of complexity; the "quiet period," traditionally a time of strictly limited corporate communication, is now often challenged by unvetted digital speculation and viral sentiment that can disrupt pricing and investor demand before the first trade is even executed. Positive sentiment on FSM can amplify interest and drive higher valuations, while negative sentiment can create skepticism and hinder financial performance.

Building momentum pre-IPO is vital. FSM offers companies a direct channel to engage potential investors, share compelling narratives, and emphasize competitive advantages. Positive sentiment creates excitement and demand for shares.

For example, Rivian's 2021 IPO demonstrated the power of social media buzz. The electric vehicle maker leveraged platforms like X.com and YouTube to highlight its sustainability mission, resonating with environmentally conscious investors. Discussions about Rivian's innovative products and growth potential generated significant excitement, contributing to one of the largest IPOs in U.S. history. Aligning its messaging with market trends, such as the demand for green technologies, ensured Rivian's narrative reached both retail and institutional investors.

However, over-reliance on FSM hype carries risks. Inflated expectations can lead to investor disappointment, increased scrutiny, and even legal challenges if promises are unmet. For instance, Uber's 2019 IPO serves as a cautionary tale of excessive hype. Despite significant online buzz driving a high valuation, the company's post-IPO financial performance fell short, causing its stock price to plummet and eroding investor confidence. This underscores the importance of balancing engaging FSM campaigns with realistic portrayals of growth potential and operational challenges.

Strong governance practices are essential to manage overvaluation risks. Leaders must balance enthusiasm generation with transparency, avoiding exaggerated claims. Grounding messaging in realistic projections and delivering on promises helps build trust and sustain long-term value post-IPO.

Collectively, FSM has become an indispensable aspect of the corporate landscape, influencing everything from image and value to governance and IPO strategies. Its ability to shape investor perceptions and stakeholder relationships has made it a critical tool for companies navigating the digital era. As the digital landscape evolves, the ability to navigate these platforms strategically is paramount for corporate success.

To succeed, companies must do more than maintain an active presence on FSM. They need to adopt data-driven approaches to monitor sentiment, identify emerging trends, and anticipate potential crises. Leveraging the insights gained from FSM can enable businesses to foster stronger relationships with stakeholders, including investors, customers, and regulators. By integrating FSM strategies into broader governance frameworks, companies can ensure alignment with corporate values while effectively managing risks.

Ultimately, the mastery of FSM is not just about capitalizing on opportunities; it is about building resilience and ensuring sustainability in an increasingly interconnected world. Those who adapt to this new dimension of corporate interaction will be better positioned to achieve long-term growth, maintain trust, and uphold governance standards in the face of rapid technological change.

Notes

1. https://www.axios.com/2018/09/07/colin-kaepernick-nike-online-sales
2. https://www.wired.com/2014/01/icahn-keeps-hammering-apple-buy-back/

CHAPTER 18

Financial Social Media Risk Management

Introduction

The emergence of social media as a dominant platform for communication and information exchange has revolutionized the financial landscape. Social media channels such as Facebook, X.com (formerly Twitter), Reddit, LinkedIn, and TikTok have become integral tools for gathering market insights, gauging sentiment, and influencing investment strategies among both retail and institutional investors. These platforms provide an unprecedented amount of real-time sentiment data that can sway investor behavior, shape market trends, and drive financial decision-making. The rapid dissemination of both accurate and misleading information has created an uncertain market environment in financial markets.

While the opportunities presented by financial social media (FSM hereafter) are vast, the associated risks are equally profound. Misinformation can spread rapidly, leading to distorted market perceptions and suboptimal investment decisions. FSM has also become a platform that can facilitate market manipulation, with malicious actors leveraging these platforms to artificially inflate stock prices, spread false narratives, or engineer pump-and-dump schemes. Furthermore, the inherent volatility of crowd-driven sentiment can result in significant market disruptions, as seen in recent episodes involving meme stocks such as GameStop and AMC, as well as cryptocurrency rallies. These challenges highlight the

Y. Zhang, *Financial Social Media*,
https://doi.org/10.1007/978-3-032-09332-5_18

pressing need for robust risk management strategies tailored to the unique dynamics of FSM.

The implications of unmanaged risks extend beyond individual investors to the broader financial system. Regulatory bodies, financial institutions, and market participants must grapple with the ethical, legal, and operational complexities of this new paradigm. This includes addressing issues such as the spread of unverified information, compliance with financial regulations, and the use of FSM data in algorithmic trading models. The speed and scale at which FSM impacts financial markets necessitate a proactive approach to risk management.

This chapter covers the critical challenges posed by FSM and outlines actionable strategies for mitigating its risks. Topics covered include the identification and prevention of misinformation, regulatory considerations, the role of artificial intelligence and machine learning in monitoring social media trends, and the importance of investor education in fostering a more informed and resilient financial community. By addressing these complexities, financial stakeholders can unlock the full potential of FSM while safeguarding against its downsides.

Understanding the Risks of Financial Social Media

Misinformation and Rumors

FSM platforms are notorious for the rapid dissemination of unverified information. In the context of financial markets, misinformation can range from false corporate announcements to exaggerated claims about stock performance. These inaccuracies often gain traction due to the viral nature of social media, creating significant challenges for investors and financial institutions alike. Rumors, amplified by trends and echo chambers, can lead to market distortions and irrational investor behavior, such as panic selling or speculative buying. The tremendous speed at which such misinformation spreads leaves little room for due diligence, often causing irreversible financial consequences.

The GameStop incident of early 2021 offers a striking example of how FSM can disrupt financial markets. The Reddit community r/WallStreetBets mobilized millions of retail investors to purchase GameStop shares, driving up the stock price by over 1700% in a matter of weeks. This collective action, fueled by a mix of memes, sentiment, and a shared goal of challenging institutional short-sellers, created unprecedented volatility. While some investors achieved life-changing gains, many others entered the market at its peak and faced significant losses as prices eventually corrected. The incident underscored the power of viral sentiment to democratize market participation while also exposing its participants to heightened risks. It also revealed the challenges regulators face in addressing such phenomena.

Two other notable incidents illustrate the market-moving power of false online posts. In 2013, hackers took control of the Associated Press (AP)'s verified Twitter account and falsely reported explosions at the White House, briefly wiping out about $140 billion in U.S. market value before the claim was debunked. In 2015, the U.S. Securities and Exchange Commission (SEC hereafter) charged a trader who created fake Twitter accounts resembling reputable news sources to spread false information about public companies, causing share prices to drop by as much as 28% before trading was halted. Both cases highlight the speed at which misinformation can move markets and the critical need for rapid verification and response mechanisms.[1]

Manipulation and Malicious Actors

Manipulation on FSM takes many forms, from coordinated pump-and-dump schemes to fake news campaigns and bot-driven amplification of narratives. These activities erode market integrity, damage investor confidence, and often result in financial harm for uninformed participants. Malicious actors leverage the anonymity and reach of FSM to orchestrate schemes designed to benefit themselves at the expense of others.

The rise of artificial intelligence (AI hereafter) has introduced a new layer of complexity to social media manipulation. Deepfake technology allows for the creation of highly realistic videos and audio recordings that can convincingly mimic influential figures. For instance, a fabricated video of a CEO announcing a fictitious merger or acquisition could cause immediate and dramatic shifts in a company's stock price. While such deep fake has not yet been widely exploited in financial markets, their potential impact underscores the importance of developing advanced detection and verification tools.[2]

Crypto currency markets are particularly vulnerable to social media manipulation due to their relatively low liquidity and high volatility. A TikTok influencer known as Jack Kay launched a meme token called

Ibiza Final Boss (BOSS). The token's market cap briefly surged from $10 million to $50 million, creating a buying frenzy. Within 72 hours of its launch, however, the token crashed by 84%, plummeting to around $9.66 million. Allegedly, the influencer earned over $100,000 from trading fees while followers suffered heavy losses. This case highlights how influencer-driven hype on social media can fuel rapid market swings and underscore the lack of oversight in crypto currency launches. The price of the crypto currency surged as retail investors rushed to buy in, only to crash when the influencer sold their holdings at the peak. This pump-and-dump scheme left countless investors with significant losses and highlighted the lack of regulation and oversight in crypto currency markets. The incident emphasizes the need for greater awareness and due diligence among participants in these markets.

Volatility of Sentiment

Unlike traditional financial indicators, FSM sentiment is inherently volatile and often driven by emotions such as fear, greed, and excitement. Online discussions can rapidly spiral into a feedback loop, amplifying market swings and creating instability. This volatility poses unique challenges for both investors and financial institutions attempting to navigate sentiment-driven markets.

Elon Musk's tweets about crypto currencies like Bitcoin and Dogecoin have repeatedly demonstrated the sensitivity of markets to social media-driven sentiment. In 2021, a single tweet from Musk announcing Tesla's decision to accept Bitcoin payments caused a sharp rise in Bitcoin's price. Conversely, another tweet expressing concerns about Bitcoin's environmental impact triggered a significant sell-off. Musk's influence, while often unintentional, highlights the precariousness of relying on social media sentiment for financial decision-making. It also underscores the need for investors to contextualize and critically evaluate such information before acting on it.

By understanding these risks in greater detail, financial stakeholders can better equip themselves to navigate the challenges posed by FSM and implement safeguards to protect market integrity.

Risk Management Strategies

Advanced Data Verification and Fact-Checking Mechanisms

The first line of defense against misinformation is robust data verification. Financial institutions and platforms can adopt a variety of measures to ensure the accuracy and reliability of information circulating on FSM:

- Automated Fact-Checking Tools: Algorithms can be deployed to cross-reference FSM content with credible sources, detecting discrepancies and flagging potential misinformation in real time. These tools leverage natural language processing (NLP hereafter) and machine learning to analyze large volumes of data efficiently.
- Partnerships with Verification Agencies: Collaborating with third-party fact-checking organizations can provide an additional layer of scrutiny. These partnerships allow financial platforms to validate claims and prevent the spread of false information.
- X.com's Birdwatch Program: X.com's Birdwatch initiative enables users to flag and annotate misleading tweets, fostering a community-driven approach to fact-checking. A similar model tailored to financial content could enhance transparency and trust in market-related discussions.
- Use of Blockchain for Verification: Blockchain technology offers a promising solution for enhancing data integrity. Immutable records of verified information, such as timestamps on official announcements, can help differentiate credible sources from fake news. By providing a transparent and tamper-proof ledger, blockchain technology reduces the risks associated with misinformation.

Sentiment Analysis Algorithms

Advanced sentiment analysis plays a pivotal role in distinguishing genuine market signals from speculative noise. Leveraging cutting-edge technologies, these tools provide financial stakeholders with deeper insights into market sentiment.

- NLP: NLP techniques analyze textual data to assess sentiment polarity (positive, negative, neutral). This helps investors gauge the general mood of FSM discussions surrounding specific stocks or markets.

- Emotion Detection: More sophisticated algorithms can detect underlying emotions such as fear, optimism, or frustration in online conversations. These insights enable a more nuanced understanding of market sentiment.
- Bot Detection Systems: To ensure the reliability of sentiment analysis, tools that identify and filter out bot-generated content are essential. Bots can distort sentiment metrics, leading to inaccurate conclusions and misguided decisions.
- Innovations in Sentiment Analysis: Recent advancements in machine learning have led to context-aware sentiment analysis models. For instance, transformers like BERT (Bidirectional Encoder Representations from Transformers) enable algorithms to consider the context of words within sentences, enhancing accuracy.
- Hybrid Models for Sentiment Accuracy: Hybrid models that combine machine learning and rule-based approaches have demonstrated significant improvements in sentiment analysis. These models leverage the strengths of both methods to better understand complex financial discussions, reducing the risks of misinterpretation.

Diversification of Information Sources

Relying solely on FSM sentiment for financial decision-making is inherently risky. A diversified approach that integrates traditional financial indicators and alternative data sources ensures a more comprehensive understanding of market conditions.

- Cross-Referencing Data: Comparing FSM sentiment with traditional metrics such as earnings reports, trading volumes, and macroeconomic indicators helps validate trends and reduces reliance on any single data source.
- Integration of Alternative Data: Alternative data, such as satellite imagery, consumer spending patterns, and supply chain analytics, can complement FSM sentiment analysis. These data points provide additional context and reduce the risks of overreacting to FSM-driven trends.

- Hedge Funds and Data Diversification: Hedge funds often adopt a diversified approach by integrating FSM sentiment, traditional financial data, and alternative data into their strategies. This multifaceted perspective minimizes risks and enhances decision-making precision.

Investor Education

Educating investors about the limitations and biases of FSM sentiment is critical for fostering informed decision-making. By equipping investors with the tools to navigate FSM-driven markets, financial institutions can promote a more resilient investment community. Here are some key educational initiatives:

- Workshops and Seminars: Interactive sessions that teach investors how to interpret social media sentiment and avoid common pitfalls can empower them to make smarter decisions.
- Guidelines for Sentiment Interpretation: Providing clear frameworks for distinguishing actionable insights from speculative trends helps investors navigate the complexities of social media-driven markets.
- Awareness Campaigns: Highlighting the dangers of misinformation, manipulation, and emotional decision-making through targeted campaigns can foster greater caution and critical thinking among investors.

By implementing these risk management strategies, financial stakeholders can mitigate the risks associated with FSM while harnessing its potential to enhance market understanding and decision-making.

Crisis Management in the age of Financial Social Media

Mitigating Crises Arising from Misinformation

Financial markets are particularly susceptible to crises triggered by viral misinformation. A proactive approach to crisis management involves several key strategies:

- Real-Time Monitoring: Leveraging AI-driven tools to track FSM platforms for emerging threats. This includes identifying unusual spikes in activity, trending hashtags, or the sudden viral spread of potentially misleading content.
- Rapid Response Teams: Assembling dedicated teams to address misinformation promptly. These teams should include communication experts, financial analysts, and technology specialists to craft immediate and effective responses.
- Transparent Communication: Counteracting false narratives with accurate, timely updates. Official channels such as press releases, verified FSM accounts, and direct communication with stakeholders can help dispel misinformation swiftly and restore market confidence.

Flash crashes, which are sudden and dramatic drops in market prices, are often intensified by a combination of algorithmic trading and FSM rumors. For example, during the May 6, 2010 flash crash, the Dow Jones Industrial Average plunged about 1000 points, nearly 9%, within minutes. Although FSM was less prominent at that time, today's interconnected platforms could amplify similar events due to the widespread use of Application Programming Interface (API) driven algorithmic trading that analyzes social sentiment in milliseconds, a practice that was not the industry standard in 2010. Effective crisis management requires close coordination among regulators, exchanges, and market participants to investigate the causes, halt trading when necessary, and disseminate accurate information to stabilize markets.

Building Resilience through Scenario Planning

Scenario planning equips financial institutions to anticipate and prepare for potential crises. By simulating various scenarios, such as (a viral fake news event, a coordinated FSM attack, or the unintended consequences of a high-profile influencer's statement), organizations can stress test their response capabilities and identify areas for improvement.

- Stress Testing Communication Channels: Ensuring that official communication channels are robust and capable of handling

increased traffic during crises. Testing these systems under simulated crisis conditions can help avoid technical failures that could exacerbate the situation.
- Simulated Crisis Drills: Conducting regular drills involving multiple departments, from IT to public relations, to ensure readiness.

Although FSM was less pervasive in 2008, its emerging role in spreading rumors about bank liquidity underscored its potential for harm. For instance, unverified tweets or posts about a bank's financial stability could have led to panic withdrawals and a loss of consumer confidence. Today, with FSM's broader reach, such rumors could escalate even faster, making it imperative for institutions to counteract them in real time. Modern tools, such as AI-driven rumor detection systems, could have helped mitigate the crisis by identifying and debunking false information before it gained traction.

Leveraging Technology for Crisis Management

Technology plays a pivotal role in managing crises arising from FSM. Tools and strategies include:

- AI-Based Rumor Detection: Algorithms that identify trending topics and assess their credibility in real time.
- Blockchain for Transparency: Utilizing blockchain to timestamp and verify official announcements, reducing the impact of fake news.
- Sentiment Analysis in Crisis Mode: Deploying advanced sentiment analysis tools to gauge public reaction to emerging events and adjust strategies accordingly.

By integrating these approaches, financial institutions can strengthen their crisis management frameworks and minimize the disruptive impact of FSM-driven events.

Ethical Considerations and Regulatory Frameworks

The regulation of FSM necessitates a careful balance between upholding freedom of speech and safeguarding market integrity. FSM thrives on open discourse, enabling users to share ideas, opinions, and strategies freely. However, in the context of financial markets, unregulated communication can lead to misinformation, manipulation, and market volatility. To address this, regulatory frameworks must aim to curtail harmful practices without suppressing legitimate discussions.

- Content Moderation Policies: FSM platforms can establish clear guidelines for posting financial content, focusing on disallowing false or misleading claims while respecting the right to express opinions. Automated systems combined with human moderation can help identify and address harmful content.
- Transparency Requirements: Mandating disclosures for posts with potential conflicts of interest, such as influencer endorsements or sponsored financial advice, is critical. Users must be aware when content is influenced by paid promotions or personal financial incentives.

The SEC has taken steps to enforce transparency on social media. In December 2022, the SEC charged eight social media influencers for engaging in a massive $100 million stock manipulation scheme, executed through X.com (formerly Twitter) and Discord platforms. These individuals cultivated significant followings by portraying themselves as successful traders. They promoted specific stocks, often while secretly selling their own holdings, without disclosing their financial incentives or their intent to sell once the prices were artificially inflated. The case underscored the need for regulatory oversight to prevent deceptive practices while preserving users' ability to engage in financial discussions.

International Approaches to Regulating Financial Social Media

Regulatory strategies for FSM vary significantly worldwide, reflecting cultural, legal, and economic differences. As FSM continues to influence financial markets, countries and regions are adopting tailored approaches to balance innovation and investor protection.

European Union: Proactive Platform Oversight

The European Union's Digital Services Act (DSA hereafter) exemplifies a forward-thinking approach, emphasizing accountability for harmful content, including financial misinformation. Key measures include:

- Mandatory Moderation Protocols: FSM platforms must detect and remove illegal or misleading financial content.
- Algorithmic Transparency: Disclosure of how algorithms amplify or suppress content is required.
- User Rights: Clear explanations for content decisions and accessible appeal processes empower users.

The DSA's emphasis on transparency and proactive monitoring aims to prevent market instability caused by misinformation while maintaining free speech protections.

United States: Focus on Fraud Prevention and Transparency

In the United States, regulators such as the SEC and Financial Industry Regulatory Authority (FINRA hereafter) focus on combating fraud and promoting transparency.

- Anti-Fraud Measures: The SEC targets pump-and-dump schemes and unregistered securities promotions.
- Fair Disclosure (Reg FD): Ensures companies share material information equally with all investors, discouraging selective announcements via social media.
- Collaboration with Platforms: Partnerships with social media companies enhance financial content moderation.

For instance, (the SEC's 2022 enforcement against cryptocurrency influencers who failed to disclose compensation underscored the importance of transparency in maintaining market integrity).[3]

Asia-Pacific: Responding to Emerging Risks

The Asia-Pacific region adopts stringent measures to address speculative financial products like cryptocurrencies:

- Singapore: The Monetary Authority of Singapore (MAS hereafter) mandates clear risk disclosures and restricts crypto promotions targeting retail investors.
- Japan: The Financial Services Agency (FSA) enforces fair advertising standards, holding influencers accountable for misleading content.
- South Korea: Amid a surge in cryptocurrency speculation in 2021, South Korea introduced strict regulations requiring influencers and exchanges to register and disclose risks. FSM platforms were also tasked with filtering false claims, reducing speculative behavior and enhancing investor protection.
- India: India's approach highlights the challenges of regulating a rapidly evolving market. While the government initially considered banning cryptocurrency promotions, it ultimately adopted a balanced strategy that combines innovation with oversight. Current regulations require influencers and FSM platforms to disclose risks clearly, allowing innovation to continue while protecting investors.
- China: China adopts a restrictive stance on FSM, banning cryptocurrency promotions and requiring strict licensing for financial influencers. Regulatory bodies, such as the China Securities Regulatory Commission (CSRC), closely monitor FSM platforms to combat misinformation and fraud, reflecting the government's cautious approach to digital assets.

In sum, the diverse regulatory strategies highlight the need for tailored solutions that reflect local market conditions while addressing global risks. Collaboration among regulators, FSM platforms, and stakeholders is essential to create a safer, more equitable financial ecosystem that fosters both innovation and investor protection.

Ethical Use of Algorithms in Financial Social Media

Algorithms are integral to FSM, driving tasks like sentiment analysis, risk assessment, and automated trading. While they enhance efficiency, their misuse can lead to significant ethical and market challenges. Addressing these concerns requires attention to bias, transparency, accountability, and misuse prevention.

Mitigating Bias

Bias in algorithms often arises from skewed or incomplete training data, which can perpetuate systemic inequities. For example, algorithms trained on data dominated by affluent demographics might undervalue diverse perspectives, leading to unfair outcomes. For example, Zhang et al. (2012) argued that the weak performance of the text classifier is primarily due to the imbalanced data, where one class (such as Strong Buy or Buy) dominates the training information. To address this issue, they proposed designing the training data so that each class contains an equal number of messages. Balancing the dataset in this way helps mitigate class imbalance and enhances the classifier's effectiveness. Thus, here are key strategies to address bias in training data:

- Diverse Data Sources: Including varied demographic and geographic data ensures balanced algorithmic insights.
- Fairness Metrics: Using metrics during model testing helps identify disparities across classes.
- Bias Detection Tools: Tools that pinpoint and address biases during development can enhance fairness.

Ensuring Transparency and Accountability

Algorithms' opaque "black box" nature makes it difficult to scrutinize decision-making processes, raising risks of misuse and reducing trust. To improve transparency, we can do the following:

- Explainability: Techniques like explainable AI (XAI) clarify how algorithms derive outcomes, such as sentiment scores.

- Documentation: Detailed records of data sources, preprocessing, and decision logic enable accountability.
- Stakeholder Involvement: Engaging developers, regulators, and end-users ensures ethical practices throughout the algorithm lifecycle.

Conducting Algorithm Audits

Regular audits assess whether algorithms meet ethical and regulatory standards. They also help identify potential risks and ensure compliance with legal requirements. Components of effective audits include:

- Ethical Risk Evaluation: Assessing algorithms' impact on diverse groups and contexts.
- Regulatory Compliance: Ensuring adherence to laws like GDPR or financial oversight regulations.[4]
- Continuous Improvement: Monitoring and updating algorithms to align with evolving standards.

Preventing Misuse and Manipulation

Algorithms are vulnerable to exploitation, such as coordinated efforts to manipulate sentiment or trading decisions through false information. Mitigation measures include

- Fraud Detection: Algorithms should detect anomalies, such as sudden spikes in sentiment linked to suspicious sources.
- Developer Guidelines: Clear ethical standards for developers can help prevent the creation of exploitable features.
- Regulatory Oversight: Real-time monitoring of algorithmic activity can deter misuse and identify manipulation attempts early.

In sum, ensuring the ethical use of algorithms in FSM requires a multifaceted approach. Addressing bias, increasing transparency, implementing audits, and guarding against misuse are essential to building trust and promoting responsible innovation in financial markets. As algorithms evolve, maintaining ethical standards will remain central to their role in fostering a fair and sustainable financial ecosystem.

Challenges of Algorithmic Transparency

As algorithms increasingly influence decision-making in financial markets, their opacity poses challenges. Stakeholders demand greater transparency to ensure these tools are not being misused.

Many machine learning models operate as "black boxes," making their decision-making processes difficult to interpret. Regulators and organizations are exploring explainable AI (XAI) to provide clarity on how algorithms arrive at conclusions. Broader implications of the Black-Box problem:

- Impact on Market Confidence: When algorithmic decisions lack transparency, investors and regulators may struggle to trust the fairness and accuracy of these tools. This erodes confidence in financial systems.
- Challenges for Oversight: Regulators often face difficulties auditing algorithms because proprietary models may be protected as trade secrets, limiting access to their underlying mechanisms.
- Ethical Dilemmas: A lack of transparency can enable unethical practices, such as covertly prioritizing certain market actors or reinforcing systemic inequities.

  Thus, the following are three approaches we can take to enhance transparency:
- Model Interpretability Techniques: Developers are increasingly adopting techniques like SHAP (Shapley Additive Explanations) or LIME (Local Interpretable Model-agnostic Explanations) to make algorithmic output more understandable.
- Regulatory Frameworks for Transparency: Policymakers are advocating for regulations that mandate minimum transparency standards, ensuring algorithms disclose key decision-making criteria without compromising proprietary technology.
- Collaborative Research Initiatives: Academic and industry collaborations are advancing the development of tools and methodologies to enhance algorithmic transparency.

In sum, efforts to address the challenges of algorithmic transparency must balance the need for accountability with protecting intellectual property. Transparent algorithms that are both interpretable and secure will likely become the cornerstone of ethical and effective financial systems.

Ongoing research, regulatory innovation, and stakeholder collaboration will be critical to achieving this balance.

Establishing Ethical Guidelines for Financial Influencers

The rise of financial influencers, or "finfluencers," has changed how retail investors access market insights. While they offer accessibility and relatability, the absence of robust ethical standards has led to misinformation, conflicts of interest, and even financial harm. Establishing clear guidelines is essential to foster transparency, accountability, and trust.

Transparency through Disclosure

Influencers must disclose sponsorships, conflicts of interest, and the nature of their advice to help audiences make informed decisions.

- Sponsored Content: Influencers should clearly indicate paid promotions to distinguish genuine advice from marketing. Hidden sponsorships can mislead audiences and invite regulatory scrutiny.
- Conflict of Interest: Any personal financial stakes or relationships with promoted entities must be transparently disclosed to avoid biased recommendations.
- Clarification of Intent: Influencers should state whether their content is educational, opinion-based, or professional financial advice. Ambiguity in this distinction can lead followers to make risky decisions.

Certification for Credibility

Certification programs can enhance influencers' financial literacy and ethical accountability, distinguishing trustworthy individuals from unqualified ones.

- Training: Programs could cover core financial principles, risk communication, and ethical practices, ensuring influencers understand and relay information responsibly.

- Independent Oversight: Third-party organizations could issue certifications, much like licensing for financial advisors, signaling credibility to audiences.
- In 2022, Australia's Securities and Investments Commission (ASIC) introduced strict guidelines requiring unlicensed influencers to either cease providing financial advice or obtain proper certification.[5]

Regulatory Oversight and Enforcement

Ethical standards must be enforceable through collaboration between regulators, FSM platforms, and financial institutions:

- Monitoring: FSM platforms should flag financial content lacking disclosures or promoting high-risk schemes.
- Reporting Tools: Audiences should be able to report unethical content, triggering investigations or audits.
- Penalties: Influencers violating standards should face fines, suspensions, or legal consequences.

In 2023, the SEC fined multiple influencers for failing to disclose compensation while promoting stocks, setting a precedent for stricter compliance.[6]

Educating Audiences

Educating the public to critically assess financial advice is as important as regulating influencers.

- Red Flags: Teach audiences to identify signs of misinformation, such as promises of guaranteed returns or lack of disclosures.
- Educational Campaigns: FSM platforms and regulators can collaborate to improve financial literacy and awareness of influencer accountability.

In sum, ethical guidelines for financial influencers are essential to protect retail investors and uphold market integrity. A combination of transparency requirements, certification programs, regulatory oversight, and audience education can ensure influencers contribute positively to

FSM while minimizing harm. As this space continues to evolve, proactive measures will be key to fostering trust and professionalism.

Collaborative Frameworks between Regulators and Platforms

The surge of financial content on FSM, driven by influencers, bots, and algorithms, has created unique regulatory challenges. Misleading information and market manipulation demand cooperative efforts between regulatory bodies and FSM platforms to uphold ethical standards, protect users, and ensure market integrity.

Co-Regulation Models

Co-regulation involves shared responsibility between regulators and FSM platforms to develop and enforce content guidelines, bridging gaps in expertise and oversight.

- Joint Policy Development: Crafting policies to identify misleading investment advice, undisclosed sponsorships, and manipulative schemes, with regulators providing the legal framework for enforcement. For example, the UK's Online Safety Bill requires platforms to work with regulators like the FCA to remove harmful financial content and ensure transparency in moderation practices.
- Enforcement Mechanisms: Combining AI tools, human oversight, and penalties for non-compliance strengthens accountability. For example, TikTok partnered with Italy's Consob to detect misleading financial videos, using keyword-based moderation and regulatory collaboration to remove thousands of harmful posts.

Verified Financial Information

Creating centralized databases of verified financial data can counter misinformation while promoting reliable content.

- Curated Content Hubs: FSM platforms can feature information from licensed institutions and credible sources to reduce reliance on unverified advice.

- Verification Systems: Labeling credible financial influencers ensures transparency and trust. For example, X.com's pilot program verified financial experts to differentiate them from unreliable sources, reducing false investment tips.
- Real-Time Market Data Feeds: Integrating accurate market data prevents manipulation by misinformation campaigns. For example, Google's collaboration with financial institutions delivers reliable stock data to users, setting a model for FSM platforms.

Flagging and Moderation Systems

Effective moderation systems combine technical tools and community engagement.

- Algorithmic Detection: Machine learning algorithms can flag patterns like exaggerated claims or pump-and-dump schemes.
- User Reporting: Enhanced reporting tools empower users to highlight questionable financial content for review.
- Independent Audits: Regular evaluations ensure moderation systems are effective and transparent. For example, Facebook's fact-checking partnerships under the EU Code of Practice reduced visibility of flagged financial misinformation.

Regulatory Sandboxes

Regulatory sandboxes allow FSM platforms and regulators to test innovative tools and policies in controlled settings.

- Moderation Tools: AI-based moderation systems for financial content can be piloted to ensure fairness and scalability.
- Transparency Standards: Testing disclosure guidelines for influencers and advertisers enhances trust. For example, Singapore's MAS sandbox encouraged collaboration to mitigate risks and improve transparency in digital finance.

Future Directions

To address evolving challenges, regulators and FSM platforms must:

- Establish Global Standards: Align moderation and disclosure practices across jurisdictions.
- Increase Transparency: Publish reports on actions against financial misinformation.
- Advance AI Solutions: Invest in tools that detect financial fraud and sentiment manipulation.

Strengthened partnerships between regulators and FSM platforms will foster a safer, transparent, and ethical ecosystem for financial content, enabling innovation while safeguarding users.

Final Thoughts

Collectively, the emergence of FSM as a transformative force in the financial landscape has redefined market dynamics, offering unparalleled opportunities while introducing significant risks. FSM platforms enable real-time access to market sentiment, democratizing financial information and participation. However, they also expose markets to challenges such as misinformation, manipulation, and the volatility of crowd-driven sentiment. Navigating this double-edged environment requires a strategic and proactive approach.

To address these complexities, financial stakeholders must prioritize the development of robust risk management frameworks. This includes implementing advanced data verification processes, leveraging cutting-edge sentiment analysis technologies, and diversifying information sources to avoid over-reliance on FSM-driven insights. Investor education plays a vital role in fostering critical thinking and equipping individuals to identify biases and misinformation effectively. Additionally, crisis management frameworks are essential for mitigating the impact of misinformation-driven disruptions and ensuring market stability.

Collaboration among regulators, financial institutions, and FSM platforms is crucial for establishing a fair and transparent financial ecosystem. Ethical considerations and adherence to regulatory frameworks should underpin all efforts to balance innovation with integrity. By fostering accountability and trust, the financial industry can effectively integrate FSM into decision-making processes without compromising market stability.

In an increasingly digital and interconnected world, the financial sector must embrace the potential of FSM while remaining vigilant against its inherent risks. A forward-looking approach that combines technological innovation, regulatory oversight, and investor education will pave the way for a more resilient, equitable, and informed financial ecosystem.

Notes

1. https://www.sec.gov/newsroom/press-releases/2015-254
2. https://www.dhs.gov/sites/default/files/publications/increasing_threats_of_deepfake_identities_0.pdf
3. https://www.sec.gov/newsroom/press-releases/2022-183
4. GDPR stands for the General Data Protection Regulation, a comprehensive data protection and privacy law enacted by the European Union (EU). It came into effect on May 25, 2018.
5. https://www.asic.gov.au/about-asic/news-centre/news-items/asic-cracks-down-on-unlawful-finfluencers-in-global-push-against-misconduct/
6. https://www.goodwinlaw.com/en/insights/publications/2023/03/03_02-sec-and-finra-to-securities-influencers

CHAPTER 19

The Future of Financial Social Media

Introduction

Financial social media (FSM hereafter) platforms will continue to play a crucial role in providing information to investors and the financial community. Understanding their evolution and future development is essential. Looking ahead, information, including government announcements, macroeconomic updates, corporate news, and investor sentiment will spread rapidly across digital media platforms, increasingly less constrained by language, time zone, geographic, or political barriers.

Investor sentiment will likely become more clearly divided between institutional and individual investors. Institutional sentiment will originate primarily from professional financial analysts, while individual sentiment will emerge from sources such as online chatrooms, trading boards, discussion forums, blogs, and other similar platforms.

This chapter explores the structural deficiencies in current FSM platforms and propose strategies to address them. The chapter concludes by discussing eleven emerging trends that are likely to shape the future development of FSM platforms.

Y. Zhang, *Financial Social Media*,
https://doi.org/10.1007/978-3-032-09332-5_19

Trend 1: User-Rating System

An effective and reliable user-rating system could significantly improve platform credibility. As discussed in Chapter 5, the anonymity of posters makes it challenging to assess their credibility, making a user-rating system essential. Such a system can reduce information asymmetry among users and prevent adverse selection that can hinder the development of sustainable FSM ecosystems. In the future, user ratings may be generated not only by peers, as seen on platforms like TheLion.com, eBay, and Amazon, but also by the platforms themselves, or through a combination of both.

For example, a FSM platform could implement an algorithm that objectively ranks users based on their sentiment about a stock and the stock's current and future performance. Greater weight would be given to predictive accuracy. This system would be fairer than the purely peer-based rating systems commonly used today, which can be manipulated by users creating multiple accounts to inflate their primary account's rating.

When this manipulation occurs, the credibility of a user's rating becomes distorted, ultimately diminishing the quality of information and the overall value of the platform. Therefore, I propose a hybrid rating system in which 60% of the credit score is based on the accuracy of sentiment predictions, 20% on the accuracy of same-day sentiment reports, and 20% on peer recommendations. The proposed 60/20/20 allocation could be adjusted depending on platform policies and goals. A higher credit score, indicating better forecasting ability, would lead to advantageous selection, as discussed in Chapter 5. Ultimately, an effective rating system would enhance the value of an FSM platform by increasing both the quantity and quality of posts and membership. In contrast, a platform without such a system would risk experiencing adverse selection, which could lead to declining user activity and eventual obsolescence. In conclusion, I predict that successful future FSM platforms will, at a minimum, incorporate effective and reliable user-rating systems.

Trend 2: Moderation Tools

As discussed in Chapter 10, anonymity often conceals online security scams. Effective management of anonymity will be crucial to the success of FSM platforms. Given that most online communication is protected by freedom of speech in the United States, innovative and effective moderation tools are essential to mitigate adverse selection and moral hazard issues.

Although users' IP addresses are not publicly displayed, web operators do record them to combat abuse and fraud. However, it is impractical to disclose these addresses to the public. Nevertheless, one IP address should be linked to a single account. It is possible to show only the last four digits of an IP address alongside a username. For example, if a full IP address (e.g., 123.45.678.910) is associated with the user "yingzhang," the last four digits could be displayed so that the username appears as "yingzhang (…8910)." This would allow readers to determine whether different usernames linked to the same IP address possibly belong to the same poster. This approach gives moderators and readers a tool to identify if multiple accounts are being used by a single individual.

Moderation teams should collaborate closely with regulators, such as the SEC and FTC, as frequent securities fraud on FSM platforms could jeopardize the websites' operations. Moderators need to be well-versed in identifying and reporting illegal activities, and they should cooperate fully by providing all relevant information when regulators initiate securities fraud investigations.

In the future, regulators may develop methods to monitor FSM platforms in real-time. Additionally, future moderation tools should allow platform moderators to privately discuss actions like banning users, issuing warnings, disabling accounts, and reporting to regulators. Moderator input would be stored in protected areas (inaccessible to regular users), which could be retrieved, reviewed, discussed, and acted upon by peer moderators.

To survive and thrive, future FSM platforms must implement effective user-rating systems and maintain robust moderation teams.

Trend 3: Value-Added Services

Value-added services play a significant role in determining the success of FSM platforms. Currently, many FSM platforms resemble traditional bulletin boards, where users primarily share information. To attract more users, some platforms are offering additional value-added services, such as internal search engines and daily rankings of the most discussed stocks. For example, TheLion.com currently provides six value-added services:

- Search Box: A search tool that allows users to find all message postings related to a specific stock ticker symbol across multiple online platforms.
- Most Popular Blogs: A constantly updated list of the most popular blog submissions from users.
- Most Active Platforms: A regularly updated list featuring the most active user-moderated platforms.
- Top Stock Discussions: A list that is continuously updated to showcase the most popular discussions across various platforms.
- Most Stock Searches: A daily updated list of the most frequently searched stocks using the Search Box.
- Most Endorsed Messages: A list that is frequently updated to highlight the messages that have received the most approval from the community.

Looking ahead, to thrive and appeal to online investors, FSM platforms will likely offer a variety of additional value-added services. For example:

- Aggregate Sentiment Reporting: While many messages already include users' self-disclosed sentiments, an aggregate sentiment for a stock over a specific time is currently unavailable. In the future, it may be possible to report an aggregate investor consensus about a stock on a daily basis or within a 24-hour rolling window, enabling readers to assess overall investor sentiment. For messages without explicit self-disclosed sentiments, suggested sentiments could be generated using artificial intelligence tools. Thus, future FSM platforms may feature two sentiment measures for each stock: one reflecting overall sentiment generated by users and text classifiers, and another based purely on users' self-disclosed sentiments.
- Broad Sentiment Index: A broader aggregate sentiment index could be created based on all stocks discussed on a FSM platform over specific time periods or in real time. This index could be either equally weighted or value-weighted, based on each stock's market value. Such an index would provide readers with an overview of investor confidence and the general market mood.
- Investor Disagreement Indices: Future FSM platforms could also provide indices measuring the dispersion of sentiments, or investor disagreement. There could be a disagreement index for each stock

as well as for the entire platform. Understanding the level of disagreement among investors could help predict market volatility.

- Posting Volume Index: An index describing posting volume would also be valuable. While some platforms currently report the cumulative number of messages, a time-series summary of daily posting volume for each stock does not yet exist. With a posting volume index, readers would gain insight into the level of investor attention.
- User Classification by Trading Style: Each user could be classified by their trading style (e.g., long-term holder, day trader, momentum trader, arbitrager, hedger, or contrarian trader). This information could be collected during registration, updated by the user, or inferred from their stock recommendations. The trading style of each poster could be displayed alongside their username, enabling readers to quickly discern whether a poster shares a similar trading style. Readers could also choose to view only messages from traders with similar styles, while blocking those from unwanted sources.
- User Interaction Features: Users could receive notifications or emails when other members "recommend," "endorse," "like," or "cite" their posts. They could also track their favorite posters, see what topics those users have posted about, read their posts, and engage in related discussions.

Trend 4: Multimedia Sharing

Plain text remains the dominant format for messages in online financial communities, and it will likely continue to be. However, other forms of communication are emerging, and FSM platforms will increasingly accept and embrace these new formats.

- Voice Messages: Voice messages are set to become a key feature in the future. They are faster and more convenient than typing for most people, which is particularly beneficial for traders during trading sessions. With voice messages, traders can multitask while making trades. If a platform requires text, voice messages can be automatically converted into text using voice-to-text transcribers. Likewise, if someone replies via text and you receive a voice notification, you can choose to listen to the message through a reverse text-to-voice transcriber. With current technology, voice-to-text and text-to-voice transcription is extremely accurate.

- Video Messages: Video messages will also play an important role in the future. With advances in data capacity, bandwidth, and Internet service, FSM platforms will not only support voice messages but also video messages alongside traditional text. While video messages may not be suitable for short messages or replies, they are ideal for longer communications. Individuals, corporations, and other organizations already frequently post video clips (e.g., many investors maintain video blogs on personal websites), so it will not be surprising when future FSM platforms support video messages for both online discussions and blogging. Users will be able to respond to video messages with video replies, voice replies, text replies, or a combination of all.
- Mobile Apps: Mobile applications are poised to transform how investors engage with FSM platforms, much like the way Facebook and X.com (formerly Twitter) have expanded their user bases through mobile access. As smartphones have become the primary device for online interaction, dedicated apps will allow FSM users to receive instant notifications, post updates, monitor discussions, and track sentiment without being tied to a desktop computer. This constant connectivity will likely increase both the frequency and immediacy of user participation, particularly during periods of market volatility when timely information is critical.
- A strong precedent is Reddit, which has significantly boosted community activity through its smartphone app by making it easy for users to browse platforms, join discussions, and contribute content from anywhere. Similarly, FSM platforms with well-designed mobile interfaces can integrate features such as personalized watchlists, live price feeds, sentiment indicators, and in-app alerts for trending topics or unusual activity. Over time, these capabilities will encourage deeper engagement, foster a more active trading community, and potentially enhance the market influence of discussions occurring on these platforms.

Trend 5: Combination of Stock-Trading and Stock-Specific Boards

Currently, FSM platforms are typically divided into two types: trading boards or stock-specific boards. A trading board functions like a chat room, allowing registered users to retrieve past messages. However, these boards list messages in reverse chronological order, making it challenging to group relevant messages efficiently. To address this issue, stock-specific boards compile messages related to a particular stock on a dedicated page.

Stock-specific boards allow users to focus on one stock at a time without being distracted by discussions about other stocks. All conversations on the board pertain to that specific stock. In my view, stock-trading boards are more suited for short-term momentum traders who want to follow trending stocks, while stock-specific boards are better for long-term, fundamental investors. However, momentum traders sometimes seek relevant information on stock-specific boards, and fundamental investors may also read posts on stock-trading boards.

The separation of these two types of boards is suboptimal. I predict that future FSM platforms will be hybrids, combining the features of both stock-trading and stock-specific boards. Since an FSM platform can only display one layout at a time, users will have the option to choose the layout that best suits their trading style. This would require a robust internal search engine and an efficient database structure. With a stock-trading layout, the platform would display all messages according to their posting time, sorted in reverse chronological order. With a stock-specific layout, the platform would display messages according to stock symbol, sorted alphabetically and by posting time. Users can also select multiple stock symbols so that the platform displays only messages related to those selected stocks.

For instance, if I am interested in discussions about two retail giants, WMT (Walmart) and TGT (Target), I could choose a stock-specific layout focused on these two stocks. The platform would display all messages related to WMT, followed by those related to TGT, or vice versa, with all messages sorted in reverse chronological order. If I want to see what people are saying about these two stocks around the same time, I could choose a flexible view, which sorts all messages related to WMT and TGT in reverse chronological order.

Additionally, future FSM platforms will likely allow users to create invitation-only, private chat rooms, where message content is restricted to those specific chat rooms.

Trend 6: Multi-Assets Boards

The United States hosts several major financial markets, including the capital market, commodity market, derivatives market, foreign exchange market, money market, insurance market, and cryptocurrency market. These financial markets are highly cohesive and interdependent, so there is little reason to separate platforms by asset type. However, most current FSM platforms focus on just one or a few types of assets.

In the future, I anticipate the emergence of websites or applications featuring integrated platforms for different types of assets. Much like "one-stop shopping," investors will be able to gather information on various assets through a single platform. This trend is already visible in some platforms. For example, Trade2win.com hosts discussion boards for stocks, indices, foreign exchange, futures and options, commodities, and money markets.[1]

HotCopper, the largest stock market platform in the Southern Hemisphere, covers a broad range of topics beyond financial assets, including religion, politics, science, music, and sports.[2] Among financial assets, it covers stocks, commodities, foreign exchange, and IPOs. With its high posting volumes and large user base, HotCopper seemingly covers almost everything.

Unlike HotCopper, where platforms are created by webmasters, TheLion.com is a platform that allows users to create their own discussion boards. One of the most popular boards, WallStreetPit, was created and is maintained by a user named "Lionmaster." TheLion.com also hosts many other discussion boards for different types of assets, including bonds, commodities, futures, and foreign exchange.

Given the existing platform frameworks (sunk costs), the cost of adding additional platforms is low, which makes this trend likely to grow. Additionally, with ongoing globalization, future FSM platforms will not be confined to just one country or region. I expect to see even larger platforms covering different markets and assets across the globe. These boards will likely feature instantaneous translation technology, allowing online messages to be translated into a user's preferred language.

Trend 7: Search Engine

The volume of information generated in FSM is staggering. Effectively managing and analyzing large datasets will be crucial for the success of future FSM platforms. The key to this success lies in powerful search engines, both external and internal. Search results are typically presented on separate pages, with messages listed based on relevancy and posting time.

Given the constant influx of new messages and the maximum number of messages displayed per page (usually between 25 and 50), new posts can be archived, meaning they disappear from the front page, within minutes, especially during trading hours. Without a powerful search engine, much valuable market information can be easily overlooked. Once a message is archived, retrieving it requires using the search function. An internal search engine is a software system that indexes content exclusively from a particular platform, creating a search results list with information only from that platform.

On the other hand, an external search engine searches for messages both inside and outside a particular platform. For example, TheLion.com features an external search box that allows users to retrieve message postings from multiple external platforms (including Raging Bull, InvestorsHub, Motley Fool, Investor Village, Yahoo! Finance, Seeking Alpha, and Google Finance) as well as TheLion.com's own platform. BoardCentral.com is another good example of a platform that extends the capabilities of an external search engine. Without a doubt, an external search engine is more powerful and preferred over an internal one, as it provides far more information to investors.

Trend 8: Social Media Aggregation

Internal searches focus on a single platform, while external searches span multiple sources. In the future, these searches may also include other social media platforms, such as Facebook, X.com, and Tumblr. Data from these platforms can be just as important and useful to investors seeking analyst opinions, investment ideas, or community sentiments about a stock or the market. However, navigating from one platform to another on the Internet can be cumbersome, so it would be highly beneficial for investors to have a single source that aggregates information from all available online social media channels.

Several websites are already working on developing social media aggregators. For instance, BoardCentral.com searches for information within two of the largest financial social communities: financial forums and stock-related tweets. The BoardCentral.com search engine scans messages from 13 popular FSM platforms, as well as tweets from X.com, covering over-the-counter and NASDAQ and NYSE-listed stocks, as well as ETFs and foreign exchange securities.

Yahoo! Finance offers a "Market Pulse" gadget, which provides a real-time stream of information from various sources, including FSM platforms, all in one place. Each stock has its own "Market Pulse" page.[3] Yahoo! Finance also features a leaderboard of "Trending Tickers on Market Pulse," helping investors identify companies generating unusual buzz. Additionally, NASDAQ offers a "Market Stream" function, a continuous, interactive stream of real-time data, news, and social commentary based on the stock you enter.[4] "Market Stream" includes reactions from financial experts to breaking news, discussions around company developments, and investment ideas on stocks, ETFs, and mutual funds shared by individuals.

To stay informed, future investors will increasingly rely on social media aggregators, making this an exciting new trend.

Trend 9: Revenue-Generating Models

Most current public FSM platforms are free and generate almost no revenue. Only a few receive money from voluntary donations, which are generally insignificant. Some private platforms, however, charge users several hundred dollars per month through subscription fees (e.g., the one run by "Tokyo Joe").

This creates a dilemma for platform operators, involving a tradeoff between retaining users and generating revenue. The switching cost for users is almost zero, as many free online platforms offer similar functions. As we all know, users and their posts are the platform's most valuable assets. Once a subscription fee is introduced, many users may simply switch to other, free platforms. This is why most current FSM platforms do not charge fees. The key is to provide value-added services and a trustworthy user-rating system. I propose several new revenue models:

- Multilayer, Progressive Membership Program: This model relies on offering various value-added services. Basic members would have the right to read and reply to original messages, but they wouldn't be able to see sentiment scores generated by text classifiers for messages without self-disclosed sentiment. To access these sentiment scores, they would need to pay a minimum monthly fee and become advanced users.

- Premium Membership: To access quantified aggregate sentiment, a member would need to pay a higher fee and become a premium user. Premium users would have additional privileges, such as setting up private chat rooms, inviting other users to join these rooms, and accessing trading signals (e.g., buy, hold, and sell) based on online discussions and/or social media feeds.
- Loyalty and Referral Programs: To enhance user loyalty and encourage active participation, administrators could implement loyalty rewards and referral programs. For instance, a user could be promoted to a higher membership level by exceeding a certain number of messages or by gaining a large following. Users could also receive financial or membership rewards for bringing in a certain number of new subscribers.
- Advertising Opportunities: Many corporations and financial institutions are interested in advertising on FSM platforms, providing another potential revenue stream.
- Selling Data to Third Parties: A small number of data mining and analytics firms collect content from FSM platforms and refine it into trading signals for resale to investors. Licensing platform data to third-party analytics or technology companies can also provide a significant revenue stream. For example, Reddit has sold its data to OpenAI for use in training large-scale artificial intelligence models, showing the commercial value of high-quality user-generated content. Ultimately, sustaining this model depends on retaining a loyal user base through value-added services and maintaining a transparent, trustworthy membership program, since the quality of the data and its market value rely heavily on active and credible community participation.

Trend 10: Mergers and Acquisitions

In the future, the FSM industry is likely to be dominated by a few monopolies through mergers and acquisitions. Currently, major social media platforms like Facebook, Reddit, Google, Tumblr, X.com, and Yahoo are among the most popular in the United States. Many of these platforms also host their own stock forums (e.g., Yahoo! Finance and Google Finance), and there are numerous stock-trading groups on Facebook and X.com.

Supporters of online platforms are likely to embrace deeper integration between FSM platforms and mainstream social media. As this trend develops, it is reasonable to anticipate more mergers among independent FSM platforms, as well as acquisitions by larger social media companies. In fact, this trend has already begun:

- Big-Boards.com: In early 2005, Big-Boards.com was one of the most popular online platforms, with over 300,000 visitors and more than one million page views per month. Unfortunately, Big-Boards.com no longer exists.
- Google's Acquisition of YouTube: Google acquired YouTube on October 9, 2006. Before that, YouTube was a popular, stand-alone video-sharing website.
- InvestorsHub.com: Founded in 2000, InvestorsHub.com was a stand-alone FSM platform in the United States until it was acquired by the UK company ADVFN in 2006.
- ClearStation: Originally a public online chat room, ClearStation was acquired by E*TRADE and integrated into the E*TRADE community. It now facilitates the sharing of trading strategies and ideas among E*TRADE investors. Access to the chat room requires E*TRADE membership, making ClearStation a semipublic chat room since its merger with E*TRADE.
- Social Media Integration: Some platforms now have their own Facebook and X.com pages, allowing investors to share their trading positions and posts via their social media accounts.

Collectively, these examples demonstrate the ongoing wave of mergers and acquisitions within the industry. This trend will continue, following the principle of survival of the fittest.

Trend ii: AI and the Future of Financial Social Media

Artificial Intelligence (AI hereafter) is rapidly transforming various industries, and FSM is no exception. The integration of AI into FSM platforms is poised to revolutionize the way investors interact, share information, and make decisions.

AI systems thrive on data, and FSM platforms are treasure troves of information. Millions of posts, comments, and discussions generated daily on these platforms provide a wealth of unstructured data that AI can analyze. By leveraging this data, AI models are trained to understand market sentiment, identify emerging trends, and even predict market movements. For example, AI-driven sentiment analysis can sift through vast amounts of social media content to gauge public opinion on a particular stock or sector, providing investors with real-time insights that were previously unimaginable.

Moreover, AI can enhance the functionality of FSM by offering personalized content to users. Through machine learning algorithms, AI can analyze an individual's past behavior, preferences, and interactions on the platform to present relevant news, discussions, and investment opportunities. This personalized approach will keep users more engaged and informed, making FSM platforms even more valuable as a resource.

Another significant impact of AI will be the automation of trading decisions based on data from FSM. AI-powered bots can be programmed to monitor social media for specific triggers, such as a sudden surge in positive sentiment about a stock and execute trades automatically. This kind of automation could lead to more efficient markets, but it also raises concerns about increased volatility and the potential for market manipulation.

Furthermore, AI will play a crucial role in detecting and mitigating the spread of misinformation on FSM platforms. By employing advanced algorithms, AI can identify and flag suspicious or misleading content in real time, helping to protect investors from being influenced by false information. This capability will become increasingly important as the volume of content on these platforms continues to grow.

Looking ahead, the integration of AI into FSM will likely lead to the creation of more sophisticated tools and features. For instance, AI-powered virtual assistants could help users navigate complex financial topics, provide tailored investment advice, or even simulate potential market scenarios based on current data trends. These advancements will make FSM more interactive and user-friendly, attracting a broader audience of both retail and sophisticated investors.

In conclusion, AI is set to be a game changer in the world of FSM. As AI continues to evolve, its influence on these platforms will grow, reshaping the landscape of online financial discussions and making them more dynamic, insightful, and responsive to the needs of the investment community.

Notes

1. http://www.trade2win.com/boards/
2. http://hotcopper.com.au/
3. For example, market pulse for AAPL is on http://finance.yahoo.com/marketpulse/aapl
4. For example, market stream for AAPL is on http://www.nasdaq.com/symbol/aapl/stream

CHAPTER 20

Literature Review for Financial Social Media Studies

Academic interest in financial social media (FSM hereafter) can be traced back to the first published study in this field in 1998. However, research in this field remains relatively new. To date, more than 180 academic journal articles have been published that directly examine FSM. Scholars from a range of disciplines including accounting, artificial intelligence, computer science, management information systems, finance, and applied statistics have contributed to this growing body of literature. This chapter focuses exclusively on research articles written in English. Papers written in other languages are excluded, although their existence is acknowledged.

Figure 20.1 illustrates the annual number of FSM-related papers from 1998 to 2025. The number of publications has generally increased over time, reaching at least 19 papers by mid-2025. Since this chapter was completed in the middle of that year, the final count for 2025 will exceed 19. Due to space limitations, this chapter provides a summary of selected papers.

To the best of my knowledge, the first study on FSM platforms was conducted by Peter D. Wysocki in 1998. Wysocki (1998) examined whether changes in message-posting volume were merely noise or related to underlying firm characteristics and stock market activity. He reported that high posting volume was indeed associated with firms exhibiting the following six characteristics: (1) high short-seller activity, (2) high market valuations relative to fundamentals, (3) low institutional holdings,

Y. Zhang, *Financial Social Media*,
https://doi.org/10.1007/978-3-032-09332-5_20

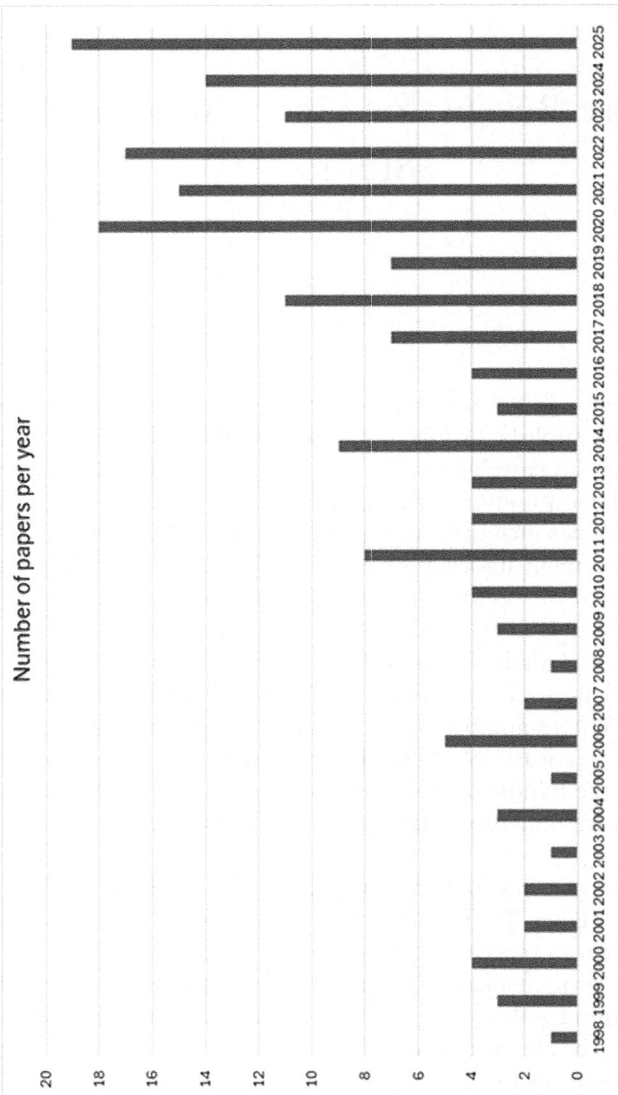

Fig. 20.1 Number of papers per year

(4) high trading volume, (5) extreme performance, and (6) high analyst following. He also found that changes in message-posting volume were related to stock market activity when earnings were announced and when stock trading volume and returns shifted. Consequently, he concluded that changes in overnight posting activity contain valuable information, and overnight message-posting volume can predict changes in next-day stock trading volume and returns.

In 1999, Wysocki continued to explore which stocks attract the most message postings. He found that both fundamental and technical characteristics of a stock influence message-posting volume. Firstly, he observed that message-posting volume is related to firm characteristics, suggesting that online traders prefer certain types of stocks. Secondly, he reported that online traders are more likely to trade stocks with higher trading volumes. Thirdly, he found that online investors pursue stocks with low institutional holdings to generate a greater impact on the stock price. Wysocki also suggested that online posters can influence public opinion about a firm through message board posts.

In his master's thesis, MIT graduate Ghanta (1999) studied whether message board activity had a statistical relationship with stock activity. He explored how these relationships vary based on message board and stock characteristics. Ghanta concluded that message boards track stock prices and trading volume, although the tracking relationship varies according to certain message board characteristics. He found that while message boards had no systematic effects on trading activity, they did increase short-term volatility for some small-cap stocks.

Bagnoli, Beneish, and Watts (1999) compared First Call analyst forecasts of earnings to unofficial, anonymous whispers posted on FSM platforms. They found that whispers are more accurate proxies for market expectations of earnings than First Call analysts' forecasts. They further argued that trading strategies based on the relationship between whispers and First Call forecasts generate abnormal returns, suggesting that whispers provide information not reflected in analyst forecasts.

Thomas and Sycara (1999) were the first to apply a text classifier, specifically the Maximum Entropy Model, to extract information from text data downloaded from FSM platforms. In addition to the text classifier, they used a genetic algorithm to learn simple rules based on numerical data, including trading volume, the number of messages, and the number of words. They discovered that although each approach demonstrated predictive power, combining the two methods predicted future stock excess returns more accurately.

In 2000, Wysocki conducted his third study on FSM platforms, focusing on unexpected changes in message-posting volume before and on earnings announcement dates. He suggested that message-posting activity can serve as a useful source of data on investor beliefs and private information about publicly traded companies. He found that announcement-period trading volume was positively associated with unexpected daily changes in message-posting volume, both before and during the earnings announcement. Additionally, the positive relationship between announcement-period trading volume and absolute returns diminished in cases of unexpected message-posting volume on the earnings announcement date.

Hirschey, Richardson, and Scholz (2000a, 2000b) conducted two studies documenting how the market responds to stock recommendations reported on Motley Fool's discussion site. In Hirschey, Richardson, and Scholz (2000a), they found that Motley Fool's buy (sell) recommendations, particularly those concerning small-cap growth stocks, lead to significant rises (falls) in stock prices on the announcement day. Both studies documented herd-like behavior among Internet investors and noted that Motley Fool's stock advice is more newsworthy than second-hand buy-sell recommendations published in traditional print and electronic media. In Hirschey, Richardson, and Scholz (2000b), they provided systematic evidence that stock recommendations published on the Internet influence prices and trading volumes, with Motley Fool buy announcements closely followed by Internet investors.

Tumarkin and Whitelaw (2001) examined the relationship between Internet message board activity and abnormal stock returns and trading volume, using data from Raging Bull and focusing on stocks in the Internet service sector. They concluded that on days with abnormally high message activity and trading volume, changes in investor opinion correlated with abnormal industry-adjusted returns. However, they found that FSM platforms did not predict industry-adjusted returns or abnormal trading volume. Tumarkin (2002) reached similar conclusions, examining the relationships between Internet message board activity and both abnormal stock returns and abnormal trading volume in the same sector.

Hittle (2001) addressed FSM platform posting activities, anonymity issues, Internet stock fraud, and SEC regulations. He emphasized that due to anonymity and unverified information, a reasonable investor cannot easily distinguish manipulation from legitimate stock movement. Furthermore, fraudsters often use the Internet to spread false and misleading information on FSM platforms to inflate stock prices. FSM platforms dedicated to investing can create a false sense of community and trust, leading unwary investors to react and invest. Once a pump-and-dump scheme is complete, the stock price often collapses, resulting in significant losses for legitimate investors.

Felton and Kim (2002) studied the Yahoo! Finance message board for Enron, and discovered that the company's downfall was foreshadowed by warnings from online posters. They examined posts from 1997 to 2001 and documented that Enron's reputation was tarnished long before its collapse. Their findings suggest that companies and regulators should pay closer attention to anonymous postings on message boards, as these may provide early signs of corporate distress.

From a practitioner's perspective, Dewally (2003) investigated individual posters' investment advice on stock forums, focusing on recommendations from misc.invest.stocks and alt.invest.pennystocks between April 1999 and February 2001. He reported that the majority of online stock recommendations were overly bullish and often followed sharp price increases. Dewally found no significant market reactions to these recommendations, with short-term returns being mostly insignificant and long-term returns failing to outperform market benchmarks.

Koski, Rice, and Tarhouni (2004) explored how FSM platform postings impact trading volatility, using data from Raging Bull and Yahoo! Finance. They argued that day traders, acting as noise traders, rely on message boards as proxies for day trading. Their findings suggested that increased message posting is associated with higher market volatility, though they found that market volatility primarily drives online posting activity.

One of the most influential papers in this field, Antweiler and Frank (2004), used data from Yahoo! Finance and Raging Bull to study the effects of FSM platforms. They created an aggregate poster sentiment index using a Naïve Bayesian text classifier and supported their findings with a support vector machine classifier. Their research highlighted that posters are likely to discuss a stock only when they hold a position in it, and that institutional structures favor long positions over short ones, resulting in predominantly bullish sentiments. Antweiler and Frank found that online discussions can help predict market volatility, with increased disagreement among messages leading to higher trading volume. They also discovered that a high number of messages predicted negative subsequent returns, though investor sentiment itself did not predict future returns. In summary, they concluded that online chatter provides valuable information, rather than mere noise.

Carson and Felton (2004) examined the role of Internet message boards in corporate governance, stressing the importance of monitoring online discussions for corporate reputations. They discussed how negative commentary and stock manipulation schemes, such as "pump-and-dump," can harm firm value. Carson and Felton emphasized the potential for rumors to spread rapidly via message boards, urging companies to pay close attention to these discussions to prevent damage to their reputations.

Das, Martinez-Jereza, and Tufano (2005) utilized language-processing algorithms to analyze over 170,000 messages posted about four stocks: AMZN, DAL, GMGC, and GWRX. Their study revealed that online discussions often contain unsubstantiated rumors, but they also serve as platforms for exchanging information quickly. The researchers found that poster sentiment levels were closely tied to posting activity, stock returns, and trading volumes, suggesting a positive relationship between sentiment and current trading volume.

Jones (2006) explored the differences in stock market behavior before and after the introduction of FSM platforms, using data from Yahoo! Finance. She observed a significant increase in daily trading volume following the establishment of a firm's message board, potentially due to new investors or increased activity from existing investors. However, daily returns were lower in the post-message board era, and market volatility increased significantly. These results remained robust even after accounting for market and industry-wide events.

Clarkson, Joyce, and Tutticci (2006) analyzed 189 takeover rumors posted on HotCopper IDs between May 1999 and March 2000, examining the market's reaction to these rumors. They found that the market responded with abnormal returns and trading volumes on the day the rumor was posted and the day before. Intraday analysis revealed significant returns and trading volume within the ten-minute interval following the rumor's posting, as well as abnormal trading volume just before it.

Gu, Konana, Liu, Rajagopalan, and Ghosh (2006) proposed a method for computing a message poster's reputation based on their past cumulative predictive accuracy. By weighting messages from posters with higher predictive accuracy, they found that sentiment from accurate posters was negatively correlated with future stock movements. They suggested a trading strategy of buying stocks with low sentiment and selling those with high sentiment, arguing that some posters possess information not fully reflected in market prices.

Liu, Gu, Konana, and Ghosh (2006) expanded on this research by examining the difficulties casual users face in distinguishing between posters and evaluating their comments. They developed a framework using Yahoo! Finance message board data to identify historically accurate posters and analyze their sentiments automatically. Their findings demonstrated that implementable trading strategies based on this information could achieve statistically significant returns, even after adjusting for market conditions and transaction costs.

Das and Chen (2007) analyzed stock board messages, primarily from providers like Yahoo! Finance. Using statistical and natural language-processing techniques, they extracted the emotive content of messages to classify authors as bearish, bullish, or neutral. Their study reported that aggregating sentiment across time series and cross-sectional data improves the quality of a sentiment index. This aggregated sentiment, when tracked across multiple stocks, correlated with returns of the Morgan Stanley High-Tech Index (MSH), suggesting a viable trading strategy based on FSM platform sentiments.

Bettman, Hallett, and Sault (2007), using data from Raging Bull and Yahoo! Finance public message boards between January 2003 and December 2006, investigated the effect of takeover rumors on the U.S. equity market. Their findings demonstrated that such rumors exert a significant impact on the market, with positive abnormal returns and increased trading volumes observed both before and after the dissemination of the rumors. However, the rumors did not significantly affect bid-ask spreads. They concluded that takeover rumors from message boards offer interesting insights into financial information dissemination but do not present economically exploitable opportunities for investors.

Sabherwal, Sarkar, and Zhang (2008), analyzing messages on TheLion.com, focused on stocks most actively discussed by online posters. They found that online posters preferred thinly traded microcap stocks, and these stocks experienced significant abnormal returns when they were among the 10 most discussed stocks. The volume of messages posted on a given day not only correlated positively with abnormal returns on that day but also predicted abnormal returns for the following day. Their study provided evidence to regulators that online discussions can affect stock prices, highlighting market inefficiencies. They suggested corporate managers, especially those of smaller firms, should monitor FSM platforms closely.

Cook and Lu (2009) refined their analysis by improving sample selection and removing noise caused by program-generated sentiments. They found that the bullishness of board messages significantly predicted abnormal stock returns up to 2 days in advance. When factoring in the credibility of posters, they found the predictive power of these messages became even stronger in both economic magnitude and statistical significance. Their conclusion was that rumormongers can spread honest but imprecise rumors, profiting from users who follow them.

In her doctoral dissertation, Letitia Meier Pleis (2009) studied how message board postings influence companies. Through an in-class experiment with 110 MBA students, she concluded that only negative postings significantly influence investors' decisions. Negative messages, often driven by short-sellers or disgruntled individuals, were shown to negatively impact a firm's reputation and value by swaying investment decisions toward selling.

Chua, Milosavljevic, and Curran (2009), using text data from HotCopper ASX stock-based discussions, developed a method to classify investor sentiment on FSM platforms. Their system, which employed a variation of the Bayesian classifier with feature selection methods, outperformed conventional classifiers in terms of accuracy and precision. This allowed investors to trade based on more reliable signals and to anticipate the market impact of new information released on message boards.

Zhang (2009) investigated the determinants of poster reputation on WallStreetPit, focusing on whether a poster's reputation was influenced by their characteristics and the stocks discussed. He found that a poster's popularity, sentiment, message quality, and follow-up opinions positively affected their reputation. Conversely, promoting stocks with high price-to-earnings ratios or those with high institutional ownership reduced the likelihood of receiving reputation credits.

Zhang and Swanson (2010) addressed the issue of bias in day traders' stock recommendations on Yahoo! Finance. Using a Naïve Bayesian text classifier, they found that day traders' "Hold" recommendations were skewed toward the buy side, indicating a bias likely caused by the predominance of long positions held by traders.

Depken and Zhang (2010) explored how the pecuniary reputation system on TheLion.com influenced adverse selection on message boards.

They found that posters with high-reputation scores were less likely to offer buy-hold-sell sentiments, and those with no reputation at stake tended to be more bearish. High-reputation posters, however, offered more accurate predictions, suggesting that reputation and pecuniary rewards can mitigate adverse selection.

Bird and Thapa (2011) analyzed investor reactions to company news via FSM platform discussions. They found that negative online discussions correlated with share price declines following negative news, while positive discussions had the opposite effect. Message-posting activity also contributed to post-announcement price drifts, indicating that these discussions could reflect speculation about upcoming announcements.

In a follow-up study, Thapa and Bird (2011) explored whether online discussions provided useful information to investors by examining the relationship between message postings and stock returns. While posting activity correlated with stock returns and volatility, they found no evidence that message boards significantly affected cross-sectional stock returns, except in distressed and momentum stocks.

Avery, Chevalier, and Zeckhauser (2011), analyzing 2.5 million stock picks from www.caps.fool.com, discovered that individual stock picks were surprisingly informative about future stock prices. A long-short strategy based on these picks yielded a 9% annual return, primarily driven by the accuracy of negative stock predictions.

Delort, Arunasalam, Leung, and Milosavljevic (2011) investigated manipulation on FSM platforms using moderated online messages. Their study found that manual moderation was ineffective at preventing manipulation, as ramping was positively associated with market volatility and volume. They noted that stocks with higher turnover and lower market capitalization were common targets for manipulation.

Sabherwal, Sarkar, and Zhang (2011) examined stocks with no material news but high message-posting activity on TheLion.com. They identified a "pump and dump" pattern, where prices rose for 2 days following high message volume and then fell for the next 2 days. Their findings underscored the importance of monitoring message board sentiment as a predictor of trading activity.

Bettman, Hallett, and Sault (2011) revisited their earlier work on takeover rumors, using both Naïve Bayesian and support vector machine classifiers to analyze 2898 takeover rumors from Yahoo! Finance between 2003 and 2008. They found that these rumors generated significant abnormal returns and trading volumes, offering investors a trading opportunity.

Hill and Ready-Campbell (2011), using stock pick data from over 3 years, demonstrated that the "wisdom of the crowd" could outperform the S&P 500 in 2008 and 2009. By giving more weight to expert opinions, they achieved even greater returns during these periods.

Oh and Sheng (2011) studied microblog sentiments from StockTwits.com, showing that these sentiments predicted both simple and market-adjusted stock returns. Their findings aligned with the underreaction hypothesis in behavioral finance, suggesting that stock microblogs have predictive power for future stock movements.

Huang, Qiu, and Wu (2012) examined local bias in investor attention using Guba.Eastmoney stock forums. They found that individual investors paid more attention to local stocks, with the bias being stronger in underdeveloped regions and for certain types of stocks. Their findings suggested that limited attention drives local bias.

Dong et al. (2012) investigated asynchronous information transmission between stock returns and message-posting volume in China. They found a two-way volatility spillover effect between stock returns and posting volume, showing that online discussions can stabilize financial markets and influence investor decision-making.

Zhang, Prombutr, and Swanson (2012) improved text classification accuracy and found a negative correlation between sentiment and stock returns. Their work discouraged investors from pursuing highly discussed stocks with overly optimistic sentiment but provided opportunities for short-sellers.

Wang et al. (2012) studied the impact of 2.85 million postings on 58 firms in the Shanghai Shenzhen 300 index. They found that online discussion often led to declines in stock returns and increased volatility, with variations in the correlation based on message length.

Park et al. (2013) examined how message boards influence investor behavior using data from Naver.com. They found that investors exhibited confirmation bias, which increased their overconfidence and led to poorer investment performance.

Berkman and Koch (2013) explored retail investor disagreement during earnings announcements. They found that retail investors contributed to pre-announcement price increases and post-announcement reversals, with disagreement linked to retail trading patterns.

Karabulut (2013) explored whether investor sentiment derived from Facebook activity can serve as a reliable indicator for stock market trends. The study highlights Facebook's potential as a sentiment data source for predicting market behavior.

Marko, Grzinic, and Padavic (2013) presented a mathematical model based on collaborative filtering, also known as "wisdom of crowds," to forecast stock market behavior. The model interprets aggregate crowd contributions to inform market predictions.

Marta, Arratia, and Xuriguera (2014) demonstrate that Twitter feeds can be used to forecast market trends, providing early evidence that social media content has predictive value for financial time series. This study helped pioneer using social media sentiment in market prediction models.

Blankespoor, Miller, and White (2014) found that when firms disseminate news via Twitter, it reduces information asymmetry among investors. They showed that using Twitter to broadcast corporate news (e.g., product recalls) mitigated adverse price reactions by keeping the market better informed.

Chen, De, Hu, and Hwang (2014) quantified the "wisdom of crowds" in investment forums based on Seeking Alpha. By text mining millions of stock posts, the authors found that aggregated investor opinions (measured by the proportion of negative words in posts) predicted future stock returns and earnings surprises. This was among the first papers to confirm that social media sentiment can predict market performance, treating online investor buzz as valuable information rather than "noise."

Gottschlich and Hinz (2014) designed a decision support system using user-generated stock polls from an online community to guide investments. Portfolios constructed from the crowd's collective recommendations significantly beat market benchmarks in terms of returns and risk-adjusted performance. This implies that crowd-sourced forecasts on social platforms can be harnessed to improve portfolio management outcomes.

Gu, Konana, Raghunathan, and Chen (2014) provided evidence that investors in virtual communities tend to cluster with like-minded others (homophily). This homophily effect means that online forums can create "echo chambers" where similar opinions reinforce each other, potentially impacting how information is interpreted and how investors respond to news.

Kim and Kim (2014) found no significant evidence that Yahoo Finance message board sentiment predicts future stock returns. This null result—attributed to differences in sample period and methodology—sparked debate, highlighting that social media sentiment effects might depend on context (time frame, platform, etc.).

Li et al. (2014) proposed a trading strategy that incorporates online media sentiment (news and social media) into quantitative models. In simulation, their "media-aware" strategy yielded an impressive +166% return, vastly outperforming a baseline, thus demonstrating the profit potential of leveraging web sentiment signals in trading.

Smailović et al. (2014) developed an adaptive sentiment analysis system for financial contexts. By continuously retraining new streams of social data, the system improved classification of sentiment in real-time. This is important because finance-related social media is a moving target—language and sentiment can shift quickly, so models must adapt.

Sprenger et al. (2014) showed that Twitter sentiment strongly correlates with stock market metrics. Specifically, bullishness on Twitter was linked to higher stock returns, increased trading volume, and lower volatility in the short term. They also observed an information aggregation mechanism: users giving above-average investment advice gained followers, suggesting the market detects and amplifies insightful voices. This influential paper established Twitter as a novel source of market sentiment and predictive signals.

Da et al. (2015) introduced the "FEARS" index, an investor sentiment metric based on the frequency of anxiety-related keywords in Google searches and media. They found that spikes in this index (indicating investor fear) predicted downward pressure on asset prices. While not a social media study per se, this work showed how online activity can proxy investor sentiment and influence markets—a concept extended to social media in parallel research.

Lee et al. (2015) examined consumer product recall announcements and found that firms engaging on social media during a crisis experienced less severe stock price drops. By proactively communicating recalls on platforms like Twitter, companies reduced information asymmetry and rumors, thereby dampening the market's negative reaction. This highlighted social media's value in corporate disclosure and crisis management.

Nguyen et al. (2015) developed a model to predict stock price direction by extracting topic-specific sentiment features from message board posts. Testing on thousands of posts for 18 stocks, their model achieved about 2% higher accuracy than using historical prices alone. The improvement was even larger (+9.8%) for the hardest-to-predict stocks. This demonstrated that mining detailed sentiments (by topic) from social media can enhance predictive models, beyond simple mood indicators.

Ackert et al. (2016) identified "opinion leaders" in stock message boards and showed that these influential users' posts carried more predictive power for stock movements than others' posts. In other words, not all forum posts are equal—a small fraction of savvy contributors provided more accurate information, and their views more strongly moved the market.

Bukovina (2016) presented an early overview of the nascent research linking social media "big data" to financial markets. Bukovina summarized initial findings across studies and pointed out that social media sentiment was emerging as a new market signal for asset prices, while also noting challenges in processing such unstructured data.

Dimpfl and Jank (2016) found that Google search volumes for financial keywords correlate with subsequent stock market volatility. High search activity signaled greater investor attention (often fear) and preceded volatile market swings. This reinforced the idea that investor online behavior (searches, tweets, etc.) contains predictive information about market risk, a concept extended to social media activity in related works.

Luo et al. (2016) developed a novel method to classify investor opinions by mapping them into an "emotion space" (a multi-dimensional sentiment framework). By moving beyond simple positive/negative tags, this approach more accurately captured nuanced emotions (e.g., optimism, fear) in forum posts. Such improved sentiment classification can lead to better sentiment signals for predictive modeling.

Checkley et al. (2017) provided evidence for the "wisdom of the crowd" in financial forums, finding that aggregated online sentiment did predict short-term stock market behavior (e.g., next-day returns). However, they also noted this predictive power didn't extend to longer horizons (weekly or monthly). In other words, crowd sentiment quickly impounds into prices but has limited long-run forecasting ability, aligning with the idea that social media mainly captures immediate reactions.

Deng et al. (2017) addressed the challenge of slang and sarcasm in finance tweets/forums by creating domain-specific sentiment lexicons. By tailoring word sentiment scores to financial contexts, they improved the accuracy of sentiment analysis on social media. This is key because off-the-shelf sentiment tools often misclassify finance jargon, so adapting them yields better measures of true investor mood.

Ho et al. (2017) showed that the impact of social media sentiment on stock returns changes over time. For example, sentiment might be strongly predictive in one year but weaker the next. Their time-series model with time-varying parameters captured these shifts, highlighting the need to continually recalibrate sentiment-based models as market regimes and social media usage evolve.

Mazboudi and Khalil (2017) found that social media activity prior to M&A announcements reduced the market's reaction when those acquisitions were officially announced. Essentially, active speculation and information leakage on social media attenuated the surprise of corporate takeover news, leading to smaller jumps in the stock price. This suggests that social media can serve as an informal information channel that levels the playing field.

Oliveira et al. (2017) quantified Twitter's value-add by showing that including microblogging (Twitter) metrics improved predictions of stock returns, volatility, and trading volume compared to models using only traditional data. They found that Twitter sentiment and message volume had explanatory power for market behavior, reinforcing that social media data enhances forecasting of various market variables (price direction, volatility, and even survey-based sentiment indices).

Zhang et al. (2017) investigated a Chinese stock forum to compare influential users ("celebrity" investors) versus typical "ordinary" users. They found that posts by reputed, or highly followed individuals contained more accurate market information than posts by casual users. This implies a hierarchy of information quality on social networks—prominent users (often industry experts or experienced traders) tend to produce content that better predicts stock movements, which the market may increasingly follow.

Bartov et al. (2018) showed that the tone of tweets about a company prior to earnings announcements predicted the company's earnings surprises and abnormal returns when earnings were released. In effect, the Twitter crowd's wisdom anticipated which firms would beat or miss earnings, demonstrating social media's relevance for fundamental analysis.

Tsukioka et al. (2018) investigated how investor sentiment influences the well-known IPO puzzles of high initial returns and long-run underperformance. Using text mining on Yahoo! Japan Finance message boards, the authors analyzed sentiment and attention for 654 Japanese IPOs from 2001 to 2010. They found that high investor attention and bullish sentiment inflate offer prices and initial returns, which are followed by price declines. The results suggest that excessive optimism partly explains IPO mispricing.

Dong et al. (2018) broke new ground by using features from social media to detect financial misconduct. By extracting sentiment, topic patterns, and network cues from platforms like Seeking Alpha and Twitter, they built a classifier that could flag firms engaged in accounting fraud with notable accuracy. This demonstrated a novel application: social media as an early warning system for corporate fraud, since suspicious firms often garner telling discussions online.

Glaser and Risius (2018) studied a social trading platform (where users publicly share their portfolios/trades) and found that increased transparency and social interaction can introduce biases. For instance, top traders attracted many followers, and those followers tended to copy trades (herding), which sometimes hurt performance. Social feedback (likes, comments) also influenced traders' risk-taking. In sum, even as social trading democratizes information, it can create social biases and herding effects that impact trader performance.

Li et al. (2018) concluded that stock microblogs (like StockTwits) are "more than just noise." They showed that if you weight messages by the credibility/influence of the user, the bullishness in posts strongly predicts stock outcomes. Heavily followed users' optimism led to abnormal returns, trading turnover, and volatility. This finding supports the idea that social media efficiently aggregates information: influential users' opinions drive a disproportionate part of market-relevant sentiment.

Long et al. (2018) developed a sophisticated machine learning approach (Universum Support Vector Machine) to better identify investor sentiment from social media text. By incorporating additional "universum" data (unlabeled examples) into training, their model more accurately classified sentiment in stock forum posts. Improved sentiment extraction like this provides cleaner signals for subsequent prediction models.

Mai et al. (2018) found that on Bitcoin forums, the silent majority (the large group of passive readers) had more influence on Bitcoin price dynamics than the vocal minority of frequent posters. Even though lurkers don't post, their collective presence (measured indirectly via views or passive sentiment) moved markets. This "silent majority" hypothesis implies that overall crowd interest (not just loud commentary) drives social media's impact on crypto prices.

Zhou et al. (2018) analyzed Weibo (Chinese Twitter) data and found that emotional indicators from social media predict stock market volatility. They also established Granger-causal links, meaning spikes in collective emotion (e.g., fear or excitement) on social media preceded and helped forecast jumps in market volatility. This was among the first papers to verify that Chinese social media sentiment has a predictive causal role in China's stock market.

Chen et al. (2019) found that when contributors (e.g., analysts or bloggers) are paid or sponsored, their stock opinions tend to be more positive and attract more attention but can be less predictive. This raises important implications about bias in social media stock tips—not all "crowd wisdom" is unbiased, and one must account for ulterior motives (the paper's detailed findings help identify when and how incentives skew online stock analysis.).

Cresci et al. (2019) uncovered large-scale spam and bot networks on Twitter's finance sphere. Malicious accounts were using cashtags (e.g., $AAPL) to "piggyback" on trending stock conversations and spread spam or pump-and-dump schemes. They developed algorithms to detect these bots. The key takeaway is that a substantial portion of finance-related tweets can be automated or manipulative, so filtering them is crucial for reliable sentiment analysis.

Gao et al. (2019) proposed a novel measure of investor attention by tracking abnormal reading volumes of posts on a popular Chinese stock forum (Guba). This Guba-based attention proxy was significantly correlated with traditional metrics (like Baidu search trends) and importantly, predicted high stock returns via reversal strategies (stocks that had attention spikes experienced short-term mispricing that corrected). Thus, online forum engagement can serve as a quantifiable predictor for trading strategies.

Shen et al. (2019) found that Twitter activity does help predict cryptocurrency market behavior. Increases in Twitter volume and bullish sentiment about Bitcoin preceded rises in Bitcoin's price and volatility. This was one of the early studies linking social media to crypto: it showed that social sentiment is a key driver in the relatively sentiment-sensitive crypto markets.

Wu (2019) developed an improved investor-attention index by separating the "organic" growth in Twitter activity (more users joining) from surges due to specific news events. Wu found that unexpected bursts of Twitter activity after company announcements led to higher cumulative abnormal returns for the stock. Essentially, when social media shines a new spotlight on a stock (beyond its usual following), the stock's price reacts positively as that attention translates into buying. This underscores the effect of social media attention as a market force.

Cookson and Niessner (2020) analyzed an online network of retail investors to investigate why investors often disagree. They concluded that disagreement was driven largely by differences in information, such as what news each investor sees, rather than by differences in fundamental investing approach. Moreover, they found that these diverging information silos, essentially echo chambers of content, significantly influenced trading behavior. This study suggests that on social platforms, the information one is exposed to, possibly through selective feeds, plays an important role in market divergence.

Ding et al. (2020) found a link between online investor discussion and stock price synchronicity. Stocks with heavy discussion on Seeking Alpha showed higher return co-movement with peer stocks and more opaque financial reporting. One interpretation is that social media can propagate generic market sentiment or narratives, causing stocks to move together beyond fundamentals. It also hints that managers of those firms might withhold some info (opacity) while the crowd speculates, thereby increasing co-movement.

Gan et al. (2020) compared the market impact of sentiment from traditional news media versus social media. They found that social media sentiment had at least as strong an effect on stock prices as news sentiment, and in some cases a more immediate effect. This highlights that by 2020, investors were closely monitoring social channels for cues, and platforms like Twitter could move markets as much as mainstream news.

Gu and Kurov (2020) showed that Twitter bearishness versus bullishness carried predictive power for market returns. For example, days with extremely negative Twitter sentiment foreshadowed market declines. They also found that Twitter sentiment helped explain trading volume and volatility, confirming that social mood swings translate into market activity. Overall, this paper established Twitter as an informationally rich environment that reflects and even drives investor expectations.

Huang et al. (2020) investigated an internal-facing social platform (such as Glassdoor or workplace forums) where employees post about their company. They discovered that employee sentiment on social media predicted their firm's future stock returns and earnings surprises—in fact, employees often knew and signaled good or bad news before it became public. This intriguing result suggests mining employee chatter as an "insider" sentiment indicator for investors (albeit one must be careful about using nonpublic info).

Jin et al. (2020) used Twitter sentiment combined with Long Short-Term Memory (LSTM) neural networks to forecast stock prices. Their model outperformed those using only historical prices, reinforcing that social media sentiment improves predictive accuracy. This paper is representative of many in this period that married deep learning with sentiment data to push the frontier of market prediction.

Kraaijeveld and De Smedt (2020) confirmed that Twitter sentiment is a statistically significant predictor of cryptocurrency price fluctuations. By analyzing millions of tweets, they could forecast short-term price direction for major cryptocurrencies better than chance. They found that crypto markets are heavily sentiment-driven, with Twitter often functioning as the "pulse" of the crypto investor community.

Lerman (2020) found that individual investors in online forums pay close attention to official accounting disclosures, such as earnings releases. Social media discussions spiked around 10-K and 8-K filings, and this attention was associated with more efficient market reactions to the news. Essentially, social platforms amplify and disseminate firms' financial disclosures, reducing information asymmetry between retail and institutional investors.

Liang et al. (2020) compared various sentiment indices (some from social media, some from traditional sources) in predicting stock market volatility in China. They concluded that indices incorporating social media sentiment provided more information and led to better volatility forecasts than those based only on, say, news or surveys. This supports the idea that blending social sentiment into sentiment indices yields a superior barometer of market risk.

Maqsood et al. (2020) proposed an LSTM model that integrates sentiment signals from local and global events (gleaned via social media) for stock prediction. By factoring in sentiment around major events (e.g., elections, pandemics) as expressed on platforms like Twitter, their model achieved improved accuracy. This reflects a growing trend of using social media to quantify the market sentiment of world events, feeding that into AI models for trading.

Xie et al. (2020) discovered that the structure of social media conversations (network cohesion) affects their predictive value. In Bitcoin forums, discussions that were less densely connected (lower cohesion) were more predictive of next-day price moves, whereas tightly knit discussion clusters tended to just reiterate the same info. This implies that a diversity of voices (less echo chamber) in social media discussions yields better "wisdom of crowds," whereas very insular conversations may generate more noise than signal.

Yang et al. (2020) focused on extreme negative outcomes and found that "panic" discussions on stock forums preceded stock price crashes in China. When message boards saw surging fear-driven posts (e.g., speculation that a company was a fraud), those stocks often experienced sharp price drops (crashes). This suggests that online chatter can serve as an early warning indicator of a coming crash, as widespread panic talk often triggers or accompanies flight from the stock.

Ahn and Kim (2021) revisited the social media–crypto link with a twist: analyzing Bitcointalk forum sentiment. They reported a null result that surprised some—Bitcoin's future returns showed no significant relationship with the sentiment of Bitcointalk posts. This suggests that not all social sentiment sources are equal: while Twitter sentiment moved crypto markets, the more niche Bitcointalk forum (perhaps due to different user base or lower frequency) did not predict prices. It underscores the importance of selecting the right platform and sentiment measure for prediction.

Al-Nasseri et al. (2021) investigated a social trading network and found that stocks held by tightly connected investor communities showed different return dispersion patterns than those held by dispersed investors. In essence, online social networks of investors can lead to synchronized trading and returns, affecting how much individual stock returns diverge from each other. This bridges sentiment and risk: if investors in a network share sentiment, their coordinated actions can increase or decrease return dispersion.

Guégan and Renault (2021) focused on frequency: they found StockTwits sentiment did predict Bitcoin returns at high-frequency (intraday) intervals, but the effect washed out at longer (daily) intervals. In practical terms, social media sentiment is very useful for short-term crypto traders (e.g., 15-minute ahead forecasting), but long-horizon investors see the effect averaged out. This aligns with crypto being news—and sentiment-driven on a minute-by-minute basis.

Li et al. (2021) employed the then-state-of-the-art NLP model BERT to gauge sentiment in social media posts about stocks. The richer language understanding of BERT allowed capturing context (e.g., sarcasm or idioms in posts) better than prior lexicon methods. This led to more accurate sentiment extraction and improved prediction of stock trends based on investor sentiment signals. It exemplifies how advanced AI language models have enhanced sentiment analysis for finance.

Liu et al. (2021) showed that an LSTM model augmented with social network data (connections and interactions among investors) outperformed an LSTM using only price data. Essentially, the model learned patterns of herding or coordinated behavior from network information. It indicates that knowing who influences whom in a social network of investors helps predict how information will propagate and affect stock prices.

Mehta et al. (2021) used a deep learning model to directly incorporate Twitter sentiment time-series into stock prediction and found noticeable performance gains. Their work underlines the consensus that social media sentiment is a key feature for modern stock prediction models, and even relatively unstructured approaches (like feeding sentiment indices into an RNN) yield benefits.

Rakowski et al. (2021) analyzed the diffusion of information via Twitter around earnings announcements. They observed that companies with greater Twitter activity (tweets and retweets) during earnings releases saw faster incorporation of that information into stock prices. In other words, Twitter accelerates investor attention and eliminates underreaction: news spreads more rapidly, and prices adjust more efficiently, when lots of investors are tweeting about it.

Selin and Taş (2021) investigated cross-country effects of social media sentiment, finding that Twitter sentiment not only affects domestic stock returns but also spills over internationally. For example, a wave of optimism on U.S. finance Twitter could lift not just U.S. stocks but also markets in Europe or Asia (especially in today's globally interconnected investor community). They also linked sentiment to changes in trading volume globally. This indicates social media has become a cross-border sentiment bridge in equity markets.

Zhang et al. (2021) found that companies with active, constructive discussions on stock forums showed improvements in productivity and efficiency (e.g., possibly due to feedback or crowd-sourced problem solving). This suggests an intriguing channel—social media as a platform for stakeholder feedback that can influence corporate behavior, not just stock prices.

Critien et al. (2022) found that combining Twitter sentiment with tweet volume about Bitcoin significantly improved price trend prediction. Notably, a surge in tweet volume often foreshadowed big moves (volatility), and sentiment helped get the direction right. This reinforced that both the tone and the sheer amount of social media discussion are key indicators for crypto price forecasting.

Goutte (2022) found that on social trading platforms, investors' actual trading actions (e.g., portfolio changes shared publicly) had more impact on asset prices than their posted words did. In other words, observing what traders do through social features is more telling than what they say. It also provided evidence of herding behavior: users tended to mimic successful traders, which affected market prices. The phrase "actions speak louder than words" rings true in social finance—trade signals from influencers carry weight.

Lang et al. (2022) found that a Twitter-based uncertainty index (constructed from analysis of tweets about oil) significantly predicted future volatility in oil futures markets. When Twitter indicated high uncertainty (e.g., lots of discussion about geopolitical risk or demand concerns), oil volatility rose. This is an important extension of social media sentiment analysis into commodity markets, suggesting traders should monitor Twitter for early signs of commodity risk sentiment.

Lee and Zhong (2022) analyzed the effect of mandated interactive investor Q&A platforms in China. They found that firms engaging genuinely (providing timely, informative answers) enjoyed lower information asymmetry and reduced stock price volatility. This study emphasizes that social media can serve as an effective investor relations channel, where proactive communication by companies leads to more stable markets and better-informed investors.

Shi et al. (2022) investigated homophily, or like-minded grouping, in a large financial forum. They concluded that investors who engaged only in echo chambers had inferior information and potentially worse outcomes, whereas those exposed to diverse opinions made more balanced decisions. In essence, hearing all parties on social media, that is, having a diverse feed, leads to more robust investment strategies, whereas too much agreement can be misleading. This highlights why echo chambers can be risky for investors.

Sun et al. (2022) found that companies with a strong retail investor following on social media were less able to get away with earnings management. The collective scrutiny by retail investors (e.g., FinTwit users dissecting financial statements) acted as a deterrent to extreme earnings manipulation. This is framed as a "victory" for retail investors: through social media, dispersed shareholders effectively monitored and disciplined corporate reporting behavior, a role traditionally played by regulators or institutions.

Zhang, et al. (2022) found that investors tend to be more talkative in relation to firms that are (1) smaller size, (2) more growth-like, (3) with lower prices and higher short interests, and (4) of higher beta. They also found that the bullish tone of investors positively affects the abnormal returns of small-capitalization stocks. However, online talk has little impact on large-capitalization stocks, except that more postings boost trading liquidity. Finally, they found online talk predicts the presence of future news regardless of firm size, with stronger predictive power found for small-capitalization stocks.

Chung et al. (2023) tackled the rising issue of fake news and false rumors in stock forums. They proposed a theory-guided deep learning model that successfully identified false information and even detected "sockpuppet" user accounts spreading it. In an era of meme stocks and misinformation, this study is timely: it shows that AI can help regulators and investors filter deception on social media, improving the integrity of the information environment.

Cookson et al. (2023) provided one of the first large-scale analyses of echo chambers in financial discussions. They found that investors who cocoon themselves in like-minded groups (following and interacting only with those who share their views) experience reinforcement of their biases and under-diversification, which can lead to market mispricing and volatility. This study has policy implications: it suggests fostering diverse views on platforms (or exposing users to counterpoints) might improve market efficiency by breaking echo chambers.

Fan et al. (2023) examined stocks dual-listed in markets like the United States and China. They discovered that social media activity contributes to faster price discovery across markets. For instance, if a piece of news broke and U.S. social media buzzed about it, the price in the U.S. market would incorporate it quickly and that information would also transmit to the stock's price overseas. Essentially, social media helps synchronize prices of the same asset across different countries, indicating a globalization of sentiment and information flow.

Heng and Leung (2023) found that discussions on StockTwits about options (calls/puts) contain valuable predictive information for both options trading volume and underlying stock returns. Unusual interest in certain options by the StockTwits community foreshadowed big moves in those options and the stock itself. This is novel in linking derivatives-market activity to social media—retail chatter about options can help predict option market flow and equity price impact.

Koch and Dimpfl (2023) presented evidence that when a cryptocurrency gets heightened social media attention, retail investors herd into it, amplifying price swings and occasionally forming bubbles They used metrics like Google searches and tweets as proxies for attention. The outcome aligns with the notion that social-driven herding is especially strong in crypto markets, where fundamentals are hard to pin down and narratives dominate.

Long and Zhong (2023) showed that the lurkers or rarely posting users on stock forums—though "silent"—influence stock prices through their collective trading. Firms followed by a large silent audience tended to have returns more aligned with the sentiment inferred from passive metrics (views, likes) than the vocal minority's sentiment. This implies investors and analysts should pay attention not just to loud opinions but also to engagement metrics that capture the silent majority's interest.

Xu et al. (2023) constructed various sentiment indices from Chinese social media and news, and found they correlate strongly with stock market movements. A composite index blending Weibo sentiment and financial news sentiment had robust predictive power for Chinese stock returns. This study reinforces for China what has been seen elsewhere: aggregated sentiment indicators that include social media signals are valuable predictors for market trends.

Zhao and Yang (2023) developed an integrated framework combining multiple deep learning models with a fusion of inputs—technical indicators, economic data, and social media sentiment. This integrated model achieved superior accuracy in predicting stock price movements, highlighting that the best forecasts often come from marrying traditional finance data with alternative data (like social sentiment) using advanced AI.

Yang, et al. (2024) examined the spillover between social media sentiment and market volatility across stocks, bonds, foreign exchange, and commodities. The results show that information mainly flows from volatility to sentiment, with the VIX acting as the most influential transmitter. Spillovers intensify during major crises such as the global financial crisis, Brexit, the U.S.–China trade war, and the COVID-19 pandemic. In turbulent periods, sentiment can switch from receiving to transmitting shocks, reflecting dominant news narratives.

Liu and Son (2024) presented the first systematic review of mainstream methods for aggregating investor sentiment from social media. It emphasizes that the choice of aggregation method is critical, as it directly affects the ability to capture market sentiment and the reliability of sentiment indices. The study discusses key methodological issues, including handling neutral sentiment and the limitations of simple aggregation. The findings offer important guidance for researchers in behavioral finance, social media mining, and micro investor sentiment analysis.

Zou et al. (2024) used GPT-4 and a finetuned BERT model to analyze emoji sentiment on Twitter and its impact on cryptocurrency markets. Emoji-based sentiment outperforms traditional text analysis in predicting price movements, helping to avoid downturns and stabilize returns. The findings demonstrate the potential of AI-driven sentiment analysis for improving cryptocurrency trading strategies.

Bradley et al. (2024) analyzed the impact of due diligence posts on Reddit's WallStreetBets. Before the GameStop short squeeze, these recommendations reliably predicted returns, cash flow news, and informed retail trading. After the event, predictive power disappeared as posts shifted toward attention-grabbing stocks, suggesting a cultural change that reduced investment quality and harmed smaller investors.

Cookson et al. (2024) compared social media attention and sentiment from Twitter, StockTwits, and Seeking Alpha. Attention is strongly correlated across platforms, while sentiment is largely platform-specific due to differences in user types and design features. The study finds that sentiment predicts positive next-day returns, whereas attention predicts negative next-day returns, underscoring the need to distinguish between the two when analyzing multiple platforms.

Buz and de Melo (2024) analyzed over 1.6 million WallStreetBets posts to evaluate their stock recommendations against more than 16,000 from major investment banks. While not all WSB picks are profitable, their average performance matches that of top banks and sometimes exceeds them, especially in identifying top-performing stocks. The results suggest WSB can be a valuable and freely accessible source of investment advice.

Chang et al. (2024) used 3605 firm-level panel data observations from China to examine how online public opinion affects stock price synchronicity (SPS). Higher attention to and engagement with posts, along with both positive and negative sentiments, significantly reduce SPS. Increases in post views, positive posts, and deviations in public opinion further amplify this reduction.

Warkulat and Pelster (2024) examined how Reddit attention from r/wallstreetbets affects investor behavior using individual trading data from a large platform. WSB attention drives uninformed and riskier trading, leading to larger portfolio allocations in new positions and significantly lower holding period returns, with peak-attention trades losing 8.5% on average. The findings suggest retail investors often react emotionally to negative user sentiment rather than relying on analyst advice.

Lachana and Schröder (2025) compared investor sentiment from social media and traditional print in predicting short-term market returns. Sentiment from Seeking Alpha outperforms that from the Wall Street Journal, reflecting the richer language and greater timeliness of online media. The results highlight social media's advantage as a source for extracting predictive investor sentiment.

Haase, et al. (2025) investigated over 28,000 explicit trading recommendations from social media platforms using NLP and large language models. Crowd-based signals significantly predict short-term cryptocurrency price movements, particularly for smaller-cap assets with recent losses, and an out-of-sample strategy based on them outperforms the CCI30 and S&P 500. The findings also reveal the role of automated accounts in disseminating trading advice and offer a targeted alternative to sentiment analysis.

Sevinç and Coşkun (2025) analyzed Twitter and Investing.com posts about stocks on Borsa Istanbul flagged for manipulation between 2018 and 2022, using a Turkish finance sentiment dictionary that includes a "suspicious" category for speculative content. The results show that social media's impact on markets varies by conditions and trading volume, with positive and suspicious content exerting stronger influence during bull markets and high-volume periods. These findings suggest that social media can amplify investor optimism, herd behavior, and speculative activity, especially in favorable market environments.

Wolfgang et al. (2025) found that Seeking Alpha author recommendations can significantly influence trading activity, with more accessible articles and easily observable characteristics more likely to attract attention. While in-depth analyses offer more valuable medium—to long-term investment guidance, they generate less immediate reader reaction. The results suggest that certain article features can be used to design potentially profitable investment strategies.

Nani and Mcbride (2025) explored “desperation capitalism,” where individuals take high-risk measures to seek economic security, a trend intensified by the 2008 financial crisis and the COVID-19 pandemic. Using r/WallStreetBets as a case study, it offers a conceptual model of the phenomenon and shows how social media shapes retail investors’ decision-making. The findings highlight the role of online communities in driving risk-taking behavior.

Cao et al. (2025) examined how the network centrality of stocks, based on investor interactions on the Eastmoney forum, affects stock liquidity. The results show that greater centrality improves liquidity by enhancing information transparency and attracting investor attention, with stronger effects from higher-quality and more optimistic discussions. The network structure also drives liquidity spillovers across connected stocks.

Li et al. examined how social media analysts (SMAs) on a Chinese financial platform strategically generate and monetize content by catering to investor preferences for free and paid material. Using a Bayesian empirical model, the authors find that a significant share of content sentiment variation is explained by this strategic catering, with SMAs adjusting decisions to balance attracting free readers and retaining paid subscribers. The results highlight how audience composition shapes SMA behavior and the potential for such strategies to reinforce investor confirmation bias.

Zhang (2025) investigated the value that investor discussion boards (IDBs) such as Stocktwits and TheLion provide to short-term traders. Using a new modeling approach, the study identifies four factors that shape this value: the board’s reputation system, the posting frequency of contributors, their ability to learn, and the rate of growth in active posters. The reputation system determines whether the value is positive or negative, while all four factors together determine its overall size, offering important insights for market participants, researchers, and policymakers.

Gerritsen and de Regt (2025) examined stock and cryptocurrency recommendations from 21 Dutch financial influencers, analyzing 453 endorsements across 243 stocks and 61 cryptocurrencies. It finds that influencers often recommend assets with strong recent performance, but these picks typically deliver negative returns afterward. The results suggest that such endorsements rely heavily on social heuristics, posing risks to investors and highlighting the need for greater caution and regulatory oversight.

Future Research about FSM Platforms

There remain several unresolved questions that future research may address. For example, in the early stages of FSM platform research, many scholars argued that online discussions were largely noise, with little predictive value. Bagnoli, Beneish, and Watts (1999) were among the first to criticize the credibility of information on message boards, noting that it often contained bias and unfounded rumors. Tumarkin and Whitelaw (2001) observed that, on days of abnormally high posting activity, changes in online investor sentiment were correlated with contemporaneous stock trading volume but did not predict future trading volume. Similar findings were reported by Tumarkin (2002). While Das, Martinez-Jerez, and Tufano (2005) found that posting activity was associated with same-period stock returns, sentiment among posters did not appear to predict returns. Koski, Rice, and Tarhouni (2004) suggested that message board information increased stock return volatility but did not provide any fundamental predictive insight into stock returns.

Later, research has suggested that online discussions do matter and can significantly influence not only contemporaneous but also future stock trading. Examples include studies by Clarkson, Joyce, and Tutticci (2006), Sabherwal, Sarkar, and Zhang (2011), Zhang, Swanson, and Prombutr (2012), Bettman, Hallett, and Sault (2011), and Oh and Sheng (2011). However, as different studies use different sample stocks, these inconsistent results may be due to variations in sample selection.

Future research should first seek to verify the predictive power of FSM platform information with respect to market movements. The inconsistent findings about the predictive power of online discussions may be attributable to the different samples used. Many studies concluding that online discussions have little predictive power rely on self-selected samples, which generally include large-cap stocks. These papers include Tumarkin and Whitelaw (2001), Antweiler and Frank (2004), Koski, Rice, and Tarhouni (2004), Das, Martinez-Jerez, and Tufano (2005), and Bird and Thapa (2010). All of these studies consistently find no evidence that message postings significantly predict future stock returns based on large-cap stock samples.

In contrast, studies finding significant effects from message board activity tend to focus on small-cap or even microcap stocks. Examples include work by Clarkson, Joyce, and Tutticci (2006), Bettman, Hallett, and Sault (2011), Sabherwal, Sarkar, and Zhang (2008; 2011), and Zhang, Prombutr, and Swanson (2012). This suggests an asymmetrical effect. While Zhang, et al. (2022) recognized this asymmetric effect due to size distortion, further research is necessary to determine whether online discussions can impact large-cap stocks.

Second, the issue of endogeneity remains unresolved. The causality between online discussions and stock trading activity is sometimes ambiguous. Several earlier studies suggest that causality flows more from market activity to online discussions rather than the other way around. Tumarkin and Whitelaw (2001) and Tumarkin (2002) concluded that it remains unclear whether message board activity causes abnormal stock returns or is simply a reaction to them. Das, Martinez-Jerez, and Tufano (2005) found that sentiment does not predict returns and that returns, in fact, drive sentiment. Koski, Rice, and Tarhouni (2004) argued that market volatility drives message board activity, rather than message board posts causing volatility.

However, Wysocki (1999) suggested that FSM platform posts could influence "public opinion" about a firm. Antweiler and Frank (2004) proposed that causality for volatility flows more from message boards to the market. Gu, Konana, Liu, Rajagopalan, and Ghosh (2006) argued that informed posters on FSM platforms provide information not fully incorporated into market prices, suggesting that message board sentiment can predict stock returns. Sabherwal, Sarkar, and Zhang (2011) found that in the absence of market news, online traders' sentiment caused positive contemporaneous returns and negatively predicted the next day's returns. Clarkson, Joyce, and Tutticci (2006) and Bettman, Hallett, and Sault (2011) documented those online rumors triggered significant abnormal returns and trading volumes. Oh and Sheng (2011) revealed that stock microblog sentiment had predictive power for simple and market-adjusted stock returns. Bird and Thapa (2010) found that unscheduled company news, when accompanied by high message board activity, led to positive return drifts and increased trading volatility.

Because none of these studies use identical samples and their statistical models differ, the endogeneity issue may stem from factors such as measurement error, autocorrelation, simultaneity, or omitted variables.

This endogeneity problem between online postings and stock trading activity calls for further investigation.

Third, while it is now recognized that some financial analysts monitor online posters' opinions, and that certain posters offer valuable insights, there remains no conclusive comparison between the accuracy and effectiveness of security valuation and forecasting by financial analysts and by online posters. A direct statistical comparison between these two sources of advisory information remains absent and should be the focus of future research.

Fourth, as proposed in Chapter 5, the value of an FSM platform can be affected by four factors: a_F, b_F, c_F, and d_F. I argue that a_F can be estimated using a cross-sectional regression model of forecast accuracy and the rankings of posters at a static point in time. Factor b_F can be measured with a panel regression model, given the number of messages posted by all authors over time. A similar panel regression structure can be used to estimate c_F for all posters over time. Factor d_F can be calculated through time-series analysis, based on the number of active users over time. Future studies can empirically measure these four factors using actual FSM platform data.

Finally, academic research on FSM is still in its early stages, there is still a long way to go. Nonetheless, a step forward has been taken in this field and a better understanding of how online discussions affect security trading and financial market benefits academicians, practitioners, and policymakers. These proposed extensions remain promising areas of future research.

Bibliography

Ackert, Lucy F., Lei Jiang, Hoan Soo Lee, and Jie Liu. 2016. "Influential investors in online stock forums". *International Review of Financial Analysis* 45: 39–46.

Admati, Anat R. and Paul C. Pfleiderer. 2001. "Disclosing information on the internet: Is it noise or is it news?" *Technical Report*, Graduate School of Business, Stanford University.

Aggarwal, Rajesh K., and Wu. Guojun. 2006. "Stock Market Manipulations". *Journal of Business* 79: 1915–1953.

Ahn, Yongkil, and Dongyeon Kim. 2021. "Emotional trading in the cryptocurrency market". *Finance Research Letters* 42: 101912.

Al-Nasseri, Alya, Faek Menla Ali, and Allan Tucker. 2021. "Investor sentiment and the dispersion of stock returns: Evidence based on the social network of investors." *International Review of Financial Analysis* 78: 101910.

Amihud, Yakov, and Haim Mendelson. 1986. "Asset Pricing and the Bid-ask Spread." *Journal of Financial Economics* 17: 223–249.

Antweiler, Werner, and Murray Z. Frank. 2004. "Is all that talk just noise? The information content of Internet stock message boards." *Journal of Finance* 59: 1259–1295.

Antweiler, Werner and Murray Z. Frank. 2006. "Do US stock markets typically overreact to corporate news stories?." *Working paper*, the University of Minnesota.

Arias, Marta, Argimiro Arratia, and Ramon Xuriguera. 2014. Forecasting with twitter data. *ACM Transactions on Intelligent Systems and Technology (TIST)* 5 (1): 1–24.

Y. Zhang, *Financial Social Media*,
https://doi.org/10.1007/978-3-032-09332-5

Alok, Kumar, and Charles M.C. Lee. 2003. "*Individual investor sentiment and comovement in small stock returns.*" *Working paper*,. Cornell University.

Avery, Christopher, Judith A. Chevalier and Richard J. Zeckhauser. 2011. "The CAPS Prediction System and Stock Market Returns." *Working Paper*, National Bureau of Economic Research.

Bagnoli, Mark, Messod D. Beneish, and Susan G. Watts. 1999. "Whisper forecasts of quarterly earnings per share." *Journal of Accounting and Economics* 28: 27–50.

Bagnoli, Mark, Michael B. Clement, Michael J. Crawley and Susan G. Watts. 2009. "The profitability of analysts stock recommendations: What role does investor sentiment play?." *Working paper*, Purdue University.

Bagozzi, Richard P., and Utpal M. Dholakia. 2002. "Intentional Social Action in Virtual Communities." *Journal of Interactive Marketing* 16: 2–21.

Bank, Matthias, Martin Larch, and Georg Peter. 2011. "Google search volume and its influence on liquidity and returns of German stocks." *Financial Markets and Portfolio Management* 25: 239–264.

Barber, Brad, and Terrance Odean. 2000. "Trading is Hazardous to Your Wealth: The Common Stock Investment Performance of Individual Investors." *Journal of Finance* 55: 773–806.

Barber, Brad, and Terrance Odean. 2001. "The Internet and the Investor." *Journal of Economic Perspectives* 15: 41–54.

Barber, Brad M., Yi-Tsung Lee, Yu-Jane Liu, and Terrance Odean. 2009. "Just how much do individual investors lose by trading?" *Review of Financial Studies* 22: 609–632.

Barber, Brad, Reuven Lehavy, Maureen McNichols, and Brett Trueman. 2001. "Can investors profit from the prophets? Consensus analyst recommendations and stock returns." *Journal of Finance* 56: 531–563.

Bartov, Eli, Lucile Faurel, and Partha S. Mohanram. 2018. "Can Twitter help predict firm-level earnings and stock returns?" *The Accounting Review* 93 (3): 25–57.

Berger, Adam L., Vincent J. Della, Stephen A. Pietra, and Della Pietra. 1996. "A maximum entropy approach to natural language processing." *Computational Linguistics* 22: 39–71.

Berkman, Henk and Paul D. Koch. 2013. "Internet chat, disagreement, retail trading, and stock returns around earnings announcements." *Working paper*, The University of Kansas.

Bettman, Jenni L., Aiden G. Hallett and Stephen Sault. 2007. "The Impact of Electronic Message Board Takeover Rumors on the US Equity Market." *Working paper*, Australian National University.

Bettman, Jenni L., Aiden G. Hallett and Stephen Sault. 2011. "Rumortrage: Can Investors Profit on Takeover Rumors on Internet Stock Message Boards?." *Working Paper*, Australian National University.

Bhme, Rainer and Thorsten Holz. 2006. "The effect of stock spam on financial markets." *Working Paper*, Technische Universitt Dresden.

Bird Ronald and Kiran Thapa. 2010. "Stock Message Board and Investors Reaction to Company News." *Working paper*, University of Technology Sydney.

Blankespoor, Elizabeth, Gregory S. Miller, and Hal D. White. 2014. "The role of dissemination in market liquidity: Evidence from firms' use of Twitter." *The Accounting Review* 89 (1): 79–112.

Bollen, Johan, Huina Mao, and Xiao-Jun Zeng. 2011. "Twitter mood predicts the stock market." *Journal of Computational Science* 2: 1–8.

Bradley, Daniel, Jan Hanousek Jr, Russell Jame, and Zicheng Xiao. 2024. "Place your bets? The value of investment research on Reddit's Wallstreetbets." *The Review of Financial Studies* 37 (5): 1409–1459.

Bradshaw, Mark T. 2004. "How Do Analysts Use Their Earnings Forecasts in Generating Stock Recommendations?" *The Accounting Review* 79: 25–50.

Breuer, Wolfgang, Andreas Knetsch, and Eric Sachsenhausen. 2025. "Influence and predictive value of Seeking Alpha articles." *Financial Analysts Journal* 81 (1): 102–128.

Buckley, Chris, Gerard Salton and James Allan. 1994. "The effect of adding relevance information in a relevance feedback environment." *In Proceedings of the* 17th Annual International ACM conference on Research and Development in Information Retrieval.

Bukovina, Jaroslav. 2016. "Social media big data and capital markets—An overview." *Journal of Behavioral and Experimental Finance* 11: 18–26.

Burges, Christopher J.C. 1998. "A tutorial on support vector machines for pattern recognition." *Data Mining and Knowledge Discovery* 2: 121–167.

Butler, Brian S. 2001. "Membership size: Communication Activity and Sustainability: A Resource-Based Model of Online Social Structures." *Information Systems Research* 12: 346–362.

Buz, Tolga, and Gerard de Melo. 2024. "Democratisation of retail trading: a data-driven comparison of Reddit's Wall Street Bets to investment bank analysts." *Journal of Business Analytics* 7 (4): 256–272.

Cao, Jie, Zhongyang Zou, Xin Yang, and Xiong Xiong. 2025. "How does social media shape stock liquidity? The role of investor online communication networks." *International Review of Financial Analysis* 103: 104236.

Cao, Run, Xun Liang, and Zhihao Ni. 2012. "Stock Price Forecasting with Support Vector Machines Based on Web Financial Information Sentiment Analysis." *Advanced Data Mining and Applications* 7713: 527–538.

Carhart, Mark M. 1997. "On persistence of mutual fund performance." *Journal of Finance* 52: 57–82.

Carson Jonathan and James Felton. 2004. "New Technology Issues for Corporate Governance: Internet Message Boards." *In* C.F. Joseph & Lufkin (Ed.), International Corporate Governance, 2nd ed., Euromoney Books, 184-194.

Chang, Kai, Mengfei Yang, Shengqi Zhou, and Guangxi Wei. 2024. "The impacts of online public opinions on stock price synchronicity in China: Evidence from stock forums." *Expert Systems with Applications* 255: 124520.

Checkley, M.S., D. Añón Higón, and H. Alles. 2017. "The hasty wisdom of the mob: How market sentiment predicts stock market behavior." *Expert Systems with applications* 77: 256–263.

Chen, Hailiang, Yu Hu Prabuddha De, and Byoung-Hyoun Hwang. 2014. "Wisdom of crowds: The value of stock opinions transmitted through social media." *The Review of Financial Studies* 27 (5): 1367–1403.

Chen, Hailiang, Hu Yu Jeffrey, and Shan Huang. 2019. Monetary incentive and stock opinions on social media. *Journal of Management Information Systems* 36 (2): 391–417.

Chen, Yangyang, C.S. Agnes Cheng, Shuo Li, and Jingran Zhao. 2021. "The monitoring role of the media: Evidence from earnings management." *Journal of Business Finance & Accounting* 48 (3-4): 533–563.

Choi Won Seug, Jeong-Mi Cho and Jungyun Seo. 1999. "Analysis system of speech acts and discourse structures using maximum entropy model." *In Proceedings of the* 37th conference on Association for Computational Linguistics, Morgan Kaufman, San Francisco, 230-237.

Chua, Christopher, Maria Milosavljevic, and James R. Curran. 2009. "*A Sentiment Detection Engine for Internet Stock Message Boards*," 89–93. Sydney, Australia: *In Proceedings of the Australasian Language Technology Association Workshop*.

Chung, Wingyan, Yinqiang Zhang, and Jia Pan. 2023. "A theory-based deep-learning approach to detecting disinformation in financial social media." *Information Systems Frontiers* 25 (2): 473–492.

Cook, Douglas O. and Xing Lu. 2009. "Information Matters, Noises Dont: Internet Message Boards Affect Stock Returns." *Working Paper*, University of Alabama.

Cook, Douglas O., Xing Lu, Ying Zhang and Tingyu Zhou. 2014. "The Asymmetric Stock Message Board Effect." *Working Paper*, University of Alabama.

Cookson, J. Anthony, and Marina Niessner. 2020. "Why don't we agree? Evidence from a social network of investors." *The Journal of Finance* 75 (1): 173–228.

Cookson, J. Anthony, Joseph E. Engelberg, and William Mullins. 2023. "Echo chambers." *The Review of Financial Studies* 36 (2): 450–500.

Cookson, J. Anthony, Lu Runjing, William Mullins, and Marina Niessner. 2024. "The social signal." *Journal of Financial Economics* 158: 103870.

Cowan, Arnold R., Nandkumar Nayar, and Ajai K. Singh. 1990. "Stock returns before and after calls of convertible bonds." *Journal of Financial and Quantitative Analysis* 25: 549–554.

Cresci, Stefano, Fabrizio Lillo, Daniele Regoli, Serena Tardelli, and Maurizio Tesconi. 2019. "Cashtag piggybacking: Uncovering spam and bot activity in stock microblogs on Twitter." *ACM Transactions on the Web (TWEB)* 13 (2): 1–27.

Critien, Jacques Vella, Albert Gatt, and Joshua Ellul. 2022. "Bitcoin price change and trend prediction through twitter sentiment and data volume." *Financial Innovation* 8 (1): 1–20.

Da, Zhi, Joseph Engelberg and Pengjie Gao. 2009. "In search of fundamentals." *Working Paper*, University of Notre Dame.

Da, Zhi, Joseph Engelberg, and Pengjie Gao. 2011. "In Search of Attention." *Journal of Finance* 66: 1461–1499.

Da, Zhi, Joseph Engelberg, and Pengjie Gao. 2015. "The sum of all FEARS investor sentiment and asset prices." *The Review of Financial Studies* 28 (1): 1–32.

Darroch, John N., and Douglas Ratcliff. 1972. "Generalized iterative scaling for log-linear models." *Annals of Mathematical Statistics* 43: 1470–1480.

Das, Sanjiv R., and Mike Y. Chen. 2007. "Yahoo! For Amazon: Sentiment extraction from small talk on the Web." *Management Science* 53: 1375–1388.

Das, Sanjiv, Asis Martinez-Jerez, and Peter Tufano. 2005. "eInformation: a clinical study of investor discussion and sentiment." *Financial Management* 34: 103–137.

DAvolio, Gene. 2002. The market for borrowing stock. *Journal of Financial Economics* 66: 271–306.

Delort, Jean-Yves, Bavani Arunasalam, Henry Leung, and Maria Milosavljevic. 2009. "The impact of manipulation in internet stock message boards." *The International Journal of Banking and Finance* 8: 1–18.

DeMarzo, Peter M., Dimitri Vayanos, and Jeffrey Zwiebel. 2003. "Persuasion bias, social influence, and uni-dimensional opinions." *Quarterly Journal of Economics* 118: 909–968.

Dempster, Arthur P., Laird Nan. M. and Rubin, Donald. B. 1977. "Maximum likelihood from incomplete data via the EM algorithm." *Journal of the Royal Statistical Society*, Series B (Methodological), 39: 1-38.

Deng, Shuyuan, Atish P. Sinha, and Huimin Zhao. 2017. "Adapting sentiment lexicons to domain-specific social media texts." *Decision Support Systems* 94: 65–76.

Depken, I.I., A. Craig, and Ying Zhang. 2010. "Adverse selection and reputation in a world of cheap talk." *Quarterly Review of Economics and Finance* 50: 548–558.

Dewally, Michael. 2003. "Internet investment advice: Investing with a rock of salt." *Financial Analysts Journal* 59: 65–77.

Dimpfl, Thomas, and Stephan Jank. 2016. "Can internet search queries help to predict stock market volatility?" *European financial management* 22 (2): 171–192.

Ding, Rong, Hang Zhou, and Yifan Li. 2020. "Social media, financial reporting opacity, and return comovement: Evidence from Seeking Alpha." *Journal of Financial Markets* 50: 100511.

Dong, Dayong, Liaoliao Li, Dan Yang, Huilin Zhu, Qilin Cao, and Lu. Yong. 2012. "Is there two-way asynchronous information transmission between stock markets and stock message boards?" *International Journal of Information Technology & Decision Making* 11: 777–792.

Dong, Wei, Shaoyi Liao, and Zhongju Zhang. 2018. "Leveraging financial social media data for corporate fraud detection." *Journal of Management Information Systems* 35 (2): 461–487.

Drake, Michael S., Darrent T. Roulstone, and Jacob R. Thornock. 2012. "Investor Information Demand: Evidence from Google Searches Around Earnings Announcements." *Journal of Accounting Research* 50: 1001–1040.

Tan Selin, Duz, and Tas Oktay. 2021. "Social media sentiment in international stock returns and trading activity." *Journal of Behavioral Finance* 22 (2): 221–234.

Ertimur, Yonca, Jayanthi Sunder, and Shyam V. Sunder. 2007. "Measure for Measure: The Relation between Forecast Accuracy and Recommendation Profitability of Analysts." *Journal of Accounting Research* 45: 567–606.

Estabrooks, Andrew, Taeho Jo, and Nathalie Japkowicz. 2004. "A multiple resampling method for learning from imbalanced data sets." *Computational Intelligence* 20: 18–36.

Evangelopoulos, Nicholas, Michael J. Magro, and Anna Sidorova. 2012. "The Dual Micro/Macro Informing Role of Social Network Sites: Can Twitter Macro Messages Help Predict Stock Prices?" *Informing Science* 15: 247–268.

Fama, Eugene F. 1970. "Efficient capital markets: A review of theory and empirical work." *Journal of Finance* 25: 383–417.

Fama, Eugene F., and Kenneth R. French. 1995. "Size and Book-to-Market Factors in Earnings and Returns." *Journal of Finance* 50: 131–155.

Fan, Rui, Oleksandr Talavera, and Vu Tran. 2023. "Social media and price discovery: The case of cross-listed firms." *Journal of Financial Research* 46 (1): 151–167.

Felton, James, and Jongchai Kim. 2002. "Warnings from the Enron message board." *Journal of Investing* 11: 29–52.

Fernandez, Raquel, Jonathan Ginzburg, and Shalom Lappin. 2005. "*Using machine learning for non-sentential utterance classification*," 77–86. Lisbon,

Portugal: *In Proceedings of the Sixth SIGDial Workshop on Discourse and Dialogue.*

Frieder, Laura, and Jonathan Zittrain. 2007. "Spam works: Evidence from stock touts and corresponding market activity." *Hastings Communications and Entertainment Law Journal* 30: 479–520.

Furey, Terrence S., Nello Cristianini, Nigel Duffy, David W. Bednarski, Michel Schummer, and David Haussler. 2000. "Support vector machine classification and validation of cancer tissue samples using microarray expression data." *Bioinformatics* 16: 906–914.

Gan, Baoqing, Vitali Alexeev, Ron Bird, and Danny Yeung. 2020. "Sensitivity to sentiment: News vs social media." *International Review of Financial Analysis* 67: 101390.

Gao, Ya, Xu Xiong Xiong, Youwei Li Feng, and Samuel A. Vigne. 2019. "A new attention proxy and order imbalance: Evidence from China." *Finance Research Letters* 29: 411–417.

Gerritsen, Dirk, and Anouk de Regt. 2025. "Influencers and Consumer Financial Decision-Making." *International Journal of Consumer Studies* 49 (2): e70037.

Ghanta, Praveen. 1999. "The effects of message board information dissemination on stock activity." *Working paper*, Massachusetts Institute of Technology.

Ghose, Anindya, Panagiotis Ipeirotis, and Arun Sundararajan. 2006. "The dimensions of reputation in electronic markets." *Working paper*, New York University.

Glaser, Florian, and Marten Risius. 2018. "Effects of transparency: analyzing social biases on trader performance in social trading." *Journal of Information Technology* 33 (1): 19–30.

Gottschlich, Jörg, and Oliver Hinz. 2014. "A decision support system for stock investment recommendations using collective wisdom." *Decision support systems* 59: 52–62.

Goutte, Maud-Rose. 2022. "Do actions speak louder than words? Evidence from microblogs." *Journal of Behavioral and Experimental Finance* 33: 100619.

Green, T. Clifton. 2006. "The Value of Client Access to Analyst Recommendations." *Journal of Financial and Quantitative Analysis* 41: 1–24.

Gregg, Dawn G., and Judy E. Scott. 2006. "The role of reputation systems in reducing on-line auction fraud." *International Journal of Electronic Commerce* 10: 95–120.

Grover, Ronald. 2000. "The perils of teeing off online." *Business Week, March* 13: 2000.

Gu, Bin, Prabhudev Konana, Alex Liu, Balaji Rajagopalan, and Joydeep Ghosh. 2006. "Predictive Value of Stock Message Board Sentiments." *Working Paper*, University of Texas at Austin.

Gu, Bin, Prabhudev Konana, Balaji Rajagopalan, and Hsuan-Wei Michelle Chen. 2007. "Competition among virtual communities and user valuation: The case of investing-related communities." *Information Systems Research* 18: 68–85.

Gu, Bin, Prabhudev Konana, Rajagopal Raghunathan, and Hsuanwei Michelle Chen. 2014. "Research note—The allure of homophily in social media: Evidence from investor responses on virtual communities." *Information Systems Research* 25 (3): 604–617.

Gu, Chen, and Alexander Kurov. 2020. "Informational role of social media: Evidence from Twitter sentiment." *Journal of Banking & Finance* 121: 105969.

Guégan, Dominique, and Thomas Renault. 2021. "Does investor sentiment on social media provide robust information for Bitcoin returns predictability?" *Finance Research Letters* 38: 101494.

Haase, Frederic, Tom Celig, Oliver Rath, and Detlef Schoder. 2025. "Wisdom of the crowd signals: Predictive power of social media trading signals for cryptocurrencies." *Electronic Markets* 35 (1): 1–23.

Hallett, Aiden. 2007. "*The Impact of Electronic Message Board Takeover Rumours on the US Equity Market*." *Working Paper*,. Goldman Sachs Australia Pty Ltd.

Hanke, Michael, and Florian Hauser. 2008. "On the effects of stock spam e-mails." *Journal of Financial Markets* 11: 57–83.

Heng, Zin Yau, and Henry Leung. 2023. "The role of option-based information on Stock Twits, options trading volume, and stock returns." *Journal of Futures Markets* 43 (8): 1091–1125.

Hill, Shawndra, and Noah Ready-Campbell. 2011. "Expert Stock Picker: The Wisdom of (Experts in) Crowds." *International Journal of Electronic Commerce* 15: 73–102.

Hirschey, Mark, Vernon J. Richardson, and Susan Scholz. 2000a. "Stock-Price Effects of Internet Buy-Sell Recommendations: The Motley Fool Case." *The Financial Review* 35: 147–174.

Hirschey, Mark, Vernon J. Richardson, and Susan Scholz. 2000b. "How foolish are Internet investors?" *Financial Analysts Journal* 56: 62–69.

Hittle, Byron D. 2001. "An Uphill Battle: The Difficulty of Deterring and Detecting Perpetrators of Internet Stock Fraud." *Federal Communications Law Journal* 54: 165–194.

Ho, Chi-San, Paul Damien, Gu Bin, and Prabhudev Konana. 2017. "The time-varying nature of social media sentiments in modeling stock returns." *Decision Support Systems* 101: 69–81.

Hong, Se-Joon. 2000. "Information-Processing Costs in Online Stock Trading." *Electronic Markets* 10: 192–196.

Huang, Kelly, Meng Li, and Stanimir Markov. 2020. "What do employees know? Evidence from a social media platform." *The Accounting Review* 95 (2): 199–226.

Huang, Yuqin, Huiyan Qiu and Zhiguo Wu. 2012. "Local bias of investor attention: Evidence from Chinas Internet stock message boards." *Working Paper*, Central University of Finance and Economics.

Japkowicz, Nathalie, and Shaju Stephen. 2002. "The class imbalance problem: A systematic study." *Intelligent Data Analysis Journal* 6: 429–450.

Narasimhan, Jegadeesh, and Woojin Kim. 2006. "Value of analyst recommendations: International evidence." *Journal of Financial Markets* 9: 274–309.

Jegadeesh, Narasimhan, Joonghyuk Kim, Susan D. Krische, and Charles M.C. Lee. 2004. "Analyzing the Analysts: When Do Recommendations Add Value?" *Journal of Finance* 59: 1083–1124.

Jin, Zhigang, Yang Yang, and Yuhong Liu. 2020. "Stock closing price prediction based on sentiment analysis and LSTM." *Neural Computing and Applications* 32 (13): 9713–9729.

Jones, Anne Leah. 2006. "Have internet message boards changed market behavior?" *info* 8: 67–76.

Jones, Charles M., Gautam Kaul, and Marc L. Lipson. 1994. "Transactions, volume and volatility." *Review of Financial Studies* 7: 631–652.

Jordan, Douglas J., and J. David Diltz. 2003. "The profitability of day traders." *Financial Analysts Journal* 59: 85–94.

Karabulut, Yigitcan. 2013. "Can facebook predict stock market activity?" *In AFA*2013 San Diego Meetings Paper.

Keasler, Terrill R., and Chris R. McNeil. 2010. "Mad Money stock recommendations: market reaction and performance." *Journal of Economics and Finance* 34: 1–22.

Khwaja, Asim Ijaz, and Atif Mian. 2005. "Unchecked intermediaries: price manipulation in an emerging stock market." *Journal of Financial Economics* 78: 203–241.

Kim, Soon-Ho, and Dongcheol Kim. 2014. "Investor sentiment from internet message postings and the predictability of stock returns." *Journal of Economic Behavior & Organization* 107: 708–729.

Kimmel, Allan J. 2004. "Rumors and the Financial Marketplace." *Journal of Behavioral Finance* 5: 134–141.

Kirilenko, Andrei, Albert S. Kyle, Mehrdad Samadi, and Tugkan Tuzun. 2011. "*The Flash Crash: The Impact of High Frequency Trading on an Electronic Market*." *Working paper*,. University of Maryland.

Koch, Sophia, and Thomas Dimpfl. 2023. "Attention and retail investor herding in cryptocurrency markets." *Finance Research Letters* 51: 103474.

Kohavi, Ron, and Foster Provost. 1998. "Glossary of Term." *Machine Learning* 30: 271–274.

Kollock, Peter. 1999. "The economies of online cooperation: gifts and public goods in cyberspace." In *Communities in Cyberspace*, ed. Marc Smith and Peter Kollock. London: Routledge.

Koski, Jennifer L., Edward M. Rice, and Ali Tarhouni. 2004. "*Noise trading and volatility: Evidence from day trading and message boards.*" *Working Paper*,. University of Washington.

Kraaijeveld, Olivier, and Johannes De Smedt. 2020. "The predictive power of public Twitter sentiment for forecasting cryptocurrency prices." *Journal of International Financial Markets, Institutions and Money* 65: 101188.

Kullback, Solomon, Richard Leibler, and A. 1951. "On information and sufficiency." *Annals of Mathematical Statistics* 22: 79–86.

Lachana, Ioanna, and David Schröder. 2025. "Investor sentiment and stock returns: Wisdom of crowds or power of words? Evidence from Seeking Alpha and Wall Street Journal." *Journal of Financial Markets* 74: 100970.

Lakonishok, Josef, and Seymour Smidt. 1986. "Volume for winners and losers: Taxation and other motives for stock trading." *Journal of Finance* 41: 951–974.

Lang, Qiaoqi, Lu Xinjie, Feng Ma, and Dengshi Huang. 2022. "Oil futures volatility predictability: Evidence based on Twitter-based uncertainty." *Finance Research Letters* 47: 102536.

Lee, Charles M.C., and Qinlin Zhong. 2022. "Shall we talk? The role of interactive investor platforms in corporate communication." *Journal of Accounting and Economics* 74 (2-3): 101524.

Lee, Lian Fen, Amy P. Hutton, and Susan Shu. 2015. "The role of social media in the capital market: Evidence from consumer product recalls." *Journal of Accounting Research* 53 (2): 367–404.

Lerman, Alina. 2020. "Individual investors' attention to accounting information: evidence from online financial communities." *Contemporary Accounting Research* 37 (4): 2020–2057.

Lewis, David D. 1998. "Naive (Bayes) at forty: The independence assumption in information retrieval." *In Machine Learning: ECML*-98, Tenth European Conference on Machine Learning, 4-15.

Li, Ding, Khim-Yong Goh, and Cheng-Suang Heng. 2025. "Strategic content generation and monetization in financial social media." *Information Systems Research* 36 (1): 61–83.

Li, Menggang, Wenrui Li, Fang Wang, Xiaojun Jia, and Guangwei Rui. 2021. "Applying BERT to analyze investor sentiment in stock market." *Neural Computing and Applications* 33 (10): 4663–4676.

Li, Qing, Tiejun Wang, Qixu Gong, Yuanzhu Chen, Zhangxi Lin, and Sa-kwang Song. 2014. "Media-aware quantitative trading based on public Web information." *Decision support systems* 61: 93–105.

Li, Ting, Jan van Dalen, Pieter Jan, and van Rees. 2018. "More than just noise? Examining the information content of stock microblogs on financial markets." *Journal of Information Technology* 33 (1): 50–69.

Li, Xiaoli, and Zhongzhi Shi. 2002. "Innovating web page classification through reducing noise." *Journal of Computer Science and Technology* 17: 9–17.

Liang, Chao, Linchun Tang, Yan Li, and Yu Wei. 2020. "Which sentiment index is more informative to forecast stock market volatility? Evidence from China." *International Review of Financial Analysis* 71: 101552.

Lidsky, Lyrissa B. 2009. "Anonymity in Cyberspace: What Can We Learn from John Doe?" *Boston College Law Review* 50: 1373–1392.

Litan, Robert E., and Alice M. Rivlin. 2001. "Projecting the Economic Impact of the Internet." *American Economic Review* 91: 313–317.

Liu, Alexander Y., Bin Gu, Prabhudev Konana and Joydeep Ghosh. 2006. "Predicting Stock Price from Financial Message Boards with a Mixture of Experts Framework." *Working Paper*, University of Texas at Austin.

Liu, Keyan, Jianan Zhou, and Dayong Dong. 2021. "Improving stock price prediction using the long short-term memory model combined with online social networks." *Journal of Behavioral and Experimental Finance* 30: 100507.

Liu, Qing, and Hosung Son. 2024. "Methods for aggregating investor sentiment from social media." *Humanities and Social Sciences Communications* 11 (1): 1–22.

Loh, Lawrence, and Yee-Shyuan Ong. 1998. "The adoption of Internet-based stock trading: a conceptual framework and empirical results." *Journal of Information Technology* 13: 81–94.

Loh, Roger K., and Ren M. Stulz. 2011. "When Are Analyst Recommendation Changes Influential?" *Review of Financial Studies* 24: 593–627.

Long, Wen, and Yanqiang Zhong. 2023. "The neglected cohort: The impact of silent majority in social media on stock returns." *Finance Research Letters* 52: 103363.

Long, Wen, Ye-ran Tang, and Ying-jie Tian. 2018. "Investor sentiment identification based on the universum SVM." *Neural Computing and Applications* 30 (2): 661–670.

Jie, Lu, and Bruce Mizrach. 2011. "*Strategic Interaction in a Stock Trading Chat Room.*" *Working paper*,. Rutgers University.

Jie, Lu. 2009. "*Essays on Behavioral Finance and Market Microstructure.*" *Dissertation*,. Rutgers University.

Luo, Banghui, Jianping Zeng, and Jiangjiao Duan. 2016. "Emotion space model for classifying opinions in stock message board." *Expert Systems with Applications* 44: 138–146.

Mai, Feng, Zhe Shan, Qing Bai, Xin Wang, and Roger H.L. Chiang. 2018. "How does social media impact Bitcoin value? A test of the silent majority hypothesis." *Journal of Management Information Systems* 35 (1): 19–52.

Mao, Huina, Scott Counts and Johan Bollen. 2011. "Predicting Financial Markets: Comparing Survey, News, Twitter and Search Engine Data." *Working Paper*, Indiana University-Bloomington.

Maqsood, Haider, Irfan Mehmood, Muazzam Maqsood, Muhammad Yasir, Sitara Afzal, Farhan Aadil, Mahmoud Mohamed Selim, and Khan Muhammad. 2020. "A local and global event sentiment based efficient stock exchange forecasting using deep learning." *International Journal of Information Management* 50: 432–451.

Marko, Velic, Toni Grzinic, and Ivan Padavic. 2013. "Wisdom of crowds algorithm for stock market predictions." *In Proceedings of the ITI*2013 35th International Conference on Information Technology Interfaces, pp. 137-144. IEEE.

Maron, Melvin Earl, and Larry J. Kuhns. 1960. "On Relevance, Probabilistic Indexing and Information Retrieval." *Journal of the Association for Computing Machinery* 7: 216–244.

Matsuo, Yutaka, Yukio Ohsawa, and Mitsuru Ishizuka. 2002. "Mining Messages in an Electronic Message Board by Repetition of Words." In *The Second International Workshop on Chance Discovery, Pacific Rim International Conference on Artificial Intelligence (PRICAI).* Tokyo, Japan.

Mavrogiorgos, Konstantinos, Athanasios Kiourtis, Argyro Mavrogiorgou, Andreas Menychtas, and Dimosthenis Kyriazis. 2024. "Bias in machine learning: A literature review." *Applied Sciences* 14 (19): 8860.

Mazboudi, Mohamad, and Samer Khalil. 2017. "The attenuation effect of social media: Evidence from acquisitions by large firms." *Journal of Financial Stability* 28: 115–124.

McCallum, Andrew K. 1996. "Bow: A toolkit for statistical language modeling, text retrieval, classification and clustering." *http://www*.cs.cmu.edu/~mccallum/bow.

Mehta, Pooja, Sharnil Pandya, and Ketan Kotecha. 2021. "Harvesting social media sentiment analysis to enhance stock market prediction using deep learning." *Peer J Computer Science* 7: e476.

Mikhail, Michael B., Beverly R. Walther, and Richard H. Willis. 2004. "Do security analysts exhibit persistent differences in stock picking ability?" *Journal of Financial Economics* 74: 67–91.

Mizrach, Bruce, and Susan Weerts. 2009. "Experts online: An analysis of trading activity in a public Internet chat room." *Journal of Economic Behavior & Organization* 70: 266–281.

Nani, Albi, and Keegan Mcbride. 2025. "Retire or get retired: Stocks, memes, and desperation capitalism on r/WallStreetBets." *Telematics and Informatics* 97: 102195.

Navarro, C.L.A., J.A. Damen, T. Takada, S.W. Nijman, P. Dhiman, J. Ma, G.S. Collins, R. Bajpai, R.D. Riley, K.G. Moons, and L. Hooft. 2021. "Risk of bias in studies on prediction models developed using supervised machine learning techniques: systematic review." *bmj* 375.

Nelson, Karen K., Richard A. Price, and Brian R. Rountree. 2013. "Are Individual Investors Influenced by the Optimism and Credibility of Stock Spam Recommendations?" *Journal of Business Finance & Accounting* 40: 1155–1183.

Neumann, John J., and Peppi M. Kenny. 2007. "Does Mad Money make the market go mad?" *Quarterly Review of Economics and Finance* 47: 602–615.

Nguyen, Thien Hai, Kiyoaki Shirai, and Julien Velcin. 2015. "Sentiment analysis on social media for stock movement prediction." *Expert Systems with Applications* 42 (24): 9603–9611.

Odean, Terrance. 1999. "Do investors trade too much?" *American Economic Review* 89: 1279–1298.

ODonnell, Susan, Kerri Gibson, Mary Milliken and Janice Singer. 2008. "Reacting to YouTube videos: Exploring differences among user groups." *In Proceedings of the International Communication Association Annual Conference (ICA* 2008), Montreal, Quebec, Canada.

Oh, Chong and Sheng, Olivia R Liu. 2011. "Investigating Predictive Power of Stock Micro Blog Sentiment in Forecasting Future Stock Price Directional Movement." *In Proceedings of the* 32nd International Conference on Information Systems, Shanghai, China.

Oliver, Bender, Klaus Macherey, Franz Josef Och, and Hermann Ney. 2003. *"Comparison of alignment templates and maximum entropy models for natural language understanding."* 11–18. *In Proceedings of the tenth conference on European chapter of the Association for Computational Linguistics.*

Oliveira, Nuno, Paulo Cortez, and Nelson Areal. 2017. "The impact of microblogging data for stock market prediction: Using Twitter to predict returns, volatility, trading volume and survey sentiment indices." *Expert Systems with applications* 73: 125–144.

Olson, Clark F. 1995. "Probabilistic indexing for object recognition." *IEEE Transactions on Pattern Analysis and Machine Intelligence* 17: 518–521.

Park, Jae Hong, Prabhudev Konana, Gu Bin, Alok Kumar, and Rajagopal Raghunathan. 2013. "Information Valuation and Confirmation Bias in Virtual Communities: Evidence from Stock Message Boards." *Information Systems Research* 24: 1050–1067.

Patell, James M. 1976. "Corporate forecasts of earnings per share and stock price behavior: Empirical test." *Journal of Accounting Research* 14: 246–274.

Paul, Asquith, Michael B. Mikhail, and S.Au. Andrew. 2005. "Information content of equity analyst reports." *Journal of Financial Economics* 75: 245–282.

Peter, Clarkson M., Daniel Joyce, and Irene Tutticci. 2006. "Market Reaction to takeover rumor in Internet Discussion Sites." *Accounting and Finance* 46: 31–52.

Pettibone, Jeanette and Heather Pon-Barry. 2003. "A Maximum Entropy Approach to Recognizing Discourse Relations in Spoken Language." *Working paper*, The Stanford Natural Language Processing Group.

Philbrick, Donna R., and William E. Ricks. 1991. "Using Value Line and IBES Analyst Forecasts in Accounting Research." *Journal of Accounting Research* 29: 397–417.

Pleis, Letitia Meier. 2009. "How Message Board Rumors Can Hurt Your Business." *Management Accounting Quarterly* 10: 34–43.

Rakowski, David, Sara E. Shirley, and Jeffrey R. Stark. 2021. "Twitter activity, investor attention, and the diffusion of information." *Financial Management* 50 (1): 3–46.

Rao, Tushar and Saket Srivastava. 2012. "Twitter Sentiment Analysis: How To Hedge Your Bets In The Stock Markets." *Working Paper*, Indraprastha Institute of Technology.

Rashes, Michael S. 2001. "Massively Confused Investors Making Conspicuously Ignorant Choices (MCIMCIC)." *Journal of Finance* 56: 1911–1927.

Ratnaparkhi, Adwait. 1997. "A simple introduction to maximum entropy models for natural language processing." *Technical Report* 97-08, Institute for Research in Cognitive Science, University of Pennsylvania.

Rawley Z. Heimer and David Simon. 2012. "Facebook Finance: How social interaction propagates active investing." *Working paper*, Brandeis University.

Rocchio, J.J. 1971. "Relevance feedback in information retrieval." In *The SMART Retrieval System: Experiments in Automatic Document Processing*, ed. G. Salton, 313–323. Prentice-Hall.

Saavedra, Serguei, Kathleen Hagerty, and Brian Uzzi. 2011. "Synchronicity, instant messaging, and performance among financial traders." *In Proceedings of the National Academy of Sciences of the United States of America* 108: 5296–5301.

Sabherwal, Sanjiv, Salil K. Sarkar, and Ying Zhang. 2008. "Online talk: does it matter?" *Managerial Finance* 34: 423–436.

Sabherwal, Sanjiv, Salil K. Sarkar, and Ying Zhang. 2011. "Do Internet Stock Message Boards Influence Trading? Evidence from Heavily Discussed Stocks with No Fundamental News." *Journal of Business Finance & Accounting* 38: 1209–1237.

Salton, Gerard. 1991. "Developments in automatic text retrieval." *Science* 253: 974–979.

Salzberg, Steven. 1991. "Distance metrics for instance-based learning." In *Methodologies for Intelligent System: 6th International Symposium*, 399–408.

Scholes, Myron, and Joseph Williams. 1997. "Estimating Betas from Nonsynchronous Data." *Journal of Financial Economics* 5: 309–327.
Schumaker, Robert P., and Hsinchun Chen. 2006. "Textual analysis of stock market prediction using financial news articles." In *Americas Conference on Information Systems*. Acapulco, Mexico.
Schumaker, Robert P. and Hsinchun Chen. 2009. "Textual analysis of stock market prediction using breaking financial news: The AZFinText System." *ACM Transactions on Information Systems*, 27: 12:1-12:19.
Sevinç, Deniz, and Metin Coşkun. 2025. "The impact of social media and internet forums posts on the stock market dynamics: a sentiment analysis using a lexical approach in Borsa İstanbul." *Applied Economics*: 1–13.
Shen, Dehua, Andrew Urquhart, and Pengfei Wang. 2019. "Does twitter predict Bitcoin?" *Economics letters* 174: 118–122.
Shi, Yong, Yuan An, Xiumei Zhu, and Fuwei Jiang. 2022. "Better to hear all parties: understanding the impact of homophily in online financial discussion." *Electronic Commerce Research and Applications* 54: 101159.
Shiller, Robert J. 2021. *Narrative Economics: How Stories Go Viral and Drive Major Economic Events*. Princeton University Press.
Smailović, Jasmina, Miha Grčar, Nada Lavrač, and Martin Žnidaršič. 2014. "Stream-based active learning for sentiment analysis in the financial domain." *Information sciences* 285: 181–203.
Sprenger, Timm O., Andranik Tumasjan, Philipp G. Sandner, and Isabell M. Welpe. 2014. "Tweets and trades: The information content of stock microblogs." *European Financial Management* 20 (5): 926–957.
Stephan, Philipp, and Rdiger von Nitzsch. 2013. "Do individual investors stock recommendations in online communities contain investment value?" *Financial Markets and Portfolio Management* 27: 149–186.
Sun, Kunpeng, Dan Wang, and Xing Xiao. 2022. "Another victory of retail investors: Social media's monitoring role on firms' earnings management." *International Review of Financial Analysis* 82: 102181.
Takahashi, Satoru, Masakazu Takahashi, Hiroshi Takahashi, and Kazuhiko Tsuda. 2007. "Analysis of the Relation Between Stock Price Returns and Headline News Using Text Categorization." *Lecture Notes In Artificial Intelligence* 4693: 1339–1345.
Thorsten, Joachims. 1997. "A probabilistic analysis of the Rocchio algorithm with TFIDF for text categorization." In *In Proceedings of ICML-97, 14th International Conference on Machine Learning, Nashville, United States*, 143–151.
Thorsten, Joachims. 2002. "*Learning to classify text using support vector machines: Methods, theory and algorithms*." New York: *Kluwer Academic Publishers*.
Bill, Tancer. 2007. "Who Still Uses Message Boards?" *Time Magazine, July* 19: 2007.

Teich, Jeffrey, Hannele Wallenius, and Wallenius Jyrki. 1999. "World-Wide-Web technology in support of negotiation and communication." *International Journal of Technology Management* 17: 223–239.

Thapa Kiran and Bird Ronald. 2010. "Reading Stock Message Board: Do Your Own Research." *Working paper*, University of Technology Sydney.

Thapa, Kiran. 2013. "Stock message board recommendations and share trading activity." *Working Paper*, University of Technology, Sydney.

Thelwall, Mike, Kevan Buckley, and Georgios Paltoglou. 2011. "Sentiment in Twitter events." *Journal of the American Society for Information Science and Technology* 62: 406–418.

Thomas, James D., and Katia Sycara. 2002. "Integrating genetic algorithms and text learning for financial prediction." In *Genetic and Evolutionary Computation Conference, Las Vegas*. Nevada, United States.

Tsukioka, Yasutomo, Junya Yanagi, and Teruko Takada. 2018. "Investor sentiment extracted from internet stock message boards and IPO puzzles." *International Review of Economics & Finance* 56: 205–217.

Tumarkin, Robert M. 2002. "Internet message board activity and market efficiency: a case study of the internet service sector using Raging Bull.com." Financial Markets Institutions and Instruments, 11: 313-335.

Tumarkin, Robert M., and Robert F. Whitelaw. 2001. "News or Noise? Internet Message Board Activity and Stock Prices." *Financial Analysts Journal* 57: 41–51.

Bommel, Van, and Jos. 2003. "Rumors." *Journal of Finance* 58: 1499–1520.

Vapnik, Vladimir N. 1995. "*The Nature of Statistical Learning Theory*." *New York: Springer-Verlag*.

Vilardo, Mark F. 2004. "Online Impersonation in Securities Scams." *IEEE Security and Privacy* 2: 82–85.

Tiejun, Wang, Junwei Ma, Xin Liu, and Qing Li. 2013. "Sense the Words: The Impact of Discussion Board Postings on the Stock Market." *International Conference on Management of e-Commerce and e-Government*: 141–146.

Warkulat, Sonja, and Matthias Pelster. 2024. "Social media attention and retail investor behavior: Evidence from r/wallstreetbets." *International Review of Financial Analysis* 96: 103721.

Welch, Ivo. 2022. "The wisdom of the Robinhood crowd." *The Journal of Finance* 77 (3): 1489–1527.

Wu, Dash Desheng, Lijuan Zheng, and David L. Olson. 2014. "A Decision Support Approach for Online Stock Forum Sentiment Analysis." *IEEE Transactions on Systems, Man, and Cybernetics: Systems* 99: 1–11.

Wu, Di. 2019. *"Does social media get your attention?" Journal of Behavioral Finance*, 20, no." 2: 213-226.

Wysocki, Peter D. 1998. "Cheap Talk on the Web: The Determinants of Postings on Stock Message Boards." *Working paper*, University of Michigan.

Wysocki, Peter D. 1999. "*Investor Relations and Stock Message Boards.*" *Working paper*,. Massachusetts Institute of Technology.

Wysocki, Peter D. 2000. "Private information, earnings announcements and trading volume." *Working paper*, Massachusetts Institute of Technology.

Xie, Peng, Hailiang Chen, and Hu. Yu Jeffrey. 2020. "Signal or noise in social media discussions: the role of network cohesion in predicting the Bitcoin market." *Journal of management information systems* 37 (4): 933–956.

Xu, Yongan, Jianqiong Wang, Zhonglu Chen, and Chao Liang. 2023. "Sentiment indices and stock returns: Evidence from China." *International Journal of Finance & Economics* 28 (1): 1063–1080.

Yang, Ni, Adrian Fernandez-Perez, and Ivan Indriawan. 2024. "Spillover between investor sentiment and volatility: The role of social media." *International Review of Financial Analysis* 96: 103643.

Yang, Xiaolan, Yu Zhu, and Teng Yuan Cheng. 2020. "How the individual investors took on big data: The effect of panic from the internet stock message boards on stock price crash." *Pacific-Basin Finance Journal* 59: 101245.

Yi, Lan, Bing Liu, and Xiaoli Li. 2003. "Eliminating noisy information in Web pages for data mining." *In Proceedings of the ninth ACM SIGKDD international conference on Knowledge discovery and data mining*, Washington, D.C. Session: Research track, 296-305.

Zaima, Janis K., and Maretno Agus Harjoto. 2005. "Conflict in Whispers and Analysts Forecasts: Which One Should Be Your Guide?" *Financial Decisions* 6: 1–16.

Zhang, Wei, Pengfei Wang, and Yi Li. 2021. "Do messages on online stock forums spur firm productivity?" *Pacific-Basin Finance Journal* 68: 101609.

Zhang, Wenbin, and Steven Skiena. 2010. "Trading Strategies to Exploit Blog and News Sentiment." *In Proceedings of the Fourth International AAAI Conference on Weblogs and Social Media*: 375–378.

Zhang, Xue, Hauke Fuehres, and Peter A. Gloor. 2012a. "Predicting Asset Value through Twitter Buzz." *Advances in Intelligent and Soft Computing*. 113: 23–34.

Zhang, Ying, and Peggy E. Swanson. 2010. "Are day traders bias free? Evidence from internet stock message boards." *Journal of Economics and Finance* 34: 96–112.

Zhang, Ying, Giao X. Nguyen, and V.Le. Steve. 2010. "Yes, Value Line Enigma Is Still Alive: Evidence from Online Timeliness Rank Changes." *The Financial Review* 45: 355–373.

Zhang, Ying, Wikrom Prombutr, and Peggy E. Swanson. 2012b. "Measuring Effects on Stock Returns of Sentiment Indexes Created from Stock Message Boards." *Journal of Financial Research* 35: 79–114.

Zhang, Ying, Lu Xing, and Wikrom Prombutr. 2022. "The asymmetric online talk effect." *Review of Behavioral Finance* 14 (2): 157–182.

Zhang, Ying. 2009. "Determinants of Poster Reputation on Internet Stock Message Boards." *American Journal of Economics and Business Administration* 1: 114–121.

Zhang, Ying. 2025. "Assessing the Value Generated by Investor Discussion Boards for Short-Term Traders." *Journal of Mathematical Finance* 15 (2): 432–460.

Zhang, Yongjie, Yahui An, Xu Feng, and Xi Jin. 2017. "Celebrities and ordinaries in social networks: Who knows more information?" *Finance Research Letters* 20: 153–161.

Zhao, Yanli, and Guang Yang. 2023. "Deep learning-based integrated framework for stock price movement prediction." *Applied Soft Computing* 133: 109921.

Zhou, Zhenkun, Xu Ke, and Jichang Zhao. 2018. "Tales of emotion and stock in China: volatility, causality and prediction." *World Wide Web* 21 (4): 1093–1116.

Zuo, Xiaorui, Yao-Tsung Chen, and Wolfgang Karl Härdle. 2024. "Emoji driven crypto assets market reactions." *Management & Marketing* 19 (2): 158–178.

The manufacturer's authorised representative in the EU is Springer Nature Customer Service Centre GmbH, Europaplatz 3, 69115 Heidelberg, Germany. If you have any concerns regarding our products, please contact ProductSafety@springernature.com

Printed and bound by CPI Group (UK) Ltd, Croydon, CR0 4YY
22/09/2026
02220956-0005